Crisiswork

ACTIVIST LIFEWORLDS AND BOUNDED FUTURES IN LEBANON

Yasemin İpek

STANFORD UNIVERSITY PRESS
Stanford, California

Stanford University Press
Stanford, California

ISBN 978-1-5036-4386-4 (cloth)
ISBN 978-1-5036-4431-1 (paperback)
ISBN 978-1-5036-4432-8 (electronic)

Library of Congress Control Number: 2025004628

Library of Congress Cataloging-in-Publication Data available upon request.

Cover design: Lindy Kasler
Cover art: Maryam Samaan, *Tree of Lebanon*, 2025
Typeset by Newgen in 10.25/14.75 Baskerville URW

The authorized representative in the EU for product safety and compliance is: Mare Nostrum Group B.V. | Mauritskade 21D | 1091 GC Amsterdam | The Netherlands | Email address: gpsr@mare-nostrum.co.uk | KVK chamber of commerce number: 96249943

Contents

Preface

This book was conceived and completed in the midst of multiple crises in the Middle East. I first visited Lebanon for two weeks in July 2010 to get a break from a research project in Syria. After the brutal repression of local uprisings led to an intense war in Syria, conducting research there was no longer an option, so I relocated to Lebanon in the summer of 2011. Like many professionals who also moved from Syria to Lebanon, I was looking for a safe place to continue my work. Witnessing many of my Syrian friends and contacts being arrested, tortured, and forcefully displaced in 2011 and 2012 made me despondently reflect on the devastating consequences of war and the systematic suppression of voices of dissent. Yet 2011 and 2012 also marked the vibrant times of what is now called the Arab uprisings that shaped many countries beyond Syria, such as Egypt, Tunisia, Jordan, Algeria, Morocco, Yemen, and Saudi Arabia. Throughout these years, Lebanon also hosted protests against its sectarian system while most of its residents, including displaced Syrians and Palestinians, apprehensively watched the growing impacts of the Syrian War on Lebanon. To develop a research project that mattered for Lebanon, I decided to *listen* to understand the experiential dynamics of the what, why, and how of what was happening.

I met with and listened to many people from diverse walks of life in Lebanon, who spoke about the country's complex crises and the bleak future they faced. Hearing shared sentiments and narratives about "Lebanon" and "the Lebanese" across diverse communities puzzled me, given that Lebanon is a country commonly portrayed as plagued by sectarian belonging and identity, and most research focuses on specific ethno-religious communities. I decided to study everyday cross-sectarian relations to understand competing notions of national identity and practices of belonging amid growing sentiments of crisis in the context of the Syrian War. My close contacts astutely connected me to activist circles that centered their projects on cultivating national belonging and post-sectarian futures. Even though they—like other residents—felt stuck in crises, these activists challenged common representations of Lebanon as a "victim of chronic crises" and mobilized with the "urge to do something."

In 2013, observing remarkably vibrant, diverse activist projects engaging with the deteriorating political and economic situation in Lebanon, I slowly found the "why" of my book project that would glue me to Lebanon for more than a decade: I wanted to understand what it meant to be an activist and to claim political agency in the crisis-laden context that inflected many aspects of activists' lifeworlds. I wanted the world to learn from the astonishingly rich conversations the people of Lebanon had about what should and could be done. As a critical, decolonizing researcher from the Middle East, I wanted to go beyond my rigorous education in Western political and social theory and interpret and theorize experiences of uncertainty and precarity in collaboration with my interlocutors. I also wanted to complicate the plethora of policy and media representations of the Lebanese, including of activists, as either used to and perpetuating crises, including sectarianism and wars, or as heroically resisting them.

The concept of crisiswork—multiscalar engagements with crises to enact change—demonstrates how crises are both forcefully experienced and yet rigorously engaged with. In drawing attention to the gray areas between failure and success and between cooptation and heroism, I highlight ambivalences and contradictions that simultaneously fashion and bound alternative futures in Lebanon. Dreams, aspirations, hope, and change characterize crisis experiences as much as fear, exasperation, despair, and stuckness do. Lebanon's history cannot be understood through the lenses of "chronic" or "worsening" crises, and Lebanese—or any other marginalized community—are not "resilient against" or "used to" crises. We must turn our eyes to contingently unfolding open-ended and historically situated struggles if we want to understand the promises and limitations of diverse activisms and their engagements with crises.

This book-length ethnography of activism in Lebanon is among the first to show the historical connections between crisis experiences and activist politics as well as the dissonances in vision and practice among a seemingly unified body of activists. Class, race, gender, sect, religiosity, age, and other forms of intersectional difference shape activist spaces. In particular, activist experiences with class inequalities reflect differential treatments by the state and the country's elites. Similarly, long-standing colonial structures and their legacies coexist with local solidarities and care in Lebanon's activist lifeworlds. Given the heavy influence of Western funding and humanitarian workers and professionals, Western geopolitical agendas have tremendously shaped Lebanese civil society. Yet, many Lebanese activists frame their work as an authentically Lebanese effort to respond to and ameliorate multilayered crises. In their repurposing of multiple civil society spaces, activists in Lebanon call our attention to the unintended consequences of globally hegemonic projects. Activist lifeworlds, which are entangled in diasporan connections, family relationships, and professional networks in Lebanon, present open-ended and contradictory processes of being political and doing politics. Thus, activism is not a monolithic practice.

While primarily focusing on the period between 2012 and 2015, *Crisiswork* lays the groundwork for understanding the expanding activist networks and political mobilizations in Lebanon since then. Against prevalent discourses of "nothing changes here," Lebanon's activists have had a long-lasting influence through their crisiswork. When they organized mass protests during the infamous Garbage Crisis in 2015, the networks and solidarities that were formed paved the way for the emergence of the Beirut Madinati political movement, which competed in Beirut's 2016 municipal elections. The mounting anger over intensifying economic crisis catalyzed the October 2019 uprisings and subsequent protests, which politicized many Lebanese and significantly expanded the repertoire of activist practices. The Covid lockdown and the devastating 2020 Beirut port explosion brought about a flourishing of activist organizations that grew stronger through new international funding. As Israel pursued a genocidal campaign against Palestinians in 2023, and its forces invaded Lebanon in 2024, diverse activist groups in Lebanon mobilized through political advocacy and humanitarian assistance, which furthered the growth of care and solidarity networks.

As I write this preface in December 2024, my Lebanese, Syrian, and Palestinian interlocutors and I are all watching the disruptions of Lebanon's fragile ceasefire with Israel, Israel's ongoing strikes on Gaza and Syria, and the uncertainty of Syria's future following the sudden fall of the Assad regime to opposition forces. Like many of them, I continue to reflect upon what activism and political agency should and could entail. Despite the various dramatic crises Lebanon has gone through in the past decade, there are significant continuities in the ways its residents understand and engage with the country's problems. As anticipations of war became tangled in actual traumatic experiences of war, ruination and poverty are still the talk of the town. Lebanese politicians continue to call for unity as they did in 2013, and Lebanese people continue to call out the corruption and incompetence of their politicians. Local political actors, including activists, are more vibrant and vocal than ever. Crisis, change, future, and nation-building—key themes in this book—are likely to remain at the center of Lebanese public debates in the coming decade. Just like the crisiswork of my interlocutors in this book, the political developments in the related contexts of Lebanon, Syria, and Palestine are likely to remain affected by the long-standing colonial ambitions of multiple geopolitical actors.

By inviting a conversation on how engagement with crises may generate new imaginations, social relations, and subjectivities, *Crisiswork* connects to struggles beyond Lebanon. The multiple and contradictory ways in which *crisis* figures as a politicizing narrative, lived reality, and quotidian embodied experience in Lebanon invite us to question how we understand and encounter *crisis* in other contexts. Lebanon is by no means an exceptional country, in either its challenges or its resources for change. Different communities in many parts of the globe articulate their collective struggles through rich idioms of crisis. Activist lifeworlds in Lebanon, which also included Syrian, Palestinian, and European activists, help us rethink the promises and limitations of projects for change in many parts of the global North and South where activists respond to distinct crises. As is the case of Lebanon, marginalized or oppositional groups across the world use invocations of crisis not only to describe a given reality but also to imagine alternative political belongings and futures. My focus on the temporal and affective aspects of crisis calls attention to how everyday experiences of suffering, violence, and precarity can surprisingly be harnessed to assert individual and collective agency.

My desire to bring to light distinct activisms, in particular ones that have been ignored by dominant theories and narratives, ultimately joins with growing calls for decolonization. Decolonization discussions predominantly focus on exposing the excessive power and privilege of the colonizers and overlook the everyday struggles of the colonized. Stories of diverse Lebanese provoke us into recognizing a plethora of other important developments happening when the long-desired systemic changes are yet to come. The crisiswork of Lebanon's diverse activists primarily targeted systemic-level change, but also designed and participated in projects on multiple scales from individual emotions to people's relationships with institutions and with each other. In order to productively think about global solidarity, we must decolonize our rigid ideas about what counts as sufficiently "political" or "revolutionary." In co-theorizing with my activist interlocutors, I ultimately advocate for a decolonizing approach to activism and political agency and push back against the dominant, Western-centric accounts. *Crisiswork*'s historically grounded account of diverse, contradictory meanings of practicing activism, being political, and imagining change offers a novel angle for understanding everyday ethical enactments of politics, community, and selfhood in Lebanon and beyond.

Acknowledgments

This book would not have come into being without the contribution of countless friends, interlocutors, and collaborators in Lebanon who have been infinitely supportive, and I apologize for being able to name only a few. Mona Sukarieh, a kindred-spirited sister, friend, and mentor, deserves the deepest gratitude. Her welcoming home and caring and wise personality have taught me a great deal about Lebanon, the Middle East, and life itself. She and her family and friends always made me feel at home in Lebanon, even at the most challenging times. Mona's niece Rana Sukarieh has also become an exceptionally supportive friend and colleague. Her cheerful and uplifting personality, along with her engaging commentaries on my writing and Middle East politics, have continually inspired me. I am also very grateful to Naziha Saleh and her family for opening their joyful house and kind hearts to me. Mazen Atat helped me tremendously to navigate the ins and outs of everyday life in Beirut, whether that meant dealing with Lebanese bureaucracy or exploring the best cafés. Berivan Aydın was an excellent friend, a fun travel buddy, and a proficient cook.

I also thank Melek El Nimer, Hiba Khodr, Ali Kayed, Haya Farah, Majd Z. Saleh, Omar Knio, Fadel Fakih, Farah Shoucair, Fadi Shayya, and Yaaser Azzayyaat for their generous friendship and unique insights into Lebanese politics and culture. Many more of my interlocutors and friends cannot be named here due to concerns about anonymity; to them and their generosity in sharing their life stories, this book owes much. I am indebted to the Department of Social and Behavioral Sciences at the American University of

Beirut (AUB) for offering me a visiting scholar position. I especially want to acknowledge Kirsten Scheid, an astute anthropologist of Lebanon located at AUB, for providing me with inspiring feedback on my initial findings in 2014 and for continuing to support this project since then. I greatly enjoyed participating in the intellectual community that Kirsten led, the Anthropological Society in Lebanon (ASIL).

At Stanford, where the research preparation and initial writing for this book took place, Sylvia Yanagisako rigorously trained me on ethnography-based theory. She raised countless empirical questions that helped me to turn messy ideas into a prose that has clarity and rigor. I am indebted to Thomas Blom Hansen's extraordinary knowledge of social theory. His sharp critiques and pertinent reading suggestions helped me to refine several key arguments in this work. Paulla Ebron has been an exceptional intellectual inspiration and academic mentor who brought up myriad cross-cultural comparisons that shaped my political and methodological positions. Our cheerful conversations and her strong grasp of anthropological critique constantly reminded me that ethnographic writing is not only a professional endeavor but can also be done with curiosity and joy, even at its most frustrating. Liisa Malkki's continuous encouragement to produce original work and good writing were central to the development of this project. Joel Beinin's interdisciplinary workshops and thought-provoking discussions regarding the Middle East provided me with a stimulating intellectual space. Suad Joseph provided generous support from the very beginning of the project. Her in-depth knowledge about Lebanon and her emphasis on conceptual rigor helped sharpen my contributions, and her "The Middle East/South Asia Studies Seminar" at the University of California, Davis, offered an intellectually nurturing space. I am grateful to all the participants in that group for their thoughtful comments in several chapters, especially to Caroline McKusick, Hakeem Naim, Tanzeen Doha, Justin Malachowski, Jean-Michel Landry, Rachel Feldman, Mehmet Fatih Tatari, and Tory Brykalski.

Many others at Stanford offered tremendous support. Şamil Can deserves profound appreciation for his intellectual rigor and analytical skills as well as his compassionate care, particularly during my long fieldwork. Sharika Thiranagama, Miyako Inoue, and Kabir Tambar offered valuable comments on the project at several different stages. Fırat Bozçalı, Jacob Doherty, Maron Greenleaf, Karem Said, Jenna Rice, and Johanna Richlin provided helpful input on the very early drafts of several chapters. Kerem Uşşaklı, Uğur Z. Peçe, Vladimir Hamed-Troyansky, Damien Droney, Mark Gardiner, Amanda Wetsel, Samuel Maull, John Moran, Byron Gray, Ian Simpson, Anna West, Hantian Zhang, Pablo Seward, Shan Huang, Kathryn Takabvirwa, Aisha Ghani, Vivian Chenxue Lu, and Aaron Hopes all provided keen insights and good company. Shelly Coughlan was an exceptionally good listener and a wise academic coach. Ellen Christensen's long hours of active presence in the department assured me that I was in good hands.

At George Mason University (GMU), I found another inspiring intellectual community. I thank Johanna Bockman, Rashmi Sadana, Cortney Hughes Rinker, Hüseyin Yılmaz, Christopher Morris, Iccha Basnyat, Alison Landsberg, Manjusha Nair, Ahmet Selim Tekelioğlu, Bassam Haddad, Hatim El-Hibri, Maria Dakake, Sumaiya Hamdani, Heba F. El-Shazli, and Peter Mandaville for their warm support. Collaborating with Vanessa Meikle Schulman, Brian Platt, Michael Malouf, Eric Ward Ross, and Christina Riley, my fellow residents at the Center for Humanities Research at GMU, has been deeply inspiring.

Several informal groups and colleagues elsewhere supported me as I completed the book. I am particularly indebted to the FRENS Writing Group led by Chris Taylor and its engaging participants Carol Ferrera, Navid Fozi, Melissa Chiovenda, Negah Angha, Yunus Doğan Telliel, Feyza Burak-Adli, and Noha Roushdy for detailed suggestions and criticisms for some of the chapters in the book. I also thank Lara Deeb, Farha Ghannam, Jarrett Zigon, Hirokazu Miyazaki, Vincent Crapanzano, Camelia Dewan, Sami Hermez, Christina Schwenkel, Michael Hathaway, and Stacy Pigg for their thoughtful comments contributing to refining my ideas in this book. I also wholeheartedly thank Corinne Segal, Rory Donnelly, Paola Bohorquez, and Aaron Neiman for their rigorous and caring reading of my work that helped me to polish my prose. In particular, Corinne's expert eye and encouraging support motivated me to keep writing. Rawan Hammoud and Hadeel Dbaibo kindly helped with the transliteration of Arabic words. Sumaya Zahid's attentive assistance in preparing the Index was invaluable. Abir Abyad provided insightful comments and feedback on the translations and the book cover. Jude Chehab generously offered two of her photos for use in the book. I am particularly thankful to the talented Palestinian artist Maryam Samaan for her stunning artwork on the book cover.

This research and writing process was made possible thanks to generous funding and support from numerous institutions. In the early phase, I benefited from the support of the National Science Foundation, Stanford's Abbasi Program in Islamic Studies, the Diversity Dissertation Research Opportunity Grant, the Graduate Research Opportunity Award, and the Department of Anthropology at Stanford. The Residential Fellowship at the Center for Humanities Research at GMU in 2021 and the Hunt Postdoctoral Fellowship by the Wenner-Gren Foundation for Anthropological Research in 2023 granted me time to focus and write. At Stanford University Press, Kate Wahl offered exceptionally generous guidance and support throughout the publication process. I was also lucky to have remarkably diligent anonymous reviewers who offered provoking yet constructive feedback that helped sharpen the book's contributions. I am grateful to Thane Hale for gracefully facilitating the submission process. Erin Ivy and her production team delivered outstanding work and were incredibly responsive and considerate. Some of the content in Chapter 3 appeared as "Bala Wāsṭa: Aspirant Professionals, Class-making, and Moral Narratives of Social Mobility in Lebanon" in *Journal of the Royal Anthropological Institute* 28 (3): 746–68; https://doi.org/10.1111/1467-9655.13764; © 2022 Wiley. Elements of Chapter 4 were first published in "Entrepreneurial Activism: Ethical Politics and Class-Based Imaginations of Change in Lebanon," *American Ethnologist* 50 (3): 474–90; https://doi.org/10.1111/amet.13109; © 2023 Wiley.

Several close friends deserve my deepest gratitude. Fırat Bozçalı has been an engaging colleague and a supportive friend since the inception of this project. Karem Said, a precious friend and a passionate colleague, has made her caring heart, wise conversations, and charming laughter available whenever needed. Reem Kambris's loving and entertaining companionship was uplifting in so many ways. Andora Rruka-Stanton's warm house and lively chats were deeply nurturing. Rawan Hammoud, Hadeel Dbaibo, Farah Zahra, Kerem Uşşaklı, and Yunus Doğan Telliel have all offered care and thoughtful insights during different phases of the project. I have received immeasurable uplifting and warmth from John Luebben and Karen Luebben, whose heartening words and smiles made me feel, "I got this." I owe a great deal to Bryan Rich's generous support. His insightful comments and edits on various parts of the book, as well as his caring friendship, have been precious. Hilal Sala's wisdom and love inspired me to keep moving forward.

Finally, I want to thank my parents Ferhan İpek and Nilgün İpek, my sister Ayşegül Alsan and my lovely niece Ebrar Alsan, my late grandmother Fatma İpek, my aunts Gülgün Turan and Süreyya İpek, and other family and friends in Türkiye for their nourishing love, which has for many years brought home to my heart.

And in my heart dwell various beloved others who remain unnamed here, yet who have wonderfully transformed research and writing from a fierce struggle into a journey of growth. This book is dedicated to them. . .

Note on Transliteration

For transliteration of Arabic words, I have followed the *International Journal of Middle East Studies* (IJMES) system, adjusted for the Lebanese dialect as appropriate. Proper names and names of places and institutions in Lebanon follow conventional English spelling in Lebanese media and common use in Lebanon. All translations are my own unless otherwise stated.

Crisiswork

INTRODUCTION

"We Must Do Something."

In early January 2014, Manal, a twenty-eight-year-old activist, invited Farah and me to what she called a "dinner for raising morale" (*ʿashā la-rafʿ al-maʿnawiyyāt*).[1] The three of us were neighbors in an apartment building in the Mar Ilyas area of central Beirut. I felt grateful for this opportunity to connect with friends at a time when several car bombings had recently shaken Beirut and led many residents to stay in their homes. In contrast to the anxious atmosphere in Farah's and my apartments, there was typically more joy and warmth in Manal's small two-bedroom apartment where she lived with her mother. Like many other Lebanese activists, Manal often organized and participated in such get-togethers to express and build solidarity with friends, relatives, and other Lebanese whose shared experiences of economic precariousness, infrastructural failure, political instability, imminent war threats, and frequent bombings characterized their daily lives. As we ate the delicious *waraq ʿinab* (grape leaves) and *kibbeh* (a meatball-bulgur wheat croquette dish) that Manal's mother had prepared for us, Manal spoke about her excitement for the new projects her activist community was developing. She mentioned that her collective had recently grown, with new activists joining them in hopes of "doing something" for Lebanon. "Lebanese youth is waking up against all this mess," she said in English, impersonating a well-off Lebanese American activist who frequently code-switched to English during her empowerment workshops at our NGO. We all laughed. Then Manal shifted her tone to firmly assert what I had been hearing from different activists: "We must do something or we will lose our country" (*Lāzim naʿmil shī aw mnikhsar baladnā*). In Manal's life, "doing something" meant advocating for women's rights as well as supporting her family and friends on a daily basis. Both her friends and I admired Manal's committed work in civil society and generous care for her loved ones.

A Shiʿi woman from South Lebanon, Manal was a warm, welcoming neighbor when we first met in the summer of 2012 in our building's elevator. She eventually became a close friend as she introduced me to activist spaces. Except for her work as a math teacher for Palestinian refugee children in summer camps funded by the United Nations Relief and Works Agency for Palestine Refugees in the Near East (UNRWA), Manal had been unemployed since graduating from the Lebanese University with a degree in economics in 2010. She was part of a feminist collective that focused on issues such as civil marriage, gender equality, and youth empowerment, and she was an active participant in advocacy campaigns, protests, and marches. She also volunteered in two youth-focused NGOs located within walking distance from her neighborhood. In addition, she helped her mother distribute food at a local charity. In 2007, a year after the July War between Lebanon and Israel, her father had suddenly abandoned the family and emigrated from Lebanon to start a new life in Australia. Manal often referred to this abandonment and the difficulties she and her mother endured afterward as central to why she became an activist (*nāshiṭ*). "I always adored how activists challenged ideas such as 'this country won't be fixed' (*haydā al-balad mā raḥ yiẓbaṭ*)," she told me during a protest against domestic violence in February 2013. For her, an activist was someone who, regardless of circumstances, believed that change was possible and tirelessly worked for it. The dinner was similarly meant to show that there was hope and a future in Lebanon.

Not all Lebanese activists had Manal's cheerful and optimistic disposition. Farah, a twenty-three-year-old Sunni woman originally from Tripoli who had lived in Mar Ilyas with her aunt since 2012, was often sad and downcast. Farah had met Manal at an empowerment workshop at a youth-focused NGO near her home, and they had become close friends through shared NGO activities. Manal saw Farah like a younger sister and cared for her as such. Farah worked as a secretary at a small construction company. During the dinner, she complained that the company had not paid her salary for three months and that her boss's casual demeanor suggested that this was business as usual. She had been looking for a new job for months and felt exhausted: "The country is in crisis (*azma*), our lives are in crisis. We work for days, months, years, only to end up where we started. You do your best, but your efforts don't take you anywhere." Manal nodded sympathetically, but added that, despite it all, she believed in Lebanon, and she insisted that Farah join the new projects in her feminist collective. While Farah, like Manal, identified as an activist because of her volunteer work, she felt that some of the collective's activities, such as public demonstrations and protests, were "too much," implying that she was not comfortable with that level of political participation. She asked Manal how she could recover her energy so quickly and remain hopeful after the bombings: "What is your secret? Yoga keeps you happy like this, right?" Manal smiled at Farah's teasing of her love for yoga and responded, "Bombs shouldn't scare us. On the contrary, they should remind us that we have a lot of work to do. Same with other crises. They simply tell us we should keep working for change. Yes, even doing yoga is changing something. Join me, it's free here from my home internet." Farah and I laughed again; we were lucky to have someone who hardly ever got tired of cheering us up.

This book explicates the relationship between crisis and political imagination by examining the diverse meanings and practices of activism in contemporary Lebanon. It asks, "How does crisis shape, and how is it shaped by, activist politics?" and "How do diverse activists imagine change differently and to what effects?" In recent years, expressing a determination to "do something" (*aʿmal shī*) about what they viewed as growing crises, various groups in Lebanon increasingly mobilized within civil society (*al-mujtamaʿ al-madanī*) and called themselves activists. Like Manal, many activists emphasized the need to address the structural and urgent problems they observed and experienced in their lives. They emphasized how the entire Lebanese political system, culture, and people's attitudes needed to change to prevent further crises. Mobilizing around ambiguous tropes such as "doing something" and "working for change" enabled them to engage both individually and collectively with what they saw as the pervasive crises plaguing the country. The root of the Arabic word *aʿmal* in "doing something" (*aʿmal shī*) could be translated into English as "to do," "to work," "to labor," "to act," or "to take action." The urge to do something, which characterized activist subjectivity in Lebanon, thus connoted activeness, yet left the contours of this activeness ambivalent. Within this ambivalent imagining of individual and collective responsibility to address crises, diverse activist lifeworlds in Lebanon took shape and generated a pluralistic yet contentious space of social and political struggle.[2]

I coin the term "crisiswork" to conceptualize the dynamic yet ambivalent idea of doing something, describing the multifaceted engagements with crises within activist lifeworlds to enact change. Crisiswork refers to activists' diverse imaginations of and responses to Lebanon's crises, which seek to transform *both* individual moralities and affects *and* political and social structures. I argue that crisiswork broadens the scope of the political by framing activism as a struggle to undo crises across political institutions, culture, and everyday life. Many activists did not see any contradiction between working for change at the individual level—that is, self-empowerment—and the structural, hegemonic level—that is, revolution. They identified crisis in all spheres of life, from infrastructure and work to family and friendship, thus extending activism beyond organizational spaces and protests into the mundane practices of everyday life. In addition to conventionally understood activist practices—such as organizing demonstrations and protests, raising awareness through media, and confronting politicians—the concept of crisiswork encompasses various other practices such as volunteering for an NGO, caring for loved ones, and doing yoga as essential aspects of an activist struggle for change in the context of crisis. Rather than approaching activism in binary terms—as either a reproduction of or resistance to hegemonic power relations—*Crisiswork* characterizes activism as an open-ended, contradictory process of multiscalar struggles against crises that generates diverse imaginations of change. As such, it reveals competing genealogies of "becoming political" as well as differences and tensions among seemingly unified activists. In doing so, it questions the naturalized dichotomies between activists and ordinary citizens and between political action and everyday practice.

In 2011, war began in neighboring Syria. This momentous event disrupted Lebanon's political and economic life in the decade that followed, leaving many Lebanese feeling stuck in recurrent crises. During my long fieldwork stay from 2012 to 2015, twenty-nine bombings and assassinations occurred in Lebanon, killing 205 people and injuring 1,796 others.[3] The heightened polarization caused by the Syrian War led to multiple demonstrations and street clashes between followers of conflicting political parties. Rumors of possible bombing targets spread rapidly, leading some Beirut residents to hide in their homes for days. Neighborhood patrols, protection rackets, and political kidnappings became increasingly common. Beirut residents often described these experiences, along with ensuing intra-family political disputes and the securitization of streets, as "living in a war." In 2014, the Islamic State of Iraq and Syria (ISIS) also began to expand its presence in Lebanon. Meanwhile, the Syrian War tremendously impacted Lebanon's economy. The country suffered a decline in foreign investment and a steady fall in GDP growth; the disruption of overland trade through Syria, as well as within the larger region, resulted in higher prices for imports and reduced exports. The poor, including Palestinian refugees, were further impoverished by economic competition with displaced Syrian workers. Between 2011 and 2018, general elections in Lebanon were repeatedly postponed; this political gridlock halted the already slow processes of legislation and reform and led to further deterioration of the country's infrastructure and public services.

It was in this context that numerous crisis narratives on the exceptionally unlucky fates of Lebanon and the Lebanese publicly circulated. The Syrian War resurrected foundational debates about Lebanon's history, identity, and long-standing challenges. Most Lebanese remembered the past as a time of "failed nationhood" characterized by colonialism, sectarianism, and war, and experienced the present as "stuck in the past" and "without a future." Rejecting these common portrayals of Lebanon as a "victim of repeating histories of violence" and "impervious to change," many activists like Manal took the new crises erupting after the Syrian War as a wake-up call for action. During this time, an increasing number of people embraced activism, joined civil society, and looked for ways to curb the negative impacts of crisis on individual, communal, and national scales. At the same time, politically experienced civil society leaders reflected on new strategies and alternative forms of mobilization. The call to "do something" gathered momentum and effectively contoured emerging forms of ethical citizenship. In the view of various activists, Lebanon's arch-nemesis—sectarianism—appeared to be intensifying, and it needed to be stopped. Yet, for many Lebanese, combating sectarianism was an arduous, if not impossible, task because the growing crises were rooted not in the contingencies of the Syrian War but in Lebanon's very foundation and historical unfolding.

Existential Crisis: Living in a Sectarian Lebanon

I heard many Lebanese describe Lebanon's main problem as an existential crisis (*azma wujūdiyya*), referring to historical struggles with the creation of a national identity and a sense of belonging. Lebanon's initial conception as a land for Maronite Christians and as a loyal European ally seeded a contested historical legacy. A close diplomatic and commercial relationship developed between France and the Maronite Catholic community during the mid-nineteenth century.[4] Following the collapse of the Ottoman Empire after World War I, the League of Nations gave France a mandate over the territory that makes up present-day Lebanon. During the 1919 Paris Peace Conference, the Lebanese delegation, led by Maronite Patriarch Elias Pierre Hoyek, successfully negotiated the creation of a Greater Lebanon (*Le Grand Liban*), which was officially proclaimed by the French High Commissioner General Henri Gouraud in September 1920. This newly designated political entity included not only the largely Christian-inhabited region of Mount Lebanon but also the ethnically and religiously diverse city of Beirut and the predominantly Muslim areas of the Bekaa Valley and the cities of Tripoli, Sidon, and Tyre. Many residents in those areas rejected inclusion in a Maronite-dominated Greater Lebanon. They saw themselves as part of the wider Arab world and instead advocated joining Syria.[5]

I heard many educated, middle-aged Lebanese recount this origin story to explain how Lebanon had been colonially designated for Maronite Christians, with the result that its diverse inhabitants had been deeply divided from the country's very inception. Most young Lebanese, on the other hand, did not like to talk about this origin story, a preference I attribute to their willingness to imagine a unifiable nation and avoid any condemning discourse against the country's Christians. Yet as several of my Lebanese activist interlocutors, including Maronite Christians, also emphasized, criticizing French colonialism should not be equated with an anti-Christian sectarian discourse. The people of the newly designated Lebanon were divided in the 1920s not because they hated other sects, but because they pursued competing political projects of collective identity and belonging.[6]

France governed Lebanon on the basis of confessionalism and established political sectarianism as an institutional system. The first modern Lebanese constitution, which was drafted under French rule in 1926, delineated a new balance of power between the various confessional groups. The constitution was specifically designed to guarantee the political dominance of France's Maronite allies, and political and social elites of the time believed that the confessional system established by the constitution would recognize different communities and diffuse sectarian discord. Thus, the "sectarian" system operating since the 1920s was celebrated by both France and numerous Lebanese elites for promoting stability by distributing power along strictly confessional lines—a model also called consociationalism. As demarcations of political power and citizenship were fiercely debated throughout the mandate period, so were definitions of national identity and belonging. Three ambiguous forms of "nationalism" existed during the French Mandate, which forcefully institutionalized confessional structures and identities: Lebanism, Syrianism, and Arabism. Through the increasing sectarianization of the state and other political institutions as well as the dissemination of competing nationalist ideologies, dynamic and overlapping communities within the newly created Greater Lebanon were reified as homogenized and monolithic identities. The Lebanese citizen was thus imagined as simultaneously belonging to Greater Lebanon and to primordial, self-enclosed sectarian communities.

In 1943, the year the Lebanese achieved national independence, an unwritten agreement referred to as the National Pact (al-Mithaq al-Waṭani) justified the allocation of parliamentary seats and certain government positions on a confessional basis. New power-sharing arrangements allocated representatives to each confessional group, favoring Christian over Muslim sects in a 6:5 ratio. These positions were proportioned according to the contested 1932 census data, which listed Maronite Christians as the majority sect, Sunni Muslims as the second-largest, Shiʿi Muslims as the third, and Druze as the fourth. In line with substantial executive powers and a highly favorable electoral law, the Maronite Christian community, who had historically established strong global economic and cultural networks, accumulated numerous privileges in both the public and private sectors between 1945 and the beginning of the long Lebanese War in 1975. These decades witnessed rapid economic growth along with rising socio-economic disparities and political conflicts across the nation.[7]

The long Lebanese War—from April 1975 until October 1990—was rooted in the complex economic, political, and cultural tensions of the previous decades and unfolded in the context of continually shifting domestic, regional, and global dynamics.[8] Two opposing camps fought each other throughout the war, each of which consisted of multiple militia groups.[9] Israel, which invaded Lebanon in 1978 and 1982 and occupied South Lebanon between 1978 and 2000, and Syria, which entered and controlled most parts of Lebanon between 1976 and 2005, were also militarily involved in the war, while many other states supported different local groups, both financially and diplomatically. The roots of this prolonged war and the destruction it caused were incomprehensible for many Lebanese I spoke to. Some commentators argued that the presence of Palestinian organizations in Lebanon after the 1967 Arab–Israeli War had increased tensions among different confessional communities. Other explanations highlighted growing economic and social inequalities, ideological differences (mainly between Lebanese nationalism and Arab nationalism), or foreign interventions. Yet all of these competing explanations agreed on one thing: Lebanon's biggest problem, and the root cause of all its crises, was sectarianism.

Sectarianism mainly refers to a confessional political system, in which the Lebanese state codes citizenship according to one's sect and personal status. There were eighteen legally recognized sects in Lebanon, each managed by a different personal status court that adjudicated many aspects of daily life, including marriage, divorce, and inheritance. Sect came to define political identity in the nineteenth-century Levant through Ottoman modernization reforms and under European influence, particularly French.[10] Far from expressing an essential, immutable culture, sectarianism was historically produced by a complex network of political parties, religious institutions, sect-affiliated militias, and charities. Sectarian identity in Lebanon differed from religious identity or theology,[11] and sectarian identities and communities were neither monolithic nor static. As much as it descriptively referred to political systems with specific institutional and legal underpinnings, the term "sectarian" was also often used to indicate fanatical cultural forms and practices, or excessive partisanship. In everyday life, many Lebanese used the words sectarianism (*ṭāʾifiyya*), racism (*ʿunṣuriyya*), and confessionalism (*madhabiyya*) interchangeably to refer to any form of social exclusion based on ethnic or religious background. In practice, though, social enactments of sectarianism in Lebanon were less indicative of religious schisms and more of modern struggles with managing citizenship, diversity, and inequality. In this sense, sectarianism in Lebanon was not at all exceptional and could be compared to racism in the United States, for instance.[12]

The long Lebanese War left an ambivalent legacy in which sectarianism and nationalism were simultaneously promoted. The order established by the Ta'if Agreement—signed in October 1989 in Taif, Saudi Arabia, following intense diplomacy by the Arab League—divided Lebanon's parliamentary seats equally between Christians and Muslims. While the agreement rhetorically called for gradual desectarianization, it effectively reinforced sectarian rifts by making political and social reform dependent on confessional power sharing. The social power of sectarian leaders over their constituencies also expanded. Because the provision of public goods and services by the post-Ta'if state was inefficient and corrupt,[13] many Lebanese learned to rely instead on sectarian political parties and ethno-religious community networks for the distribution of resources.[14] The Lebanese state came to be understood as absent because of the primacy of these parties and networks in delivering various benefits to diverse residents.

Nevertheless, the Lebanese state as such was not absent or weak, as it was typically characterized by many commentators, including Lebanese activists. Rather, it manifested itself as a capitalist spectacle, increasingly so after the 1990s. It was "an agile state that mobilized billions of dollars, mainly from the Lebanese diaspora, Gulf investors and foreign donors,"[15] creating a banking and real-estate bubble that eventually exploded in 2019. During the 1990s and 2000s, the Lebanese state was very present in its forceful promotion of privatization and foreign investment, as it favored the banking, financial, real estate, and service sectors over the agricultural, industrial, and manufacturing sectors. These policies resulted in "neoliberal sectarianism," in which sectarian divides were reinforced as new forms of poverty, inequality, and internal displacement emerged along both inter-sectarian and intra-sectarian lines.[16] In the context of a neoliberal sectarian state, the further erosion of public institutions and people's calls for a strong state were simultaneously reinforced.

Desiring a strong, functioning nation-state and unevenly encountering a "present-absent" state characterized everyday life in Lebanon. As in the case of other post-colonial states with long histories of war, most of Lebanon's citizens, including the majority of the activists, profoundly longed for a modern state that would establish some sense of order and normalcy. The Lebanese state was perhaps absent in its failure to deliver on these longings; however, it was present in the lifeworlds of activists and other residents. Run by a small circle of political elites, the Lebanese state was a differential state that worked through the sectarian system—not despite it—presenting distinctive forms of presences and absences to hierarchically situated groups in Lebanon. While some Lebanese blamed the state for not defending them against the recurrent Israeli aggression, others articulated grievances about not being protected from certain Lebanese groups that were armed. The Lebanese state also actively safeguarded Lebanese citizens from refugees and migrant workers, whose mobilities and public appearances were strongly policed by various state authorities. In this regard, activists' and other residents' encounters with the Lebanese state were uneven.

In parallel with the entrenchment of neoliberal sectarianism and its asymmetrical manifestations, *al-ʿaysh al-mushtarak* (coexistence) and *al-waḥda al-waṭaniyya* (national unity) became official goals of the Lebanese state. Through amnesty laws and the promotion of a "No Victor, No Vanquished" rhetoric, the political elite cultivated the image of a unified Lebanese nation while protecting wartime religious and political leaders from accountability. As a result, a sort of state-sponsored amnesia characterized post-war public life in Lebanon, despite some civil society activists' strong advocacy for public memorials and truth commissions to facilitate transitional justice.[17] The Taʾif Agreement thus deepened the generalized sense of existential crisis and aggravated the common sentiment that Lebanon was inevitably prone to instability.

The post-war decades witnessed several periods of intense political polarization and violence. Nevertheless, because of widely circulating official campaigns, many Lebanese grew up in the 1990s and 2000s learning that belonging to the nation was superior to belonging to a sect. During the 1990s, the Lebanese government implemented the Education Reform Plan with the aims of fostering national identity and belonging in all schools and of disseminating "authentic Lebanese values" such as nonviolence, tolerance, liberty, and democracy among youth.[18] This plan was largely unsuccessful, mainly because of the tensions in reconciling Lebanese and Arab nationalism.[19] In the context of increased social polarization following the assassination of Sunni Prime Minister Rafiq Hariri in 2005, education reforms further focused on creating "an overarching, preferably uncontroversial feeling of national belonging to foster social cohesion and facilitate social reconstruction."[20] The post-war generation had to negotiate the collective, familial, and individual effects of trauma stemming from the unresolved questions of historical memory while responding to calls for national unity and patriotism. During the 2000s, many young Lebanese strongly endorsed both confessional and national identity, which reinforced the sentiments of existential crisis.[21]

Crisis As Generative and Experiential

Questioning how political and social elites frame challenging collective predicaments, recent scholarship has investigated how invocations of crisis discourses by those in power may limit public conversations and foreclose certain political possibilities.[22] For instance, it has been argued that neoliberal regimes and their privileged actors often name aggravating economic and social problems at a given time as crisis in ways that conceal the historical causes of these problems, normalize existing conditions, and ultimately undermine the possibilities for critique, dissent, and progressive change.[23] In these scholarly analyses, the concept of crisis articulates not a collective experience but an expert judgment on social reality—a political technology that justifies the actions and rationales of the governing elites as well as the status quo.

In Lebanon, however, crisis narratives were invoked by not only policy-making bodies, experts, journalists, and academic circles but also the country's residents in general. In addition to being a depoliticizing discourse used by various Western and local elites, crisis in Lebanon was also a politicizing narrative, a lived reality, and an embodied experience. Lebanese commonly understood "crisis" as a social fact—a condition that was tied to the nation's unresolved and accumulated historical, political, and cultural problems, directly shaping their daily lives, their identities, and their sense of belonging. Many activists not only talked about crises but lived through them, engaging with their multilayered impacts in ways that imagined alternatives to the status quo. This engagement was not depoliticizing—on the contrary, crises became generative of various forms of political and social action, and efforts to respond to crisis led to the emergence of new notions of activism and politics.

Focusing on how diverse actors' multiscalar practices of "undoing crises" coalesce into new ways of being and acting, I theorize crisis as generative of competing activist lifeworlds. Illuminating diverse and contradictory meanings of being an activist and doing politics, *Crisiswork* helps us understand how new political imaginations and (un)belongings continually arise in contexts of ongoing precarity. Precarity does not only constrain livelihoods; it can also generate new forms of world-making. People's struggles with precarious circumstances are inherently indeterminate and thus can lead to unexpected (dis)connections and (dis)attachments, both empowering and debilitating.[24] Such "unpredictable encounters" can be transformative for precarious subjects as well as formative of other multitemporal relations that escape the linear narrative of progress.[25] Many Lebanese activists, for instance, connect through shared temporal experiences of stuckness, hopelessness, or trauma. Indeterminate encounters may also generate contingent exchanges of ethical visions. In different activist spaces, many Lebanese are introduced to new kinds of moral selves—such as the professional, expert, patriotic, volunteer, entrepreneurial, cosmopolitan, hopeful, or optimistic self. All of these aspirational selves, seeking to engage with Lebanon's crises, are understood and embodied in different ways, resulting in ambivalent and open-ended activist lifeworlds. Many of my interlocutors oscillated between cynicism and faith, and between despair and hope.[26]

Crisiswork's methodological focus on the experiential dynamics of crisis and activism moves forward scholarly and policy conversations on crisis, which tend to focus on single, discrete, and noteworthy economic transformations and ensuing forms of governance reforms. Lived experiences of complex issues, such as past traumas, precariousness, unemployment, violence, infrastructure failure, identity struggles, and restricted mobility rights inform crisiswork. Crises in Lebanon have affective, temporal, and bodily dimensions in which daily struggles with uncertainty and vulnerability take place. Everyday invocations of crisis in Lebanon make references to past, present, and future[27] and are wrapped in affects such as fear, anxiety, worry, confusion, and hope.[28] My activist interlocutors frequently shared memories of violence—particularly from the long Lebanese War and the public conflicts that erupted between 2005 and 2014—to describe the long-term effects of Lebanon's crises on people's health and well-being. Social suffering was experienced as embodied individual suffering, often through forms of bodily pain.

I draw on phenomenological approaches to understand how everyday experiences of suffering, violence, and trauma may propel crisiswork inflecting all spheres of everyday life.[29] *Crisiswork* foregrounds embodied experiences of crises and activism work, including the narrativization of these experiences, to understand ethical and political lifeworlds. Many activists complained of headaches, muscle aches, anxiety, and depression after incidents such as street clashes and bombings. These recurrent, embodied experiences were more than physiological side-effects of precarious living—they prompted individuals to revise their political visions and future plans. Moments of enunciating, "I can't take this anymore" (*mā ādir itḥammal ba'ā*), a phrase I frequently heard from my interlocutors, were also moments of imagining alternative ways of living and being.[30] Routinized forms of bodily suffering made many question their loyalties to certain political actors or factions and search for more supportive and trustworthy ones, and led others to contemplate emigration. Many activists emphasized that embodied traumas of current or historical political crises directly inspired them to engage more explicitly with political issues through activism. Publicly sharing their embodied suffering through phrases like "I can't take this anymore" affectively bonded people and communities and turned crisis into a shared intersubjective experience that fostered solidarity and collective agency.

Lived histories of war significantly shape sentiments of crisis among activists and other residents of Lebanon. Through remembrance of traumatizing events or through the anxious anticipation of violence, "war remains constantly present" in political and everyday life in Lebanon, even in the absence of an ongoing conflict.[31] As several ethnographies of Lebanon have also convincingly argued, wars were not only destructive, but also generative of lifeworlds.[32] Embodying and narrating war were inherent to activist socialization even in seemingly "apolitical" activities like volunteering for children with cancer or attending empowerment workshops. It was not uncommon to witness a participant suddenly begin recounting a story about their family's struggles with violence, fear, displacement, or poverty during a self-empowerment workshop at a local NGO. When a group of activists formed tighter bonds and spent time with each other outside of activist spaces, they shared intimate stories of how their families' and their own experiences with war motivated them to "do something for Lebanon."

Though multiple crises affect political and social structures as well as everyday life in Lebanon, they are rarely seen as ordinary occurrences, and many Lebanese have actively criticized and engaged with multiple crises on a daily basis for a prolonged time. Various scholars, including anthropologists, have suggested that crises were a normal part of life in Lebanon, and that people no longer saw crises as extraordinary.[33] Such ideas of "chronicity of crisis" or "normalization of crisis" capture the prolonged nature of multiple social, economic, and political problems and challenge the assumed distinctions between crisis and normalcy. However, activists' multiscalar engagements with Lebanon's crises and the diverse subjectivities that these engagements bring about reveal that, despite this depiction of crises as recurrent, constant, or uninterrupted, they are hardly experienced as banal or normal.

The idea of normalization of crisis can also be complicit in deeply problematic Orientalist representations of non-Western societies as passive and compliant. For example, the 2011 *New York Times* article "For Lebanese, Crisis Has Become a Way of Life" claims that ordinary Lebanese are not sufficiently worried about the nation's current crises, a situation the article explains as "exhaustion," "healthy cynicism," and "weariness."[34] Similarly, the 2015 *Wall Street Journal* article "Lebanon Marks a Year Without a President With a Shrug" portrays Lebanon as indifferent to its own political crises and gridlocks.[35] Such articles systematically characterize Lebanese political actors and ordinary citizens as habituated to crises and unwilling to engage with them. A wide range of elite actors whom I interviewed—leading Lebanese politicians and bureaucrats; journalists; managers of youth programs in major Lebanese banks, consultancy companies, and universities; and representatives of local and international NGOs and donor agencies—similarly described Lebanese people as caught up in sectarian relations and not interested in changing the status quo. Western aid workers and volunteers who participated in Lebanese NGOs and grassroots organizations frequently complained to me that Lebanese in general "accept the situation" and "do nothing." Such complaints resonate with Orientalist narratives—often unreflectively articulated by local elites—which depict non-Western peoples as static, passive, obedient to power, and thus in need of saving.[36] *Crisiswork* offers a more nuanced view of Lebanon by documenting how its people actively engaged with crises and demonstrated political agency in multiple ways.

What Is Activism?

Crisiswork invites a critical examination of the predominant definitions of activism and activist politics. Many liberal scholars and policy-makers in the West typically use the term "activist" to refer to idealistic and even heroic individuals, distinguishing them from ordinary citizens. Whereas ordinary citizens are understood to focus on their individual lives in compliance with the rules of the system, activists are seen as politicized individuals who make an organized effort to change the system by visibly exercising resistance in the public sphere. Many consider rallies, demonstrations, and public protests as the true and authentic forms of political struggle. The *Cambridge Dictionary*, for instance, defines an activist as "a person who believes strongly in political or social change and takes part in activities such as public protests to try to make this happen."[37] This assumed distinction between those who comply with the system and those who seek to change it ignores other forms of political engagement. In Soviet Russia, for instance, "normal people" saw anti-state activists' public efforts as silly and uninteresting, but they were neither pro- nor anti-state and demonstrated dissent in creative ways.[38] Growing far-right mobilization in Europe and North America shows that activism is not limited to those who oppose state power or capitalism and can be enacted by groups who want to fortify those systems or expand authoritarian agendas.[39] As also compellingly documented by numerous anthropological works, it is difficult to distinguish between power and resistance, or to neatly place activists in either category.[40] In contemporary Lebanon, almost everyone, not only activists, is anti-system, anti-sectarian, or anti-state in rhetoric. But people's understanding of "the system" and visions for change vary remarkably—a situation that creates ambivalent articulations of political agency and moral selfhood. Nevertheless, similar to liberal Western commentators, many middle-class Lebanese activists widely invoked a difference between those who sought to change the existing system and those who did not to distinguish activists from others.[41] *Crisiswork* suggests that the difference between an activist and a non-activist is not always clear or straightforward. In civil society circles in Lebanon, being an activist was less a durable identity than a contingent description of the very act of taking action—doing something.

Paying attention to the intricacies of the multiscalar politics of "doing something" to engage crises ultimately expands established ideas about political action. Many in the West understand activists' political engagement as separate from, or even opposed to, the fulfillment of daily life needs and the concerns of the private sphere. Hannah Arendt's theory of politics, which relies on the distinction between the private and public spheres in ancient Greek life, is emblematic of this understanding. According to Arendt, the *polis* (city-state, state, nation, or society) is distinct from, and superior to, the *oikia* (household). The *polis* represents a public space for a political community, in direct opposition to the *oikia*, which is characterized by the satisfaction of the daily needs of life.[42] The *polis*, for Arendt, is where one could truly exercise one's reason, potential, and creativity, as she saw the public sphere as the proper place of political action. Arendt's related classification distinguishes between labor, the struggle to meet our biological needs; work, the production of socially needed goods and services; and action, the free and plural articulation of collective futures. In Arendt's thinking, action is superior to work and labor. According to her, while work and labor focus on necessities, action is where transformative sociality among people takes place and where imagining and acting for change become possible. Action is where "new beginnings" occur; it is "the political activity par excellence."[43]

While Arendt's narrow Western-centric understanding of political action, and the hierarchical distinctions it entails, have received a fair amount of critique,[44] both scholarly and public discussions on activism are still strongly shaped by these ideas. Yet, as emergent approaches from the global South reveal, "the production of the political can be understood not by trying to predefine the ontologically political but by attending to the contingent and different ways in which the political gets differentiated from the putative non-political."[45] Going beyond Western-centered definitions of the political will also make possible more inclusive and nuanced understandings of activism. For activists in Lebanon, the idea of "doing something" to address crises and experiential work on change contoured activism, rendering seemingly apolitical practices political and politicizing even self-proclaimed "non-political" activists.

Crisiswork contends that activist struggles against crises, meant to continually refashion lifeworlds and selfhoods, can also generate politicization as activists push back against the constraints imposed by hegemonic structures, expand degrees of freedom and agency, and configure alternative ways of being and acting. By politicization, I refer to the deliberate processes of continually exposing oneself and others to alternative modes of thinking, feeling, and acting as well as to the processes of socializing, caring for, and building solidarities with diverse communities for the purpose of implementing discursive and practical strategies and tactics to generate desired social and political changes. Diverse activisms in Lebanon were explicitly geared toward creating change in all spheres of life; however, the activist efforts toward producing change were open-ended, and therefore, they could be politicizing or depoliticizing. Activism, in this regard, was not an inherently political or apolitical practice.

Nāshiṭ, the Arabic word for activist, has a broader meaning than the English term "activist." It connotes not only working for systemic change, but also being socially active and serving others. Moral responsibility is ingrained in the word *nāshiṭ*; it encompasses patriotism and ethical citizenship but also day-to-day practices of care for family, community, and oneself. Petra—an environmental activist in her early thirties from a middle-class Maronite Christian family and who took pride in her strong Arabic—explained to me the root for *nāshiṭ*, *na-sha-ṭa*, as connoting the multivocal meanings "to be active," "to work on something," and "to work for a good cause." She emphasized how a *nāshiṭ* was someone who would actively intervene to change any problematic circumstances in her immediate world. One day, during a birthday party, as she witnessed my puzzlement at hearing another activist say, "I am an activist in everything I do," Petra explained:

> Who is an activist? Are we only activists when we are on the streets protesting the government, or when we distribute food to the poor and refugees? Of course not. Activism can be anything. Remember the workshop last week in our collective? Didn't we discuss how everything is political? It's the same for activism. Everything is activism as long as you *do something* [emphasis added] to change things for better, whether in the system, in your personal life, or in the lives of others. For instance, I need to take care of my stress now with yoga, reading, etc. so that I'll be able to go to the protest next weekend. Revolution is a life-long task. Maybe our grandchildren will see the revolution.

The phrase "doing something" encompasses much more than changing political structures and includes other activist goals such as "helping people live a dignified life," having a "character," and "raising people's morale." It evokes ethical qualities such as taking responsibility, evaluating social norms critically, and giving people hope.[46] It highlights the importance of "small things" (*ashyāʾ ṣaghīra*) such as being kind, helping people find jobs, supporting one's family, and supporting good actions by good people. Thus, many Lebanese activists understand activism as a multiscalar political and ethical endeavor in the present that fosters a belief in positive change and a responsibility for working individually and collectively toward that change.[47]

These notions of activism emphasize a type of "work" for change and to undo crises—what I call crisiswork—that encompasses and even transcends Arendt's categories of labor, work, and action. As a "healing artist," Petra earned her money through commissioned works for various Lebanese NGOs, a labor that she approached as part of her activism, as it helped Lebanese recover from politically inflicted traumas. She also saw helping her mother with housework as related to her activism insofar as it lightened the burden of the sectarian system's patriarchal structures on her mother. Additionally, she understood various leisurely practices—such as going out with her activist friends or going dancing with her boyfriend—as forms of activism because such activities alleviated the overwhelming emotional impacts of political crises, which she directly associated with sectarianism: "I refuse to be suffocated with all the negativity or fear the media shows us. We sometimes need a break from the news or negative people."

Even though Petra knew that "sectarianism" as a political structure would not change as a consequence of her individual activist practices, she hoped to experience, and hence actualize, change by reducing some of the negative footprints of sectarianism in her life and the lives of others. She believed that through her activism, her and others' experience of sectarianism could change. It was from Petra that I first heard the famous statement by Audre Lorde, an American black feminist theorist: "Caring for myself is not self-indulgence, it is self-preservation, and that is an act of political warfare."[48] Like other activists, Petra also focused on advocacy, protests, raising awareness, and imagining alternative political futures with her activist friends. Yet, she did not distinguish these activities from her quotidian efforts to practice care for herself and others as a way to assuage the debilitating effects of crises. All of these activities were part of Petra's activism, as they expressed her efforts to break out of intensely constraining circumstances and of building a dignified life.[49] Yet, Petra and other activists did not see all routine activities as activist practices; rather, intentional acts to mitigate the effects of crises at various scales were understood as part of activists' politics.

In its focus on how everyday life is generative of activism,[50] *Crisiswork* incorporates family and kinship into its theorization of political subjectivity and activist lifeworlds.[51] In Lebanon, extended kinship ties and the moral idioms generated within these relations significantly shaped one's quotidian interactions with the state, politics, economy, and society.[52] Many activist interlocutors emphasized how their family histories and kinship relationalities were formative of their political identities and explained that familial experiences with war, violence, and poverty had politicized them since their childhood. Some understood their activism as continuing their parents' activist projects, such as the pursuit of Lebanese unity or the Palestinian cause. Others framed their activism as a reaction against their family's reliance on sectarian ties and understood practices like refusing to vote for their families' preferred parties as part of their activist commitments. The "refusal to cooperate with projects initiated by others," such as consuming negative media news or voting for the candidates supported by one's family, sought to disrupt sectarian formations on a daily basis.[53] In a place where "everyday sectarianism"[54] is a lived reality—necessitating kinship networks in order to access basic infrastructures such as electricity, education, and medical care—everyday activism against sectarianism constitutes essential crisiswork.

Because sectarianism is commonly understood as both an ethical and a political problem, activists struggle to undermine sectarianism by simultaneously working on both political structures and individual moralities. Through fostering what I call "ethico-political dispositions"—embodied capacities that are believed to generate empowerment and agency—activists sought to manage "negative" (*salbī*) affects such as stuckness, despair, and fear of war. They articulated notions such as willpower, hope, and autonomy as essential to asserting "life" and to articulating new future horizons against Lebanon's systemic crises, which were described as "killing" its citizens. Similar to protesting, advocacy, or volunteering, many mundane practices such as reading a book, doing yoga, and spending time with friends were viewed as part of activism because they helped cultivate the "right" dispositions for "good" citizenship in an imagined future nation. Activists worked on their affects on a daily basis, not only individually but also through socializing with and caring for each other. In this sense, cultivating ethico-political dispositions is a form of "affect management"—a process of ethical cultivation imbued with political motivations and implications.[55] Cultivating ethico-political dispositions thus becomes a form of "biopower from below"[56] and of "self-constitution of national subjects (i.e., subjects without a clear political authority subjecting them)."[57]

As anthropologist Tania Ahmad suggests, demands for normalcy are important for understanding contemporary configurations of moral and political subjectivity.[58] Activism in Lebanon sought changes both to the existing power structures and to dispositions and feelings, aiming to enact alternative political projects with the potential to bring about normalcy, stability, well-being, and a livable life for oneself and others. By cultivating well-being and a sense of normalcy, activists sought both to render Lebanon livable in the present and to build capacities to enact change when suitable conditions arise in the future. Thus, as they prepared for a future revolution, for systemic change, activists also sought to experience change in the present time and invite others to do the same.

Crisiswork, with its emphasis on affects and ethico-political dispositions, joins the "subjective turn," which brings into view individual activists' experiences and deeply personal accounts of their political practices. Ethnographies contributing to the subjective turn examine how activists have worked on their subjectivities to defy dominant power structures.[59] They study "politics from the granularity of human experience, often focusing on unexpected locations and configurations of contest and contestation."[60] Highlighting experiential aspects of activism, many ethnographies convincingly show that, while numerous collectivities around the world may not call what they do "political," their practices do create potential for desubjugation and critiques of existing political structures.[61] Questions such as how to live a good life or how to carve out belonging are crucial to challenging, subverting, or evading unjust systems of power.

Crisiswork, however, departs from other works situated within the subjective turn in its emphasis on difference. Most ethnographies of activism that focus on subjective experiences suggest that while tensions, disagreements, and conflicts among activists are ubiquitous, it is more productive to focus mostly on emergent solidarities and resistance.[62] For instance, Maple Razsa, a leading proponent of the subjective turn, acknowledges the existence of conflicts and disagreements among activists but underscores his deliberate choice of an "affirmative ethnography" that highlights the contributions and strengths of the activist politics of the researcher's interlocutors. Thus, much of the existing work on activism focuses on collective subjectivities and shared personal experiences.[63] As I followed my key interlocutors' participation in distinct yet interconnected activist spaces, however, I came to understand that Lebanese civil society, as a shared field of alternative politics, hosted diverse activist lifeworlds with numerous competing visions and practices of doing something, often with incompatible or contradictory meanings and implications.

A Decolonial Approach to Activism

Activism in Lebanon is a field of translocal encounters that generates both new technologies of power and subversive appropriations of these technologies.[64] Lieba Faier and Lisa Rofel propose the term "encounter" as a productive response to calls for decolonizing both ethnographic methodologies and anthropological theorizations. Studying everyday activism in Lebanon offers an ethnography of encounters that focuses on "how culture-making occurs through unequal relationships involving two or more groups of people and things that appear to exist in culturally distinct worlds."[65] A focus on encounters pays attention to everyday engagements across difference. Activist spaces proliferate new encounters among diverse residents of Lebanon and a variety of transnational actors that render crisiswork a site of both "political intervention and political invention."[66] In particular, recent political mobilizations and ethical debates among activists in Lebanon are situated within a series of translocal encounters among Western donors and humanitarian workers, diasporan Lebanese, local elites, and activists from diverse classes. The concept of translocal encounters emphasizes "processes of negotiation, resistance, awkward resonance, misunderstanding, and unexpected convergence."[67] It offers a nuanced approach that attends to both the co-constitutions of long-standing power structures *and* alternative imaginations. *Crisiswork* deploys a decolonial practice that develops three distinct yet related critical perspectives on the study of activism in Lebanon.[68]

First, I engage with my interlocutors as co-intellectuals who can and do recognize, interpret, and critique power imbalances and inequality. Decolonizing anthropology requires, among other things, "taking seriously the critiques and theories of anthropology's peripheral allies, such as feminist activists and policymakers," and "using the frames of reference of those being studied."[69] Going beyond "giving voice," a decolonial approach recognizes our interlocutors' capacity to participate in academic interpretation and analysis[70] and promises a more culturally situated, experiential, and grounded understanding of activism. By approaching my activist interlocutors in Lebanon as co-intellectuals, I build on and contribute to decolonizing methodologies that challenge the epistemicide of colonized subjects' knowledge[71] and advocate for a more collaborative knowledge-production process between researchers and the communities they study.[72] Activists in Lebanon inhabit a continual mode of critical reflexivity in their engagements with state institutions, donors, international organizations, and other NGOs and activists. Taking seriously their critical analysis resists extractive anthropology and invites the reader to go beyond learning *about* others and to begin learning *from* and *with* others.[73]

Second, I emphasize the ongoing legacies of colonialism in shaping present political contestations and spaces of activism and highlight the complex flow of influences, interests, and policies at play shaping Lebanon's civil society.[74] Western "humanitarian" interests in Lebanon have a long history. What Ussama Makdisi calls the "foundational encounter" between Anglo-American Protestant missionaries and the Arab world during the nineteenth century was the point of origin of US ideological and political influence in the Middle East.[75] Through the 1990s, as Arab nationalism began to decline and most nations in the region began to adopt neoliberal and

US-friendly regimes, Western powers became primarily concerned with migrant and refugee communities whose mobilities they saw as a threat, in particular following the wars in Afghanistan, Iraq, and Syria.[76] Following the end of the long Lebanese War, Western donors robustly promoted civic activism in Lebanon in line with their geopolitical agenda to create Western-friendly political actors across the Middle East who would align with Western geopolitical interests. During my fieldwork, I heard many high-level Western actors, including ambassadors of major European states, publicly encourage activism among Lebanese youth and denounce apathy as the most insidious problem. After the outbreak of the war in Syria in 2011, donors' focus shifted toward the formation of patriotic citizens who would want to stay in the country and work toward resolving Lebanon's crises.

Promoting activism in this sense was also a key strategy of population mobility control from the global South to the global North. The dynamics of Western funding for activism in Lebanon supports anthropologist Catherine Besteman's insight that contemporary border control takes place not only through physical and legal enforcement at border gates or in refugee camps but also at sites of humanitarianism and civil society.[77] By fostering discourses of patriotic citizenship that would dissuade people from emigrating, Western promotion of activism functioned as an "emplacement project"[78] that designated certain spaces for certain people and hindered population movements, deploying racialized rationales.

Third, in tracing often unseen hierarchies, rifts, and instances of dissonance within seemingly unified movements, I take the question of difference among activists seriously. A wide range of Western and Lebanese observers typically depict Lebanese politics as a complicated set of relationships between "the people" and "the political/sectarian elites" and portray activists as a univocal and synchronous movement defending the interests of "the people" from the "political elites." In contrast, I approach activism in Lebanon as "a space that is *internally* marked by cultural difference and the heterogeneous histories of contending peoples, antagonistic authorities, and tense cultural locations."[79] As historians of Lebanon document, diverse genealogies of "peoplehood" and "change" have informed social and political movements in Lebanon,[80] and Lebanese civil society has not emerged in isolation from the country's political divisions. Events such as the assassination of Rafiq Hariri in 2005 and the Syrian War significantly polarized activist networks in ways that both revealed *and* effectuated ideological and programmatic fissures.

A focus on difference and heterogeneity exposes both the plurality of political imaginations as well as invisibilized social hierarchies and ideological tensions and inconsistencies. It complicates common scholarly conceptualizations of civil society activism as "anti-politics"[81] and instead reveals competing notions of the political and unexpected moments of politicization.[82] Avoiding normative appraisals grounded in extraneous or transcendental criteria allows a productive examination of differences, conflicts, and incongruences among and within activists. Hence, rather than judging their politics as fragmented, chaotic, or disabling, I focus on how activists craft distinctive, ambivalent, and fluid subjectivities. Prioritizing solidarity and resistance in studying activism risks producing a monolithic portrayal of activist struggles and oversimplifying activists' identities. Instead, being attentive to how class, sect, race, gender, generation, and other social positionings and individual trajectories shape activist spaces enables us to see how multiple forms of historical injustice and struggle play out in contemporary crisiswork.[83] Tensions and conflicts render visible social hierarchies and mechanisms of exclusion that may constrain the durability and resilience of solidarity alliances. For example, I realized toward the end of my fieldwork that many participants in activist spaces were Palestinian and Syrian refugees, a fact unknown to the Lebanese in the group. Their preference to hide their ethnic identities enabled them to avoid mistreatment and exclusion, but this also furthered their own historical silencing and perpetuated asymmetries of power. The fact that these refugees recognized that their participation was conditioned on concealing their ethnic identities and outsider status is one illustration of how activist spaces may also be complicit, however unwittingly, with the very patterns of exclusion they struggle to overcome.

Class Hierarchies and Their Subversions

Civil society (*al-mujtamaʿ al-madanī*) is often used by scholars as a broad term that comprises a wide range of associations (*jamʿiyyāt*) in Lebanon—from faith-based and secular nongovernmental organizations, grassroots initiatives, collectives, cooperatives to professional organizations, labor unions, trade unions, and syndicates. Various research centers and educational consultancy companies in Lebanon also consider themselves as part of civil society, and their participants self-identify as activists. From this perspective, the everyday lives of many Lebanese are entangled in multiple registers of civil society. Nevertheless, the "civil" in civil society is also widely understood to indicate that its members were substantially different from the political elite, who were involved in the long Lebanese War and continued to dominate Lebanese politics. Imagining families and confessional communities as perpetuating sectarian narratives, many activists believed that civil society played a unique role in bringing together diverse Lebanese to craft potential solutions to the nation's multifarious crises.

Self-identifying as members of non-partisan, non-sectarian, and independent groups, many activists—the focus of this book—did not consider those groups arranged by or affiliated with established parties or religious institutions as part of civil society, which they imagined as a space distinct from both the state and sectarian institutions.[84] Many activists also distinguished between "civil society organizations" (*jamʿiyyāt al-mujtamaʿ al-madanī*) and "nongovernmental organizations" (*al-munaẓẓamāt ghayr al-ḥukūmiyya*). In their view, civil society organizations were founded by Lebanese and operated in Lebanon, whereas NGOs could be established by either Lebanese or foreigners and could have local, regional, or global focus and reach. Accordingly, the term "NGO" carried more neutral and institutional connotations, whereas "civil society" signified localness and organicity while excluding international NGOs.[85] Imagining Lebanese civil society as an indigenously grown site of political action that truly represented the Lebanese people, many activists took pride in its vibrancy.[86]

My activist interlocutors came from diverse backgrounds and upheld different political orientations, yet they all emphasized that being part of civil society was key to their self-identification as activists. Most of them were not focused on a specific social or political cause, such as environmentalism, gender rights, or anti-capitalism. Instead, they saw themselves as responsible citizens who were concerned with all of Lebanon's problems. Viewing the Lebanese state and most political elites as sectarian, incompetent, and corrupt, activists dreamed of radical, systemic changes to sectarianism as a pervasive system inflecting all political and cultural life. Few had clear visions of alternative political formations, but many shared vague aspirations for a system resembling European social democracy.

Most activists were members of multiple NGOs, movements, and coalitions and collaborated with each other on numerous projects. For example, a feminist grassroots activist could collaborate with other activists on projects related to public spaces, electoral reforms, or youth empowerment. An activist focusing on climate change might shift their focus to refugee rights in a matter of months. Such flexibility was partly related to the short-term nature of funding, but it also expressed activists' willingness to contribute to different social causes. There were many large-scale events, such as workshops, trainings, and public demonstrations, where diverse activists could meet and network with each other. Several cafés and bars in Beirut's cosmopolitan neighborhoods were well-known gathering places for activists. Typically, when I hung out with an activist interlocutor at a public space, we would unexpectedly come across many other activists. While participation in civil society spaces had distinct implications for different social classes in Lebanon, the spaces where activists pondered post-crisis futures were also spaces for urban sociality, leisure, and relaxation.[87]

This book highlights the heuristic potential of the concept of "class" as an analytical tool for studying competing forms of civil society politics and diverse activist lifeworlds. Through a historically situated theorization of inequality, I analyze class in Lebanon as a socio-economic condition, a structure of feeling,[88] and specific sets of cultural practices, social and symbolic capital, and moral narratives. Employing an intersectional approach, I show how class was entangled with race, gender, generation, religiosity, sect, and legal status, and how resources and capabilities to engage with Lebanon's crises were unevenly distributed among different communities. Even though most of my interlocutors did not have a coherently articulated "class identity" or "class consciousness," they were deeply cognizant of socio-economic disparities in Lebanon and how they themselves were situated within them. I use the terms "low-income activists" or "aspirational middle classes" to refer to Lebanese activists who came from economically disadvantaged families. In this group, I also include Syrian and Palestinian activists who were part of NGOs and grassroots organizations led by Lebanese. Most of these activists were either unemployed or underemployed. Although they held university degrees and aspired to join the middle class, they systematically struggled with economic hardship and experienced various forms of economic precariousness. There were important differences among low-income activists in terms of how they viewed activism. Some of them saw the networks offered by civil society as a path toward becoming middle-class professionals. Others focused mainly on working toward their political goals.

With the term "middle-class cultural elites" or "middle-class activists," I refer to urban Lebanese activists who enjoyed moderate to high household income and were educated at elite Western and Lebanese universities. They had strong diaspora connections, were typically multilingual in Arabic, French, and English, and were active within Lebanese civil society. They were cultural elites in the sense of mobilizing their class privileges to claim leadership in forming the modern culture of the country in order to "oppose the rulers and to lead the subjects."[89] Partha Chatterjee's articulation of middle-classness as a hegemonic political subjectivity is useful for understanding how highly educated and well-off Lebanese positioned their membership in civil society as a marker of distinction from the political and economic elites of the country—whom they deemed "sectarian"—as well as from the larger society and non-activist citizens, whom they viewed as in need of political education and guidance.[90] Middle-class activists worked in a range of professional occupations, such as humanitarian workers, academics, teachers, consultants, architects, urban planners, designers, bankers, and managers. Some of them proudly referred to themselves as "technocrats" and believed their expertise in professional fields made them particularly effective in activist work. I include diaspora returnees within the category of middle-class activists. During the Syrian War, many diasporan Lebanese (*mughtaribīn*) returned to Lebanon and became involved in activist projects.[91] Articulations of modernity and middle-classness were inherently tied to the diasporic culture in Lebanon.[92]

In addition to recognizing hierarchies and tensions traversing activist spaces and networks, a focus on classed subjectivities and practices also reveals that activism can become a contentious space for class-making, and that marginalized groups could appropriate civil society spaces for class mobility. Most civil society initiatives in Lebanon were historically dominated by cis-gendered, urban, middle-class men, but low-income Lebanese men and women, LGBTQ communities, and non-citizen groups from different parts of Lebanon increasingly claimed a place and a stake in civil society and forged cross-sectarian and cross-class connections in navigating Lebanon's crises.[93] Precariously positioned activists from different class, racial, and gender backgrounds appropriated civil society in ways that creatively exceeded the calculations of Western donors and local elites—resulting in the formation of "counter-emplacements."[94] For example, many unemployed Lebanese and non-citizens (e.g., Palestinian and Syrian) activists could improve their job prospects—and chances of success in their applications for emigration to Western countries—by demonstrating their involvement in civil society. Activists from marginalized communities also repurposed neoliberal technologies such as professionalism and entrepreneurship for cultivating class mobility and solidarity. Given that unemployment constituted a fundamental part of precarious activists' lived experiences of crisis, enhancing the probability of securing a stable job could become an essential component of crisiswork. Attention to different rationales, effects, and implications of activism reveals that crisiswork entailed multiple modalities of being political, becoming political, and doing politics. Different activist lifeworlds generated diverse crisis narratives that led to distinct imaginations of the state, citizenship, belonging, change, and agency.

In its double focus on emergent possibilities and obstacles hindering activists' struggle for change, *Crisiswork* resists a common expectation among many scholarly and non-scholarly readers to choose between an "optimistic" or a "pessimistic" account. In her thought-provoking article "Dark Anthropology and Its Others: Theory Since the Eighties," anthropologist Sherry Ortner contrasts what she calls "dark anthropology"—which focuses on issues such as power, domination, and oppression, and their negative effects on people' experiences—with "anthropologies of the good," or ethnographies that react to "dark anthropology" by focusing on positive themes such as happiness.[95] While cautioning against drawing a sharp line between dark anthropology and anthropologies of the good, Ortner suggests that ethnographies of activism can bridge these two opposite poles of anthropological thinking.

By producing accounts that offer both nuanced cultural critiques of existing structures of power *and* alternative imaginations emerging from and challenging these existing structures, *Crisiswork* invites the reader to sustain a productive tension between pessimism and optimism. I find both optimism and pessimism in activist lifeworlds. Many Lebanese activists shaped and were shaped by both colonial and decolonial visions and practices. Rather than assessing Lebanese activisms' capacity to create "real change," this book focuses on the ambivalences and contradictions constituting crisiswork.

Research (Dis)Empowered by Crises

When I began my long fieldwork in 2012 to study everyday cross-sectarian relations and belonging in Beirut, I had little idea how popular activism was becoming among Lebanese or how it was shaped by invocations of crisis. My earlier visit for exploratory research in 2011 had helped me familiarize myself with Msaytbeh, a diversely populated neighborhood in central Beirut in terms of class, sect, and political background. Conducting neighborhood-based research in Msaytbeh as an entry point to my long multi-sited ethnography in 2012 allowed me to participate in the everyday routines of communities with different sectarian, political, and economic backgrounds. My interlocutors saw me as an enthusiastic Turkish female researcher based at a prestigious university in the United States. Once they were convinced that I was not an agent of the US government, Turkish government, or any political group, people seemed to appreciate my voluntary choice to do research in Lebanon.

The main streets in Msaytbeh were lined with small clothing shops, fast-food eateries, and modest apartment buildings, half of which had been recently rebuilt. The aura of a stable middle-class neighborhood was overshadowed by highly politicized and militarized spatial configurations. Most side streets were decorated by party flags and pictures of martyrs from specific sects. Each of the three neighborhoods in Msaytbeh I stayed in had a highly visible army barracks guarded by an armed soldier, overseen by young men sitting on street corners, smoking water pipes, and watching those who walked by. Sometimes these soldiers and young men asked the passersby, especially young men from other neighborhoods, to present their identification cards, and briefly interrogated them about their identity. The heavy presence of sectarian symbols undoubtedly reinforced complex sentiments of fear, belonging, loyalty, and indifference among many. But there was more to everyday life in the neighborhood and the larger city.

When I told my initial contacts that my research was about everyday relations between different confessional communities and the issue of belonging, some suggested that I talk to activists, who "love talking about these issues." I met and conducted interviews with a wide range of self-identified activists, such as unemployed NGO volunteers, leftist intellectuals, representatives of collectives and social movements, humanitarian workers, and the returning Lebanese diaspora. These activists participated in civil society spaces ranging from institutionalized organizations, such as NGOs, university clubs, and consultancy companies, to grassroots formations such as collectives, coalitions, and movements. I accompanied my interlocutors to cafés, bars, university campuses, workplaces, hiking trips, public events, protests such as rallies and marches, house parties, and family gatherings and spent time with their extended families. This initial phase of research helped me recognize both the pervasiveness of crisis narratives and the diverse genealogies of activism. For example, some activists claimed inheritance to the vibrant activism for the Palestinian cause unfolding through the 1960s and 1970s, which positioned Lebanon as a significant hub for the leftists of the global South. Others, such as some from the middle-class returnee Lebanese diaspora, embraced the entrepreneurial ethos of Silicon Valley.

In order to better understand diverse experiences of activism, I undertook in-depth interviews with activists from various sect, class, and gender backgrounds; volunteered in several youth-focused feminist and environmental NGOs and collectives; led focus group discussions with and administered surveys to various activists; and conducted media analysis of Facebook and WhatsApp groups. To further contextualize civil society engagement within translocal policy-making processes, I interviewed leading Lebanese politicians and bureaucrats, intellectuals, journalists, program managers of social entrepreneurship programs in major Lebanese banks and universities, representatives of international organizations and donor agencies, and Western aid workers who were active in civil society. I also amassed a textual archive from local newspapers, NGO booklets, and public event brochures and pamphlets.

My research process was profoundly impacted by political crises related to the Syrian War. When I began my long fieldwork in the summer of 2012, the Lebanese Shiʿi Miqdad clan was kidnapping Syrian, Saudi, Qatari, and Turkish citizens in Lebanon to pressure the governments of these countries to help free Lebanese Shiʿi pilgrims kidnapped by the armed opposition in Syria. As my Turkish partner and I endeavored to keep a low profile and remain vigilant, I had to restrict my ethnographer's drive to go everywhere and meet everyone. This vigilance dissipated after a couple of months, as I found creative ways to hide my Turkish identity when needed. However, the increasing number of public bombings in 2013 endangered my field stay. As the US Department of State issued serious travel warnings throughout that year, my program at Stanford encouraged me to suspend my research. Particularly in light of my ambiguous status as a Turkish national affiliated with a US institution, the university feared I could become a liability if Lebanon's instability worsened. I was required to demonstrate that I could safely navigate Lebanon's crises, had solid local connections, and was ready to leave immediately if required.

From my perspective, however, I was a privileged visitor in Beirut. Unlike many of my interlocutors, I could afford to move between neighborhoods, stay at home as much as I needed, or exit the country at will. Thanks to the welcoming and supportive networks I cultivated, I seldom felt fearful during my stay in Lebanon and viewed the American threat metrics as unreasonably exaggerated. As I increasingly became more engaged with diverse groups of people, I did feel vulnerable, challenged, and confused, but I also felt cared for, loved, and supported. Participating in my interlocutors' crisiswork led me to experience Lebanon as a place of continual political and ethical learning. A central aspect of this learning process was that imagining post-crisis futures could open up some doors while closing others.

Lifeworlds Within Bounded Futures

Imagining non-sectarian (*ghayr ṭā'ifī*) futures, many Lebanese activists articulate deep longings for a unified national identity and a functional nation-state.[96] This is not surprising, given that endorsing nationalism has become the *sine qua non* of political discourse in post-war Lebanon.[97] In particular, civil society actors view national belonging as a panacea for the detrimental effects of sectarianism. In the futuristic politics of activism, Lebanese identity and citizenship become aspirational narratives with temporal, affective, and ethical dimensions. Similar to urban middle-class Lebanese during the early twentieth century who imagined "uniting on the basis of who they might be rather than who they were,"[98] diverse Lebanese activists search for belonging in the future while frequently experiencing unbelonging in the present. Lebanese activists' crisiswork is an example of how national identities, civic cultures, and vibrant public conversations can be forged by fluid, incoherent networks of civil society.[99] While opposition to sectarianism and cultivating national identity have been formative of Lebanese civil society, activist projects often have contradictory implications. Rather than focusing on whether activists challenge sectarianism or reproduce it, I examine how they are historically situated within the cultural, socio-economic, and political dynamics of sectarianism while they actively critique and seek to undo sectarianism.[100]

As activists seek to counteract narrowing horizons of expectation by invoking alternative future imaginations and rebuilding individual and collective forms of agency,[101] these imaginations of future and agency could become bounded by various processes. Activists' crisiswork is a futuristic project of generating a hopeful new generation of active Lebanese citizens who would believe in and work for change. Yet this work for change is contingent and open-ended. Activists' crisiswork is "a project always on the threshold of becoming" and is not necessarily geared toward a foreseeable outcome like a revolution.[102] Meanwhile, not all "becomings" are linear or positive. In their ambivalent call for "doing something" and "creating change," diverse activists in Lebanon often eschew meaningful discussions about "failure," thereby suppressing potential trajectories that might arise out of individual and collective practices of self-reflection. Excessive futurism could hence become self-defeating in its continual orienting of subjects to forward-looking projects that hardly build upon their collective past experiences.

More importantly, alternative future imaginations become restricted when Lebanese activists actively avoid addressing the exclusion of racialized communities whose crises and sufferings they rarely acknowledge or grieve. Colonial legacies and historical injustices often play out in present struggles in ways that limit future imaginations. Not all demands for "doing something" express concerns with the suffering of Lebanon's Others. In 2012, a few months before I traveled to Lebanon for my long fieldwork stay, my Lebanese teacher in California—from whom I learned the Lebanese dialect of Arabic—told me that she and her family had recently been preparing to return to Lebanon to help "save the country" from Syrian refugees and the negative impacts of the Syrian War. After that, I systematically observed how "doing something" could also bound futures when "doers" excessively blame outside forces for undermining the possibilities of Lebanon's unification and growth.

Crisiswork, hence, also generates self-victimization. Many activists blamed the urban poor, refugees, and migrant workers for obstructing Lebanon's nation-building project. Seeing Lebanon and Lebanese as exceptionally victimized by incommensurable crises, many activists turned a blind eye to others' problems. After 2011, and as Lebanon became host to the largest number of refugees per capita in the world, as well as to sizable numbers of migrant workers from the global South, the growing precarity of these newcomers evidenced the impacts of racial capitalism. In blaming racialized communities as precipitating Lebanon's crises or in simply refusing to attend to their urgent needs or to listen to their experiences, many activists hindered solidarity possibilities that could inform and expand visions of a more inclusive political community. Many activists also consistently downplayed how intersectional dynamics such as class, gender, race, and religion could factor into the collective imaginations of future and agency. Crisiswork, therefore, is also generative of bounded futures.

The Book and You

Thank you for your interest in this book. Whether you know plenty, nothing, or something in between about crisis, activism, Lebanon, anthropology, or decoloniality, I wholeheartedly welcome you. I wrote this book for anyone who, regardless of their level of knowledge or expertise, is curious about the complexities and ambiguities of everyday life in Lebanon as experienced by activists. Crisiswork, the open-ended processes of activist struggle for undoing crises and enacting change, offers a unique window into the broader political, economic, and cultural dynamics of contemporary Lebanon. In this sense, this book is about both Lebanese activists and broader Lebanese society. It is also about politics and ethics in relation to lived and perceived crises.

The ethnographic research that undergirds this book does not delimit Lebanon by territory, sect, class, or ideology. Instead, it documents open-ended encounters among multiple actors from different locales and identities. In delineating the various ways in which crises generate complex responses and engagements, each chapter details how diverse groups in Lebanon—most under conditions of precarity—simultaneously embrace and contest competing modalities of political agency, ethical citizenship, and affective selfhood. While Western donors and local elites praise Lebanese civil society for fostering "shared identity and culture" and "civic activism," *Crisiswork* shows that Lebanese activists *live* such abstract dreams, and their endless deferral, in ambivalent ways. Diverse activists' modalities of crisiswork are deeply rooted in the contingencies of everyday life. As you turn these pages, you will gain an understanding of the manifold and interrelated experiences of crises that activists contend with as well as the various class-based activist projects that seek to address such crises through work on active citizenship, professionalism, social entrepreneurship, and sustaining hope. In reading through the many stories of Lebanese and non-Lebanese engaged in crisiswork, you will learn how, in the very pursuit of the elusive ethos of change, multiple lifeworlds emerge.

This book is also a humble invitation to experience solidarity and empathy with others even if, or precisely because, their suffering and struggle may seem far away from some of you. I ask that you think and feel together with my interlocutors and me, and that you reflect on the complexity of these activists' experiences of crises and on the profound meaning of sustaining a struggle for alternative presents and futures, often amid precarity and fear. Reading these textured stories of competing ways of "doing something" will familiarize you with the differential experiences of crisis constituting contemporary Lebanon. But these stories will also, I hope, defamiliarize you from your certainties about identity, activism, and politics.

In reading stories that oscillate between national unity and communal belonging, working for change and preserving the status quo, hope and despair, and inclusion and exclusion, you will recognize the contradictory pressures that activists experience in their daily lives. *Crisiswork* requests that you notice the convergences between your own lives and the complex lifeworlds that Lebanese inhabit, which would facilitate meaningful pathways to new, translocal connections and solidarities. As we reflect together on the political and ethical ambiguities that many Lebanese face while creatively navigating crises, perhaps we can all learn from and continue to build on crisiswork, in Lebanon and elsewhere.

ONE

Crisis Narratives

I was walking through Hamra—a cosmopolitan touristic neighborhood in Beirut hosting numerous hotels, cafés, restaurants, and shopping areas—in December 2013 when a smiling, sportily dressed, and well-groomed woman in her early twenties handed me a survey. The title read, "What's the Problem of the Lebanese?" (Figures 1 and 2). Speaking in the Lebanese dialect of Arabic, the surveyor introduced herself as an activist and requested that I take five minutes to fill out the survey, which would contribute to research for an NGO project. Pointing at two other surveyors standing a few meters ahead of us, she added that all three were students at Lebanese American University (LAU), a gesture I interpreted as an effort to convey their respectable, middle-class social status. I happily accepted the request, as I was in no hurry to go anywhere and was interested in how NGOs interfaced with the public. After reading the pamphlet and being struck by both its questions and their focus on Lebanon and the Lebanese, I told the young surveyor that I was not Lebanese but very much liked the survey, and I asked her if I could keep a copy after returning the one I had filled out. She kindly acquiesced and continued to distribute pamphlets to others.

The survey is anonymous and includes a brief confidentiality statement. The questions and instructions appear in both English and Lebanese Arabic, and both versions have some grammatical mistakes, which led me to guess that the young surveyors had prepared the pamphlets themselves (I frequently saw grammatical mistakes in Arabic and English texts prepared by diverse NGO members in Beirut).[1] One of the pages has demographic

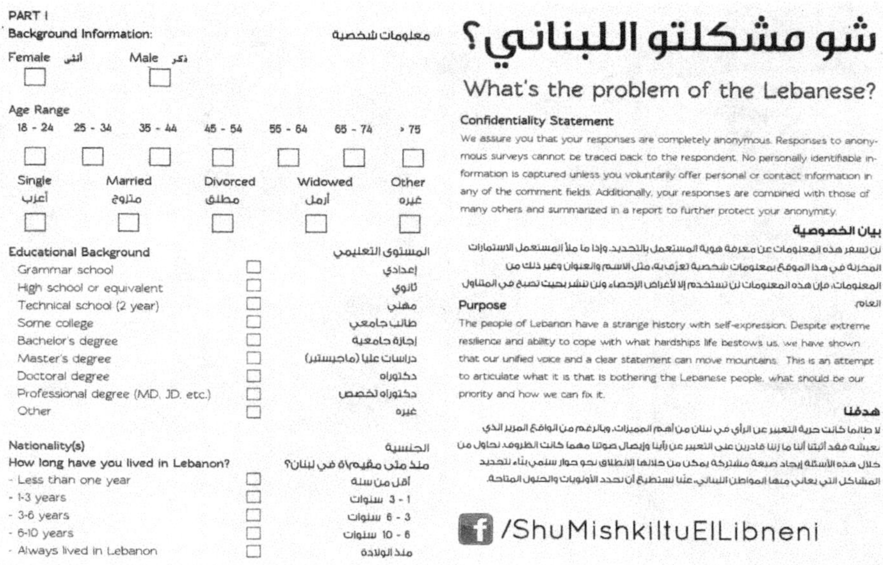

FIGURE 1. Public Survey distributed in Hamra Street, Beirut, December 2013. The front side.

questions about gender, age, marital status, educational background, and nationality. In contrast to many other forms and documents prepared by the state and private institutions, the survey does not ask about confessional background. As the question on nationality indicates, the survey was open to non-Lebanese as well, and I saw surveyors explaining to several English-speaking tourists that they could fill it out, even as the survey's wording suggests that its main focus is Lebanon and the Lebanese.

The reverse side of the survey asks fifteen questions about Lebanon's problems, which encourage the participants to share their emotions and opinions about the nation's past, present, and future, as well as the unique traits of its people. One question inquires about people's "pride" to be Lebanese and another about the Lebanese's "big flaw." While most questions are neutrally formulated, the question, "Do you think Lebanon will ever be independent, self-sustaining and sovereign?" conveys a political message that Lebanon is not presently an independent, self-sustaining, and sovereign country. While inviting people to think more deeply about the country's problems, the survey itself identifies a problem and calls into question the state of nationhood in Lebanon.

I did not interview the surveyors, but I observed them for about two hours and noticed that they gave the pamphlet primarily to well-dressed, urban,

What's the problem of the Lebanese?	NO لا	Neutral عادي	YES نعم	شو مشكلتو اللبناني؟
1. Happy with Lebanon?				1. مبسوط بلبنان؟
2. Optimistic about the future?				2. متفائل للمستقبل؟
3. Proud of your nationality?				3. فخور بهويتك؟
4. If you could immigrate, would you?				4. ازا بصرلك تهاجر بتهاجر؟
5. If yes, where to?				5. لوين؟
6. What do you think our priorities as a nation should be?				6. شو بنظرك الاولويات لبناء وطن؟
7. One thing you love about Lebanon.				7. شغلي بتحبا بلبنان؟
8. One thing you hate about Lebanon.				8. شغلي بتكرها بلبنان؟
9. Describe Lebanon in ONE word.				9. وصوف لبنان بكلمة وحدة.
10. Do you think Lebanon will ever be independent, self-sustaining and sovereign?				10. بتعتقد الو لبنان بيوماً ما ممكن يكون قائم بحد ذالو؟
11. Who is at fault? Who do you blame?				11. على مين بتلقي اللوم؟
12. Do we have any unique traits? What are they?				12. بنظرك عنا مميزات؟ شو هيي؟
13. What is our big flaw?				13. شو توكنا؟
14. If you could change one thing in the history of Lebanon, what would it be?				14. ازا ممكن تغير شي بتاريخ وطنك شو بتغير؟
15. What do you foresee?				15. شو بترتئي؟

FIGURE 2. Public Survey distributed in Hamra Street, Beirut. December 2013. The back side.

middle-class, and secular-looking young people. Some of these people refused to take the pamphlet, while others agreed to fill in the survey quickly. The three young surveyors seemed enthusiastic about what they were doing and did not look discouraged when people turned down their requests. As they waited for people to fill in the surveys, they discussed the submitted ones together in conversations that became passionate at times.

The pamphlet, in English, explains its purpose as follows:

> The people of Lebanon have a strange history with self-expression. Despite extreme resilience and ability to cope with what hardships life bestows us, we have shown that our unified voice and a clear statement can move mountains. This is an attempt to articulate what it is that is bothering the Lebanese people, what should be our priority and how we can fix it.

This statement does more than explain the purpose of the survey. It begins by qualifying "the people of Lebanon" as having "a strange history with self-expression." The following sentence does not unpack what makes that history "strange" but continues to make other statements about Lebanese history, pointing to shared "hardships" without explicating what those are. It also does not clarify what "unified voice" refers to, nor how such a voice functions. The last sentence explains that the purpose of the survey is to provide an opportunity to articulate what bothers the "Lebanese people" and explore new ways to fix their problems.

The word "priority" implicitly acknowledges that there could be many problems, and the survey seeks to identify the most important ones. While the very practice of surveying signals a quest to seek diverse perspectives about Lebanon and the Lebanese, the purpose statement offers its own viewpoint on the topic by describing the Lebanese as resilient in the face of hardship—able to unify and fight when needed. In effect, the survey invites city residents to imagine themselves as part of a unified and strong collective that needs their insights and efforts. It also signals that Lebanon's problems, once well understood, can be fixed. The survey, thus, is a perfect example of middle-class activists' crisiswork, which invokes shared crises and seeks to respond to them by calling for ethical citizenship—the willingness to do something for Lebanon's crises.

The Arabic version of the purpose statement is significantly different from the English version in its wording and tone. I share my translation below to offer a better understanding of how the surveyors conceived of their project:

> Freedom of expression has always been one of the most important features of Lebanon. Despite the bitter reality we live in, we have proven that we still can express our opinion and make our voice heard, whatever the circumstances. With these questions, we are trying to find a common ground on which we can proceed toward a peaceful and constructive dialogue to identify the problems that the Lebanese citizens suffer from. Publicly we can determine the priorities and available solutions.

Both versions express the difficult conditions of life in the country and the ability of the Lebanese to make their voices heard. They convey urges to speak and make others speak. In the Arabic version, Lebanon is characterized as a place where freedom of expression prevails—in contrast to the English version, which labels the history of such freedom "strange"—and there is a clearer goal for the project: finding common ground through peaceful and constructive dialogue. It reflects more clearly the language of middle-class–led conflict resolution and peacebuilding efforts that characterized many civil society initiatives in the country. Rather than asserting an existing "unified voice," the phrase "trying to find a common ground" in the Arabic version depicts national unity as an aspiration. Also, the preference in the Arabic version for "Lebanese citizens" over "Lebanese people" expresses a more nationalist undertone, as many residents of Lebanon do not have Lebanese citizenship.

Yet both surveys express curiosity about Lebanese perspectives on Lebanon and seek to instill a sense of citizenship, national identity, and belonging. By asking participants to reflect cognitively and emotionally on the past, present, and future of the country, the survey questions such as "Happy with Lebanon?" and "One thing you hate about Lebanon?" invoke an intimate relationship between a resident and Lebanon, calling upon the residents of the country to imagine themselves as Lebanese who deeply care for and actively engage with Lebanon's history and problems. What do these calls mean at a time when many residents worry about frequent bombings, increased political polarization, and declining economy?

I call conversations that develop around these kinds of existential questions—such as "What's happening to Lebanon?" and "Who are Lebanese?"—*crisis narratives.* Such narratives form a temporal account as a way of making sense of an intense and eventful period, evoking existing problems and suggesting a need for intervention in the process. As exemplified in the survey, crisis narratives are attempts to reckon with life in Lebanon and articulate the strains of individual and collective experiences in the country. The survey represents the past and the present as times of struggle, asking the respondents to imagine the future as a time when these problems could be solved. By asking these questions, the survey seeks to build a shared narrative that represents affective and temporal experiences of collectively living in Lebanon.

Narratives are stories of change that convey "the temporal character of human experience."[2] Crisis narratives are attempts to weave the past, present, and future together in ways that invite conversations on identity, belonging, and change. But narratives do more than organize happenings sequentially—they connect seemingly disconnected phenomena in ways that help us with meaning-making. Even though the world is not arranged as such, people often perceive it in narrative form, and through narratives, people make sense of the world around them and who they are.[3] As conveyed in the surveys, crisis narratives invoke a political subject who experiences multiple national problems, yet who looks for ways to solve them. Crisis narratives call for crisiswork—"doing something" about crises—and they foster public conversations about what could be done.

Crisis narratives come into being when subjects collectively seek an answer to the question, "What is happening?" In this sense, crisis narratives are modes of knowledge-making, particularly with respect to periods that are perceived as unusual, dramatic, or uncertain. Lebanon's vibrant public culture creates numerous spaces for generating and exchanging crisis narratives that respond to urgent questions. By building accounts of, and searching for explanations for, perceived experiences of crisis, many Lebanese participate in public and private conversations about the history of the country that are entangled with temporal practices of remembering, forgetting, imagining, and anticipating.

Crisis narratives also foster world-making, which, as a collective process, imagines new possibilities through "evoking socio-political transformation."[4] Crisis narratives facilitate world-making by generating a multiplicity of open-ended ways of experiencing the world and striving to change it. Talking about Lebanon's problems and potential solutions to them through crisis narratives produces a contested social terrain on which different accounts of history-writing and future-imagining take place and compete. Different lifeworlds generate diverse crisis narratives, resulting in distinct modes of crisiswork with competing imaginations of state, citizenship, belonging, change, and agency. While middle-class activists, like the NGO surveyors above, portrayed shared experiences of struggle and searched for common ground, low-income activists, alongside other low-income residents, emphasized the structural constraints that created inequalities and exclusions; in particular, how Lebanon's state formation created asymmetrical and differential experiences of crises. Despite participating in the shared cultural world of civil society, their crisis narratives were based on lived experiences of everyday hardship and marginalization, whereas middle-class activist narratives were mainly based on abstractions.

Unlike middle-class activists, low-income activists did not see Lebanese civil society as the primary agent of change. Instead, their crisis narratives exposed often-ignored structural inequalities and called upon the Lebanese state to serve and protect all of its citizens. Attention to competing, open-ended, disjunctive, and contradictory crisis narratives of diverse actors in Lebanon reveals that activism is not a monolithic practice and that crisiswork involves multiple modalities for being political and ethical with divergent practices of citizenship and belonging.

Social Life of Crisis Narratives

Talking about the problems of Lebanon and the Lebanese was a common everyday practice for diverse residents of Beirut. Taxi drivers, shopkeepers, janitors, and Syrian refugees, as well as my neighbors from diverse confessional and class backgrounds, fervently spoke at length about how there was no state (*mā fī dawla*), no government *(mā fī ḥukūma*), and no order (*mā fī niẓām*) in Lebanon, and how everyone was sectarian (*ṭā'ifī*), self-interested (*maṣlaḥjī*), and a liar (*kadhdhāb*). My shared-taxi rides (*sarvīs*), one of the most popular transportation arrangements in Beirut, were rife with conversations about crisis (*azma*) and chaos (*fawḍā*) on the frequent occasions when Beirut's notorious traffic jams provided passengers ample time for an enjoyable chit-chat.[5] Complaining about electricity cuts, water shortages, rising consumer prices, unemployment, and other familiar problems gave many Lebanese an opportunity to engage in social and political conversations with strangers without the risk of straying into controversial topics and potential confrontations. For diverse Beirut residents, talking about both Lebanon's larger and everyday problems generated possibilities for sharing discontent and enabled various forms of sociality, solidarity, and care.

The versatility of the Arabic word for "crisis," *azma*, helps explain its frequent usage to describe a variety of problems. Contemporary use of words that can be translated as "crisis" in different languages commonly refer to an aberration: a situation in which things are perceived as not normal or as they should be.[6] In ancient Greek society, the term *krisis* (crisis) denoted a "singular moment of decisive judgment." In current times, "crisis" in English mainly describes a condition of demise and exception, often in reference to major, prolonged problems in economics, finance, politics, or diplomacy.[7] *Azma* has a much broader historical use.[8] In AD 545, *azma* was used to denote hardship.[9] The well-known thirteenth-century Arabic-language dictionary *Mukhtar al-Sihah* by Muhammad ibn Abu Bakr Al Razi defines *azma* as "distress and drought."[10] In contemporary Arabic, many circumstances that cause distress can be called *azma*, including prolonged problems or issues of varying scale and severity. For instance, one common term for heart attack is *azma albiyya* (heart crisis), with crisis symbolizing the intense distress felt in the heart. Similarly, *azma nafsiyya* (psychological crisis) is used for a wide spectrum of mental disorders and psychological distress. In Lebanon, I heard these usages as well as phrases such as *azmat sayr* (traffic crisis) and *azma bil*

ʿalāʾa (relationship crisis). Depending on the context, *azma* could mean crisis, hardship, distress, struggle, scarcity, shortage, deadlock, or conflict.

As the historical genealogy of *azma* reveals, crisis narratives in Lebanon were not limited to well-known political or social events or those featured in media. For many Lebanese, the word was intrinsically entangled with the everyday problems of Lebanon and Lebanese. A minor problem on an ordinary day could easily be called a "Lebanese problem" and tied to the crises the country was going through. When a water tank in one's building was quickly depleted or a car cut off one's rightful passage, many interpreted such incidents as "Lebanese problems" rather than as isolated incidents. Oftentimes, a conversation about a personal experience related to family, romance, work, or fun could quickly slide into negative commentaries about Lebanon and its people. The association of daily problems and personal experiences with the larger crises of the nation facilitated a proliferation of public conversations about Lebanon and the Lebanese among diverse communities.

Lebanon's problems—and strategies for fixing those problems—were topics that many Lebanese encountered in intimate spaces of family and friendship from a very early age. Growing up during the long Lebanese War (1975–1990) and afterwards, many heard their families speak about war and current political affairs. Many of my interlocutors told me that they formed their first political opinions by listening to older, male family members discuss politics. In elementary and high schools, while institutional policies and curricula discouraged discussion of war and politics, young Lebanese were exposed to a variety of accounts of the past from their friends, most of whom came from families of the same sect or political orientation. Through extensive participation in popular training programs on leadership, conflict resolution, problem solving, and communication offered in all levels of schooling, young Lebanese were taught that their country had many problems and that they were expected to do something about them.

Given this shared cultural history of continually discussing "Lebanon," many Lebanese interlocutors displayed an impressive mastery of articulating Lebanese problems and solutions. I listened to a myriad of proposals from different groups on how to "fix" (*ẓabbiṭ*) Lebanon. The very practice of hearing political and religious leaders, family members, neighbors, teachers, activists, foreign and local experts, media figures, and many others discuss how Lebanon's crises created a dynamic public space, which invited the public to reflect on Lebanon and the Lebanese. These reflections were ultimately generative of the complex and contradictory field of crisiswork, in which activism was conceived and practiced as an act of ethical citizenship to undo crises within both the political system and everyday life.

While talking about Lebanon and its problems was an everyday practice for diverse Beirut residents, people from urban educated groups—particularly middle-class activists—had a more purposeful project to make others talk about the state of affairs in the country in order to cultivate sentiments of national identity and belonging. Young activist surveyors in Hamra were not alone in their efforts to invite people to imagine themselves and others as Lebanese. Between 2012 and 2014, I frequently came across local and international journalists conducting interviews with cameras and microphones in popular Beirut neighborhoods such as Hamra and Ashrafieh. These TV and newspaper representatives often asked seemingly random people on the street their opinions about day-to-day political events or general problems in Lebanon. Activists, NGO workers, and high school and college students also took this approach, asking passerby in popular corners of the city whether they had a few minutes for a short interview or survey about life in Lebanon. I met about twenty Lebanese activists who either had produced an amateur documentary on everyday life in Lebanon or planned to do so.

Civil society organizations, which were key to the dissemination of crisis narratives, had a massive presence everywhere, from cities to remote towns and villages. In day-long or multi-day events, such as empowerment workshops, skill trainings, and weekend retreats in Beirut or in Lebanon's mountain resorts, many Lebanese from different backgrounds came together to discuss the country's problems. Various Lebanese NGOs conducted one-on-one interviews with citizens and convened town hall meetings that brought together representatives of different groups. Lebanese civil society networks also created open public forums in cafés and bars in Beirut, and activists invited representatives of different communities to discuss Lebanon's problems in open areas and local associations' offices in villages.

The Lebanese media—particularly programs that targeted urban educated groups—was central to facilitating conversations about the nature and essence of the Lebanese.[11] As the young activist surveyors in Hamra did, influential media figures encouraged Lebanese to reflect, both cognitively and emotionally, on the country and its people. They not only collected random opinions and feelings but also actively shaped public conversations. "Lebanese are not extreme people (*mutaṭarrifīn*); they are moderate (*muʿtadilīn*)," said a participant in a January 13, 2014, episode of the popular Lebanese Broadcasting Corporation International program *Kalam al-Nas* during a conversation about how Lebanese felt about the recent bombings in Beirut. Lebanese social media conversations, particularly on Twitter and Facebook, were saturated with discussions on the characteristics of the Lebanese and the problems of Lebanon. Media and social media—both of which were lavishly consumed in Lebanon—facilitated people's imagining of both a nation with ample problems and a people with certain shared qualities.

Several local publishers, targeting urban middle-class audiences who were fluent in English and who could afford the high price tag, released entertaining books that focused on what they viewed as the shared characteristics of the Lebanese. For example, the introduction to *You Know You're Lebanese When. . .* (2011) describes Lebanon as "a motley mix of strong family ties, lifestyle, allergy to following rule and order, and a tendency to 'show off'" and the Lebanese as "a proud, resourceful people whose country is a strategic strip of land on the Eastern Mediterranean."[12] *"Life's Like That!": Your Guide to the Lebanese* (2008) offers page-long descriptions in English of a range of archetypical Lebanese figures, such as "service driver," "civil servant," "*arguileh* smoker," and "corniche jogger," that carefully avoid any identification based on ethnicity, sect, or political orientation.[13] Both books, prepared by well-educated middle-class Lebanese authors, journalists, and artists, list "shared characteristics" of the Lebanese, such as being addicted to plastic surgery or going to many nightclubs in one night. Their portrayals of most characters as urban, middle-class, and secular provide a restricted representation of Lebanese people's socio-economic, religious, and political backgrounds. Many of my Lebanese interlocutors contested the essentialized characters in such portrayals as simplistic and reflective of an urban elite classism. Regardless of their veracity or the level of endorsement they receive, such narratives expand public conversations about Lebanese identity and belonging, inviting Lebanese to be part of what presented itself as a national conversation on the country and its inhabitants. Perhaps more significantly, they portray Lebanese as a homogeneous entity with shared characteristics and problems.

Even though the predominant public discourses of urban middle-class elites framed crises as shared problems that impacted all Lebanese in the same way, many Lebanese perceived, interpreted, and experienced those problems through the lenses of their socio-economic backgrounds and political alignments. Crisis narratives were classed, gendered, racialized, and generational.

Political, confessional, and religious orientations shaped how people articulated accounts of everyday and broader problems and positioned themselves vis-à-vis the imagined nation and other groups. Moreover, no one had a complete, coherent, and consistent narrative. Crisis narratives were open-ended and dynamic, continually undergoing processes of contestation, revision, and cooptation. Critically examining competing activist enactments of crisis narratives reveals that the idea of shared Lebanese struggles with constant crises was a convenient abstraction to imagine a unified civil society. In reality, civil society was inherently fractured with classed experiences of belonging and unbelonging.

Middle-Class Activists' Crisis Narratives

MAKING LAWS, NOT WARS

On July 9, 2013, a car bomb hit Bir al-Abed, a southern, predominantly Shiʿi suburb of Beirut, severely injuring more than fifty people. The incident marked the first attack on Shiʿa-populated south Beirut after Hizbullah officially sided with Syrian president Bashar Assad in the Syrian War against "extremists." Despite political differences, Lebanese politicians and the public alike commonly referred to the bombing as a watershed development that would move Lebanon toward further polarization and violence. Comparisons to the long Lebanese War abounded. Lebanese President Michel Suleiman said the bombing reopened the "black pages" of the war. Key political leaders, including Speaker Nabih Berri, caretaker Prime Minister Najib Mikati, and Premier-designate Tammam Salam, issued statements that called for national solidarity, asking Lebanese to end their disputes and unite.[14] Like other acts of violence, the bombing at Bir al-Abed became grounds for proliferating crisis narratives about national unity and the nation's history.

Lara, then a thirty-two-year-old middle-class Lebanese activist who worked at one of Beirut's United Nations branches as a project manager, texted me after the bombing and suggested that I meet her at the Starbucks café in Verdun, an upscale Sunni-majority neighborhood in central Beirut. I had contacted Lara about a week before to check on her, but she had not responded, as she had been very busy completing a project report. Because of the bombing, another friend of hers had canceled a meeting they had been planning, and Lara did not want to stay at home. She felt overwhelmed by her family's political discussions at home and wanted to go out. She liked to go to the Starbucks in Verdun; it was near her house, and Verdun was relatively safe even during such moments of tension.

Like many other public places that day, the café was not crowded. When Lara arrived at the table where I was waiting, she was very nervous and upset. Most of the people on her mother's side of the family were Shiʿa and lived near the bombing site. Her mother had panicked after being unable to reach Lara's maternal uncle, who worked near the site, for a few hours. Like most residents of Shiʿa-populated parts of Beirut, her mother blamed the bombing on foreign agents and their "extremist" Sunni allies in Lebanon who supported the ongoing insurgency against Syria's President Assad. Lara felt sorry for her mother and relatives, but unlike them, she blamed Lebanese sectarianism in general rather than Sunni extremists in particular. "People always think of their sect. If we don't have a national identity, then there's nothing to unite us," she commented, interpreting both bombing and bombed groups as operating with sectarian logics. Lara did not support Hizbullah and was critical of Hizbullah's involvement in Syria and its support for the Syrian regime. She was also worried because one of her distant cousins, as with many other young Shiʿi men, had been training to fight for Hizbullah in Syria. Lara was especially upset because she believed that Hizbullah's involvement in Syria would further polarize Lebanon and undermine its economy, and she complained that young fighters in the ranks of Hizbullah, her distant cousin included, had little idea what they were fighting for.

After the long Lebanese War ended in 1990, Hizbullah was the only militia group that had been officially permitted to keep its weapons and defend South Lebanon against the ongoing Israeli occupation. After Israel's withdrawal from South Lebanon in 2000, Hizbullah controversially retained its weapons. In the context of the increased political polarization that followed the assassination of Prime Minister Rafiq Hariri in February 2005, the debates over Hizbullah's role in Lebanese politics have intensified. Two competing political coalitions that emerged in this process—the Sunni-led, pro-Western March 14 coalition and the Shiʿa-led, anti-Western March 8 coalition—rekindled debates about the country's geopolitical policies and national interests.[15] Disagreements between the opposing political camps generated new conflicts in the following years. Political tensions mounted in May 2008 when the pro-Western government removed the pro-Hizbullah airport director and shut down Hizbullah's telecommunications networks, resulting in brief but intense street clashes in different parts of Beirut and an unexpected seizure of central Beirut by Hizbullah. These "Events of May" ended with the Doha Agreement on May 21, 2008.

On the topic of Hizbullah, many middle-class activists had views closer to those in the March 14 coalition, although they called themselves "independent" (*mustaqill*) to emphasize their non-sectarian and non-partisan identities. Lara saw Hizbullah's weapons as a major obstacle to Lebanon's formation of a functioning modern state. While those in the March 8 coalition viewed Hizbullah as protecting Lebanon against Israeli and other threats to the nation, those closer to the March 14 coalition emphasized that Hizbullah had used its weapons against other Lebanese in May 2008 and might do so again. Moreover, similar to many other middle-class Lebanese activists I met, Lara believed that Hizbullah controlled the army, most of the state institutions, and the borders. Some activists also criticized Hizbullah for representing Iran's interests rather than Lebanon's, while others were concerned about Hizbullah's promotion of an Islamic milieu to the country's Shiʿi youth.

Thus, in the hegemonic middle-class activist imaginary, Hizbullah obstructed the building of a sovereign nation-state with rule of law, shared identity, and other liberal principles. The majority of liberal or leftist middle-class civil society activists were explicitly critical of Hizbullah. Some middle-class activists from diverse confessional backgrounds, however, supported Hizbullah or did not see it as a major problem. Given the dominant anti-Hizbullah stance within civil society, however, such activists told me that they self-censored and refrained from bringing up this issue in collaborative spaces with others.

Lara lived with her parents in an upscale and well-maintained high-rise building in an upper-middle-class neighborhood of central Beirut. While legally registered as Sunni in Lebanon's patrimonial confessional system, given that her father was Sunni, she refused to identify as a Sunni or a member of any sect. She self-identified as a secular citizen and was proud that her mother was Shiʿi and one of her sisters was married to a Maronite Christian. After studying political science at AUB, she went to a prestigious university in London for her master's studies in public policy. I had first met her in the summer of 2011, when she was passionately working for the Smoking Ban Campaign and on other advocacy campaigns for civil marriage and electoral reform. She had struck me as a self-confident and elegant woman, always dressed in chic outfits with her hair and nails done.

She liked to lavishly enjoy the cosmopolitan life in Beirut, going to trendy cafés, bars, and artistic events.

Like several other middle-class activists I met, Lara actively supported the smoking ban, yet she was, herself, a smoker. As I listened to her political comments about the incident, Lara quickly glanced at the other customers as she lit her cigarette. I initially thought that she was concerned about being reprimanded for smoking by a customer or a café manager. Instead, she criticized the café owner and the state:

> No one enforces the law, you see? Everyone smokes here because the café owner doesn't care, and even he himself smokes. [Silence] I sometimes call the phone line [referring to the line that was set up for smoking ban violation complaints] and they don't do anything either. It's a law, but no one follows it.

Since the early 2000s, middle-class Lebanese had fervently participated in public health initiatives and civil society advocacy campaigns for a smoking ban in Lebanon. The public health rhetoric disseminated through civil society activism, academic institutions, and media campaigns constantly referred to "European standards" and cited countries like Türkiye as successful examples of Middle Eastern states that had banned smoking in public places. Lebanon ratified the World Health Organization Framework Convention on Tobacco Control in 2005 and banned smoking in enclosed public spaces in 2011. Middle-class activists, Lara included, referred to this ratification and ban as being among the few major achievements of Lebanese civil society.

Lara and other middle-class activists who both smoked and worked on the smoking ban saw themselves not as hypocritical or lacking willpower, but as victims of a corrupt state that failed to properly govern public life. Despite being committed to "doing things differently," they could also revert to the ways of those they criticized for not doing anything. For Lara, socializing and trying to achieve normalcy counted as part of her activist work that day; so did criticizing the state's failure to enforce the smoking ban, even as she evaded responsibility for not following it herself.

Between 2012 and 2014, I often heard middle-class Lebanese in Beirut, including activists, wearily refer to non-implementation of the ban as an example of "how things work in Lebanon." Ratification of the smoking ban, for middle-class activists, symbolized Lebanon's ability to establish the standards of a civilized nation. Yet many believed that noncompliance by restaurant, bar, and café owners, as well as state officials, rendered the ban almost ineffective. Its sporadic enforcement in most parts of Beirut incited further NGO activism and civil campaigns that targeted the state's absence and the lack of public respect for the law, and praised the institutions complying with the law as ethical actors.[16] Media outlets and public forums focused on non-implementation to call attention to "corrupt" state institutions that rendered the law ineffective. In addition to middle-class activists like Lara, other middle-class Lebanese also vehemently criticized the negligence and unwillingness of state institutions and officials to implement the law.[17]

Non-implementation of the smoking ban, similar to Hizbullah's keeping its weapons, infuriated many middle-class activist Lebanese. Both cases reminded them how far Lebanon was from their ideal of a civilized nation that had a functioning state and rule of law. They mourned that, despite tremendous efforts by responsible citizens and activists to elevate Lebanon to higher global standards, corrupt political actors stubbornly clung to power and favored petty self-interest over the nation's interests. These opinions were reflective of cross-sectarian civil society activism in Lebanon, the leading members of which were middle-class, secular, urban Lebanese. Their crisiswork proposed that Lebanon's crises would be overcome not through war, fighting, or supporting existing political parties but through forceful reforms in the politico-legal structure and changes in the culture.

CIVILIZING THE CULTURE

During one of our commutes in his car from downtown Beirut to his office in the Mar Mikhael neighborhood of Beirut in November 2013, Safa pointed out the lax traffic police who did not stop cars that violated red lights. As we moved very slowly in traffic, Safa also showed me reckless car and motorcycle drivers who spoke on cell phones while driving and commented, "This is a typical day in Lebanon. Surely, you know. We live in a jungle."[18] He smiled sarcastically, speaking with undertones of disgust, frustration, and cynicism. He then began talking about the absence of the state and rule of law in Lebanon. Like many other middle-class activists I had met, he criticized the ineffectiveness of the Lebanese state in maintaining public order and the "incivility" (*balā adab*) of Lebanese people who displayed improper manners in traffic and in public more broadly.

When I interviewed him in 2011, Safa, then a thirty-two-year-old architect, was one of the leading activists who advocated for enhancing public spaces. Brought up in a middle-class Maronite Christian family, he went to prominent French-language schools and the prestigious, private, French-language Saint Joseph University. He identified as secular and leftist and did not support any of the existing political parties. He had completed a master's degree in urban studies in France before returning to Beirut in 2006. Although he had a demanding job in a transnational private company, Safa was an active member of four NGOs that respectively focused on urban development, public spaces, waste management, and environmental sustainability. Like other middle-class Lebanese activists, he consistently dressed stylishly in a smart, casual style, spoke English and French fluently, and was a skillful public speaker.

Despite focusing on mobilizing society against existing political actors for system-level change, Safa and his middle-class activist friends also criticized the "culture" and "uncivil" people as being obstacles to change. For them, Lebanon's problems were both structural (related to the state, law, and institutions) and cultural (related to what they called a lack of civility among urban residents). I heard Safa and many other middle-class activists referring to public scenes that involved soldiers and police catcalling young women, pedestrians spitting on the street, car passengers throwing garbage on the road, and drivers violating traffic rules as essential features of life in Lebanon. During our short walks around the Hamra and Corniche areas in Beirut, many middle-class Lebanese activists pointed to cars with loud music, drivers parking on pedestrian pavements, or people throwing garbage on the street as representing city residents' ignorance and lack of ethical citizenship. Depending on activists' confessional backgrounds and political orientations, the targets of their criticism diverged. While some mainly complained that Lebanese Shiʿi residents lacked the cultural and aesthetic tastes of Beirut's urban culture, others criticized Syrian refugees for disrupting the city's cosmopolitan culture, sharing stereotypical portrayals of Syrian men staring at women with short dresses and Syrian street children unrelentingly begging.

Any residents who were low income or from outside the city could be framed as not properly belonging to Beirut if they were perceived to lack particular manners or tastes. I heard diverse middle-class activists comment negatively on others, including low-income participants in the workshops and trainings they led as well as work colleagues and distant relatives, whom they viewed as not knowing how to dress or behave in public. For them, those who lacked "civic culture" and "social etiquette"—phrases I frequently heard in

Arabic, English, and French—were constitutive of Lebanon's crises, and civil society spaces could help foster civic culture and well-mannered citizens.

Such class-based commentaries about the absence of proper social norms among urban residents are common in many countries. I heard many middle-class residents in Istanbul, Ankara, Palo Alto, Fairfax (Virginia), Damascus, and Aleppo—cities that I lived in long enough to observe the public culture—condescendingly make judgments about the "inappropriate" or even "threatening" behaviors of the urban poor, migrants, and refugees. The self-orientalizing gaze of the local elites toward less privileged groups is a common feature of social life in many global contexts.[19] As ethnographies that focus on different parts of the world have also pointed out, urban middle-class identity is often asserted through disapproving discourse over perceived breaches of social etiquette.[20] In the context of Lebanese middle-class activism, narrating a nation in crisis as a social practice "operated as a ritual of belonging and distinction that returned the middle class to a privileged position within the national imaginary."[21] Yet their crisis narratives convey not a desire to preserve the status quo, which is the case for many other middle-class communities in the world, but a desire to enact changes to move forward Lebanon's incomplete state-making and nation-building projects.

In their crisis narratives, middle-class activists placed themselves in a superior ethical position as responsible and informed citizens and claimed the authority to evaluate and act upon Lebanon's problems. They believed that, through cultivating skills to live in a "civilized" urban public culture, Lebanese could develop an authentic sense of citizenship and belonging. The "lack of national consciousness," in their view, could be overcome by creating a civic culture, as modeled in the Western countries, that instilled orderly and good manners in public and suitable interaction with others in society. Yet, as Safa's and others' comments illustrated, this imagination of civic culture was class-based. Middle-class activists' class-based criticisms not only perpetuated existing social hierarchies but also obscured how middle classes have privileges such as being able to navigate Beirut quickly, safely, and with little anxiety about eliciting respect or recognition. They had better cars, their neighborhoods had more functional infrastructure, and they had access to more reliable connections to help them if they breached any traffic laws. These middle-class criticisms also comprised privileged accounts of *banal crises* that felt bothersome to them but did not cause a significant or continuing burden. Middle-class activists experienced multiple crises, but often not in life-altering ways.

Not all middle-class activists approved of condescending discourses. I met with middle-class activists who were critical of the "classist" style and commentary of their activist friends. They similarly confirmed my observation that the great majority of Lebanese middle-class activists perpetuated elitist discourses that characterized the hegemonic culture of Beirut's cultural elites. Yet very few of them questioned narratives about the superiority of Western civilization and the need for Lebanon to emulate it.

LAGGING BEHIND THE WEST

As we entered his office that day in November 2013, Safa began talking about how, the previous week, his brother had to change a tire on his car because of potholes on the highway outside of Beirut. Adding that several other Lebanese friends had the same problem, Safa commented, "I'm tired of these Lebanese problems (*mashākil libnāniyya*). They never end. Sometimes I feel I'm used to them, but then Lebanon surprises me again."

What made potholes on a highway a specifically Lebanese problem for Safa? Because we had become comfortable discussing politics over the last few months, I wanted to provoke him a bit to find an answer to this question:

YASEMİN: How are potholes a Lebanese problem?

SAFA: Potholes are just an example of how public infrastructure is terrible in Lebanon. I lived in France for three years. I visited other European countries as well. Roads and public spaces are very well-maintained there. There are so many public parks, large pavements, and public transportation. There are laws. There is a respect for citizens and human life.

YASEMİN: But we have potholes in highways, even in California, one of the most developed states in the U.S. in terms of urban infrastructure. I know some Americans also complain about them. So, I don't think this is a Lebanese problem.

SAFA: But Yasemin, there is a state there that can take care of them. The American state is very well-known. It is a very strong state. My cousin studied for his doctoral degree in the US. People living there know that the state will fix those problems eventually, and the state does fix them. But there's no one to take care of those problems here [in Lebanon]. The state is terminally absent (*al-dawla ghayba nihā'iyyan*). You must belong to a political party to receive services. You know, we are not citizens.

Middle-class activists like Safa viewed Lebanon's crisis through a continual comparison with Western countries. They frequently invoked an image of a civilized and developed Western country—often the United States, Canada, or a West European country—in civil society activities or casual outings to encourage everyone to imagine a prosperous future Lebanon. Most of them had experiences of either studying at Western universities or visiting Western cities. They talked about those experiences as making them recognize what Lebanon lacked but could attain. Major Western cities had vast public parks and public transportation systems, whereas Beirut and other Lebanese cities did not. Traffic was well regulated and citizens interacted with each other civilly in European cities, but Beirut was chaotic, and its residents were violent and hostile to each other. European citizens cared about the environment, but Lebanese did not. These contrasting images were evoked both to discuss Lebanon's problems and to envision a future in which these problems were overcome.

The nation's crisis, for middle-class activists, was Lebanon's failure to progress to the level of Western nation-states, which were imagined to have a functioning state apparatus, sovereignty, rule of law, civic culture, and citizenship rights.[22] The urban middle-class imaginary desired a Lebanon similar to European countries, and that desire manifested as a daily frustration with Lebanon's not-being-like a European country. Issues such as potholes were considered exceptional problems in this imaginary not because they happened only in Lebanon but because they symbolized the Lebanese state's lagging behind an idealized sovereign and developed modern state.

The striking incongruence between Lebanon's high-quality education system and the country's poor infrastructure development and overall governance emerged as a key aspect of the middle-class crisis narrative. I heard several middle-class activists, including an NGO representative on a prominent TV show for youth and women, mention a stark contrast within the World Economic Forum's Global Competitiveness Index of 2013–2014. In this ranking, out of 148 countries, Lebanon ranked last in electricity supply, last in public trust in politicians, 147th in favoritism in the decisions of government officials, and 142nd in overall infrastructure quality. Yet, in the same report, it ranked fourth in math and science education and thirteenth in overall quality of education.[23] Many commentators used these statistics to argue that Lebanese, given their exceptionally superior educational skills and competencies, deserved a better political system and public services. They drew upon and perpetuated the discourses of exceptionalism that viewed Lebanon as significantly distinct, in both its superiorities and its problems, from other countries in the region.[24] In discussions regarding the potential of the nation in the face of crises, many experts and commentators used the word "Lebanese" to refer to well-educated, middle-class urban groups whose credentials, qualifications, and accomplishments outshined the "failed state" of the dysfunctional sectarian regime. Segments of society with less income or education, by contrast, were viewed as perpetuating the crises that were believed to emanate from Lebanon's failed state.

Middle-class crisis narratives evoked a sense of social bargain in which good education and hard work should be rewarded with a good life. After studying hard in university, middle-class activists felt pride in having done their part, had high expectations for a good life, and self-righteously criticized the state and some parts of society for failing to fulfill these expectations. Because middle-class activists, such as Lara and Safa, viewed themselves as adjacent to an imagined civilized West, they saw in themselves the authority to guide the Lebanese state and society toward progress and development. Their critiques of Lebanon's system, society, and people imagined a nation that was in need of intervention from people like themselves, who were considered capable of reversing the unfavorable course of history. Thus, their crisiswork unwittingly limited activism to middle-class, educated citizens with proper social and cultural capital. It also sidelined other narratives that called attention to historically accumulated hierarchies and inequalities and that questioned the moral superiority of the West.

Counterhegemonic Crisis Narratives

> One task of the critic is to give voice to those
> who do not have authority to have their crisis
> acknowledged and to thus contribute to bringing
> to existence untold crises: the crises of the dominated.[25]

DIFFERENT LIVES

On a warm evening in April 2014, a movie screening in one of the large auditoriums of AUB was suddenly interrupted by a power outage. Some young people in the audience applauded and said in English, "Welcome to Lebanon," which earned a laugh from other audience members. The sarcastic phrase—often said in jest when a problem suddenly erupted in daily life—was meant to convey that the proper functioning of the movie was, in fact, an exception in Lebanon, and such infrastructural problems were the norm. The sudden power failure was viewed not as surprising but as representative of shared problems that characterized everyday life in Lebanon. While we waited for the movie to resume, most of the audience checked their smartphones and others talked to their friends. The experience of a sudden interruption in a fancy auditorium in the country's top university was not received as an unusual event. After a few minutes, a generator started working and the movie resumed.

The movie, *Beirut Oh Beirut*, was part of the Limelight Film Festival. The program commemorated the internationally renowned Lebanese director Maroun Baghdadi, who had produced poignant documentaries of everyday life in Lebanon during the 1970s and 1980s and had passed away in 1993 at the age of forty-three. The movie focused on the struggles of four young Lebanese as Lebanon's political landscape shifted following the country's defeat in the 1967 Arab–Israeli War. I was watching the movie with Nour, then a twenty-nine-year-old, female, Shiʿi Lebanese activist who was a graduate student at the university. Nour commented on the applause and chanting of the young men when the power went off: "They consider this an electricity problem. For them it is a joke. I can't laugh, unfortunately." Nour was referring to our conversation the week before in which she had said that her apartment building in Chiyah, a Shiʿa-dominated, low-income neighborhood in south Beirut, suffered from many hours of power outages. She found it hard at times to charge her laptop sufficiently to complete her class assignments and was upset that some of her professors and friends at AUB did not believe her excuses. One of her classmates even teased her, saying, "Oh, we were thinking you [residents of south Beirut] had free electricity," referring to an urban myth that residents of south Beirut did not pay for government services. Expressing frustration with such comments, which she considered ignorant, classist, and arrogant, Nour described spaces such as the AUB and LAU campuses—located in west Beirut and upscale neighborhoods in central Beirut—as part of a "bubble" that had long been disconnected from the reality of life in the rest of Beirut and Lebanon. For her, the privileged residents of these spaces had comfortable lives, were not impacted much by Lebanon's crises, and knew little about "different lives" (*ḥayāt mukhtalifa*).

Nour was from a low-income family that had been displaced to Chiyah from downtown Beirut in the mid-1990s after the massive reconstruction of the city center by the Lebanese real estate company Solidere.[26] She had vivid childhood memories of family problems associated with the displacement. Her father had suffered from chronic distress, especially after he lost his small shop and an important part of his social community, and from cancer, both of which contributed to his death in 2001. After that, Nour struggled with depression and spent most of her time in the small two-bedroom apartment she shared with her mother and younger sister. When their house was hit during the 2006 July War in the Israeli bombings that destroyed thousands of buildings and displaced almost a million people in south Beirut and South Lebanon, Nour experienced the resulting suffering as a wake-up call and decided that her main life goal would be to help children traumatized in war.

After studying psychology at the Lebanese University, a poorly funded and low-ranking public university in Beirut, Nour began working in 2011 with an international humanitarian NGO that focused on children with trauma. After the funding for the project she had been working on stopped in early 2012, she was unemployed for about a year. During this time, she attended NGO workshops and trainings, which were proliferating in her neighborhood and across the broader city. She then found a paid position at a local educational consultancy company that targeted refugee children and worked there until 2016. There, her coworkers pressured her to obtain a master's degree to find a good job in civil society. Having been awarded a scholarship from a local charity and AUB, she began her graduate studies in education at AUB in fall 2013, an event Nour described as essential to building her self-confidence. "People treat you differently when they hear you're from AUB," she told me once, referring to a link between educational advancement and social prestige.

I met Nour in January 2013 during a leadership workshop offered by a local NGO in central Beirut. She was the only woman who wore the hijab among the twenty mixed youth group participants, and she seemed shy and nervous during the small group activities in which we collaborated. When I saw her again in February 2013 at a fundraiser for Palestinian refugee children organized by a Muslim charity organization in south Beirut, she looked more relaxed. Her long, loose, pastel-colored dress did not stand out, as many other women in the event room wore similarly modest clothing. She chatted with me for about an hour, expressing appreciation for my support for the

Palestinian cause. Having co-organized the event, she was pleased that I had come and encouraged me to bring my friends to other gatherings. We began to hang out more, and thanks to her generous invitations, I had an opportunity to attend several educational events in south Beirut organized by locally influential Shiʿi activists and community leaders.

Nour was active in several NGOs in south Beirut and was an enthusiastic participant in cross-sectarian civil society networks. While she was mainly interested in the psychosocial problems of disadvantaged children and youth, Nour also joined meetings and protests that focused on public spaces and environmental development and was an active member of a civil society coalition focusing on these issues. As a cheerful and energetic person who liked participating in and organizing social events, she invited her friends, including me, to hiking events, free NGO workshops, theater plays, and movies—going to Maroun Baghdadi's movie was her idea. She liked to explore new activities and meet people, and she enthusiastically posted about these activities on social media. She did not like to go to protests and demonstrations, a preference she explained to me as resulting from her fear of witnessing violence. Yet she did not shy away from sharing political messages and publicly criticizing various political figures in parliament, particularly those affiliated with the March 14 coalition.

While Nour was on good terms with all of her colleagues and activist collaborators, I noticed over time that her close activist friends embraced "the Palestinian cause" (*al-qaḍiyya al-filasṭīniyya*), sided with the March 8 coalition, and either supported or were neutral toward Hizbullah. They were from different sects, and some identified as "secular," meaning that they did not practice any religion and did not like to be associated with a sect. They were all from low-income backgrounds, though they and Nour did not identify as "low-income" nor have an explicit class consciousness. Nonetheless, they were aware of the specific struggles of coming from a "modest family" (*ʿā'ila mutawāḍiʿa*), which they frequently contrasted with the privileges of urban middle-class groups. In particular, they contrasted the poor infrastructural services and absence of public spaces in their neighborhoods with the glamorous and well-maintained corners of the city, such as the AUB campus, downtown Beirut, and some parts of Christian-dominated Ashrafieh.

Having lived in neighborhoods in the "bubble" that Nour referred to and also in low-income neighborhoods, I observed firsthand the different experiences of infrastructural problems, particularly power outages. Most residents in Beirut and its suburbs used the electricity supplied by Électricité du Liban (EDL) and paid private generator operators. Although the official regulation for electricity cuts in central Beirut was three hours per day, in predetermined three-hour intervals from 6 a.m. to 6 p.m., the duration and timing of the daily cuts varied considerably in reality. The allocation of electricity cuts between city districts and neighborhoods was based on rather ambiguous sets of political alliances and access to strong community figures.[27] In the five different apartments I stayed in between 2011 and 2014, I observed that the electricity cuts did not follow the prescribed times. I witnessed discrepancies in the provision of these services between neighboring streets. It was also publicly known that streets near prominent political figures' houses usually had fewer electricity and water supply cuts. In contrast, many suburbs of Beirut that had strong political identities, such as the Shiʿa-dominated Dahiya neighborhood and Sunni-dominated Tarik al-Jadidah neighborhood, were subject to many hours of cuts during intense periods of political tension within the government.

In Beirut's suburbs, electricity and other infrastructural services were mainly controlled by private vendors, some of which were mafia-like entities that were associated with local political figures. It was more challenging to access such services there than in central Beirut, especially for households, like Nour's, that lacked regular income, connections to local political figures, or a mediating male figure in the immediate family. In fact, the locations that some middle-class Beirut residents stereotyped as stealing state electricity were the ones that struggled the most to access it. I observed Nour and others being unable to take showers, charge phones and other electronic devices, or refrigerate food—all because of power outages that could last up to twenty hours a day.

In contrast to the middle-class activists who believed that the crises of Lebanon resulted from the absence of a functioning state, national identity, and citizenship, low-income activists like Nour focused more on the uneven distribution of Lebanon's crises and how structural inequalities and injustices affected people's everyday lives. Rather than imagining "Lebanese people" as homogenously affected by Lebanon's structural problems, they highlighted unaddressed discrepancies in the ways those problems affected diverse communities. Like middle-class activists, Nour desired a functioning nation-state and a common national identity, but found these goals hard to achieve in

Lebanon. "In this country, there's everything except the people (*al-shaʿb*)," she told me once. She continued, "This is a sad but true reality."

Nour's story is a good example of how experiences of crises were uneven and laden with social and other hierarchies. Common complaints such as "there is no state" meant different things for different groups. Nour viewed the Lebanese state as unable to protect her and her community from Israeli attacks and as neglectful and discriminatory in providing infrastructural services. This is why she viewed Hizbullah's political and military power as offsetting the weakness of the Lebanese state rather than contributing to it. There were also many low-income activists who were politically situated within the March 14 coalition and were highly critical of Hizbullah. Yet, like Nour, they did not see civil society as the leading agent for state-building and nation-building despite sharing the middle-class activists' desire for a strong and functioning state.

In contrast to middle classes who primarily blamed Lebanese culture for the absence of national unity, Nour and her friends centered their criticisms on colonialism. They frequently criticized Western states, in particular the United States, Britain, and France, for hypocritically and selfishly pursuing colonial ambitions. Similar to other activists, they understood Lebanon's problems as being rooted in a politically institutionalized sectarian system that was in need of radical structural changes. But they mainly blamed the West for perpetuating sectarianism in Lebanon through policies that, for instance, condoned Israeli aggression and supported historically privileged Maronite Christians.

Low-income activists' lifeworlds included a daily struggle with the differential treatment that they and the urban poor received from the state and cultural elites. Nour's and her friends' experiences with middle-class–dominated civil society and their comparison of their lives with those of people from social milieus such as AUB and downtown Beirut informed them about the "different lives" people lived in Lebanon as well as the prejudices people in those places could hold. This knowledge about "different lives" also gave them a unique sense of power. "They [middle class activists] don't come to Dahiya, but we [activists living in the southern suburbs of the city] go everywhere. We talk to everyone. But not everyone is open-minded. Some activists have many prejudices," Nour told me. She saw her ability to navigate different—and even hostile—spaces in the city as a proof of her authentic and patriotic activist identity. Like many low-income activists, she felt empowered by her crisiswork and identified as a non-sectarian and respectable member of civil society, which had long been dominated by urban middle-class elites. On the other hand, low-income activists' experiences of invalidation could also produce sentiments of unbelonging.

INEQUALITY AND UNBELONGING

In July 2013, Nour and I visited Yara, a secular activist in her late twenties who was one of Nour's closest activist friends. Yara's family's apartment was located in a crowded and low-income neighborhood in Dahiya. Because Yara had to help her elder sister with childcare, she requested that we meet there instead of Hamra, the neighborhood Nour and Yara liked the most because of its mixed nature and nice cafés. Yara's mother, a Lebanese Armenian Catholic, had married Yara's Shiʿi father after they met at a mutual friend's wedding party. Her parents identified as secular and leftist and did not see Lebanon's sectarian laws as an obstacle to their union. Yara was very proud of her parents for building a successful family despite the absence of support from their extended families and some of their friends. After showing us a photo album of her parents and extended family, Yara brought us tea and desserts and asked if we needed anything else. She then turned off the TV, which had been tuned to a local news program at very low volume, and asked us, "Do you want to listen to some Lebanese nagging?" Nour giggled and replied, "Always ready."

Yara began complaining about the NGO where she had volunteered for more than a year, which focused on creating public spaces in Beirut. She was upset that the management had failed to uphold its promise to offer her a paid position. She had been unemployed since obtaining her bachelor's degree in English language and literature at the Lebanese University in 2010, and her only income came from tutoring high school students. She was also skeptical about the benefits of the paid job she had been promised, as some of her friends working at NGOs did not receive their salaries regularly. Then, she began talking about how some of the activists who advocated in principle for expanding public spaces in Beirut did not understand or care about the differences between Beirut's neighborhoods. "People here [in Dahiya] have nowhere to go," she said. Noticing that Nour and I were nodding sadly, she continued, "There are cafés, but not everyone can afford them. This is why we need to build small parks and outdoor spaces here, but no one cares." Nour nodded and mentioned how public beaches in Lebanon were so dirty that many were afraid of getting cancer, but the state, in particular the Beirut municipality, did not care to clean them. Yara responded, "I agree with you one hundred percent. There're many reports on the pollution crisis, but the state doesn't do anything. Because rich Lebanese can go to nice beaches, or to Türkiye, Cyprus, and other countries for a beach vacation."

As other middle-class activists working on public spaces did, Yara believed in the importance of civil society activism, doing advocacy work, and cultivating a sense of citizenship. Yet, in contrast to middle-class activists who sought to apply abstract liberal principles to what they viewed as an uncivil Lebanese society that failed to live up to those principles, Yara and her friends emphasized the lived experiences of differences and inequalities within the society. Thus, in their advocacy work, low-income activists focused their activism on claiming social rights and public visibility for communities they viewed as marginalized, going beyond targeting "Lebanese problems."

Most middle-class activists conceptualized crisis as a set of circumstances that resulted from a deviation from Lebanon's path to an idealized modern state and society. Their accounts of "Lebanese people" were often based on outside observations and shallow public encounters. Even though they experienced problems such as potholes on a highway or water shortages, they did not experience them continually. Also, middle-class activists believed that Lebanon had exceptional problems and wanted to empower the state and society to address them. By contrast, low-income activists did not view Lebanon as struggling with exceptional problems because they lacked the high expectations associated with elite education and continual self-comparison with the West. Instead, they associated Lebanon's problems with the country's asymmetries of power and structural inequality. Nour and her low-income activist friends drew on their lived experiences of hardship and marginalization—as well as the lived experiences of people they had intimate and deep interactions with on a daily basis—to talk about the specific problems they or their communities experienced.

Many low-income activist women were also more critical of hegemonic gender norms, and their crisis narratives were significantly shaped by these norms. When I praised her chic attire during one of our get-togethers in March 2014, Yara responded, "Thanks, but I am far below Lebanese standards." She looked sad and distressed. I asked what she meant, and she responded that she felt different from many of the Lebanese women around her, and that some of her colleagues, friends, and family members made negative comments about her appearance and personal grooming. I was surprised to hear that. I had thought that Yara, who dressed in the smart causal style typical of middle-class civil society activists, generally looked chic and well groomed. She, Nour, and I shopped together at outlets for international brands such as H&M that produced affordable casual attire for urban professionals. Seeing my confusion, she explained that because she did not have a nose job, wear makeup, have regular manicures and pedicures, and could not afford a designer bag or designer shoes, she considered herself poorly groomed compared to other Lebanese women around her. She cited several examples of bullying comments in which colleagues or relatives mocked her as not looking like a proper woman. Yara interpreted these pressures on appearance as a Lebanese problem rather than a failure on her part:

> When I went to the Philippines last month for a workshop, I realized this was a Lebanese problem. We focus so much on appearance. We like showing off (*maẓāhir*). People outside [of Lebanon] are not like that. They simply liked who I was, and instead of focusing on my appearance, they appreciated my work, abilities, and character. They did not care how I looked.

Knowing how deeply Yara loved Lebanon, I was struck by how she felt more accepted and comfortable in the Philippines. She did not explain this comfort by mentioning the exceptionality of Filipino hospitality or kindness but by discussing her liberation from feeling inferior and not accepted in Lebanon. She emphasized how excessive Westernization corrupted the Lebanese psyche, particularly among the elites in Beirut. For Yara, the "Lebanese problem" was not about lagging behind an idealized Western culture; rather, it referred to the hegemony of a distinctly Westernized elitist culture in Beirut. Some of my female middle-class activist interlocutors also voiced complaints about the pressure on appearance. They saw this pressure, however, not as reflecting hegemonic culture but as reflecting a "traditional mentality" held by "judgmental" people in their families and social circles. It did not cause them to experience feelings of social disapproval or unbelonging.

Yara's comparison between Lebanon and the Philippines also presented an interesting contrast with middle-class activists' comparison between Lebanon and Western countries. While many middle-class activists viewed themselves as embodying Western standards and were concerned that Lebanese culture lagged behind those standards, Yara and many low-income activists articulated experiences of being judged and looked down upon based on those same standards. In a way, middle-class activists unbelonged to Lebanon by comparing their lives with the West, while low-income activists unbelonged to Lebanon by not receiving approval from the dominant culture's norms.

While it is imperative to bring to light accounts like Nour's and Yara's, one must also be cautious against romanticizing their activism just because it represents marginalized voices. Similar to middle-class activists, Nour, Yara, and other low-income activists constructed essentializing narratives about other communities and activists in opposing groups. Nour and her friends imagined all middle-class Lebanese, including middle-class activists, as colonized by the West, both materially and psychologically. Moreover, some of them had an exaggerated view of infrastructural conditions in more privileged parts of the city. Many middle-class neighborhoods in Ashrafieh and Hamra struggled with severe water shortages and electricity cuts. One of my middle-class interlocutors had to move from her apartment in the Geitawi district of Ashrafieh in November 2013 because of the unreliability of the private companies that provided water; the municipality at the time provided water only every other day. When I anonymously shared this experience with Nour, she shrugged it off and told me, "Don't believe everyone, dear (*ḥabībtī*), people lie all the time." This was one instance among others in which she refused to empathize with other communities whom she construed as uninterruptedly enjoying certain privileges. Some of Nour's friends also believed that those who opposed or criticized Hizbullah did not care about the Palestinian cause, a claim that contradicted my observations. I met many activists from varying class and sect backgrounds who were politically closer to the March 14 coalition and disliked Hizbullah but were still very invested in the Palestinian cause. Some of them criticized Hizbullah supporters for monopolizing pro-Palestinian advocacy. Thus, despite their efforts to voice different lives and experiences, low-income activists like Nour could also perpetuate the prejudices and stereotypes that contributed to Lebanon's political polarization.

SUSTAINABLE ACTIVISM

I frequently heard middle-class activists complain about other participants' lack of "motivation" and "commitment." In particular, they criticized the "inertia" and "carelessness" of low-income activists who were unwilling to immerse themselves in NGO work or other collective activities. These middle-class activists believed that the Lebanese needed more motivation and commitment, which could be achieved by setting goals and passionately pursuing them. There was some truth to this "lack of motivation" analysis. In many instances, I heard both my low-income and middle-class interlocutors refer to lost or insufficient motivation as an explanation for their delaying, quitting, or neglectfully doing a task. Nevertheless, what appeared to be insufficient motivation or commitment was mainly related to certain ways of perceiving one's position and power vis-à-vis social structures and to different ways of imagining crisiswork. Unlike middle-class activists, most low-income activists did not view civil society as the main agent of change. Instead, they called upon the Lebanese state and elites to be more active in creating a more equal and just society.

Many of my low-income activist interlocutors believed that devoting a sizable effort to a project might be futile and result in fatigue and disappointment rather than in concrete results. In two different instances, I was reminded by my low-income activist interlocutors that I unnecessarily tired myself when undertaking tasks that were more profound than they seemed. In one instance, I wanted to finish a 10 km (roughly 6.2 mile) "Fun Run" race that was part of the annual Beirut Marathon in November 2013.[28] I was running a shorter version of the marathon with seven low-income activists from a small collective working for gender equality, with whom I had been collaborating for more than six months. The activists had been excited about this national event for several weeks. We had several long conversations about the planning of the event, its significance in bringing together "everyone" (*kill al-ʿālam*, referring to Lebanese from diverse confessional backgrounds), and the excellent publicity opportunity for the collective. I was also excited, given the activists' enthusiasm and that it would be my first race. I physically and mentally prepared myself to complete the 10 km run. Yet the other members of our team decided to stop for coffee about two miles before the finish line when several members felt very tired. I initially thought they would resume after a rest, so I continued running. We had already taken several short breaks.

When I texted them after finishing the race, I learned they were still in the café, so I went to meet them. They all congratulated me and asked how the finish line was. Some of them teased me in a friendly way for my "ambition" and "firmness." They seemed content with their decision to quit the race and chat. Fuad, a bright and energetic young Sunni man in his late twenties, looked at me with a serious face and said, "I really like what you did. You show us how we must pursue our goals no matter what. But, you know, we lost our belief in this country long ago." He paused for a few seconds and then, looking at the others, continued:

> In the marathon the previous year, I crossed the finish line. But I didn't feel happy. I felt very weird. I kept asking myself why, what is this for, and what changed? Our problems are so deep that I couldn't even feel I accomplished something for one day. This year, I joined the marathon because I wanted to spend time with you all.

I felt that Fuad's emotional sharing touched all of us. Many agreeing comments followed it, starting with "you're right" (*maʿak ḥaqq*). One activist, Fuad's close friend, added that "no matter how much work one does for this country, it [Lebanon] would remain in the same place and not progress." Another activist, who self-identified as queer and focused on LGBTQ rights, added, "We don't have more equality and freedom when we run." The group had a long and lively conversation about how Lebanon's problems were too deep to be solved by Lebanese citizens' efforts.

In many other instances, I observed Fuad and others in the group speaking and acting with passion and commitment. They enthusiastically participated in protests and demonstrations and interacted with representatives from state institutions and local and international NGOs in an engaging manner. They were often very passionate for change and felt empowered to contribute to it. So why did they find completing the race futile, even disappointing?

Changing something in Lebanon had not been my motivation for finishing the race. I had not even established any connection between my run and Lebanon. For others in the group, though, their individual run and Lebanon were inherently connected. As a popular annual activity for many Lebanese since its inception in 2003, the Beirut Marathon was highly loaded with the patriotic goals of bringing together diverse groups and cultivating in them a sense of ethical citizenship. The marathon took place every year, including years that witnessed intensified political conflicts and eruptions of public violence in Beirut. Many private companies, NGOs, political parties, and state officials supported the marathon, and Lebanese from all ages and socioeconomic backgrounds enthusiastically participated. Indeed, while running the marathon in November 2013, at different junctures of the race, I greeted and chitchatted with dozens of my interlocutors from various parts of Lebanon. The motto of the 2013 marathon was "Run for Lebanon," and many well-known public figures, including politicians and their families, joined to show their support for Lebanon. Mainstream media channels reminded everyone that Lebanon had been going through a difficult period and that "we should all run for Lebanon." Lebanon's then-first lady Wafaa Sleiman stated that the marathon was a message to the world that "Lebanon is stronger than the challenges it faces."

Fuad and his friends had an ambivalent relationship with the patriotism of the event. They were not against the organizers or the patriotic messages. They just did not believe in the idea that by running a marathon they could change Lebanon. Instead, Fuad's experience of completing a marathon was an ironic reminder of how much there still was to accomplish. In a way, he and others in the group offered a subtle critique of how the marathon associated Lebanon's progress with individual strength and resilience.[29] By refusing to "run for Lebanon," Fuad and other low-income activists in the group were, in a way, protesting the hypocrisy of a post-war neoliberal Lebanese state that expected considerable patriotic affective and bodily investments from its citizens, even as it upheld sectarianism and offered little to low-income citizens.

Middle-class activists also criticized the Lebanese state while at times refusing to exercise individual responsibility, as seen in Lara's blaming of the state for citizens' smoking in public. However, they rarely questioned their individual capacities to enact change or scrutinized the Lebanese state's differential treatment of its citizens. Fuad and his friends believed that it was the state and urban elite who owed low-income Lebanese an effort for change, rather than vice versa. For them, a change to the structures of power that unevenly burdened them was the first priority. In addition, feeling tired during the marathon symbolized to the low-income activists in the group the myriad ways that they had been making an effort in civil society and their individual lives with no concrete results. Nevertheless, rather than feeling despair or resignation, Fuad and his friends preferred to enjoy their time and maintain their dignity and well-being. Having casual time together in NGO spaces helped them process crises as an intersubjective experience that can be tackled better by connecting through shared grievances and hopes. In this sense, their "half-hearted efforts" compellingly balanced their commitment to working for Lebanon through collective morale building and working on themselves through leisure. Crisiswork, in this sense, needed to be continually "recharged" through seemingly non-political practices.

During a two-hour beach cleaning event that I joined in February 2014, which was hosted by an environmental advocacy NGO, I was similarly teased for "overdoing it." We met at the NGO office located in Hamra and drove to Ramlet al-Bayda, a public beach close to the Msaytbeh neighborhood. Ramlet al-Bayda was the only public sandy beach in Beirut and was visibly dirty despite the cleaning efforts of various local and international NGO volunteers. The beach's visitors were mainly low-income residents of the city's periphery who could not afford fees for private beaches. After about half an hour of collecting large chunks of waste, the other participants in the group began taking pictures and chatting. Feeling moved by the beach's vastness and the garbage that covered it, I wanted to continue cleaning for a while longer. I contemplated that following my interlocutors would have been a wiser anthropological practice. Still, I had been enjoying the waste collection, and stopping after half an hour felt discomforting. Also, I had been with the same group for over a year, and some of them were close friends by then. I decided to stop being an anthropologist momentarily and continued cleaning the beach.

After ten minutes or so, Aya, then a twenty-six-year-old Druze woman from a low-income family, and Mazen, a Syrian Lebanese Sunni man in his early twenties, came toward me, smiling. Aya wore a beige cable-knit sweater and tight black pants, while Mazen wore a fitted green T-shirt and blue jeans. Their clothes were slightly dusty because of the wind, and they were trying to shake the dust off as they walked toward me. Mazen said, "You tired yourself too much, enough. Look, the beach is too big. We can't cover it all even if we worked day and night for months." Aya added, "It frustrates me to see how our work does not solve the problem. And, also, it is not our responsibility, the state must work on it. Come and have fun with us!" I nodded, agreed with them, and added, "I just wanted to do my best."

Aya, who studied health and environment at the Lebanese University, explained to me at length how Beirut's waste problem was caused by various serious infrastructural problems, pointing out the piles of landfills, nearby sewage outlet, and water discoloration within sight. She tried to convince me of the severity and depth of the problem, interpreting my continuance of the beach cleaning as well-intentioned but naïve enthusiasm. She gave examples of previously "failed" projects in which she and others at the NGO had worked wholeheartedly. Mazen elaborated on Aya's point, saying how their group had collectively reflected on the "inconsequentiality" (***bidūn natīja***) of their advocacy work and the disappointment it caused, a process that made them realize that their approach was not "sustainable" (*mustadām*). Aya nodded, adding, "You do your best, you work hard, but those efforts do not take you anywhere."

Aya was particularly upset that the many NGO projects had achieved so little for disadvantaged neighborhoods in Beirut, where she and her family lived. She also warned me that, if I continued tiring myself in this way, I would soon be disappointed and lose all my motivation. As did Fuad, Aya believed that excessive individual efforts would lead to fatigue and resentment if they did not achieve substantial change and would serve as a reminder of the enormity of the problems at hand. It was not that low-income activists were especially cynical or lacking in idealism. Rather, given their lived history of struggles, they had a more tangible understanding of how structures could be resistant to change as well as more experience in dealing with failure and disappointment.

"Doing something," a key idea in crisiswork, thus also meant recognizing the limits of civil society activism for many low-income activists like Aya and Mazen. They were as committed as other activists to their crisiswork, yet by avoiding doing "too much" and managing their fatigue, they reminded themselves and others of the structural problems and the responsibility of the political class. In the days after our excursion, I noticed that my "naïveté" unexpectedly earned me respect. Some group members expressed their appreciation for my "passion to help a country that I wasn't born in, and where I won't live in the future." Our contrasting practices in this case could each be seen as ethical for expressing different kinds of virtue. While the low-income activists praised my passion to do more cleaning as reflecting "selflessness" and "genuineness," they were also happy with their own choices to leave the cleaning earlier than planned and spend time having fun. By doing so, they avoided frustration and disappointment and reminded themselves that the Lebanese state must be called to action.

Despite inhabiting shared lifeworlds of civil society-centered crisiswork, diverse activists had asymmetrical experiences of crises, which generated different modalities of crisiswork. Like middle-class activists, low-income activists believed in and enthusiastically worked for "change" and subscribed to a notion of ethical citizenship that stipulated "doing something" for Lebanon's crises. Yet, they believed that being able to maintain well-being and dignity was also essential to this change in a country where crises had unevenly burdened them and their communities. Middle-class activists might perceive traffic jams or electricity cuts as irritating reminders of Lebanon's exceptionality, but low-income activists often experienced such crises as relentless and exhausting. Similar to infrastructural access, leisure resources were also unequally distributed. Whereas middle-class activists had the time and money for leisure activities such as working out at high-end gyms, traveling to popular vacation destinations, and eating at cosmopolitan restaurants, many of my low-income activist interlocutors worked long hours in low-paid positions such as bartenders, cashiers, and hotel clerks.

The participants in Fuad's and Aya's groups had motivation and commitment—contrary to middle-class activists' complaints—but they pursued a more sustainable activist practice in which they were able to continue their crisiswork without feeling unfairly burdened. Aya and other low-income activists enthusiastically organized and attended community-serving activities such as beach cleaning. However, they perceived the moment of tiredness as a signal they had done "enough" public service, and it was time for much-needed "fun." Hence, it was at that moment that Fuad and his friends ended their race, and Aya and her friends ended their beach cleaning. Already exhausted by the historically unequal distribution of resources, such as infrastructural access and leisurely time, low-income activists viewed it as too large a sacrifice to become tired as unpaid volunteers. They preferred to volunteer in a way that lightened their burden, rather than increasing it. Despite being a form of exploitative unpaid labor, volunteerism, at least in this context, also became a "free" leisurely activity.

I reflected frequently on the diverse ethical choices made by my interlocutors in their crisiswork. Many times during my fieldwork, low-income interlocutors' approaches to activism helped me to let go of my recurrent anxieties about how well I was doing as an ethnographer and as a guest in Lebanon. Their feedback on my understanding of productivity and accomplishment—which had focused on completing self-assigned tasks—led me to develop a more sustainable approach to fieldwork research. Learning to be less ambitious about completing all of my research goals and daily tasks enabled me to become more competent in dealing with unforeseen circumstances and their consequences for my work.

Uncertainty and unresolvedness characterized Lebanon's political and social landscape, yet many activists navigated this challenging landscape with diverse imaginings of change. Like experiences of crisis, imaginations of change in Lebanon's civil society were diverse, ambivalent, and contradictory. A multiplicity of crisiswork practices emerged as civil society networks were mobilized to transform young Lebanese into citizens that designed and participated in multiscalar projects to address crises of state, society, and the self. As middle-class activists imagined Lebanon's problems as others' problems or everyone's problems, Lebanon's crises became an exteriority that called for multiscalar interventions.

TWO

Imagining a Multiscalar Change

On December 27, 2013, a bombing in downtown Beirut targeted the convoy of former finance minister Mohammad Chatah, who was a senior advisor to the Sunni-majority party Future Movement's then-leader Saad Hariri. The attack killed Chatah and seven others and wounded more than seventy. While the March 14 coalition believed that Hizbullah and the Syrian regime orchestrated the assassination because Chatah had been an outspoken critic of both, the March 8 coalition claimed that the assassination was the product of a foreign plot to divide Lebanon. As previous bombings in 2013 had done, the attack rekindled debates about political conflicts, sectarianism, and the impacts of the Syrian War on Lebanon.

Yet this time, one of the killed civilians became the focus of public attention: sixteen-year-old Mohammad al-Chaar, who had posed for a group photo with his friends in front of the bomb-laden car a few minutes before it detonated.[1] The group selfie, which displayed four smiling young Lebanese men, was widely shared on social media. Severely injured by the explosion, al-Chaar died in the hospital the following day. His funeral, held on December 29 at the Khashoggi Mosque in Beirut, was attended by thousands of people.[2] Many young Lebanese from diverse confessional and class backgrounds empathized with al-Chaar, whose final recorded moments of enjoyment in the company of friends reflected their own lives. The killing and funeral of al-Chaar received intense local and international coverage—perhaps more than those of Chatah—and became a symbol of patriotic martyrdom and the innocence of the young victims of Lebanon's crises.[3] On news media and social media, activists and other Lebanese from diverse confessional and political backgrounds expressed their fading hopes for Lebanon's future and their concerns about the fate of the country's youth.

Several days after the blast, the intense public shock, anger, and fear slowly began to dissolve and, in many parts of Beirut, people returned to the empty streets. Some young activists took issue with the recurring instances of violence and sought to mobilize the public. On December 30, they launched the "I'm not a martyr" (*Ana mish shahid*) campaign on Twitter and Facebook. With the campaign, activists demanded a dignified life without the continual threat of violence and fear of death.[4] In the following days, many young Lebanese posted photos and messages on social media with the hashtag #notamartyr. Through vigils, demonstrations, and testimonies, they shared their fears of losing their loved ones and of spending the rest of their lives under the shadow of war, as well as their need for safety, normalcy, and belonging.[5]

In addition to creating venues for collective mourning, the sentiments of crisis triggered by the explosion facilitated collective mobilization through civil society. Leading activists in the "I'm not a martyr" campaign extended their message into a larger protest against Lebanon's political system, which they viewed as forcing Lebanese to live under the constant threat of death—through not only indiscriminate bombings but also poverty, corruption, infrastructural failure, pollution, and other crises. These political critiques publicly held the Lebanese state responsible for its failure to safeguard citizens and to provide political stability, economic and social development, and justice. Yet many Lebanese had little trust that the state would address these structural issues in the short term. Hence, they celebrated civil society activism as a unique site for imagining multiscalar transformations in society, the politico-legal system, and Lebanese subjectivities through which to address the nation's multiple and interrelated crises and, in the long term, build viable futures for the country's youth.

The collective sentiment of crisis that led many Lebanese to engage in civil society activism articulated itself in a strong, yet ambivalent drive to "do something." During the week of the attack and the funeral, I heard the following sentences over and over from many of my friends and neighbors: "We need to do something," "I want to do something," "I cannot stay silent," "We have to change things," "My heart is aching," and "This is unbearable." In the following weeks, many of them joined well-known local, youth-focused NGOs to "do something." Others continued searching for "people of conscience" with whom they could build political alliances. Given their mistrust of political parties, many viewed civil society as offering more effective venues to voice dissent and work toward change. There were also many Lebanese who reacted to the latest explosion with anger, hopelessness, or avoidance, which they expressed with sentiments such as "I hate this country," "I don't want to live here," or "I don't want to talk about the incident." Yet, it was precisely this widely circulating cynicism—typically voiced as "nothing changes in this country" (*walā shī byitghayyar bi-hayda al-balad*)— that led others to search more intensely for viable alternatives for change. The call to "do something" in the face of growing crises soon became central to public imaginations of ethical citizenship.

Civil society—a decades-old space constituted by various local and transnational actors—was widely celebrated as an ideal space to usher in change in Lebanon. Activists viewed civil society as particularly suitable to foster the formation of a non-sectarian youth, and eventually a post-sectarian future nation. All of the civil society spaces that I visited in Beirut, from unregistered collectives and movements to registered NGOs—and despite major differences in their political outlooks, areas of focus, and targeted communities—used similar idioms to convey the values of agency and responsibility in working toward change. This political outlook was more reflective of those groups led by urban middle-class Lebanese, who were civil society's leading and influential participants, but also applied to those led by low-income activists. The official goals of many youth-targeting projects, the focus of this chapter, included agentic formulations such as "motivating citizens to actively participate in public projects," "advocating reforms," "working for change," and "believing in change." How did diverse Lebanese activists imagine and enact change? What were the political possibilities and limitations of their work for change?

Crisiswork through civil society-led projects targeted multiscalar transformations in the politico-legal system, society, and selfhood, which were intended to curb the effects of sectarianism on Lebanon's political system and everyday life. Various local and transnational actors saw the active participation of Lebanese youth in civil society as essential to national unity—a major goal for cross-sectarian Lebanese civil society since the heightened political polarization and public violence that had followed Prime Minister Rafiq Hariri's assassination in 2005. Western-funded, youth-focused civil society projects in Lebanon typically defined a "youth" as someone between the ages of fifteen and thirty. These projects approached the youth as "victims" of the sectarian system who were in need of empowerment. However, many Lebanese use the Arabic word for youth, *al-shabāb*, to refer to a much larger group, those aged seventeen to forty. It is also sometimes used synonymously with "people" (*al-nās*) and refers mainly to an agentive population spanning from as young as sixteen to as old as fifty. Several activists criticized the age criteria of donor agencies and Lebanese state institutions and suggested that anyone who believed in and worked for change must be considered young.[6] Many of my civil society interlocutors between the ages of eighteen and forty-five proudly self-identified as "young activists" and viewed Lebanese civil society as mainly led by youth and for youth. In their view, the Lebanese youth were ideally positioned to practice active citizenship and become agents of change, as they were less damaged by the legacy of the Lebanese War.

The crisiswork of Lebanese activists thus sought to change the country by harnessing the agency of the country's post-war generations. In so doing, Lebanese activists pursued multiscalar projects to promote active citizenship among the youth. These activists had diverse backgrounds, though the prominent actors leading youth-focused projects were mostly middle-class. Low-income activists, as discussed previously, were more skeptical about the possibility of "fixing" Lebanon from within and emphasized the prominence of colonial legacies, structural inequalities, and power differentials reproduced by the Lebanese state. Despite their skepticism, they still continued to participate in multiscalar civil society efforts and believed in the promises of active citizenship (*al-muwāṭana al-faʿʿāla*).[7]

Examining middle-class imaginations of multiscalar changes reveals how hegemonic understandings of crisiswork across civil society centered particularly on bringing about change at the scales of the state and legal system, culture, and selfhood. Many Lebanese middle-class activists worked closely with state institutions and international organizations to enact new laws and policies, with the ultimate aim of transforming sectarian political structures. They viewed the formation of a non-sectarian society and selves as inseparable from building a non-sectarian political system. In this vein, some of them also encouraged themselves and others to overcome the "negativity" caused by the overarching effects of sectarianism—the anxiety and embodied pain associated with disillusionment and resignation. In this sense, institutions, communities, and individuals all became sites for imagining change in Lebanon.

Even though civil society activism originated as a colonial project that rested on collaboration between the Lebanese state, international organizations such as the UN, and the male, middle-class leaders of Lebanese civil society, other political possibilities opened up through the mobilization of young Lebanese as active participants in civil society. In civil society, just as crisis and activism were ambiguously framed and enacted both in abstract and concrete ways, change was also often understood and pursued in ways that dynamically yet incoherently fused abstract dreams with concrete projects. The ambivalences and contradictions of crisiswork show the dynamic and open-ended nature of middle-class–dominated civil society activism in Lebanon and its multiscalar imaginations of change to shape the country's youth and, hence, the future.

Western-Funded Civil Society

In the 1990s, following the long Lebanese War, contemporary Lebanese civil society emerged as a major political actor under urban middle-class leadership. Particularly through rights-based advocacy associations that focused on human rights, gender, and the environment, various middle-class activists challenged the sectarian politics of the state and its political parties and assumed a key role in Lebanon's post-war political and social reconstruction. Their politics was situated within Lebanon's emergent neoliberal sectarian system, in which institutionalized sectarian politics, neoliberal economics, and civil society activism were intertwined. Powerful international institutions such as the World Bank, United Nations, and European Union promoted the formation of civil society organizations and NGOs in Lebanon as essential components of "good governance," in line with neoliberal privatization policies and post–Cold War democratization rhetoric in many other parts of the world. Thus, since the 1990s, increased collaboration among international institutions, Lebanese state institutions, and civil society organizations has shaped institutional frameworks for social and political change in Lebanon.

Donor dependency and the institutionalization and professionalization of civil society organizations were prominent features of activism in Lebanon, as they were in many other parts of the world.[8] One of the major consequences of donor dependency was the increased prominence of the NGO format. In addition to facilitating smoother interactions among multiple stakeholders, the NGO format was preferred by activists because it offered respectable and well-paying jobs within the humanitarian and development sector. Many young Lebanese saw NGOs as preferred spaces for volunteering, activism, and paid work as well as promising career venues. Despite critiques from some local activists regarding the potentially harmful effects of donor dependency and the NGOization of politics, NGOs are ubiquitous in Lebanon and continue to be key actors in Lebanese civil society.

The rising political and social polarization in Lebanon that followed Rafiq Hariri's assassination in 2005 and the July War with Israel in 2006 accelerated the growth of cross-sectarian civil society. Given the US-led global war on terror in the aftermath of 9/11, Shiʿi and Sunni Muslim religious groups in Lebanon were already under scrutiny. Targeting what they framed as the "violent" and "backward" culture within Arab and Muslim communities, Western donors supported local non-partisan NGOs in Lebanon as ideal venues to instill Western liberal democratic norms and values.[9] After 2006, and increasingly after the onset of the Syrian War, the growing political power of Hizbullah and the flourishing of various "extremist" Sunni Islamic groups in Lebanon further alarmed many Western actors. By promoting liberal values such as civic activism, gender equality, and tolerance through cross-sectarian civil society, Western funders, in particular the US-based donor agencies, hoped to curb the anti-Western rhetoric of powerful Muslim political actors in Lebanon.

Many Lebanese activists criticized the United States Agency for International Development (USAID), a major donor to Lebanese civil society, for prohibiting recipient NGOs from offering services to Hizbullah-affiliated communities. USAID's designation of Hizbullah—and thousands of fellow citizens who were seen as Hizbullah's constituency—as "terrorists" was unacceptable to them. Other US donor agencies, such as America-Mideast Educational and Training Services, Inc. (AMIDEAST), targeted Shiʿi youth through various trainings or cultural exchange programs with the explicit aim of turning them into pro-Western allies. Several activists interpreted such policies as producing conflict and polarization among Lebanese people. A leftist activist interlocutor who worked with a prominent youth-focused NGO referred to the US donor policies as "colonization with a human face" (*istiʿmār bi wajh insānī*). Activists who criticized US donors emphasized that, in contrast, European donors—such as the Norwegian Embassy or the Anna Lindh Foundation—refrained from imposing such intrusive restrictions on the projects and agendas of the NGOs they funded. Despite differences in donors' policies regarding funding conditions, all the representatives whom I met from US and European donor agencies in Lebanon expressed concerns about Hizbullah's political and social power. Most of these representatives were Lebanese citizens who had grown up or attained higher education in the West. They primarily associated dangerous sectarianism with pious Muslim groups—particularly Hizbullah followers—even though members of all confessions in Lebanon could embrace "sectarian" discourses or identities.

Western-funded projects promoted youth participation in cross-sectarian civil society, particularly through projects related to conflict resolution, peacebuilding, environmentalism, development, gender rights, and human rights.[10] For example, the World Bank Country Office in Lebanon decided on "Youth in Governance" as the theme for the "Lebanon Development Marketplace 2006." For this global project, launched in 1998 and implemented country-wide in 2000, the World Bank partnered with the United Nations Development Programme (UNDP), the United Nations Children's Fund (UNICEF), the British Embassy in Beirut, and the Lebanese Transparency Association (LTA) to encourage "youth participation" and "good governance" in civil society.[11] Thirteen civil society organizations received a total of US$230,000 to encourage the youth to become "actively and effectively involved in the reform drive towards good governance," to execute projects designed to enhance youth participation in civil society and advocacy work, and to forge youth empowerment and positive youth-to-youth interactions and collaborations.[12] For example, KAFA (enough) Violence and Exploitation—a well-known Lebanese feminist NGO—received US$19,767 to establish youth clubs in different regions of Lebanon that would promote gender equality and nonviolence among the Lebanese and Palestinian youth.[13]

As exemplified by the Lebanon Development Marketplace project, Western donors offered remarkable financial and technical support for advocacy, development, and empowerment projects in Lebanese civil society, in particular from 2006 until 2012, the year in which transnational funding in Lebanon began to prioritize the Syrian refugee crisis. Among the largest of these Western interventions was the Lebanon Civic Support Initiative (LCSI), which was launched by USAID's Office of Transition Initiatives (OTI) in September 2007 for "harnessing the desire among many Lebanese to defuse sectarian tensions."[14] During interviews I conducted in 2014, several

Lebanese activists who worked for the LCSI highlighted that the OTI was key to strengthening Lebanese civil society and empowering youth to be active participants in public life through activism. According to them, the funding made it possible to attract many young Lebanese to civil society and train them in the skills needed to "become independent members of society" and "create change" in the country.

Western-funded civil society projects had long-lasting impacts on activist politics in Lebanon.[15] Despite the end of the LCSI in 2014 because of the prioritization of funding for Syrian refugees, various civil society actors continued to share the past experiences of successful NGOs and initiatives with a new generation of activists, emphasizing the potential of Lebanese activism and the hope for change. Between 2013 and 2015, a civic activism toolkit published by OTI in Arabic and English was widely distributed to Lebanese NGOs through half-day interactive training sessions (Figure 3). This thick toolkit included detailed descriptions of case studies of projects in which NGO activists successfully improved the conditions in their communities. It also shared lessons from these projects and offered concrete tips for future activism. Turning the well-designed pages of the toolkit, which was printed on high-quality paper and included many photos

Civic Activism Toolkit

YEF

USAID
FROM THE AMERICAN PEOPLE

مؤسسة مخزومي
Makhzoumi Foundation

Makhzoumi Foundation Certifies that

Yasemin Can

has attended the

Civic Activism Toolkit Interactive Session

On Friday March 14th, 2014
Beirut – Lebanon

Trainer
Cedric Choukier

Makhzoumi Foundation
Samer El-Safah

FIGURE 3. My certification for attending a Civic Activism Toolkit session on March 14, 2014.

of activist projects, I noticed that all of the youth-focused NGOs I volunteered at and visited during my fieldwork were included in the toolkit and described at length.

Even though Western geopolitical agendas sought to foster Lebanese activists who endorsed Western liberal values, as it did in different parts of the global South, many Lebanese organizations and activists went beyond emulating Western values. For example, despite acknowledging the support of USAID, the introduction of the toolkit emphasized that the case studies showcased "the experiences of the innovative and resilient Lebanese civil society," and that these experiences could inspire both the Western and Arab worlds: "It is crucial to expand the transfer of information and experience to flow in multiple directions: East to East and also East to West. [. . .] We believe that this toolkit will be instructive to civil society activists in the West, as well."[16] A leftist activist interlocutor, who had contributed to the writing of the toolkit, told me in April 2014 that the toolkit's authors had been keen to show that Lebanese civil society was not a passive follower of Western knowledge and norms just because it received money from the West, and that Lebanese activists could inspire the rest of the world. His remarks exemplify how some middle-class activists contested Western dominance and claimed Lebanese autonomy in executing civil society projects even as they acknowledged their financial dependence on the West.

Thus, not all civil society organizations and activists, including those who received Western funding, shared Western geopolitical interests such as countering the influence of Hizbullah and other religious or political authorities on Lebanese youth. Many activists I spoke to were aware of their donors' geopolitical interests and approached their relationships with donors strategically. These were mostly pragmatic activists who believed that they could promote their own agendas regardless of donors' expectations. Also, many of my low-income activist interlocutors told me that they came to the interactive toolkit sessions to receive certificates that would enhance their résumés and applications for jobs at NGOs. Most of them were aware of US and broader Western interests in funding and promoting local NGOs. They were not alarmed by donors' influence, however, because they understood donors' roles and positions within the long and ongoing histories of Western colonialism in Lebanon and were confident that the Lebanese could repurpose donor agendas for their own interests. Other activists sought to explicitly reform Hizbullah's constituency through projects that promoted human and gender rights. Hizbullah, in their view, was an Iranian-backed militia whose actions contradicted Lebanese national interests and values. These activists saw their programmatic vision and goals as aligned with Western donors' agendas. There were also numerous activist organizations that refused to receive funding from USAID and other US donors, viewing this choice as a badge of their independence. Hence, Lebanese activists' different engagements with Western funding mobilized competing ideologies.

Local Elites Promoting Activism

Western donors were one among various actors promoting activism among the youth in Lebanon. With diverse and competing motivations, a wide range of local elites from different political backgrounds, including policy-makers, scholars, and intellectuals, promoted non-sectarian and non-partisan NGOs, collectives, and social movements in Lebanon. They supported civil society projects that encouraged young Lebanese from different sects to interact and eventually develop a shared identity as "citizens." The Lebanese media similarly promoted young activists' participation in cross-sectarian civil society as the basis for creating a reconciled Lebanese society through fostering patriotic sentiments over sectarian loyalties. Prominent local media channels, such as LBC, MTV, and OTV, frequently hosted the young leaders of NGOs and grassroots movements and praised them as courageous activists for change. Other local institutions—such as universities, high schools, educational consultancies, banks, and other companies—provided incentives for young people to participate in cross-sectarian civil society. Hence, both Western donors and various local elite institutions enthusiastically promoted the idea that change could be achieved through civil society.

Structural obstacles within Lebanon's political system also led to the construction of civil society as *the only* venue through which multiscalar change could be accomplished. I heard many activists illustrate the sectarian system's debilitating control over the country's youth by pointing out how electoral laws de facto hindered citizens' right to vote. The majoritarian electoral system in Lebanon allocated seats by sect at the district level and encouraged voting for the political party associated with local patrons. There were no pre-printed ballots; instead, parties prepared their own ballots, a system that enabled parties to track voters' choices. In what was often called "vote-buying," many Lebanese citizens voted for candidates in exchange for access to services such as infrastructure, employment, and schooling.[17] In many cases, parties offered direct payments and gifts to their constituencies prior to the elections. Ballots were carefully monitored by local patrons to ensure that each family member was eligible to vote for their own candidates. Activists complained that they, like many other Lebanese, were forced to vote according to the cliental networks in the towns of origin where they and their families were embedded. Anthony, a middle-class Maronite Christian civil society activist who designed educational projects for the youth, told me during an interview in March 2014:

> Elections are just a lie. They buy your vote for $100 and a box of food for sustenance (*kartūnat al-iʿāsha*). No one votes based on their political opinions. If you vote on your opinion, your family will get into trouble with the sectarian leaders, and you'll get into trouble with your family. And no one wants that to happen.

For many activists, the inability to vote as they desired epitomized the absence of proper citizenship or political agency in Lebanon. Voting for a different party—or even abstaining from voting—could be noticed, be taken as a sign of disloyalty, and adversely affect one's entire family's livelihood. Hence, voting created troubling ethical and political conundrums for activists. Because one's voting district was based on one's place of origin, activists who moved—in many cases, to Beirut—often found they did not support any of the candidates in their voting district and were unable to vote for the party they actually supported. Changing one's voting district was an enormously bureaucratic—according to some activists, impossible—task.

Since the 2000s, several NGOs and international institutions had exerted pressure on the government to change the electoral laws. This pressure resulted in the ratification of a new electoral law in 2017 that introduced preprinted ballots and preferential voting. But many policy-makers and activists complained that the new arrangements still divided electoral districts along confessional lines and favored major parties, and thus failed to achieve the ideal of proportional representation. Given the perceived impossibility of enacting change through elections, most activists focused their crisiswork on strengthening civil society's interface with the state.

Creation of a New Political Culture

During my visit to Lebanon in the summer of 2011, I noticed that most civil society projects focused on youth.[18] I later heard from leading Lebanese activists, scholars, journalists, and policy-makers that the youth were the group most impacted by the country's crises. Their common complaints were that many young Lebanese, particularly low-income Lebanese, were controlled by sectarian parties and groups; that educated, bright Lebanese youth were forced to emigrate because of economic and political crises; and that many of the remaining educated youth were politically apathetic. Nevertheless, these actors still believed that Lebanese youth were more open to change than were older generations. Many activists referred to the family as a calcified structure whose elderly members were controlled by their lived histories, their memories of conflicts, and polarizing party politics. They believed that young people were more willing to engage with other communities and that civil society spaces fostered such engagement. Youth in Lebanon, similar to youth in other global contexts, were perceived by various political and social actors, including activists, as both a peril and a promise—a volatile entity that needed to be contained and a source of optimism for the future of the nation.[19]

In the context of post-war Lebanese nation-building, the youth became a key focus of intervention by civil society and other political actors. The "Youth Advocacy Process" (YAP) was initiated in 2000 after meetings between several youth-focused NGOs, the newly established Ministry of Youth and Sports, and the United Nations Youth Task Force. The goal of the initiative was to design a national youth policy through collaboration among diverse representatives from youth organizations, civil society, and state institutions. To that end, YAP built platforms designed to transform Lebanese youth into active citizens who participated in advocacy, lobbying, and policy-making. The booklet issued by YAP (Figure 4) emphasized that the initiative aimed to provide youth "with opportunities to participate in the public sphere as decision makers" and to "reinforce youth's roles in society and make their voices get through in the continuously deteriorating situation in Lebanon," among other goals.[20] YAP's promotion of active citizenship projects underlined the urgency of empowering the youth to better cope with intensifying crises and reinforced the pervasive public portrayal of most young Lebanese as controlled and silenced by sectarian structures and culture.

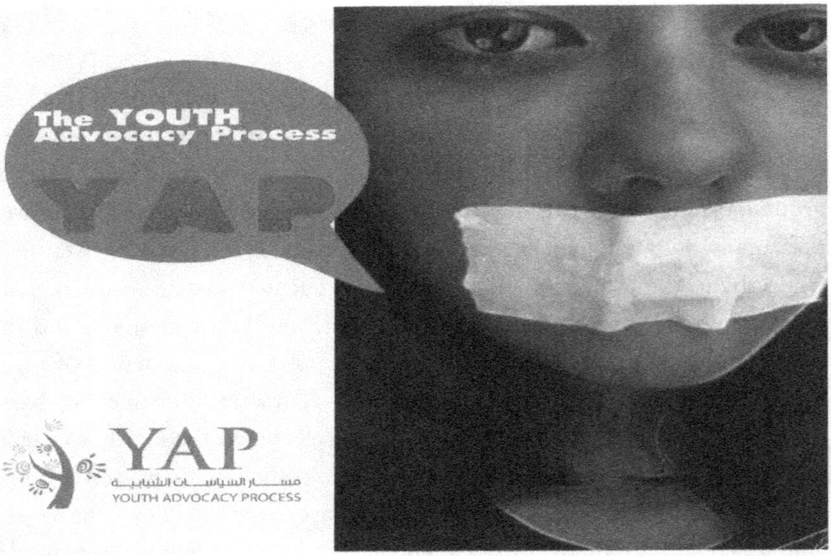

FIGURE 4. Cover page of a booklet issued by YAP. The English content was followed by an Arabic translation. It was provided to the author by MASAR in May 2014.

Kamal Shayya played a leading role in YAP's creation. Shayya was the co-founder and president of MASAR, a prominent local NGO that began working in 2007 on youth development. Since beginning his career in the late 1970s, he had worked at several international institutions and UN agencies and had gained experience in human rights, development, and emergency relief. Shayya's work since the early 1990s had focused on Lebanese and Palestinian youth. At the time of my fieldwork, he was widely known and regarded as an expert on youth and social development across civil society networks, international organizations, and academic circles. During a long interview in May 2014 at MASAR's office in Beirut, he described YAP as manifesting civil society actors' belief in the Lebanese government's responsibility to enact change: "We wanted partnership with the state because we wanted the work to also come from inside the government and not just from civil society." Shayya thus believed, as did many other experienced civil society activists, in the need for a strong and well-functioning liberal state.

Similarly to several other leading civil society activists, Shayya described himself as a patriotic person (*waṭanī*) and expressed a longing for Lebanese unity. He criticized Western states' meddling in Lebanese politics and civil society's dependence on Western funding. Nevertheless, he spoke positively about MASAR's collaboration with several European donors and organizations, which he described as respectful of MASAR's autonomy. For instance, MASAR's partnership with the National Council of Swedish Youth Organizations (LSU) was key to developing its youth policy framework and other youth policy projects. Shayya described the meetings with various Swedish civil society organizations and government agencies as productive because MASAR "took what is fit for Lebanon and adapted it before putting it into use." As did several activists engaged in the civic activism toolkit project, Shayya viewed Lebanese activist projects as a potential model for other interventions in both the Middle East and the West. He also underscored the bidirectional flow of learning. For example, he described how the exchange with local activists instructed European collaborators on the multiple and ongoing effects of colonial histories and global power asymmetries on Lebanon's current circumstances.

YAP was one of the major projects that brought together the Lebanese state, civil society, and international institutions to deliberate about good governance and reforms. The Ministry of Youth and Sports, the United Nations Population Fund (UNFPA), UNICEF, MASAR, and the Beyond Consultancy Group were the main architects and facilitators of the national youth policy-making process. Other contributors included major local NGOs that focused on issues of gender equality (such as KAFA), NGOs that focused on family (such as the Lebanese Family Planning Association), and government institutions. Thanks to my initial acquaintance in the summer of 2012 with a high-ranking UN staff member in Beirut who believed in the importance of my research project, I was able to arrange meetings and interviews with numerous UN representatives, state officials, and NGO leaders who had been active in the national youth policy-making process. Those meetings enabled me to understand not only how the youth was at the center of Lebanese civil society's vision but also how civil society activists imagined themselves as leaders for cultural, economic, and political change.

YAP was founded in 2000, but it gained momentum in the context of the post-2006 polarization and the consequent surge of concern about the youth. The document "National Advice over the Youth Policy," approved by the Lebanese Council of Ministers in 2007, set the guidelines for the design of workshops with youth groups across Lebanon. In 2009, the Lebanese NGO "Youth Forum for National Youth Policies" (also known as the Youth Forum) was established to deliberate on the formulation of youth policy and to monitor its implementation. In 2009 and 2010, the Youth Forum and seventeen Lebanese ministries facilitated hundreds of workshops that brought together over a thousand young Lebanese who were recruited through political parties, NGOs, schools, universities, syndicates, and municipalities. All major political parties sent young representatives to help draft policy recommendations. Despite several political parties' initial hesitation to join a process they viewed as controlled by the Sunni-led Ministry of Youth and Sports, they all eventually agreed to participate and sought to make their own contributions to the national document. Under the supervision and facilitation of civil society activists and communication experts, Lebanese youth from competing political and confessional groups discussed a range of socio-economic issues and collaboratively wrote policy recommendations.

In April 2012, the Lebanese Council of Ministers approved the National Youth Policy, which officially committed the Lebanese government to nationally agreed policies aimed at improving the lives of the country's youth—defined as Lebanese citizens between the ages of fifteen and twenty-nine.[21] The document included 137 policy recommendations on five policy areas—health, education and culture, labor and economic participation, social integration and political participation, and emigration—that provided a roadmap for the Lebanese parliament and the Ministry of Youth and Sports. Many middle-class activists understood their active supervision, coordination, and facilitation as an essential contribution to the National Youth Policy, one that symbolized civil society's leadership in Lebanese politics, nation-building, and state-making.

Various Lebanese political actors, including civil society activists, commonly referred to national youth policy-making as a rare instance in which a long-term, large-scale project successfully brought together differentially positioned stakeholders with conflicting agendas. My activist interlocutors considered this experience of successful collaboration exceptional given both civil society's lack of confidence in the government's political will and the activists' lucid awareness of the challenges of negotiating across power differentials, conflicting interests, and hidden agendas. I frequently heard civil society activists, international funding agency representatives, and Western humanitarian workers in Beirut complain about how major infrastructure and development projects, which had substantial funding from international organizations, preemptively failed or were aborted as a result of disagreements among Lebanese state actors. For example, a large-scale NGO project to provide accessible public water was delayed for two years because politicians sought to influence which towns and villages would receive access to public water. Civil society actors commonly viewed the sectarian system—in which confessional political parties and community groups exercised arbitrary power in distributing services and resources to their constituencies—as a major obstacle to executing national-scale projects that would benefit all Lebanese citizens.

Even though many activists viewed the approval of the National Youth Policy document in 2012 as an exceptional success, I heard numerous complaints about the policy-making process and its impacts. This included frustrations over the limitations and inconsequentiality of the final document and over the uneven and tense nature of the negotiations. More radically, some of the UN staff and NGO representatives involved in the process, whom I met in 2013 and 2014, described the National Youth Policy document as a "failed" agreement. They lamented their "wasted efforts" because the Lebanese parliament would probably not enact concrete laws and reforms to implement the agreed policies. Many activists also emphasized that disagreements on a variety of major issues resulted in compromises that diminished the transformative impact of some policies. In particular, many were upset that the document avoided some of the most pressing issues for the country's youth, such as gender inequality and the situation of Palestinian youth in Lebanon's refugee camps. Some other participants felt that their voices had not been adequately acknowledged or integrated into the final document. For instance, I heard several civil society participants complain that NGOs, which were distracted by a funding shortage, were less active than the political parties. Nonetheless, even frustrated participants and fierce critics of the process expressed their appreciation of the channels that had been created for diverse Lebanese youth to engage with both each other and multiple stakeholders on a wide range of political and economic issues.

The youth policy process was one of the few national projects that was revisited in subsequent years. In 2017, UNFPA, UNICEF, and the Ministry of Youth and Sports agreed to task the Beyond Consultancy Group with developing a National Youth Action Plan based on the National Youth Policy. The Beyond Consultancy Group made twenty priority recommendations that could be applied through 179 interventions between 2019 and 2021; however, the process was delayed because of further political crises and Covid-19.

Building on these recommendations, in 2022, UNFPA and UNICEF published the "National Youth Policy Action Plan," which presented the government with an "operational framework for the National Youth Policy to better address youth issues," to be implemented between 2022 and 2024.[22] The document encouraged public institutions (in particular the Ministry of Youth and Sports), Lebanese civil society organizations, international organizations, and donors to continue collaborating on interventions related to migration, health, employment and economic participation, social integration and political participation, and education and cultural participation.

The activists involved in the national youth policy-making process believed that, despite its limitations, the process accomplished significant changes in the lives of the youth who participated. They were especially proud that their platforms offered young Lebanese, whom the activists imagined as confined to their confessional lives, the skills to find "common ground" and "live together." Given their view that changing Lebanon's youth meant shaping the country's future, many activists understood the process as essential crisiswork: cultivating youth as active and ethical citizens would transform social structures, cultural practices, and subjectivities in order to bring about a better Lebanon.

ACTING LIKE A CITIZEN

The activists who facilitated the National Youth Policy process particularly emphasized how the participating youth learned to "act like citizens" (*taṣarraf ka-muwāṭin*). By this, they meant prioritizing the national interest over the interest of one's sect and patronage networks and expressing one's demands and opinions in a peaceful manner. Thus, many activists viewed the National Youth Policy—which had been approved by Lebanese youth representing the major confessions in the country, numerous NGOs, political parties, ministries, and international and local experts—as a unique testament to the ability of the Lebanese to find common ground. They also proudly emphasized that the bottom-up policy-making process was the first of its kind in the Arab region, showcasing how Lebanese youth could skillfully practice democracy when given the chance to do so. For these activists, the bottom-up approach meant that, rather than merely make abstract demands, the Lebanese youth and civil society undertook concrete efforts: writing policy papers with concrete solutions, practicing negotiation and advocacy, and lobbying government actors. The National Youth Policy was hence celebrated by various activists for turning active citizenship from an abstract dream into a concrete and affectively embodied experience.

Lebanese youth's experiences of active citizenship, many hoped, would reverberate across their families, social networks, and political parties. During a birthday party at a small bar in Hamra in March 2013 for a well-known local activist, I saw Ali, a middle-class, secular Shiʿi feminist activist in his late twenties. As he asked how my research had been going, he looked excited at learning that I had recently interviewed several activist participants from the Youth Forum. Ali, whom I knew from several protests organized by feminist activists, had been one of the Youth Forum workshop facilitators, and he felt nostalgic about his experiences. He recalled how new it felt for the youth from political parties to comfortably speak about their problems and to be heard for the first time in their lives: "We created a culture of discussion, expressing individual opinions, and respectfully listening to others' opinions, all of which are non-existent in most Lebanese political parties." Like other workshop facilitators I spoke to, Ali believed that providing spaces for "civic engagement" for the "sectarian" youth in political parties would eventually help broaden the horizons of society. He mentioned examples of youth party representatives who became close friends with other participants in non-partisan NGOs, and even with members of conflicting political parties. Activists like Ali believed that the process of coming together and enjoying sustained interactions with youth from other confessional backgrounds allowed many young Lebanese to overcome the sectarian barriers created by politicians.

Ali also emphasized that young Lebanese from conflicting parties cultivated a patriotic identity by realizing they had common problems and developing a "shared youth perspective," as well as a more critical outlook toward their party leaders and families. When I probed him about what that "youth perspective" meant, he described it as focusing on the common needs of the youth, the obstacles they face, their success stories, and the problems they encounter in political parties, NGOs, and everyday life. He remarked, "The government was surprised how the son [*ibn*] of Quwwat [the Lebanese Forces, a key Christian Party in the March 14 coalition] and the son [*ibn*] of Hizbullah [a key political party in the March 8 coalition] could agree on various issues and together pressure the government." He believed that sustained engagement with "others" who held conflicting political positions counteracted many young people's unquestioned loyalty to their party leaders. In September 2013, another activist who oversaw meetings between youth from different political parties told me, "Over time, they [the youth from different political parties] learned not to be afraid of each other anymore, and their political leaders couldn't scare them with the idea of the other." These comments reflected a widely shared idea among activists: when young members of different political parties and sects begin to imagine themselves as young Lebanese citizens with shared problems, rights, and responsibilities, their loyalty to the nation would surpass their loyalty to their sects. Because I did not talk to any young members of the parties who had participated in those meetings, it is hard to assess the validity of activists' observations about how young members' attitudes changed. However, the activists' observations illustrate how civil society is imagined as "saving" the Lebanese youth from the control of sectarian political parties.

Activists' valorization of civic engagement perpetuated a middle-class fantasy of self-enclosed communities in which members of different confessional groups rarely interacted with each other or were incapable of doing so in non-conflictual ways. This fantasy further reified the notion that familial and group allegiances hindered the formation of meaningful political alliances and consensus about public matters. In the different neighborhoods where I lived in central Beirut, however, I consistently observed that, despite the prevalence of sectarian relationalities, many ordinary citizens were part of several cross-sectarian networks and had working relations with neighbors and coworkers from different sects and political orientations—an observation confirmed by other anthropological research in Beirut.[23]

While the idea of Lebanese confinement to sectarian communities certainly does not capture the complexity of social life in Beirut, it epitomizes middle-class activists' celebration of civil society as *the* unique venue where peaceful cross-sectarian interactions among otherwise isolated or adversarial groups could take place. In this sense, equating cross-sectarianism with civil society dismisses the multiplicity of everyday cross-sectarian socialities and solidarities that exist outside of civil society networks. Moreover, the idealization of civil society as transcending sectarian culture also obscures the multiplicity of relationships and practices that link civil society to the political class. Many civil society organizations in Lebanon had direct affiliations with confessional parties, and sectarian elites coopted various non-partisan and non-sectarian NGOs.

Despite recognizing the complex entanglements between civil society and other political actors, many activists still imagined civil society as inherently removed from, and therefore beyond the reach of, the nation's corrupt, sectarian politics. This purist notion glossed over complex forms of inequalities that undergirded civil society networks. As a case in point, the idealized abstraction of a non-sectarian Lebanese citizen as liberal, Western-looking, and secular often led to the automatic delegitimization of low-income activists. In middle-class activist circles, low-income activists' open display of religious markers such as hijab or religious allegiances to leaders such as Hassan Nasrallah de facto marked them as sectarian and unwilling to change. Moreover, the very desire to rise above the messy political relationalities they attributed to sectarianism led various activists to identify their work as non-political, thus uncritically endorsing technocratic frameworks of change as ideologically neutral. Crucially, the coding of technocratic interventions and related practices of expertise and professionalism as "neutral" became central to middle-class crisiswork.

Policy-Making as a Non-Political Scientific Process

The Youth Economic Forum (YEF) was a prominent independent and non-partisan local civil society organization that was founded in 2007. Several UN representatives and academics in Beirut praised YEF as a key actor that promoted activism and facilitated youth participation in policy-making. YEF contributed to the national youth policy process briefly, but its major success was in effectively training diverse groups of youth in policy writing, lobbying, and advocacy. During an interview in July 2013, Cedric Choukeir, YEF's then-vice president, politely and graciously welcomed me into the organization's meeting room. He seemed very eager to talk about YEF's activities. His well-ironed, light blue cotton shirt and dark blue chino pants fit perfectly with the chic business casual style adopted by most male professional civil society activists. He was one of the few civil society actors I met who preferred to speak with me in English, which he claimed was his preferred language for professional meetings. Cedric had a master's degree in local human development and international cooperation from the University of Florence. When I met him, he occupied active roles in various local civil society organizations and served as the director of the World Youth Alliance's Middle East Chapter, which was based in Hamra. We met twice in his Hamra office, and I also encountered him on various occasions when he served as a trainer, expert speaker, or participant in various civil society spaces. Cedric was highly respected within civil society circles, and I heard many activists praise his professionalism, hard work, and experience.

YEF's main goal was to train young Lebanese to design effective public policies. The founders of the organization included experts with graduate degrees in political science, economics, and public policy. The forum emerged as part of the post-2006 mobilization that encouraged active citizenship and working for change among youth. The idea for the forum originated when then-Finance Minister Jihad Azour, in collaboration with civil society activists, organized and hosted a series of meetings in 2006 and 2007 where youth from diverse backgrounds discussed socio-economic and other major problems of Lebanon. I heard several of my civil society interlocutors refer to Azour, an economist with a doctorate in international finance from the Paris Institute of Political Studies, as a strong supporter of Lebanese civil society. Like several of my activist interlocutors who worked with the youth, Cedric believed that Azour supported youth empowerment initiatives as part of his efforts to strengthen civil society and that Azour genuinely wanted to engage with the youth by establishing direct channels for dialogue. Cedric emphasized that the core idea behind these meetings was "to open up a space of dialogue between young people."

Following the meetings, a group of young Lebanese activists founded YEF in October 2007 with the support of the Lebanese government. The new organization's mission was to train diverse groups of young Lebanese to devise effective policies that would address economic issues such as unemployment and solid waste management. Many Lebanese college students who were majoring in a variety of disciplines—such as political science, environmental science, economics, business management, and engineering—participated in these meetings. In these settings, the major goal of YEF was "capacity-building," in order to generate concrete and workable solutions for the country's crises. YEF also supported activists in local advocacy NGOs, which were among its major partners. YEF training sessions instructed activists in advocacy NGOs on how to "represent the interests of the public sector" through developing skills such as reviewing existing policy analyses, conducting sustained policy analyses of their own, and devising effective policy recommendations for reforms. For Cedric, the word "policy" helped distinguish concrete interventions from abstract ideals, and it articulated specific short-term and long-term objectives at the national level.

Cedric also proudly underscored YEF's ability to "reach out" to diverse audiences. For instance, after recognizing that most of its trainees were from Beirut and its suburbs, YEF sought to include a more diverse body of participants by reaching out to young people in other major areas—such as Tripoli, Bekaa, and Nabatieh—as well as by speaking with representatives of the youth branches of local political parties and NGOs. Also, many local NGOs contacted YEF for training, and donors sometimes required NGOs to receive training from YEF. Cedric described their training as a "purely scientific," technical process that used factual analysis and instructed participants to rely on factual analysis as the grounds for the advocacy and lobbying processes. He emphasized that YEF merely provided tools, templates, and techniques, and that it was up to the trainees to decide what to advocate for and how. In short, YEF wanted change and helped the Lebanese youth enact it, but it refrained from openly discussing what change entailed or should entail.

In describing public policy-making as a politically neutral, scientific process, Cedric claimed that his organization was not a "political NGO." He noticed that I looked confused by this statement and encouraged me to ask for any clarifications. I smiled and asked him to explain what "political NGO" meant exactly, given that YEF did many important political activities. Cedric explained that YEF did not deal with "sensitive issues," such as "security issues," and that it explicitly refrained from advocating for specific political agendas. He emphasized the importance of not taking political positions:

> We don't have a political agenda and we don't choose one policy over the other. We don't mind if we have two policy recommendations that are completely contradictory, as long as the process to develop them is based on an ethical approach and professional manner.

Cedric viewed the content of a policy as far less important than its procedural framework. He hoped that once the Lebanese learned to develop concrete solutions that favored public interests over familial or sectarian interests, it would become possible to agree on which solutions would work better for the nation. The invoked distinction between "public" and "confessional" interests perpetuated the fantasy of enclosed sectarian communities that inherently conflict with other communities and overdetermine members' everyday lives.

In Lebanon, as in other global contexts in which technical procedures in political matters are standardized and depicted as universally valid regardless of contextual particularities, middle-class members of civil society widely viewed the procedures of policy-making as implementations of neutral professional knowledge.[24] Their technocratic approach, which claimed impartiality and neutral distance from any political agenda, construes technical knowledge—and the frameworks offered by Western-trained professionals and organizations like the World Bank and the UN—as inherently objective and above sectarianism. By clearly distinguishing "policy" from "politics," YEF and similar organizations in Lebanon aimed to draft policies that many parties could agree to. While the underlying purpose of this distinction is to prioritize consensus over disagreement, its emphasis on neutrality, professionalism, and technicality renders activist work as a matter of technical expertise that participants could learn to implement in standardized ways, devoid of context.

From this perspective, the main contradiction in YEF's conceptualization of policy-making as a technical and scientific process is that, while it concedes that different actors could hypothetically devise competing policy recommendations, it anticipates that the use of standard templates and guidelines would lead actors to formulate similar policies for a given problem. This highly systematized procedural framework reduces the scope of policy-making to a mechanical operation that any technical expert, independent of context-specific knowledge, would be able to implement. In doing so, it obscures how situated power asymmetries and conflicting political ideologies could impact the formulation, implementation, and reception of policies. As a case in point, Azour, who was a member of the International Monetary Fund (IMF) Advisory Group for the Middle East, was seen by many in Lebanon, including various independent activist groups, as a pro-Western, Maronite Christian, liberal politician rather than as a neutral, patriotic technocrat, which is how Azour saw himself. Hence, the very notion of technocracy as a non-political, neutral form of crisiswork that could operate above Lebanon's messy sectarian politics itself constitutes a particular political discourse. Just as the "national" policies of Azour and other politicians were "political," in the sense that the policies reflected specific ideological alignments, any policy proposed by young Lebanese participants would reflect particular political commitments.

Despite the contradictions and limitations inherent in YEF's crisiswork, the YEF activists' refusal of the word "political," and the concomitant emphasis on expert knowledge, could also expand possibilities of action. As

Cedric did, many Lebanese activists claimed that their participation in civil society was "not political" (*mish siyāsī*). Paradoxically, avoiding the word "political" in describing their activism was a strategy that enabled activists to distinguish themselves from existing political actors while navigating complex power relations, a process that could potentially enhance their political reach. In her study on student activism in Serbia, Jessica Greenberg convincingly argues that discursive claims to being apolitical could be "rhetorical techniques and ethical strategies for remaining socially engaged in contexts in which such engagement is deeply suspect."[25] In Lebanon, like in many parts of the world, public distrust in formal politics and politicians was rampant.[26] The word politics often carried negative connotations of sectarianism and corruption, and calling someone "political" (*siyāsī*) implied they were sectarian and corrupt.[27] Similarly, when someone used the words "sectarian" or "corrupt" to describe a person, a relationship, or a practice, the immediate connotation was that dirty politicians were involved in unethical conduct. By claiming that advocacy or policy-making processes were "not political," many civil society actors sought to portray their work as "non-sectarian" and outside of existing political structures and political party agendas.[28] YEF thus instructed participants to apply technical procedures of deliberation and policy-making in order to create a space for activism that could not easily be dismissed as sectarian. When activists like Cedric presented policy-making as a "scientific process," they carved out a legitimate and acceptable space for young Lebanese to engage in politics.

Seemingly depoliticizing discourses, such as active citizenship and "not being political," became "paradoxically crucial to the production of new political publics."[29] Between 2006 and 2013, diverse actors from civil society and the state interacted to create an exceptionally vibrant political space in which Lebanon's crises were publicly discussed and Lebanese citizens were called to "do something" to abate these crises. Activists engaged closely with the parliament and ministries and organized roundtables and townhalls that brought together local community and state representatives. A reputation for being non-political enabled activist organizations like YEF to collaborate with the existing political parties and Lebanese actors from diverse sectarian and social backgrounds. Acting as neutral, independent, and non-political experts, many middle-class activists claimed to rightfully represent the interests of the people thanks to their professional knowledge and skills as well as commitment to public interest.[30]

After two years of collective discussions, sixty-four activists, who were all YEF trainees, collaborated under the name "The Reformists Platform" to publish a booklet listing thirty-three policy briefs on eleven different sectors. The booklet, titled "33 Ideas to Improve Lebanon," was launched at the Lebanese Parliament Library on November 11, 2011, and more than thirty young YEF trainees visited the parliament that day to share their policy briefs with various ministers and parliamentarians. "33 Ideas to Improve Lebanon," which was published in both English and Arabic, was widely distributed among civil society, academic, and policy-making institutions as well as Lebanese state institutions. Multiple local and international advocacy NGOs I visited in Beirut used it as a reference book to devise new projects. The thirty-three ideas included concrete projects that targeted "human development" and "economic development" in fields such as urban planning, the environment, education, culture, energy, and telecommunications. For instance, the fourth idea, "reviving the railway system," described how railway investment had been paused throughout the long Lebanese War, explained the manifold effects of not having railways on various economic sectors and on Lebanese communities, and proposed strategies for reviving the old system.

Even though most of these ideas were never implemented, the process reinforced the activists' belief that Lebanon's problems could be solved under the leadership of well-educated, non-partisan, and patriotic members of civil society. Many activists agreed that Lebanon's problems had solutions, but the political class was not willing to implement them. Thus, they perceived their crisiswork not only as timely and urgent but also as effective and superior to existing political venues.

The technocratic approach that shaped middle-class crisiswork relied on market-driven development to reform the state. As in the case of other neoliberal, translocal development projects,[31] Lebanon's post-2006 governmental interventions—in particular the projects of youth activism—reduced numerous political and social issues to technical matters that could be resolved by expertise and skills. Various complex problems were framed as solvable by bolstering the professional competencies of educated, local youth who were guided by Western-trained local elites. As a result, new local social hierarchies were produced. The experiences of diverse local groups were treated as secondary to the visions of the local elite, and some of those groups were discredited as sectarian or affiliated with terrorism. The technocratic approach, which asserted that collaborations between patriotic, competent, and well-intentioned activists and politicians could solve Lebanon's long-standing political and social problems, also downplayed the extent to which Lebanon was impacted by regional and global forces. In doing so, it offered false promises of growth and development actualized through crisiswork.

As the collaborative framework among Western donors, civil society, and the Lebanese state lost its traction during the Syrian War, some experienced activists highlighted the significance of maintaining a belief in change in the face of growing disillusionment and resignation. According to some, the frustrations resulting from the stuckness of policy-making and advocacy work made it even more urgent for crisiswork to focus on individual and collective care as well as on well-being.

Resisting Negativity

I met Hala, a Sunni middle-class activist in her mid-twenties, in the summer of 2012 at a workshop in Beirut on public policy advocacy organized by a prominent, local environmental NGO. When she was in college, Hala had briefly participated in the youth branch of the Future Movement party—a Sunni-led party that represented the majority of Lebanese Sunnis and was a key participant in the March 14 coalition. She was disappointed, however, by what she described as the party's "corruption" and "same old mentalities." By contrast, Hala found civil society to be flexible and open to new ideas. In 2010, while working at a local bank, she began to volunteer for an independent and non-sectarian Lebanese environmental advocacy NGO in her spare time. She identified as an independent activist and explicitly refused to affiliate with existing political parties or with the March 8 and 14 political coalitions. She proudly identified as both Lebanese and Arab and was very critical of Israel and Western countries' support for Israel. She was also critical of other countries in the region, including the Gulf countries, Iran, Syria, and Türkiye, for interfering in Lebanese politics. Hala was disillusioned with both Western donor representatives and Lebanese politicians with whom she had engaged in advocacy campaigns. She believed that only the joint effort of young Lebanese in independent civil society would achieve the desired political and social change.

Two weeks after the attack on Chatah's convoy, Hala asked me to promote the collective she had just founded, which would focus on Lebanese youth. She also complained about the absence of support for her collective from her family, whom she described as extremely pessimistic and negative. I had not heard from Hala during the last few months of 2013—one of the most politically tense periods of my fieldwork—so I was excited when she asked to meet at a popular café in Hamra frequented by activists. After giving each other a warm hug, we ordered our coffees and found a quiet corner in the otherwise crowded café. Hala told me that she planned to continue volunteering at the environmental advocacy NGO but felt that there was more to do than advocacy and lobbying: "I want to do more than waiting for government action. I can't see Lebanon like this. We all live on the verge of death."

Hala believed that, in addition to putting pressure on the government to implement effective policies through advocacy, activists should cultivate a sense of positivity and a belief in change during difficult times. She talked at length about her many activist friends who had been struggling with disillusionment and hopelessness as they observed the country being "once again" shattered by sectarian polarization and fears of war: "Protests, advocacy, lobbying, campaigns, conflict resolution, peacebuilding. . .we tried everything. Now that the situation in the country is worse than ever and we are back to ground zero, it's very important to focus on raising our spirits. Enough with negativity (*bikaffī salbiyya*)." Through her collective, Hala wanted to create an alternative political space where young people would be trained to teach skills, such as photography, painting, and gardening, for the purposes of empowerment and collective healing. She believed that everyone could become a teacher and, in so doing, actively build a community that believed in and worked for change. She wanted to teach chess while learning to code and play the piano. Caring for others and for oneself, Hala believed, would foster a sense of well-being at a time when many activists struggled with fading hopes for change. In the context of a protracted war and the constant threat of violence, such activist efforts to feel well through resisting negativity became a highly charged ethico-political demand that shaped public imaginations of change.

Hala also believed that engaging with others through fun and low-effort activities would transform young Lebanese, providing them with both a sense of purpose and an outlet for their long-accumulated frustrations. "They try to divide us, kill us, and kill our future, but we will continue to live and be strong. We have the power to change things," she stated resolutely. She then began talking about political developments. Like many others, she was angry that, almost a decade after the assassination of Rafiq Hariri, killings of politicians like Chatah continued with impunity. Hala did not want to leave Lebanon, as several of her cousins and friends had, and she attributed this preference to her deep care for the nation and its future. She hoped that her collective would make other young Lebanese feel empowered to change Lebanon. Toward the end of the conversation Hala remarked that even if her initiative were to fail, she wanted to continue to try new forms of civil society engagement because she needed to do something to stay sane. Her voice began to shake and her eyes became teary as she said, "All my friends are depressed. I can't stand that." She had looked anxious and fidgeted with her chair throughout the meeting, so I was not surprised when she cried silently. We sat quietly for a minute or so and then left the café and began walking toward the seaside.

Hala was not alone in her willingness to fight against negativity. In fact, idioms of positivity and negativity were prevalent in many public conversations in Beirut, particularly among the educated middle classes. They extensively complained about the ubiquity of negativity in the media, everyday life, and relationships. Yet, activists like Hala sought to do more than complain about the overwhelming effects of negativity. They framed the practice of cultivating positivity as an essential component of crisiswork. Accordingly, activists promoted positivity, mental health, and well-being in order to protect themselves and others from sinking deeper into fear and anxiety. To that end, many of my activist interlocutors, who had diverse confessional, class, and political backgrounds, practiced physical activities such as yoga, exercise, and meditation and encouraged their loved ones to do so.

In March 2014, as we walked toward her apartment for dinner after participating in a large march against domestic violence, Hala expressed her deep concern about the horrific stories of abuse shared by several protesters during the event. Yet she was also pleased to meet a feminist activist who offered free mental health support to victims of domestic violence. Emphasizing the importance of taking care of one's mental health, Hala continued,

> I spend a lot of time in meditation. When I'm about to lose my peace, I go up to mountaintops and meditate. I'm a Muslim, but I spend a lot of time in churches and holy sites. Especially, during days when fear and hopelessness prevail, I just sit in quietness. Until I find my peace again. [. . .] Everyone is very pessimistic in this country, but an activist cannot be pessimistic. We must be positive and believe that things can change.

For activists like Hala, practices such as hiking, meditation, and yoga were more than tools for self-care to become and stay healthy, productive, and positive. They viewed those practices as politically charged efforts to counteract the "negative" (*salbī*) affects, such as stuckness, fear, and anxiety, that were induced by Lebanon's accumulating crises. Observing that their efforts to create non-sectarian policies and culture had failed in the short run, activists like Hala viewed cultivating a positive mindset, and mental health broadly, as a means to safeguard their belief in the possibility of change. Many activists endorsed staying "positive" (*ījābī*) as an ethical and political duty to protect oneself against overwhelming feelings of disillusionment and hopelessness. Cultivating positivity promised more than relief from the suffering of prolonged conflict and violence; it was seen as working toward and facilitating belief in political change.[32] Activists placed value on cultivating positivity to enhance their agency, which they described as acting with a sense of purpose and direction. Accordingly, only by embracing and practicing positivity could one persistently believe in and work for change under extreme and debilitating circumstances.

Activists believed that embodying and displaying a positive attitude were essential, not because positivity was intrinsically virtuous, but because it expressed active resistance to the pervasive, public affects of pessimism and negativity emanating from sectarianism. Practices such as visiting holy sites, meditating, practicing yoga, and hiking helped activists build positive ethico-political dispositions—embodied capacities that they believed translated into empowerment and agency. As Hala's plan to create a space for self-empowerment and collective healing exemplified, many activists sought to cultivate empowering ethico-political dispositions among the country's youth to ensure that they would retain some sense of normalcy and to promote a vibrancy for change across Lebanese civil society. They described negativity as a "normal" (*ʿādī*) and "natural" (*ṭabīʿī*) response to adverse conditions; yet at the same time, they approached negative affects as a contagious illness that needed to be contained. They hoped that resisting structures of negativity would allow them to continue to believe in the possibility of change and to execute their activist projects.[33] Through working on their cognitive, embodied, and affective circumstances, activists felt they were actively fighting against sectarianism and other structural problems, rather than merely preparing to fight.

Many activists considered yoga as the best cure for fear and anxiety during tense periods of public violence and polarization. Yoga classes in Lebanon date back to the 1960s, and the practice gained popularity after the 2000s.[34] Even though yoga had historically been an urban middle-class practice in Lebanon, many activists with diverse economic, confessional, and political backgrounds told me that they practiced yoga and meditation at home and followed internet training classes. Low-cost yoga classes were also available in different parts of Beirut, and various civil society organizations, such as NGOs and collectives, offered free yoga classes.

Beirut residents practiced yoga for various reasons—to look trendy, reduce stress, feel spiritual, get in shape, or relax. Most of them did not connect doing yoga to political agency. Yet for many activists, yoga was part of their efforts to create a livable, dignified life in Lebanon. They did not consider yoga as inherently political, yet they all emphasized that it helped them continue to invest in activism. For instance, a small group of activists with whom I volunteered at a middle-class youth advocacy NGO frequently reminded each other to relax through meditation or yoga. During moments of confusion, frustration, anxiety, and sadness, practicing yoga or meditation together, even for as little as fifteen minutes, made them feel grounded in a community.

As anthropologist Michael Jackson points out, in the face of unknown, uncertain, or disconcerting and shocking circumstances, individuals and groups strive to construct meaning, regain control, alleviate anxiety, and restore agency.[35] In such circumstances, rituals provide a sense of orderliness and agency and sustain the hope that "subjective transformations (in attitude and affect) will prompt objective changes (in their political climate)."[36] Taking seriously people's efforts to change how they feel and think, Jackson builds on anthropologist Bronislaw Malinowski to suggest that "what is at stake in critical times is not simply *doing* things the right way but *being* in the right frame of mind when you are doing them."[37] From this perspective, activists' valorization of yoga, meditation, and similar practices can be interpreted as an effort to bring themselves to the right frame of mind in order to better cope with the public affects of fear and anxiety. For many of my activist interlocutors, changing how they lived by working on their habits, beliefs, affects, attitudes, and manners offered them ways to mitigate the traces of crises in their bodies and minds and to restore a sense of normalcy to their lives. These efforts became central to crisiswork as they articulated resistance to a system that was widely understood as killing its citizens.

Cultivating positivity was not necessarily an individualistic practice. Many activists cultivated positivity by socializing with and caring for others.

They highlighted the significance of caring for oneself, one's loved ones, and the larger community. Such care was believed to offset the systematic undermining of Lebanese well-being by political actors. Hala and many other activists saw civil society spaces as helping Lebanese collectively heal from the trauma of the multiple crises the country had experienced since 2005. Several Lebanese activists told me that they experienced individual and collective healing through their NGO activities and they used politically charged idioms of resilience and resistance to characterize these healing experiences.[38]

Cultivating positivity through practices such as teaching new skills and doing yoga was not inherently political or apolitical. As an open-ended process, practicing positivity may lead to individualism and depoliticization or to solidarity and politicization. In Lebanon, one could observe both trajectories. For most activists, nevertheless, a focus on being positive did not mean that one had to abandon one's efforts to change legal and political structures. In fact, it meant sustaining the strength to continue in the collective struggle, even under often desperate conditions. Through discursively highlighting the importance of cultivating positivity as an individual and collective practice, as well as embodying a positive mindset, activists like Hala also sought to model restorative practices for younger generations. I heard several middle-class activists praise Hala for staying positive and for motivating them to stay in Lebanon and work for change. They pointed out how positive Lebanese activists "made them interested in civil society" or how they became their "best role models" because they showed that disillusionment and resignation were not inevitable.

Just as technocracy, expertise, and professionalism promised middle-class activists alternatives to existing ways of doing politics, positivity and well-being represented ethical and meaningful ways of inhabiting crises in Lebanon. Ultimately, these activist efforts to materialize alternative modes of being and doing rendered "change" as an always unfinished, non-linear, and contradictory process that could nevertheless be affectively felt in the present, rather than as an event or a future goal. Many of my interlocutors mentioned feeling that "something had changed" during their collective participation in various civil society activities, including advocacy, policy-making, and doing yoga. While they knew that crises were still unfolding, they worked actively and deliberately to transform the very experience of these crises. In demonstrating that civil society engagement could uniquely actualize the very experience of change, middle-class activists claimed moral and political authority to lead change through their crisiswork.

Many low-income Lebanese, on the other hand, had different motivations for and experiences in participating in civil society and engaging in crisiswork. Like middle-class activists, they sought better futures for Lebanon's youth and believed that this could be accomplished through multiscalar changes. Yet they understood and worked for "change" in ways that did not necessarily align with middle-class activist politics. In challenging the ethical and political underpinnings of middle-class fantasies of sectarianism, various young low-income Lebanese repurposed middle class-led NGOs, and the ideas of "professionalism" these NGOs promoted, for social mobility. In doing so, they presented alternative practices of empowerment, sociality, care, and solidarity.

THREE

Aspirant Professionals

Dana was deeply upset on the day I visited her apartment in a low-income neighborhood in the Msaytbeh region of central Beirut in May 2013. Her application for an internship as the front office manager of an upscale hotel had been rejected. She believed the reason was her "not professional" (*mish profesyonnel*) answer to the interview question, "Who is your favorite political leader?" The interviewer's face suddenly changed when Dana hesitantly replied, "Obama," and he did not ask any further questions.

Dana and her mother Nadine had moved to Beirut from a poor town in North Lebanon after Dana's father died suddenly of a heart attack in 2010. Dana was planning to graduate from the Lebanese University, a low-ranking public university in Lebanon, with a management degree in June 2014. Several of her university friends explained to her that company representatives asked such questions with the expectation of hearing "neutral" names like Mahatma Gandhi or Nelson Mandela—figures who would not be viewed as symbolic enemies by any group in Lebanon. Her friends had learned job interview techniques and productive ways to engage diverse audiences from empowerment NGOs and urged Dana to participate in one of these organizations. Nadine, a Sunni woman in her early fifties, shrugged at Dana and offered a different explanation for the rejection of her application: "This is because our *wāsṭa* [intermediary connection] was not strong enough, everything wants a *wāsṭa* here [in Beirut]" (*kill shī baddu wāsṭa hūn*). Dana responded, "I don't think it was all about *wāsṭa*." Even though Nadine insisted on her explanation, she nevertheless agreed to let Dana join We Grow, the NGO where I had been volunteering since February 2013.

Dana represents what I call "aspirant professionals": young, low-income, university-educated activists who seek to learn professional skills and become part of urban professional networks by participating in empowerment NGOs. I met hundreds of aspirant professionals from different confessional backgrounds who volunteered for NGOs or participated in free soft-skills workshops offered by these organizations. They were typically unemployed or underemployed activists who engaged in learning professionalism and networking with urban middle-class professionals as a means to upward social mobility. Most of them came from families who lived in rural areas of Lebanon or had recently migrated to Beirut, like Dana and her mother. Concerned about their limited familial support for social mobility, low-income educated Lebanese, particularly those with rural origins, were intrigued by the vibrant NGO world of Beirut and the popularity and prestige of this world. As unemployment was a fundamental constituent of low-income communities' lifeworlds, the practice of embodying a "professional" self to enhance their probability of securing a stable job, and upward social mobility more broadly, constituted a key component of low-income activists' crisiswork.

Middle-class activists in Lebanon celebrated professionalism as a defining feature of an ethical citizen whose dependence on merits and competencies qualifies them to participate in crisiswork. They promoted professionalism as a moral alternative to reliance on *wāsṭa*, a practice they associated with a corrupt, sectarian political system. They hoped that, as more Lebanese became "professional," a non-sectarian public culture that relied on meritocracy would emerge. However, low-income activists, in particular those with rural origins, appropriated NGOs for class mobility in ways that contested urban elites' separation of *wāsṭa* and professional networks. Aspirant professionals came from economically disadvantaged families and struggled with economic hardships, but they had university degrees and aspired to join the middle class. They saw the professional trainings and networks offered by NGOs as a path toward becoming middle-class professionals and as a means of distinguishing themselves from other low-income communities.[1]

The participation of low-income communities in NGOs was not a mere emulation of middle-class values or the self-interested, individualistic pursuit of a better life. Rather, striving to become "professional" through NGO engagement constituted class-making—a relational and dynamic process of pursuing upward social mobility that generates new moralities, subjectivities, solidarities, and practices of crisiswork. In seeking to counteract the negative effects of Lebanon's crises, educated low-income communities pursued economic, cultural, and political capital through their participation in NGOs. Class-making through NGOs enhanced low-income livelihoods within a declining economy. Through their participation in empowerment NGOs, low-income young Lebanese could increase their chances of finding a job in Lebanon and elsewhere. In doing so, they could repurpose neocolonial agendas of powerful actors, such as donor agencies, that seek to raise patriotic youth that would not emigrate to the West. Low-income groups' simultaneous appropriation of both *wāsṭa* and professionalism also led to alternative political and ethical modalities of crisiswork that aligned with yet transcended dominant middle-class activist frameworks of crisiswork. Appropriated by diverse residents of Lebanon, NGOs became sites for building cross-sectarian and cross-class care and solidarity, which enabled their participants to create alternative communities, selfhoods, and forms of belonging. The pursuit of professionalism and social mobility in empowerment NGOs also led to unexpected forms of politicization.

Low-income groups' simultaneous appropriation of both *wāsṭa* and professionalism led to alternative political and ethical modalities of crisiswork that aligned with yet transcended dominant middle-class activist frameworks of crisiswork. NGOs also became sites for building cross-sectarian and cross-class care and solidarity, which enabled their participants to create alternative communities, selfhoods, and forms of belonging. Hence, class-making also meant the making of new activist lifeworlds with new relationalities and socialities.[2]

Examining low-income activists' personal accounts of their experiences as contextualized in complex lifeworlds reveals that crisiswork through NGOs had diverse and contradictory rationales and implications for different classes in Lebanon. Approaching "class-making" among activists as a contested, open-ended, and contingent process that involves the pursuit of both individual and collective interests recognizes how differences in intersecting social categories, such as sect, legal status, urbaneness, generation, and gender profoundly shape Lebanese civil society. As the dialogue between Dana and her mom indicates, experiences within NGOs shaped and were shaped by other spaces of everyday life and by the translocal histories of political polarization and inequality.

We Grow: From Conflict Resolution to Empowerment

We Grow was founded in 2006 by a small group of students from elite universities in Beirut who wanted to display solidarity against the growing social polarization that followed the assassination of Rafiq Hariri. After securing a large amount of transnational funding around 2010, We Grow evolved from an NGO focused on conflict resolution to one that focused on empowerment and was also committed to community service. The path to empowerment, as articulated by the group's webpage and leading figures, was framed as becoming "professional volunteers" (in English)—that is, as learning and practicing soft skills to serve and develop one's community. We Grow offered mainly two types of activities: community-oriented volunteering, such as cleaning beaches and visiting elder care centers, and free professionalization workshops on topics such as stress management, goal setting, and time management. Dana and I, as well as the many other volunteers, participated in both types of activity, which took place on a weekly basis. In contrast to some other youth-focused NGOs that offered good salaries and positions, We Grow did not have any paid positions. All participants—including the founders, project coordinators, and workshop trainers—were volunteers.

As with many participants in other Lebanese NGOs, most participants of We Grow self-identified as activists and viewed themselves as an active part of Lebanese civil society. Unlike activists in explicitly political NGOs, such as environmental and feminist advocacy organizations, most activists in organizations like We Grow carefully presented themselves publicly as non-political. Yet, through the extended time I spent with them outside of NGO spaces, I learned that they closely followed the news, formed their own political opinions, criticized the sectarian system and its major political parties, and participated in several mass protests. Like other activists, they believed that the political system in Lebanon was in need of radical change and had hopes that their upward mobility could also enhance their political agency. They avoided political discussions in NGO spaces because they prioritized the need to build and maintain "professional relationships" with people who belonged to different sects or had conflicting political positions. In this way, they strategically deployed professionalism as a tool for fostering cross-sectarian connectivity—a shared goal among various forms of crisis-work in Lebanon.

Most We Grow participants, including volunteers and workshop attendees, belonged to low-income families of multiple sects outside of Beirut. The founders, president, and group leaders, on the other hand, were from middle-class Sunni families in the city. They were graduates of AUB and LAU, both of which promoted civic engagement and participation in NGOs as part of their Anglo-American educational curricula. Their graduates claimed distinction as professionals through their superior quality of education, commitment to civic culture and community service, and strong access to English-medium global educational networks. They framed their NGO participation in terms of ethical citizenship and leadership for change, including the mentoring of Lebanese youth. Low-income youth made up the majority of volunteers and workshop participants in the several empowerment NGOs in which I actively participated in Beirut. Given their precarious economic situation, low-income youth hoped that their involvement in these NGOs would increase their likelihood of finding a job in the private or NGO sector. Like Dana, many low-income educated Lebanese in Beirut increasingly believed in and circulated narratives such as "professionalism is required for getting a job" and "NGOs are helpful in learning professionalism."

Balā Wāsṭa as Professionalism

In January 2014, in a group meeting at the office of We Grow, Dana asked if any of us knew someone who could help her connect with the Children's Cancer Center of Lebanon (CCCL) for our next community outreach event. No one from the CCCL, a popular host for NGO community outreach events, had responded to Dana's phone calls or emails. Fadi, a low-income Shiʿi male activist in his late twenties, suggested, "I think my brother knows someone who works there. I can ask my brother." Sara, a twenty-four-year-old middle-class Sunni female activist who was the group leader, expressed clear disapproval of the idea: "Sorry, but I don't think this is moral (*akhlāqī*). We Lebanese use a *wāsṭa* everywhere, for finding jobs, internships, getting our work done in ministries. At least for our activities in the organization, we should not use a *wāsṭa*. Let's leave *wāsṭa* in our families." She went on to say, "One of the skills we try to cultivate here [at We Grow] is behaving like a professional (*professionnel*) and being a professional necessitates not using *wāsṭa*. We're trying to create a difference here." Later on, Sara asked Ziad, the twenty-six-year-old president of We Grow, to reach out to the CCCL.

Ziad arranged a visit for the group using his professional networks: a college friend had previously worked at the CCCL.

What made it morally acceptable for We Grow to rely on Ziad's friend but not on a volunteer's family member? Middle-class activists in Lebanon viewed the pervasiveness of *wāsṭa* as a symbol of sectarianism because *wāsṭa* was seen as inextricably rooted in sectarian political parties and in the kinship structures that supported those parties. Professionalism, in contrast, was celebrated as a moral subjectivity imagined as the practice of relying on one's knowledge, skills, and ability to develop networks that were independent of sectarian relationalities. Middle-class activists viewed professionalism as a cure for nepotism, corruption, and other problems associated with the sectarian system.[3] Professionalism promised an alternative modality of citizenship *balā wāsṭa* (without *wāsṭa*). This is why Sara and other middle-class activists in cross-sectarian NGOs such as We Grow understood relying on a family member to support NGO activities as an unethical practice that contradicted the professionalism of their activism. Instead, they promoted receiving help from friends and acquaintances in one's professional networks. Given that Fadi's brother was considered a *wāsṭa*, whereas Ziad's friend was considered a professional connection, it was the latter whose assistance was acceptable and preferred, even though the nature of the help was identical.

Wāsṭa, in Arabic, means "mediation," "intercession," or "connection." Lebanese used the term to describe both the person who mediates and the process of mediation through which a social exchange takes place. As a process, *wāsṭa* could be defined as "the intervention of a patron on behalf of a client or clients to obtain a service, a benefit or other resources for the client."[4] A person was said to "have a *wāsṭa*" (*ʿindu wāsṭa*) if they had such a patron in their family or extended kinship group. The Lebanese state was historically decentered in service provision, which made political parties and ethnic-religious community networks central to the distribution of resources through *wāsṭa*. Political parties and community networks regulated many aspects of social life, such as employment, schools, and infrastructure and provided extensive social services—ranging from healthcare to poverty relief—to families that pledged their allegiances to them. As part of the clientelist patronage system, kinship groups mobilized sectarian affiliations in accessing the resources and services offered by parties.

During and after the long Lebanese War (1975–1990), familial relationships continued to be central to a person's sense of security and access to resources. Being a member of a family with strong *wāsṭa* resources facilitated access to a variety of benefits, including passports, work permits, loans, school and university acceptance, and good doctors. Having unreliable family and kinship ties was a significant source of anxiety and material precarity for many Lebanese, especially for those from low-income communities. Despite Sara's assumption that all Lebanese used *wāsṭa*, my low-income interlocutors struggled with limited access to it. Wealthy groups typically had better *wāsṭa* resources, though some low-income communities did have access to an effective *wāsṭa*, for example, through a member of parliament or a religious figure connected through their extended families.

Sara represented a particular politics of Lebanese civil society that sought to transform sectarianism by cultivating "non-sectarian" (*ghayr ṭā'ifī*), "universal" practices, such as professionalism, to replace "sectarian," "local" practices such as *wāsṭa*.[5] Middle-class activists increasingly targeted *wāsṭa* as a corrupt practice that perpetuated sectarian social formations. They commonly complained that, despite having acquired degrees and skills from elite universities, they continued to depend on family ties to obtain jobs and promotions and to navigate the bureaucracy. They perceived such dependence as undermining the value of meritocracy and also as increasing their families' level of control over their lives, impacting decisions such as who they could marry, befriend, and vote for. When middle-class activists shared with me that they had used *wāsṭa* for a specific purpose in the past, they spoke as if they were revealing an embarrassing secret and explicitly asked me not to disclose their use of *wāsṭa* to anyone else. Their frustration with dependence on family ties was not merely a claim to independent adulthood. To them, using family connections also meant dependence on the religious and political leaders from whom their families sought assistance. When their parents engaged in social exchange practices, such as home visits, phone calls, and gift exchanges, with political and religious figures to secure a benefit for them, the middle-class Lebanese activists felt guilty for reproducing the very corrupt political system that they wanted to change.

The Lebanese media also portrayed *wāsṭa* as an entrenched social illness responsible for the hopelessness and resignation experienced by many university-educated young Lebanese. For example, in an article titled "Widespread Favoritism Takes Toll on Economy," the English-language Lebanese newspaper *Daily Star* claimed that "Many university graduates prefer to seek employment abroad instead of seeking a *wasta* in Lebanon."[6] Local media and online forums were filled with debates and commentaries that characterized *wāsṭa* as a defining feature of "corruption," "backward traditionalism," "nepotism," and "sectarianism." In these public discussions, *wāsṭa* was seen as more serious than mere favoritism—it symbolized the sectarian system itself, a pervasive and insidious social malaise growingly intolerable for the youth of the nation.

Activist Lebanese popularized critiques of *wāsṭa* on social media. For example, the activist initiative Bala Wasta was founded in November 2012 by Nay Boustany, a young Lebanese woman, to raise awareness about the problematic nature of *wāsṭa* and to encourage companies to hire people based on their qualifications. Bala Wasta was popular with young, university-educated Lebanese, especially between 2012 and 2014. Around a dozen of my young interlocutors from both middle-class and low-income backgrounds followed the group's page and shared its posts on their own Facebook pages. An article titled "Bala Wasta: No Connections, All Work," which was published on a popular website, praised the group as follows:

> Bala Wasta stands for exactly what its title means: without connections. After being unable to find a job with a Bachelor's degree and two Master's, Boustany decided to form a collective with the aid of other Lebanese individuals in similar situations. Fighting off the increasing trends toward immigration and political corruption, Bala Wasta's next goal is to create an accreditation system for recruitment processes, implementing an auditing process to make sure there are no instances of *wasta*. A group we can all get behind, Bala Wasta serves as a refreshing reminder that there are hardworking people who actually exist in Lebanon. Now let's just get them hired.[7]

The article is a good example of widespread portrayals of *wāsṭa* as the root cause of political corruption and youth emigration in Lebanon. Boustany is simultaneously praised as an exceptionally hardworking and successful Lebanese and described as a victim of a corrupt system that undervalued people like her. Even though there is no explicit reference to undeserving or immoral people, the idea that "there are hardworking people who actually exist in Lebanon" depicts the current system as undermining meritocracy and therefore as denying access to qualified, deserving applicants who did not use *wāsṭa*. The imagined abstraction of "we" in the "group we can all get behind" conveys an implicit sense of national unity among different sects and political opinions, yet its class-based celebration of higher education subtly excludes uneducated and undereducated young Lebanese. The abstract and universalizing idioms of non-sectarianism and meritocracy conceal both the class-based particularism of middle-class crisiswork and the historically accrued and state-sanctioned inequalities in Lebanon.

Bala Wasta Facebook postings often focalized, in the first person, the individual voice of an educated youth expressing their right to work and their demands for respect and recognition. For instance, a posting shared by the Bala Wasta Facebook group on April 6, 2015, and displayed on the Facebook profiles of several of my interlocutors, showcased a shadowed face accompanied by the appeal that their identification as a member of a certain sect not be taken into consideration by specific public actors: "I am Lebanese. It is my right to be employed without *wāsṭa*. My religion does not determine my capabilities. I respect my sect, but you must respect my diploma and my knowledge." Similarly, another Bala Wasta Facebook group posting from November 12, 2012, stated, in the Lebanese dialect of Arabic, written in both Arabic and Latin letters, "We want to be employed without *wāsṭa*." In both cases, the demand to be employed without *wāsṭa* is framed as an appeal for recognition of one's hard work and knowledge as the only legitimate grounds for employment suitability decisions. Both postings establish a clear boundary between one's sect as a private matter ("I respect my sect") and one's professional qualifications as a public matter ("you must respect my diploma and my knowledge"), with the potential implication that using *wāsṭa* marks the recipient, by default, as unqualified and undeserving. These demands are articulated in the name of an abstract young, university-educated Lebanese citizen who identifies as a member of a certain sect but requests that this identification not be taken into consideration by specific public actors. Despite claiming to represent and act for all the Lebanese, the middle-class notions of professionalism and meritocracy and the public–private binary these notions invoked ultimately invisibilized those communities with little to no access to both *wāsṭa* and educational opportunities.

Discourses of condemning *wāsṭa* were also prevalent in other Arab-majority countries and were articulated by transnational organizations such as the World Bank.[8] In Lebanon, however, condemning *wāsṭa* articulated a particular frustration with being legally, institutionally, and culturally defined as a member of a religious sect. Middle-class activists imagined an abstract non-sectarian public identity that operated independently of family and kinship relations that they associated with sectarianism. Yet, their abstractions of non-sectarianism and national unity disavowed their privileged connections as well as the concrete experiences of inequality faced by many others.

Balā Wāsṭa as a Lived Experience of Inequality

Aspirant professionals appropriated professionalism in complex ways that transcended the binary opposition between professionalism and *wāsṭa*, and between the public and the private, with the latter commonly understood as the family. They were very comfortable discussing how sectarian structures affected their lives. Consider Khaled, a hardworking Druze Lebanese activist from a low-income family. Like many other low-income Lebanese, he did not have a reliable *wāsṭa*. Khaled was twenty-eight years old when I first met him in 2014. At the time he was volunteering in two local NGOs while working part-time as a waiter at a local restaurant. By 2016, he was disappointed at not being able to find a stable job, despite his undergraduate degree in electrical engineering from a small private university and years of active participation in NGOs. Despite his frustrations, Khaled chose to continue to participate in civil society networking. As was the case with many other low-income activists, he believed that such networking efforts would eventually lead him to better opportunities. In the summer of 2017, Khaled moved to Germany to work as a case manager for a transnational NGO that focused on Syrian refugees. He was very happy to see his efforts finally starting to pay off. He regularly sent half of his salary back home to support the university education of his younger brother. In the summer of 2018, he told me on WhatsApp, "if he [my brother] can't finish university, no NGO can help him." His comment reflected his awareness that Lebanese youth without university education or English fluency found it very hard to find a job. Khaled also connected his brother with different networks in Beirut that he had built through his NGO participation and helped him find a part-time job with the bureaucracy. To help his brother resolve an interpersonal dispute at the university, Khaled even connected him with an influential Shiʿi political party representative he had met at an NGO event. By finding a *wāsṭa* for his brother, and acting like a *wāsṭa* in his own right, Khaled effectively fused his professional networks with his kinship ties.

Supporting a family member in ways that blended professional networks and *wāsṭa* ties is a form of restitutive justice, which counters the marginalization produced by Lebanon's dysfunctional state and uneven distribution of *wāsṭa* resources. Similarly to Khaled, many low-income Lebanese activists viewed professional positions and networks as means of supporting their families rather than as a way of becoming autonomous from them. Khaled's story also reveals that, for low-income Lebanese activists, becoming a professional did not inherently contradict becoming a *wāsṭa*—a strong, resourceful, and connected individual on whom many people could rely. This sentiment is perfectly articulated in an image Khaled shared with me in 2016, which read "Work until you become the *wāsṭa*," with *wāsṭa* typed in Arabic letters. In this framework, *wāsṭa* indicates not a reliance on sectarian ties accessed through one's family but rather the achievement of assuming the role of a provider through hard work. Becoming a *wāsṭa*—in contrast to relying on a *wāsṭa*—could function as a marker of adulthood, agency, and social prestige, in a way similar to how professional success marks adulthood, agency, and social prestige for middle-class cultural elites.[9]

For low-income activists with limited *wāsṭa* resources, *balā wāsṭa* represents less an ethical project of citizenship and more a lived experience of inequality. In their critique of *wāsṭa*, they focused on its uneven distribution in society and the difficulties they endured in its absence rather than on how it contradicted "professional" ways of being. From their moral perspective, refusing to use *wāsṭa* signaled privilege, not necessarily virtue. As shown by their support for the Bala Wasta movement, they were critical of how *wāsṭa* as a social institution perpetuated sectarianism. Their precarious economic situation, however, made it unrealistic to reject *wāsṭa* resources when they were available. In fact, most low-income activists suspected that even middle-class Lebanese used *wāsṭa* when necessary, despite their very public opposition to the practice—an intuition that many of my middle-class interlocutors confirmed in private.

Two memes from the popular Facebook account Lebanese Memes that Khaled shared with me further validate the existence of this double standard. One states, "Keep Calm and Call Someone Who Has Wasta." The other one challenges the audience to accept *wāsṭa* and to make use of one's father's connections after claiming the futility of applying for a job through hiring websites: "Would you use your wasta if you have a chance to? If so, why do you complain about wastas?" These posts, both with texts in English, affirm a widely shared belief in the centrality of *wāsṭa* in "getting things done" and specifically in finding a job. They also invite young Lebanese to reflect on the very contradictions inherent in the practice of *wāsṭa*. While the former meme portrays *wāsṭa* as the only solution to frustration with unemployment, the latter contrasts the effectiveness of using *wāsṭa* with professional ways of applying for a job and suggests that even people who criticize *wāsṭa* use it when it was available.

Despite its potential to mobilize diverse groups against corruption and sectarianism, middle-class activists' *balā wāsṭa* narrative naturalizes individual success and conceals the intergenerational transference of class-specific skills, urban competencies, aesthetic tastes, and other historically acquired privileges that are intrinsically embedded in the middle-class professional ethos. Aspirant professionals, on the other hand, did not strictly distinguish between *wāsṭa* and professional networks, despite their exasperation with and criticism of the sectarian system. For them, *balā wāsṭa* was a lived experience of inequality that they struggled with on a daily basis. Navigating an unjust system that disadvantaged those without *wāsṭa* or elite educational credentials, they developed support systems that crisscrossed family, friendship, and professional networks. They also challenged the invisibilized social hierarchies that were systematically obscured by middle-class practices of crisiswork. While middle-class cultural elites could fall back on their *wāsṭa* connections when their educational credentials proved unhelpful, aspirant professionals with limited family support had to continually (re)build their own infrastructures of social mobility to tackle multilayered crises in Lebanon.

"Weak" Families and NGOs

I met Nadine and Dana in the summer of 2012 through a mutual friend, Nadine's next-door neighbor. Dana was Nadine's only child, and Nadine had several medical issues that prevented her from taking care of herself and Dana. I joined our mutual friend as she regularly visited Nadine to help with food and day-to-day needs. During our visits, Nadine frequently complained that she lacked strong kinship and *wāsṭa* connections. She had no regular income, and she and her daughter relied on some modest savings and Dana's part-time job in a supermarket. Nadine's late husband's family no longer wanted any contact with them, and Nadine's only *wāsṭa* was her sister's husband, who worked as a low-ranking officer in the Ministry of Finance. He had promised Nadine that he would arrange for a high-ranking officer in the ministry to call the hotel manager about Dana's internship application, but Nadine was almost sure that he had not kept this promise. In Nadine's narrative, weak family relations were central to making sense of her misery; she believed that having a proper *wāsṭa* would have elevated her quality of life. Nadine felt betrayed by her sister and her sister's husband because she viewed their promised intercession not as a favor but as reciprocation for Nadine's years of caring for their children. In Nadine's moral narrative, her family did not reproduce "sectarianism" but supported each other through long-term reciprocal relationships.

Dana was not unique among aspirant professionals in her limited access to urban resources through family and kinship ties. In a survey that I conducted with around forty volunteers at We Grow in 2013, I found that 90 percent came from low-income families.[10] Most of those families were working-class, with incomes below the poverty line, and around 20 percent struggled with severe poverty. My extended participant observation in another youth-focused NGO in Beirut similarly revealed that most young NGO participants were from low-income families with limited resources. Even some of the middle-class NGO participants told me that they came to the NGOs because their parents did not know many people in Lebanon—for reasons such as having recently moved back to Lebanon or being disconnected from their extended families—and that they struggled to find jobs or access various resources. Many of the young unemployed and underemployed Lebanese I met in youth-focused NGOs did not have the support of a father figure or of a father's extended family. Their father had either passed away or abandoned the family. In some situations, the father worked outside of the country, and even though he provided some financial support, his broader kinship ties were no longer effective.

In youth empowerment NGOs, the striking presence of young Lebanese without fathers could be situated within the recent context of protracted conflicts and economic crises in Lebanon. In her study on the French Mandate in Lebanon, historian Elizabeth Thompson writes about the "crisis of paternity" after the First World War, in which family norms were disrupted because of famine and military conscription.[11] Many women began heading households, a process that displaced men from their traditional roles as providers and accelerated the formal education of girls and entry of women into the workforce. The protracted conflicts and economic crises that followed the long Lebanese War had a similar impact, especially among low-income communities. The families of some of my interlocutors disintegrated during the Lebanese War because of the killing, disappearance, or migration of their fathers or other men in their extended families. Others were displaced from their villages or neighborhoods or had their fathers emigrate for work as a result of the July War of 2006 and the intermittent political clashes, assassinations, and bombings that followed. They all referred to these events as shaping the precarity of their families and their lifeworlds more broadly. These personal histories show that a particular crisis of paternity factored into the popularity of NGOs in Lebanon and that it significantly shaped the lived experiences of various crises among their participants.

NGOs provided these precarious groups with avenues for "feeling" middle-class. Well-equipped NGO offices created a classy spatial and affective experience with high-quality training tables, expensive tech equipment—such as cameras and laptops—and kitchens with free snacks. Aspirant professionals proudly shared their NGO activities on social media, posting pictures from group meetings in global café chains, such as Gloria Jean's, and from weekend group trips to popular hiking destinations and upscale mountain resorts in Lebanon. These seemingly middle-class activities did not necessarily require participants to spend money. In We Grow group outings and my larger fieldwork, I consistently observed many of my low-income interlocutors sitting in upscale cafés or bars, with their middle-class friends, without ordering anything. This did not, however, prevent them from updating their Facebook status to display their ability to participate in the cosmopolitan life of Beirut. Thus, for educated low-income activists, well-funded local and international NGOs offered social spaces where they could participate in the widely celebrated middle-class, urban culture of Beirut.

Aspirant professionals also viewed NGOs as a gateway to emigration. Many in Lebanon experienced globalized precariousness more palpably as the Syrian War burdened Lebanon's economy. As a consequence, an increasing number of aspiring professionals sought to emigrate to Western countries. Dana and other volunteers at We Grow praised the NGO's active email listserv, which frequently shared ads for jobs and internship opportunities in local and transnational NGOs, cultural exchange programs, and training sessions in larger Middle Eastern and Euro-Mediterranean countries. Several volunteers at We Grow traveled to the United States and Euro-Mediterranean countries as part of prestigious exchange programs that were funded and administered by international NGOs. The ability to receive visas and travel through NGO networks furthered one's chances of emigration in the long run. Also, all of my interlocutors emphasized that NGO trainings and volunteer work in civil society stood out on one's résumé for job applications and visa applications to various embassies. They pointed out that almost all application forms and interviews for global companies included questions about civic engagement and that their participation in cross-sectarian NGOs like We Grow rendered them patriotic, responsible, and caring in the eyes of employers and other evaluators.

Given the ongoing legacies of the global war on terror—which reinforced the treatment of young Arabs as potential terrorists by Western institutions—the embassies of Western governments, as well as transnational organizations and companies, looked for proof of participation in cross-sectarian civil society to measure an applicant's civility and hence decide on the threat metrics of young Middle Eastern applicants.[12] Several representatives of Western donor organizations with offices in Beirut told me that they funded youth-focused NGOs because raising civic-minded citizens might eradicate youth extremism and prevent future conflicts in Lebanon and the larger region. After the Syrian War, Western embassies in Beirut implemented more thorough screening procedures and denied visas to many young applicants. Moreover, receiving work and other types of visas to the Gulf countries became more difficult because of the rapidly changing geopolitical landscape, which rendered many precarious groups in politically unstable places, such as Lebanon, as liabilities. Cognizant of both the expectations and restrictions of Western institutions, as well as of the private sector in Lebanon and elsewhere, aspirant professionals saw participation in credible cross-sectarian NGOs as helping them create a non-threatening profile.

Professionalism as Middle-Class Urban Respectability

I use "professionalism" as a locally defined category, which indexes a particular middle-class subjectivity that involves performing specific sets of symbolic capital, moral dispositions, and cross-sectarian relationalities. Many Lebanese did not necessarily link professionalism to a specific profession or occupational domain.[13] In Beirut, the English word "professional" and the French word "*professionnel*" indexed social approval and urban respectability and could express a wide range of meanings and tastes. In colloquial Lebanese, a place such as a restaurant, a person, a commodity, an activity, certain manners, and even the color of one's hair or nails could be called "professional." As for people, factors such as prestigious education, sect, gender, urbaneness, and global connectedness defined idealized models of professionals. As an adjective, describing someone or something as "professional" signified a middle-class subjectivity characterized by respectable behavior and high-class manner appropriate to Beirut's cosmopolitan culture. For example, We Grow's use of the term "professional volunteers" referred to those who volunteered in a respectable and high-class way and not to any particular profession or occupation. Accordingly, professionalism was equated with "symbolic capital" that marked "distinction"[14] and professionalization with the "process of struggle over the attainment of professionalism as symbolic capital."[15] Professionalism as symbolic capital referred to the "*ability* to give symbolic weight to certain educational resources, to codes of conduct and. . .to the ability to *make* a difference."[16]

Ziad embodied the locally idealized middle-class subjectivity of professionalism. His strong educational background, job, and NGO career, coupled with his aesthetic choices in urban tastes, rendered him respectable. People who knew him described him as an extremely hardworking person who was motivated primarily by a desire to make social impact rather than to attain financial gain. Although he participated in several other NGOs, he cared most about We Grow, as he was its co-founder and president. He told me that he liked seeing active members of We Grow become more professional and that he had created additional professional positions, such as "social media coordinator" and "campaign manager," to make members feel more professional. Ziad was widely esteemed by many aspirant professionals for his mastery of the "professional look." He was always stylish and well groomed in collared shirts, blazers, tailored sweaters, and leather shoes. Having mastered Western business attire, he wore a suit and tie in formal settings and larger public events and business casual style in daily life. He chose upscale restaurants and cafés in Hamra, a cosmopolitan cultural hub in Beirut, to both conduct business meetings and socialize with friends.

When I first met him in 2012, Ziad was twenty-four years old. In addition to serving as the president of We Grow, he worked as a manager in a major local bank and was otherwise an active member of civil society. He self-identified as both a civil society activist and an entrepreneur. Ziad had developed an interest in the NGO sector as an undergraduate studying chemical engineering at AUB, where he was deeply impacted by the professionalization trainings and professional networks that he encountered. Explicitly identifying himself as a youth leader, he regularly used social media, specifically Facebook and Twitter, to share educational posts on empowerment and leadership. Many around him respected him as a young leader who facilitated youth empowerment and positive social change. He often gave media interviews and represented "Lebanese youth" in prestigious youth programs, workshops, and training sessions held in major cities in Euro-Mediterranean countries. Having established themselves as successful professionals, members of the middle-class cultural elites, like Ziad, sought to mentor young Lebanese on how to conduct themselves professionally in diverse social settings. Branding themselves as patriotic, ambitious, and determined risk-taker, decision-maker, and problem-solver, they embodied the locally valorized, gendered ideal of a strong political leader who worked for Lebanon.

In their modeling after the aesthetic, affective, and moral dispositions performed by people like Ziad, low-income NGO participants channeled their becoming professional into an ongoing crisiswork that sought to transform both their selfhoods and unequal social structures. As her close friend, I was struck by how participation in We Grow gradually changed Dana. When I first met her in 2012, she was a quiet and shy woman who constantly spoke of her anxieties about her future. Three months into her participation in We Grow, however, she expressed feeling more self-confident and comfortable with public speaking. She repeatedly told me, her friends, and her mother that the NGO activities, by significantly improving her résumé and social media profile, made her look "professional." She was also excited to collect certificates of completion from professionalization workshops and training sessions and to file them together for her future job and internship applications.

In her pursuit of individual flourishing, she also vocally challenged structural constraints that unevenly impacted marginalized groups like refugees. One evening in late October 2013, Dana and I attended an engaging two-hour workshop at We Grow titled "Master Your Colors." The trainer spoke at length to an audience of around thirty young people about how to strategically use colors to boost one's professional profile. Dana enjoyed the workshop and actively participated in it. When we left the We Grow office at 8 p.m., she and two other participants in our group discussion continued discussing their experiences with choosing the right colors. One of them, Walaa, a young middle-class Syrian woman who was a first-time participant at a We Grow event, began talking about how, the week before, several friends from AUB had teased her for wearing a bright orange blouse. The orange color was associated with the Free Patriotic Movement, a major Christian-majority party in Lebanon. Walaa added that she had moved to Beirut the year before to receive an economics degree and that she had been slowly learning local political symbols as well as how some Lebanese joked about them. She often felt out of place in Beirut and hoped that workshops like "Master Your Colors" could help her better adapt to the city and its culture.

Dana and the other participant showered Walaa with sympathy and advised her not to take such incidents personally, bemoaning how sectarianism permeated every aspect of life in Lebanon, especially in Beirut. Then, because it was Walaa's first time in the area, they told her which alleys and streets to avoid given the risk of bombings, protests, or clashes. She expressed her gratitude before getting into her aunt's car, which was waiting for her in the main street. After Walaa left, Dana and others spoke briefly about how the "complicated system" in Lebanon was often more ruthless for refugees.

Dana then received a call from her mother. We hurried to her home, which was luckily only a ten-minute walk away. Dana expressed frustration with her mother:

> Image and appearance are very important for companies. The first impression is very important. They [referring to job interviewers] want to see your motivation, culture, manners, style. . .they want someone presentable (*mrattaba*) and discerning (*btifham*). . .who doesn't want that? My mother doesn't understand these things.

Nadine was not happy with Dana's participation in evening workshops because of her long-standing skepticism regarding their benefits. Like the parents of other low-income activists, Nadine regarded NGO volunteering as a waste of time. Nevertheless, Dana, like other low-income participants, believed that professionalization workshops would help her become *mrattaba* and *btifham*—colloquial Arabic words widely used to describe appropriate self-presentation and knowledge, respectively. Not fully translatable into English, the terms *mrattaba* and *btifham* refer to a person's respectability and prestige and connote the moral ideas of "doing things rightly" and "doing good." Someone *mrattaba* and *btifham*, as expressed through the ways they look and behave, would elicit respect and trust. Unlike the English and French words for "professional," which were mainly used by educated urbanites, *mrattaba* and *btifham* were used by Lebanese from all social backgrounds.[17] Professionalism in Lebanon thus had complex global and local genealogies, and an aspect of becoming "professional" entailed learning to navigate the complex local, national, and neoliberal expectations of professionalism.

In NGOs like We Grow, professionalization workshops, such as "Master Your Colors," construed empowerment as a way to increase competitiveness in a volatile job market. Skills-based workshops and training sessions in Lebanese NGOs, universities, and workplaces adopted a neoliberal ethos of "self as a business," which treated job candidates and workers as "bundles of skills."[18] Youth leaders and workshop trainers like Ziad resembled neoliberal career consultants and career coaches, who advised job seekers to develop a personal brand, reflect uniqueness, and be flexible. Many low-income activists also pursued respectability in their efforts to enhance their professional skills. They believed that working on developing new skills and refashioning their selves were not sufficient to achieve respectability—they also needed to learn how to navigate Beirut's class and sect-based hierarchies for their particular crisiswork of class-making.

Building Cross-Sectarian Networks

I use the term "network" to refer to a widely used, local vernacular category. Instead of the Arabic words *shabaka* (network) and *majmūʿa* (group), most university-educated activists in Beirut used the English words "group," "circle," and "network" interchangeably to represent different sets of people they associated with. The word "network" refers locally to a social universe distinct from family and kinship—though not necessarily excluding of these intimate circles—constituting relatively enduring forms of cross-sectarian social interaction. These networks could potentially facilitate connections to different services and resources in the city. Aspirant professionals constantly talked about the significance of "building networks" for professionalism, using English words like "network" and "networking" in otherwise Arabic conversations. They carefully strategized about which civil society venues would enhance their ability to network and participated in many public events to network with prominent figures. Many participants at We Grow and other NGOs asked me and other participants how we had initially connected with a given organization. Assessing the differential networking capacities among participants and comparing them with one's own was a common feature of social relationships based through NGOs.

Everyone at We Grow praised Ziad's extensive professional network, which included colleagues, friends, and acquaintances from diverse confessional and international backgrounds. Ziad knew many people in high positions at various Lebanese and international institutions. When Dana applied for an internship at a prestigious local consultancy company, Ziad's strong reference letter helped her get the position. While the content of professionalization workshops laid out approved codes of conduct in work and other urban settings, the middle-class trainers and leaders were idealized by aspirant professionals as both the embodiments of professional manners and potential connecting nodes to professional networks in the city.

Sahar—a young, low-income Shiʿi woman who was one of Dana's closest friends at We Grow—traveled two hours from a Shiʿa-majority village in South Lebanon to Beirut every other week to attend the NGO's meetings and workshops. Sahar justified this effort as necessary to "building her own network" (*bibnī al-network tabʿītī*) and "investing in getting to know people" (*bistathmir bi-l-taʿarruf ʿal-nās*):

> Here [at We Grow] I learned professional manners, how to dress, how to speak, and how to use English words while speaking in Arabic. These are very important skills in professional life. But you also need to know how to deal with other people (*taʿāmul maʿ al-ākharīn*), ways of speech, and etiquette. [. . .] Meeting people is important too. Think about Ziad or Sara or you. People in NGOs are more professional and have more connections. They know many people.

For Shiʿi Lebanese like Sahar, NGOs offered strategies for negotiating predominant norms of urban respectability. Most Sunni and Christian middle-class Beirut residents considered Shiʿi neighborhoods outside of Beirut as "chaotic" and "dirty" and viewed the dress codes and accents of Shiʿi residents as incompatible with the cultural and aesthetic tastes of Beirut's urban culture.[19] My Shiʿi and other aspirant professional interlocutors who had rural origins told me that their local accents, outfits, and manners could indicate their place of origin and mark them as not belonging to the city. They praised NGOs for helping them navigate Beirut's elitist, high-culture landscape of education, work, and leisure.

Through their participation in We Grow and other NGOs, precarious young activists sought to learn how to tactfully interact with diverse sectarian and class groups in Beirut. They hoped that, if they could better perform professionalism, their ideas, speech, and manners would not be associated with any political or sectarian position. Through the process of becoming part of middle-class urban networks in Beirut, aspirant professionals aimed to cultivate a presentable self for the gaze of urban residents who evaluated the aspirants' sectarian, class, and political standing. Thus, in addition to promising upward mobility, professionalism as symbolic capital could provide a protective mask from the elitist gaze of Beirut. The ability to successfully connect to cross-sectarian networks and develop working relationships with other communities promised those from low-income communities a respectable and agentive self, capable of engaging effectively in crisiswork.

Many aspirant professionals also emphasized that, through the NGOs, they enjoyed meeting and interacting with people from other sects. Some of them underscored how they had made friends with people from other sects for the first time in an NGO, describing this experience as unique and revealing. They explained how the villages and city neighborhoods where they grew up, as well as the secondary schools and universities they attended, were mostly homogeneous in terms of sect composition. Even those whose neighborhoods and schools had been more diverse claimed that intense political polarization had impeded close contact with members of other sects. The opportunity to interact and network with other communities through NGOs and to engage in cross-sectarian collaborations promised a substantial political capital for authentically claiming non-sectarianism and patriotism.

Prominent NGOs like We Grow also offered additional networking opportunities with other NGOs and actors in the city. Aspirant professionals highlighted that collaborating with NGOs and other grassroots networks in community-oriented volunteering activities helped them expand their networks. We Grow organized many activities in collaboration with other NGOs and grassroots networks. Dana and I were part of a group of twelve volunteers in one of We Grow's units. We collaborated with other NGOs in a wide range of activities in different parts of Lebanon, such as distributing *iftar* (the daily breaking of the fast for Muslims during Ramadan) to orphans and refugees, visiting elder care centers, and cleaning beaches. It was not unusual for NGOs in Beirut to collaborate with each other on various public events and community-oriented projects. Also, many We Grow participants eventually became active members in other NGOs. When Dana began to volunteer in January 2015 at a Red Cross branch in Spears near Hamra, she was delighted at the opportunity to meet new people and collaborate with new international and local NGOs. She was also well aware that volunteering at the Red Cross enhanced her résumé. "My life has changed since becoming an activist. I feel stronger and more hopeful," she told me on Skype in the summer of 2016.

Low-income activists' investment in their NGO participation exceeded its strategic or instrumental value. Strengthening their cross-sectarian professional networks within civil society enabled low-income activists to embody publicly valorized notions of ethical citizenship and claim a space within the middle-class dominated field of crisiswork in Lebanon. Volunteering in activities that served disadvantaged communities rendered low-income activists as genuinely "doing something for the nation." Like other forms of activism, volunteering conveyed the value of being considerate of others, beyond one's family or sect, and hence of being more patriotic. I consistently observed participants at We Grow and other empowerment NGOs expressing happiness and joy after each charity activity we joined. Some of them explicitly mentioned feeling they were "much better people" when they served others. Hence, low-income activists attributed an intrinsic ethical merit to volunteering and enjoyed practicing care for both vulnerable communities and other members in We Grow.

"A Family We Choose"

George, the trainer for the day's workshop, arrived half an hour after his training session was scheduled to begin, visibly out of breath as he probably ran to not be too late. After gently hanging his coat on the hanger on the office door, he stood firmly behind the hardwood lectern. Exuding confidence and smiling, he began talking enthusiastically. He had been stuck in traffic because of temporary checkpoints that were screening cars on several main streets between his apartment in Ashrafieh—a major Christian-dominated neighborhood in Beirut—and We Grow's office close to Hamra. George's body language became more animated as he began to talk about a fancy black Mercedes with tinted black windows, which stopped suddenly in front of his car at a major intersection downtown. At that moment, George feared that someone might attack the Mercedes, which probably belonged to a "big guy," and that he would become a casualty. His cheerful and vivacious storytelling captivated his audience of seventeen young participants, who had been a bit frustrated with his delayed arrival. When he commented on how he felt at that moment, the audience readily burst into laughter: "Let me transmit my message before I die, oh uncle!" (*khallīnī waṣṣil my message abl mā mūt yā ʿammī!*). The word "message," pronounced in English, referred to the moral and civic creed he had planned for the workshop.

George's "emotional intelligence" workshop in mid-January 2014 took place amid heightened political tensions. Several car bombings had taken place recently. On January 2, a car bombing in Haret Hreik, a Hizbullah-dominated area in south Beirut, had killed six people and wounded sixty others. On December 27, a bombing in downtown Beirut had killed Mohammad Chatah—a former finance minister and senior advisor to Saad Hariri, the then-leader of the Sunni-majority Future Movement party—and seven others and wounded more than seventy. George, a practicing Maronite Christian man, later told me privately that, when meeting a workshop audience he surmised was predominantly Muslim, he would emphasize that he shared their fears and concerns about living in uncertain and violent times. He explained his efforts at building friendly relationships with diverse confessional communities in the country as a commitment he developed through his relationship with his Shiʿi fiancée and while working with several human rights NGOs as an experienced activist.

Thus, George hoped that the joke about the Mercedes would make him relatable to his audience, who did not know much about him but probably inferred from his full name that he belonged to a well-known Maronite Christian family. The audience, most of whom indeed had a Muslim background, seemed to quickly bond with George, who humorously embodied an anxious Lebanese citizen concerned about frequent bombings. The laughter at his joke stirred an interesting conversation among the participants about how Lebanese people had recently become very "paranoid" (in English). Several participants cited examples from their families, neighbors, or random people in the streets who had started to avoid the central districts in the city or who had become suspicious about every unfamiliar car parked in their street. Other participants were more concerned about normalizing violence in Lebanon than becoming paranoid. One of the participants commented, "We live with these bombings. It [the bombing] has become something normal" (*biṣīr shī ʿādī*). Another young man commented that a "blast happens, and we continue" (*byiṭlaʿ infijār, mnkammil*). Another one added, with a solemn resignation, "Yeah, we are used to it" (*Ah, mtʿawwdīn*).

I was amazed at how, in a matter of minutes, George cleared the air of boredom and stiffness and created a stirring conversation that drew everyone's attention. His dexterous style reflected his charisma. He was a self-confident, intelligent, friendly, and articulate trainer. But perhaps, more importantly, as a thirty-four-year-old experienced public speaker who interacted with diverse communities in Lebanon, he knew how to connect with people by invoking crises as shared experiences. In contrast to many middle-class activists whose crisiswork denigrated low-income communities for being sectarian and uncivilized, George approached all participants as equally valued members of civil society.

George's success was one of many instances I observed in We Grow workshops in which the abstraction "we Lebanese" could instantly create a connection among strangers. The recognition that a random bomb could kill bystanders regardless of their sect, political view, class, or gender created a sentiment of shared vulnerability. The use of "we" language helped George keep the group engaged throughout the two-hour session. Particularly, his continued message that shared crises in Lebanon made everyday life challenging "for all of us" made participants feel comfortable and accepted. George used PowerPoint slides that listed problems, such as wars, economic crises, and competitive culture, under the ahistorical title of "planet disorder," another abstraction that helped imagine shared crises. Then he remarked, "Changing the world starts with changing ourselves," a truism in all such workshops. He continued by summarizing several well-known books, such as *Emotional Intelligence* by Daniel Goldman and *The 7 Habits of Highly Effective People* by Stephen Covey, as apt resources to change ourselves.

However, in George's presentation, changing oneself was inherently tied to having meaningful social relationships with and caring for others. Indeed, George continued his talk with critiquing the single focus on individual success and happiness that he saw as characteristic of education in Lebanese families and schools. Asserting that "our parents do not teach us any emotion about others but fear and hatred," George emphasized the need to develop an emotional self-understanding to become more open, loving, and empathic:

> Our education system works on our brains, not on our emotions. Our families also gave us very narrow visions of life. So, we grow up and don't

know what to do with others and about our complex emotions toward them. We need to work on our emotions to have successful relationships in life.

Throughout the workshop, George shared practical tips about transforming our emotions and attitudes so that we could better survive in a world with multiple crises, both individually and collectively. These strategies ranged from stress management to cultivating a positive attitude and curiosity about strangers. In one of the major group exercises, he asked participants to pick three habits to try out in their personal lives that would better cultivate their emotional intelligence and then to discuss in groups strategies to preserve these habits. During this exercise, Dana and Radwa, a low-income Shiʿi woman from Saida, seeded their long-term, close friendship. As one of the four participants in their group activity, I noticed how the exercise made Dana and Radwa realize that they shared the same "bad" habits. Both feared meeting new people and being judged by them. They shared their experiences of how some people in Beirut could be judgmental based on one's appearance and accent as well as small details, such as where one ate, shopped, and so on. "Everything is political here," said Radwa, referring to how people in Beirut tried to place others in ready-made political and sectarian identities. They talked about the hatred, fears, and worries people had about others and tied these to political issues, such as the bombings and corruption. They shared how they had been struggling with chronic headaches, stress, and insomnia, which they explicitly related to Lebanon's crises. Dana and Radwa decided to adopt three habits from a list that George had distributed earlier: keeping a diary, meeting at least one new person each week, and wearing a bracelet to help them be cognizant of when they felt emotionally triggered. They also decided to support each other and exchanged phone numbers.

In the following months, I saw Dana and Radwa regularly spend time together—they went to movies, cafés, and shopping malls. In the summer of 2015, after saving money for a year and convincing their respective parents, they went for a short trip to Istanbul. Through NGO activities, I witnessed other young women develop connections with each other that gradually evolved into close friendships. In particular, for young women like Dana, who wanted to meet new people, socialities built within NGOs could turn into meaningful relationships. The seemingly simple interaction of exchanging useful tips about issues such as improving self-confidence or preparing a strong résumé could later develop into a stronger bond, one based on active support and care. These workshop activities thus sometimes enabled the participants to build intimacy through the recognition that they struggled with similar problems.

Soft-skills workshops thus could unexpectedly generate spaces to vent about crises in Lebanon, criticize political structures and social norms, and share worries and vulnerabilities. In numerous youth-focused empowerment workshops, self-care and caring for others were often presented as inseparable features of an ethical citizen. Even though the idea of caring for others mainly referred to community work for those in need, and empowerment workshops were explicitly designated as "non-political" spaces, workshop participants frequently exchanged political commentaries. What typically began as an abstract lesson on topics such as emotional intelligence, positivity, and self-worth could transition into animated political discussions about the nation's concrete crises. Low-income communities were particularly skillful in critically engaging with liberal and neoliberal abstractions that contradicted their rich quotidian experiences with contextually situated problems.

The content of George's presentation could be called "neoliberal" in the sense that it focused on personal responsibility and that it persuaded the participants to become, and see themselves as, a "bundle of skills." His course materials were from popular Western psychologists and self-help gurus who typically deemphasize structural constraints and celebrate individual agency. Yet, as exemplified by George's efforts to connect with the Muslim members of the audience and to foster a love for other communities—and in the aftermath, by Dana and Radwa's friendship—the workshops did more than instill skills for self-responsibility and self-care. In the process of working through their shared affects of fear and vulnerability, aspirant professionals repurposed empowerment workshops into unexpected spaces of crisiswork that fostered sociality, care, and solidarity as a means to enact new publics and collectivities. Practices of self-care and caring for others were intertwined with professionalism and volunteerism in their crisiswork.

I frequently observed how NGO participants built lasting friendships and formed affective and intimate bonds that resembled family relations. Spending time together through different activities often turned collaborators into friends who could be relied on in difficult times. Several months into our active involvement, the more regular participants in the volunteer unit in which Sara, Fadi, Dana, and I participated began seeing each other as friends. Increasingly, we spent additional time after each club activity in cafés or each other's homes. We went to camps and picnics. We joyously celebrated each member's birthday with surprise parties in popular cafés and bought each other gifts.

This closeness was about not only sociality and fun but also caring for each other. After each of the bombings and explosions in Beirut in 2013 and 2014, the group members immediately checked WhatsApp to make sure the others were safe. We carefully avoided openly praising or criticizing any political group, such as Hizbullah or the Future Movement party, to prevent confrontations that would undermine the friendly atmosphere in the group. Many of them mentioned that politics undermined the friendships they had come to rely on and expressed apprehension at the potentially distancing effects of discussing recent crises unfolding in the country. I heard from many NGO activists participating in organizations like We Grow a version of the statement, "We know and respect each other's views, but there is no use in discussing them." They prioritized maintaining professional and friendship networks over influencing others' political opinions. Here, the main goal of their crisiswork was to maintain their bonds through accentuating the shared experiences of crises affecting all of "us" while minimizing known tensions and disagreements.

Activists at We Grow genuinely supported one another, even in the midst of strong political dissension. When a Shiʿi member who was known to support Hizbullah shared her prolonged conflict with a sibling or pressures from marriage or work, everyone in the group offered specific suggestions despite their strong dislike for Hizbullah and its followers. Listening to these suggestions, I, alongside others, learned useful strategies for dealing with "difficult people." The group also visited the apartment of a dedicated member who was a strong supporter of the Future Movement party, because his mother had undergone a serious surgery. I heard several members commenting on how the group raised their morale and spirituality. Even middle-class participants like Sara, who viewed NGOs as professional spaces distinct from the family, told us once, "We are a family here, a family we choose."

"We Need NGOs"

Youth-focused empowerment NGOs in Lebanon became central to the moral, imaginative, discursive, aesthetic, and experiential dimensions of class-making through their cultivation of the ethos of professionalism.

Crisiswork in these NGOs shaped and was shaped by intersecting spheres of everyday life such as family, university, and work as well as by the local histories of conflict and crisis. In contextualizing NGOs within the larger political and social landscape, it becomes apparent that participation in NGOs could have diverse and contradictory rationales and implications for different classes. The personal accounts that low-income activists in Lebanon gave of their participation in NGOs reveal how precarious communities appropriated hegemonic discourses, such as empowerment and professionalism, in multiple and non-determined ways that could bypass or challenge the calculations of international donors and local elites. They did not merely become patriotic and market-oriented individuals but also accomplished class mobility and forged cross-sectarian, cross-class, and cross-ethnic connections. Low-income activists used professionalization workshops to work on their affects, bodily dispositions, and manners, while also acquiring practical and useful strategies to navigate their experiences of marginalization in daily life. They could support their families through skills and networking opportunities that offered individual success, and they could also build friendships and foster solidarity and care for a wide range of communities. Boundaries between professionalism and friendship, and between public and private spheres, were continually crossed. Given the open-endedness of social relationships in Lebanese civil society as well as the continual precarity of many communities, professional networks built through NGOs could be mobilized to foster national solidarity, and familial connections could be used to help friends from different sects or classes. Yet, how did low-income activists' efforts translate into upward social mobility, and to what effects?

For many aspirant professionals, promises of professionalism did not translate into real opportunities. In 2016, for example, Dana complained to me that Lebanon's economic situation made it very hard for her to find a stable and long-term job. Her NGO experience and the support of people like Ziad helped her find some positions, but they were all temporary and carried no social benefits; in some instances, she was unable to collect her salary for months. Dana left her underpaid job in a small company in January 2017 and began making plans to emigrate. In the following month, I assisted her with her applications to several graduate programs in European countries. I connected her with some of my colleagues, helped her polish her documents, and wrote reference letters for her. Unfortunately, her applications to graduate schools in 2017 and 2018 were not accepted. She continued to volunteer in NGOs while working as a human resources assistant for a very low salary in a small company.

In December 2018, when I submitted a reference letter for her application to a graduate program in Canada, Dana wrote to me, "Thank you, you are a good *wāsṭa*." She was half-joking, of course; yet, clearly she did not find it inappropriate to tease me about being a *wāsṭa*, but rather considered it a cute way to express her gratitude. Like Khaled's meme that read, "Work until you become the wasta," Dana's comment pointed out the ambiguities of being a *wāsṭa* and being a professional connection: someone like me could be called a *wāsṭa* if they used their professional skills and connections as a resource to help a friend get a job. In this sense, *wāsṭa* referred to a position of power and influence that did not necessarily connote "nepotism," "corruption," or "sectarianism." Through such alternative narratives, aspirant professionals reconstrued *wāsṭa* as being irreducible to kinship or sectarian patronage. Their appropriation of professionalism as a dynamic, contingent, and context-specific process of class-making contested both their families' idea that no one could do anything *balā wāsṭa* and middle-class cultural elites' celebration of professional success *balā wāsṭa*.

As Lebanon's economic crisis deepened in 2020, many of my aspirant professional interlocutors tried desperately to find *wāsṭa* connections through their wider kinship ties while simultaneously volunteering in at least three different NGOs to improve their résumés and their likelihood of social mobility. Even though many of my interlocutors criticized NGOs for being "coopted by the system" and for failing to bring substantial change, they continued to rely on them to help navigate Lebanon's economic crisis.[20] Aspirant professionals' lived experiences of protracted conflicts, unemployment, and "weak" families were formative of their crisiswork strategies. They did not simply emulate the middle-class ethics of crisiswork; they repurposed the concepts of *wāsṭa*, professionalism, family, friendship, nation, networks, and care in ways that formed new socialities and solidarities. Many of them maintained their ties with Lebanese activist networks even after securing stable jobs. They participated in protests, formed and engaged in new solidarity networks, cared for others, and reflected upon ways to change things. In the process of reframing their lived crises as a shared, intersubjective experience, they continued to cultivate multiple forms of togetherness, including national solidarity, professional networks, and close friendships.

Class-making, which was central to low-income communities' crisis-work, was also central to other political and cultural practices of crisiswork. Some of my low-income activist interlocutors were also interested in social entrepreneurship, a practice that leading middle-class activists invoked as a promising tool for systemic change in Lebanon. Similar to aspiring to professionalism, aspiring to social entrepreneurship conveyed ambivalent and contradictory motivations and implications. Like volunteerism, social entrepreneurship was promoted by middle-class activists as a concrete tool for achieving abstract dreams of change and ethical citizenship in Lebanon. Yet diverse activists employed distinct political and moral calculations in their pursuit of entrepreneurship, which resulted in not only contradictory but also problematic enactments of political agency.

FOUR

Entrepreneurial Activism

In September 2011, Gilbert Doumit, a prominent Lebanese civil society activist, presented his vision for social change at a TED Talk in Beirut. The key to transforming Lebanon's politics and creating alternatives, he suggested, lies in combining the figures of the entrepreneur and the activist:

> How am I going to be able to influence on a system level? When are we going to have solutions for our problems that are on a country level? When are we going to have a better health care system, education, electoral system, decentralization? [. . .] Politics means three *c*'s, at least in Lebanon. It is about conflict, corruption, and confessionalism. Every time we talk about politics, immediately I can think of wars, sectarian tensions, corruption in public institutions, bribery, under-the-table deals. [. . .] Why, when we use the word *politics*, it cannot be about finding creative solutions to our problems, better managing our public institutions? Is that difficult? So why politics is always linked to negative connotations? [. . .] Is there a different way to practice politics? I started searching. [. . .] *Based on my business experience, part of me as an entrepreneur and part of me as an activist, I realized if we bring these two concepts together, there might be something in it. I would call these outstanding individuals political entrepreneurs.* [. . .] *Imagine if we mix these two concepts together in one individual.*[1] [emphasis added]

Gilbert, whom I came to know during my fieldwork, sought to encourage his audience, most of whom were educated middle-class Lebanese, to rethink politics as a field of positive change. Later in the talk, he emphasized the possibility of radically transforming the political and social systems in both Lebanon and the larger Arab region. Against what he considered Lebanon's immoral politics of sectarianism, Gilbert proposed a new way of conducting politics—combining entrepreneurialism and activism. Gilbert's career embodied this approach. He co-founded Beyond Reform and Development (BRD)—a consultancy and training company that advised government institutions, civil society organizations, and international and local NGOs on policy-making and leadership development in the Middle East and North Africa. BRD was a key facilitator in the national youth policy-making process, and many of its salaried employees were also well-known activists within Lebanese civil society. Having co-founded more than ten influential grassroots movements and NGOs in Lebanon, Gilbert was a widely acclaimed activist and a mentor to hundreds of activists from different social and political backgrounds. He taught social entrepreneurship courses in prestigious local universities, had degrees from public management and entrepreneurship programs in Europe and the United States, and had been a fellow at Yale University. He also helped establish Beirut Madinati (Beirut, My City), an independent political movement that achieved surprising success in Beirut's 2016 municipal elections. In May 2018, he entered the Lebanese parliamentary elections as an independent candidate.

Gilbert's idea of combining entrepreneurialism and activism was not a random creative proposal. It was representative of a particular ethico-political framework of crisiswork that gained traction in Lebanon's cross-sectarian civil society after 2011, as the Syrian War destabilized Lebanon's already fragile economic and political system. Since 2012, when I began my long fieldwork, I have heard many activists and other Lebanese invoke entrepreneurialism and activism together as a cure for Lebanon's myriad crises. Even though many Lebanese did not use Gilbert's term *political entrepreneur*, they framed Lebanon's problems and proposed solutions in a similar way.[2] In recognizing that an increasing number of Lebanese were simultaneously defining themselves as activists and entrepreneurs (Figure 5), I came to ask the following questions: What explains the combination of activism and entrepreneurialism in Lebanon? How do entrepreneurial activists engage in crisiswork? What kinds of ambivalences or contradictions does this engagement raise?

The political and moral leadership envisioned and practiced by activists like Gilbert centered on uniquely qualified "individuals" who could embody

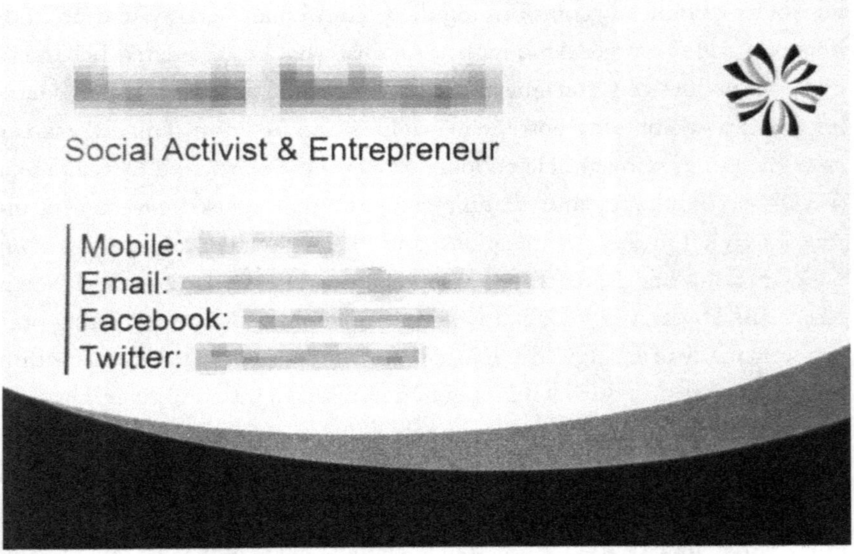

FIGURE 5. A business card given to me by one of my key interlocutors in Beirut, April 2013. I met many young Lebanese who held business cards like this one, which identified them as activists and entrepreneurs.

an alternative model of "politician" and finally deliver the change that the Lebanese had long awaited. As showcased in Gilbert's TED Talk, the combination of entrepreneurialism and activism explicitly targeted a direct engagement with Politics with a capital P—the formal politics of government institutions, political parties, and elected officials. While Lebanese civil society activism had long engaged with state institutions from the outside, particularly through advocacy work and public protests, Gilbert called on activists to take leadership roles in official decision-making structures and public institutions in order to effect change from within the system. Targeting the prevalent negative perceptions of Politics as sectarian and corrupt, he suggested that ethical citizens bring entrepreneurial values to their activism to effectively transform the system and counter sectarianism. Other Lebanese activists also pursued systemic change, but entrepreneurial activists emphasized an individualistic approach to creating change, urging ethical citizens to become leaders in official institutions in order to effect change to the system from within. The increasing recognition of civil society activism's limitations further motivated entrepreneurial activists to directly engage in Politics.

In many global contexts, cultivating entrepreneurial dispositions has been a key feature of neoliberal agendas, which have favored individualistic ideas of self-transformation and self-responsibility over a collective model of social and political rights.[3] The primary goal of neoliberalism, defined as a specific mode of governance rather than an economic doctrine, has been to create self-reliant subjects who would not make substantial demands on the state nor expect systemic change.[4] The neoliberal subject, thus, is "not a citizen with claims on the state but a self-enterprising citizen-subject who is obligated to become an entrepreneur of himself or herself."[5] Entrepreneurial activists in Lebanon, however, enthusiastically sought to change the state and the system. They were among the most outspokenly "political" activists in Lebanon. Rather than withdrawing from political activism, entrepreneurial activists used entrepreneurship to effectively participate in electoral politics and other arenas of Politics.[6]

What I call "entrepreneurial activism" refers to a form of "ethical Politics" that draws on complex global and local genealogies of activism and entrepreneurialism to animate systemic change. Leading civil society activists like Gilbert aimed to provide alternative moral vocabularies of political subjectivity, deftly combining globalized projects of social entrepreneurship with local legacies of entrepreneurial culture and leftism. Entrepreneurial activists strongly endorsed both the idea of change through direct involvement in Politics and the fostering of moral individuals transcending the "typical Lebanese," who were imagined as enclosed in sectarian communities. Unlike some other civil society activists, they did not see any problem with activists asserting "political" identities and becoming alternative politicians. They passionately pursued change both within the Politics of the state and the character of the individual. The crisiswork of entrepreneurial activism presented an ambiguous and open-ended "ethical Politics" that brought together diasporan and local Lebanese to foster social and political mobilization.

While transformation of selfhood was a shared tenet of all forms of crisiswork in Lebanon, entrepreneurial activists placed the individual moral transformation at the heart of their crisiswork. Later in his talk, Gilbert proposed *irāda* (willpower) as the authentic moral feature of political entrepreneurs. He emphasized that *irāda*, the only Arabic word in his otherwise English-language talk, could not be translated into English. The translation, I suggest, is difficult because the term brings together several different ethical dispositions linked to the concepts of autonomy and agency. *Irāda* can be translated as "willpower," "volition," "command," "determination," "self-control," "dedication," or "autonomy." In this context, it connotes an ethos of autonomy from the negative influences of ongoing crises, according to which one maintains a belief in positive change and asserts agency to work toward it. Entrepreneurial activists also associated being a successful entrepreneur with stable resource generation and financial autonomy, which to them promised a more autonomous activist life that did not depend on funding agencies. Autonomy was a central ethico-political disposition that entrepreneurial activists sought to cultivate in their crisiswork, yet it entailed significant ambivalences and contradictions. While entrepreneurial activists presented autonomy as a patriotic, non-sectarian individual moral characteristic, they practiced it differently. For instance, class-based understandings of financial independence encompassed competing moral frameworks of autonomy among entrepreneurial activists.

In celebrating the idea of social entrepreneurship, which sees business as a vehicle for social and political change, entrepreneurial activists hoped to bring in concrete, tangible projects to address Lebanon's crises. They were not against pursuing individual profit or self-interest; however, they also saw entrepreneurial initiatives primarily as novel spaces of crisiswork that directly engaged with societal problems such as infrastructural failure, unemployment, and gender inequality. Idioms such as start-up, accelerator, and innovation evoked the thriving entrepreneurial culture of California's Silicon Valley, promising tangible, rather than abstract, models of change and development that had worked in other parts of the world and seemed replicable in Lebanon. Unquestionably believing in the global "success" of entrepreneurship, entrepreneurial activists commonly dreamed of establishing business projects that would help Lebanon catch up with prosperous nations.

Given that not all activists had immediate resources to start enterprises or companies, entrepreneurialism was also an aspirational subjectivity that could nevertheless be affectively embodied and felt in the present. Many low-income Lebanese activists celebrated entrepreneurialism as a positive "spirit" and "mentality." As various ethnographic studies have shown, entrepreneurialism goes beyond business-related or profit-oriented practices and increasingly fosters new modes of selfhood among diverse global communities of artists, refugees, and others.[7] In the Lebanese case, it was interlaced with ideas of activism and change.

Genealogies of Entrepreneurial Activism

The semiotic richness of the Arabic words for entrepreneurship helps explain how the pairing of entrepreneurialism and activism captured the idea of leading change through ethical Politics. Lebanese used two Arabic words for entrepreneurship that connoted new beginnings: *rāʾid* (a leader with a different way of doing things, be it in business, science, or another field) and *mubdiʿ* (someone who has brought forth a new idea or an original way to do their work). Initiating (*ibdāʿ*) and effectively leading new projects was viewed as common to both activism and entrepreneurialism. Both *rāʾid* and *mubdiʿ* have broader meanings than the English term *entrepreneur*, which is defined as a risk-taking figure who founds and manages a business and derives from the French verb *entreprendre* (to undertake). The two Arabic words were used for both the founders of activist social movements and the leaders of new companies, and they strongly connoted ideas of newness and change. Those words are helpful in understanding the linguistic imagination of entrepreneurship as a local concept that marked leadership for change, which interlaced individual moral change with systemic change. Entrepreneurial activists envisioned that individuals with unique character and leadership skills would precipitate systemic change through their crisiswork.

Many Lebanese understood entrepreneurship as a positive characteristic of their national identity and local culture and saw the entrepreneur (*rāʾid* or *mubdiʿ*) as an inherently patriotic and ethical citizen. The invocation of ancient Phoenician history as the origin of Lebanese national identity by various political and intellectual groups rendered entrepreneurship an authentic component of local heritage and a symbol of growth and prosperity, even for those communities that did not identify with the Phoenician past. The image of the Phoenician trader, who was believed to have spread culture and prosperity across regions, portrayed Lebanon as an entrepreneurial nation throughout history. Many of my interlocutors told me they had learned in elementary and high school that entrepreneurialism was a defining feature of the Lebanese, one that helped the Levant and regions beyond it prosper. Scholarly articles have also characterized entrepreneurialism as an essential part of Lebanese national culture and history.[8] This deep conviction of the "Lebaneseness" of entrepreneurialism led many Lebanese to proudly embrace the word "entrepreneur" and aspire to become one. Thus, when Western-funded NGO projects began to disseminate neoliberal notions of social entrepreneurship in Lebanon during the 2000s, many Lebanese were ready to embrace them, seeing entrepreneurship as more tangible, effective, and patriotic than other circulated notions such as active citizenship and peacebuilding. Though many activists were not entrepreneurial and several of them explicitly criticized this approach for its emphasis on the neoliberal concept of individualism, entrepreneurial activists were influential in Lebanese civil society.

The surprisingly high number of entrepreneurial activists who self-identified as leftist also elucidates how entrepreneurship was widely seen as a progressive and revolutionary subjectivity. During the 1960s and the first half of the long Lebanese War of 1975–90, Lebanon became a regional hub for the complex ideology of Arab leftism, which wedded ideas of Arab nationalism, socialist revolution, and Palestinian liberation. After the end of the Lebanese War, many leftists became involved with NGOs, viewing civil society as a strategic site to build a non-sectarian state and society through nationalism and secularism.[9] The integration of leftist movements into civil society activism after the 1990s led to new exchanges between globalized liberal human rights discourses and the legacy of leftist movements in Lebanon.[10] Neoliberal notions of entrepreneurialism have shaped Lebanon, as well as many other parts of the world, as exemplified in Gilbert's participation in several educational programs in the United States and Europe that promoted neoliberal values. Yet, some of the same activists who were trained by neoliberal projects were raised as patriotic leftists by their families. The complex activist lifeworlds show how entrepreneurial activism could combine—often in ambivalent and contradictory ways—an individualistic pursuit of market-based capitalistic models with a collective pursuit of activist mobilization.

Though Gilbert did not identify as a leftist, several in his team and many of his activist mentees I conversed with did. I met about forty entrepreneurial activists from the middle class and the aspirational middle class who identified themselves as leftists. Despite its variances, leftism in Lebanon was mainly characterized by secularism and anti-sectarianism.[11] Leftist entrepreneurial activists often idealized Western Europe–style representative democracy, which upheld secularism, social justice, the rule of law, and individual freedom, as an alternative to Lebanon's sectarian political system. I also met about a dozen entrepreneurial activists who rejected leftism and secularism and emphasized their religious and conservative identities, even though they also explicitly opposed the sectarian system.[12] In contrast to some other leftist civil society groups in Lebanon that associated the problems of sectarianism with global capitalism, both leftist and non-leftist entrepreneurial activists did not criticize private markets or global institutions more broadly.[13] Compared to anti-capitalist leftist groups, leading entrepreneurial activists, both leftist and non-leftist, were more visible and influential within the public sphere—media, educational institutions, NGOs, and social and grassroots movements. Leftist entrepreneurial activists believed that entrepreneurial skills would help activists to effectively challenge political and legal structures, mobilize political action, protest the government, and achieve change on a grand scale.

Entrepreneurial activists shared several commonalities with other Lebanese activists. All the entrepreneurial activists I met played active roles in broader civil society, including as humanitarian workers, volunteers, and empowerment workshop trainers and participants. They centered their activism on reducing the dire impacts of crises and creating livable futures in Lebanon. As did many other participants in civil society, entrepreneurial activists self-identified as activists, worked or volunteered in community-oriented NGOs, went to protests, and participated in grassroots movements. Entrepreneurial activists, like other civil society activists, came from diverse class backgrounds and had no common ideological formation. While some middle-class activists worked at or actually owned entrepreneurial initiatives, aspirational middle-class activists dreamed of becoming entrepreneurs and leading entrepreneurial initiatives.

Entrepreneurial activists' crisiswork differed from other frameworks of crisiswork primarily in its strong emphasis on individual moral character and direct involvement in Politics, but also in its focus on effective leadership for change and tangible solutions. The emphasis on leadership envisioned what they saw as a more active practice of crisiswork, one that went beyond participating in a collective movement or project and magnified the potential impact of a single individual who could lead others toward change. Entrepreneurship, for many civil society activists, also promised effective and tangible solutions to Lebanon's growing economic and political crises.[14] Social entrepreneurship training sessions offered by various NGOs, universities, and grassroots movements in Lebanon conveyed to many activists that within a defined period of time, they could devise concrete projects that could effectively solve a specific problem in Lebanon while developing a sustainable revenue system. A successful enterprise promised activists both financial autonomy and leadership for change.

Serving Lebanon Through a Social Enterprise

Fadia and I first met in early 2013 at a workshop on stress management at a local NGO in central Beirut. A Maronite Christian woman in her mid-twenties from a low-income family in Bekaa, Fadia introduced herself as an activist, entrepreneur, dreamer, and artist. Having received an undergraduate degree in physics from AUB in 2011, she had been unemployed for two years and was spending most of her time volunteering in NGOs that advocated for women's empowerment and gender equality. Fadia held a leftist, anti-imperialist, and open-minded approach to these issues. She frequently referred to the intellectual heritage of Arab socialism envisioned by her late father, a journalist and staunch Arab socialist who had been killed for his pro-Palestinian position during the Lebanese War. Fadia was an impressive intellectual who fluently spoke English, French, and Arabic. She was also fluent in philosophy, psychology, global literature, and fine arts, and she liked discussing her ideas and projects. Fadia and I quickly became close friends, and I enjoyed her company throughout my stay. We had many common interests, including the Lebanese author Khalil Gibran, Arabic literature, traveling, and movies.

In March 2014, Fadia and I went to a conference on the role of NGOs in Lebanon organized by AUB's Center for Civic Engagement and Community Service (CCECS) (Figure 6). CCECS promoted the nonprofit sector, social entrepreneurship, and especially youth empowerment initiatives and NGOs. I saw many of my activist interlocutors from multiple NGOs in the conference hall, and there was substantial interest from academic and media institutions as well. After the conference, I asked Fadia what she liked about entrepreneurship and why she defined herself as an entrepreneur. Her response demonstrates how in Lebanon, entrepreneurialism was conceived of as a force for the greater good—in part because NGOs were understood to be entrepreneurial projects:

FADIA: An entrepreneur sells a product and service for a social cause. He makes a profit, but it is for a social cause. Think about the conference today. I was so excited. You saw the hall, many people attended. *That's because people want to do something* [*al-ʿālam baddun yaʿmlū shī*; emphasis added]. This is the reason why NGOs and entrepreneurs are growing. Think about the title of the conference: "Mind Your Business, Heart Your Community." Very nice. An NGO

FIGURE 6. Cover of the eleven-page booklet distributed to all participants at a conference titled “Mind Your Business, Heart Your Community,” American University of Beirut, March 2014. On several pages of the booklet, the terms “social enterprise” and “NGO” are used interchangeably.

is also a business. One needs to be business-oriented to grow and to be impactful. And then the heart. Everyone thinks of himself only. No one thinks of this country. I love Lebanon. I want to serve people. It gives me a purpose, a dream.

YASEMİN: So, your dream is to serve Lebanon?

FADIA: Yes, most definitely [*akīd*]. I want to start my own company. I want to have a big consultancy company. Then I will be able to influence others and change the system.

Multiple consultancy companies (including Gilbert's) that worked on issues such as development, education, gender, and human rights were prominent civil society actors in Lebanon. Daleel Madani, which was the largest civil society portal in Lebanon and fostered cooperation among civil society actors, listed dozens of consultancy companies as civil society organizations working on Lebanon's problems. Low-income activists like Fadia dreamed of founding a consultancy company for several reasons. First, owning a company would provide them with stable income and employment, allowing them to generate a sustainable livelihood. Second, as a company owner, they would have the power to engage with Lebanon's problems by taking an active leadership role in both crisiswork and Politics. Finally, as a company founder, their income and power would be autonomous from "corrupt" sectarian institutions such as *wāsṭa* (intermediary connection). Lebanese entrepreneurial activists distinguished themselves from other activists by claiming more autonomy and power, and from other entrepreneurs by claiming to be oriented toward national service and political change.

Fadia also viewed her entrepreneurial dream to have a consultancy company as continuing the work of her father, whom she saw as a martyr for the Palestinian cause. She explained to me at length how she thought Israel's economic success drew from its strong entrepreneurial ecosystem, and she stressed that "we [Arab nations]" must do the same. To support her point, she opened her laptop and showed me several media and scholarly articles in English. Published in credible Western outlets, these articles analyzed how Israel became a "start-up nation" where both the government and families inculcated a culture of entrepreneurialism in children. Even though I was puzzled with this admiration of Israel coming from someone who advocated for, and whose father had been killed for supporting, Palestine, I thanked Fadia for educating me on Israel's rich entrepreneurial ecosystem and asked her more questions about the role of entrepreneurialism in addressing Lebanon's crises. She praised the tangible nature of activities enacted by social entrepreneurship projects and contrasted them with other civil society projects and activities that she characterized as inconsequential. She also complained about how Lebanese entrepreneurs overseas, whether in Iraq and the UAE or further abroad, contributed to the national development of other states instead of Lebanon. She hoped that as more entrepreneurs joined civil society, and more activists integrated entrepreneurialism into their crisiswork, Lebanon could become a stronger country that could protect itself against Israeli aggression and reduce its financial and other forms of dependence on countries such as France, Saudi Arabia, and Türkiye.

As I listened to Fadia talk about these dreams, I considered how entrepreneurial activists' patriotism rested on a teleological understanding of development that sought for Lebanon to replicate the entrepreneurship-based economic system of other states—including settler colonial states such as Israel. Thus, they curtailed the imagining of alternatives to market-based growth models as well as how these models often rested on overtly favorable Western support. I kept quiet, however, mindful that my critical anthropological analysis might sound cynical and even disrespectful to Fadia.

Sensing my skepticism about the benefits of entrepreneurship, Fadia invited me to her office to meet her colleagues. Since May 2013, Fadia had been working for a small local start-up that offered consultancy services to other Lebanese companies for software development. She felt extremely fortunate to find a job that aligned with her personality and political goals, comparing her company with other entrepreneurial initiatives that served Lebanon. A week after the conference at AUB, I joined Fadia in her aged Mercedes, and we drove to her office, which was in a small business district in Mount Lebanon. The office had two rooms and a small kitchen. Because of the presence of various personal items such as blankets, combs, perfume bottles, and slippers, it seemed like a living space to me.

I met and interviewed five employees as well as the owner of the company. They were well-educated members of the aspirational middle class in their late twenties and early thirties—people who defined themselves as activists and entrepreneurs, and who dreamed of serving Lebanon. Two of them participated in an independent feminist collective and went to demonstrations in favor of gender equality and civil marriage law, while another went to rallies for expanding public spaces in Beirut. The owner of the company was a passionate man in his early thirties and seemed happy to hear that I wanted to better understand the importance of entrepreneurship for Lebanon. During our long conversation he emphasized that there had been a "cash crisis" in the country for a while and that many of the company's customers could not pay for the services they received, rendering him unable to regularly pay employees' wages. Nevertheless, Fadia and her coworkers emphasized that they had *irāda*, which motivated them to work more than twelve hours a day on most days of the week, even though they were economically strained and often felt stressed. They were willing to wait with optimism for a time when the company would do better; they understood this as an expression of their ethical commitment to serving Lebanon.

During our lunch break, we sat around a plastic table on the patio of the office. Accepting me as a close friend of Fadia, the group comfortably shared intimate stories of how their familial and personal experiences with war motivated them to "do something for Lebanon" through entrepreneurship. Zeina, a secular low-income Shiʿi activist in her early thirties, dreamed of opening a laughter yoga studio for people struggling with mental health issues owing to war and conflict. She was first introduced to laughter yoga therapy at a workshop in the feminist collective she was part of, and she was convinced of its therapeutic impact. When I asked Zeina why she focused on mental health, she shared a story of her younger brother's severe traumatization by Israeli bombings during the July War of 2006. She added that she knew many young Lebanese who struggled with mental health issues, and she wanted to serve them through entrepreneurship. Like Fadia's story, Zeina's story reveals that lived histories of war shaped the experiences of entrepreneurial activists and their dreams of using entrepreneurialism to solve Lebanon's problems. Likewise, Gilbert and other activists from his generation said that their experiences of war, poverty, violence, and trauma made them continually think of alternative social, economic, and political solutions. For those activists, being entrepreneurs meant seeking tangible solutions to the lived realities of war, working for political change, and continually building their own moral capacities.

Fadia volunteered briefly for Live Love Lebanon, an initiative launched by several young middle-class Lebanese in 2012 that had a considerable media presence. The bracelets and other products the movement produced with the motto "Live Love Beirut" quickly became a global phenomenon and spread to other global cities: Live Love Paris, Live Love Dubai, Live Love

San Francisco, and so on. In 2014, Lebanon's Ministry of Tourism partnered with Live Love Beirut and included the brand in its official campaign advertisements. Many of its followers described Live Love Lebanon as a social enterprise, social movement, or community that aimed to unify Lebanon. For several supporters of Live Love Lebanon I talked to, the movement was a perfect example of how activists could use entrepreneurialism to help Lebanon. These kinds of social movements, which were also social enterprises, had proliferated since the 2010s. Local elite institutions, including the major universities AUB, LAU, and Saint Joseph, promoted youth social entrepreneurship in order to foster civic activism and the related idea of loving and serving Lebanon. Fostering love of and belonging to Lebanon and Beirut was part of the urban middle-class cultural milieu, rather than being unique to entrepreneurial and other civil society activists.

Yet loving and serving Lebanon could have different meanings. "Live Love Beirut: A Story of a Movement," a video in English posted by one of the co-founders of Live Love Beirut in 2015, begins with a quote from the American civil rights activist Maya Angelou: "Nothing will work unless you do."[15] It then displays graphic scenes of young men blocking roads and burning tires in Beirut in the summer of 2012. Even though the video does not identify the street protesters or comment on the nature of the protests, the time stamp of summer 2012 provides a clue: On many occasions throughout that summer, Shiʿi men in south Beirut protested the kidnapping of Lebanese Shiʿi pilgrims in Syria that May. In a few other instances, Sunni protesters in other parts of the city also burned tires to express solidarity with Sunni political leaders and institutions. There were also protesters who burned tires not to express any political allegiance but to protest electricity cuts. As dramatic background music enhances the affective impact of the text in the video, we learn that such scenes prompted the middle-class educated founders of the group to come up with a solution: "The usual for Lebanon. We were sick and tired. It had to stop. We had to show the world the Beirut we knew. We couldn't find hope. So we had to create it with you." The "we" and "you" referred to innocent Lebanese bystanders in Beirut whose lives were disrupted by the tire burners. In the rest of the video, we watch able-bodied, urban, middle-class, and secular-looking young Lebanese in sporty outfits hiking in Lebanon's mountains, having fun, volunteering, and making and selling bracelets to "help Lebanon" and "share the beauty of Lebanon with the world." As the video reports the movement's rapidly growing success and impact, we are told that Live Love Lebanon helped increase revenues for the country through tourism and fostered hope for many Lebanese. In positioning young urban secular Lebanese as working for the nation and representing its true essence, and juxtaposing them with what were portrayed as uncivil protesters who tarnished Lebanon's reputation, Live Love Lebanon presents a class-based love of the nation.

Entrepreneurialism as a Unique Character and a Spirit

Fadia suggested that I interview Salem, a leading figure in Live Love Lebanon and several other Lebanese NGOs. When I invited Salem for an interview in November 2013, we already knew each other well, since we had collaborated in several workshops and had about forty mutual activist friends. Salem, an ambitious activist in his late twenties who self-identified as secular, leftist, and independent, had grown up in a middle-class Sunni family in Beirut. Like other leftist entrepreneurial activists, he dreamed of witnessing the abolition of the sectarian system and the founding of a secular constitution.

Salem had become disillusioned after studying economics at AUB and working in the banking sector for a year. He decided to serve Lebanon and do things "that had more influence on society." Dedicating himself to youth empowerment and political advocacy, he became a prominent member of several locally influential civil society organizations and political movements within a few years. Like Gilbert, he had participated in a leadership program at a prestigious university in the United States and had received awards from several institutions in Lebanon for his outstanding leadership skills and initiatives. He explained why entrepreneurs were the leaders that Lebanon had long sought: "We need good models, good leaders. People who have a unique character [*shakhṣiyya*] such as activists and entrepreneurs who are non-sectarian [*ghayr ṭā'ifiyyīn*], patriotic [*waṭaniyyīn*], and autonomous [*mustaqillīn*] from any sectarian, familial, or other bonds."

Salem invoked the Arabic concepts of *shakhṣiyya* and *mustaqill* to describe an ethical citizen who would be a good political leader for the country and role model in society. He characterized both entrepreneurs and activists as having *shakhṣiyya*, distinct from both the sectarian and corrupt older generations and people who were apathetic about change. For Salem, having *shakhṣiyya* also meant being *mustaqill* from one's sectarian community. Someone *mustaqill* would act according to their individual choices rather than allow sectarian structures and relationalities to control their lives. They would have *irāda* and resist dominant sectarian social norms that would pressure them into unwanted situations such as marrying within their own sects or voting for political candidates representing those sects. Someone with *shakhṣiyya* would be "non-sectarian" and "patriotic," refuse to be pigeonholed into a sectarian identity, and demonstrate a capacity to create an alternative culture. While these moral vocabularies had a longer history of portraying patriotic subjectivity in Lebanon, entrepreneurial activists invoked them together to imagine themselves as rightful leaders for political and social change.

The ideas of having *shakhṣiyya* and being *mustaqill* articulated an ethical Politics that could be enacted by entrepreneurial activists in order to lead the revolution that Lebanon had long awaited. Particularly in the aftermath of the Arab uprisings, many activists in Lebanon invoked entrepreneurialism as a revolutionary political subjectivity. Some even stretched the term *entrepreneur* to include Mohamed Bouazizi, who sparked the Tunisian Revolution in 2011 by burning himself to death on the street after being humiliated by state authorities. Bouazizi had been a poor street vendor saving for a truck to grow his business. Lebanese activists, however, referred to Bouazizi as an entrepreneur for not only the job he did but also his courage in individually rising up against the system that had denied him a decent life. I heard many Lebanese praise Bouazizi for acting differently than the rest of his society did and for beginning something new. Thus, entrepreneurialism also meant displaying ethical qualities such as hard work, perseverance, and courage in service of grand-scale change in the country.

Entrepreneurialism in Lebanon was not a response to the questions of "Who am I in the world?" and "How do I wish to live and feel?" that were raised by entrepreneurial subjects in other contexts.[16] Rather, it was a response to the questions "What can I do for Lebanon?" and "How can I shape the future of Lebanon?" Entrepreneurialism through start-ups and NGOs was increasingly prized by activists and the larger society for the ethical disposition of patriotism it promised. Many activists who were paid professionals or unemployed NGO volunteers similarly called themselves entrepreneurs and dreamed of founding an NGO, social enterprise, or consultancy company. As "aspiring entrepreneurs," they could "feel entrepreneurial"[17] by serving Lebanon in NGOs, even while working as waged laborers or being unemployed. Invoking loose and sometimes contradictory definitions of entrepreneurship, low-income entrepreneurial activists emphasized that a job was qualified as entrepreneurial, and a person as an entrepreneur, not necessarily by the content of one's work but by one's "mentality" and "spirit" of loving Lebanon and working for change. Nevertheless, as aspiring entrepreneurs, they also dreamed of a future where they would have more financial autonomy.

Financial Autonomy

Diverse Lebanese activists founded companies or start-ups as sustainable solutions to the increasing financial difficulties their NGOs began to experience after international funding shifted to projects for Syrian refugees in 2012. They viewed consultancy companies as venues where they could undertake similar activities to those of NGOs, but with financial independence and more autonomy. They described to me how Western funding had been relatively easy to access but had come with various conditions and restrictions that frustrated most activists. Some of them said they had been engaged in debates about reducing dependence on Western donors even before the donors began focusing on Syrian refugees.

Ahmad, a middle-class activist, was born in the early 1970s to a poor Shiʿi family that was displaced from a village in South Lebanon to Beirut following the Israeli Occupation of Lebanon in 1982. He founded an educational consultancy company in 2012 when the arts entrepreneurship project he had been working on at an international NGO ended because of funding issues. He had a master's degree in educational leadership from a prestigious US university, had vast experience with Lebanese civil society, and had worked professionally or volunteered in seven different international or local NGOs since 2006. He could have easily found another paid position in another NGO at the time, but he believed that having his own company would grant him more autonomy and social prestige and eventually help him take a leadership role in Lebanon. He founded his company with the financial support of his wealthy uncle, who lived in Australia, and employed several close friends, all well-educated activists with whom he had collaborated for a long time. Like other entrepreneurial activist owners of companies and start-ups, Ahmad also viewed his initiative as creating employment opportunities for highly qualified Lebanese people in the country. When I met him in March 2013 in the office of his consultancy company, he told me, "I'm doing here [in the consultancy company] exactly what I was doing in NGOs.

But now, I don't have to deal with the budget problems and donor constraints. Everyone is regularly paid and is very good at their work. At the same time, we're autonomous in every aspect." Here, one sees how Salem's and Ahmad's conceptions of autonomy differed; Salem would have found Ahmad's reliance on his uncle problematic because he considered reliance on family in professional life as reproducing sectarianism, yet he was not as concerned as Ahmad about being dependent on Western funding.

Ahmad was proud of his family and maintained good relations with them. But he preferred to hide from many in civil society the fact that his family supported Hizbullah. He explained his choice to me as a way to protect himself from "judgmental people." Because of a family connection, Ahmad had also received a scholarship from the Hariri Foundation to study business administration at AUB. Unlike many middle-class entrepreneurial activists, he did not see family members' support for each other in personal and professional life as reinforcing sectarianism. He was aware, however, that such details might render him "sectarian" or "political" in the eyes of many Lebanese, including activists. He wanted to keep his good reputation, which allowed his company to cater to a wide range of groups.

As I spent more time with Ahmad and his activist friends, who shared Ahmad's political views, at the company, I observed that their motivation for crisiswork was similar to that of Gilbert, despite their different socioeconomic backgrounds and political orientations. As with Gilbert and other middle-class activists of his generation, growing up during the long Lebanese War led Ahmad to continually ponder how to help Lebanon and how to fix its problems: "Since I was five years old, I used to imagine and make my own scenarios about how to create change. I would ask myself questions and think of answers." He framed his life journey as a "continual search" (*baḥth mustamirr*) for viable political solutions to Lebanon's problems. Ahmad eventually concluded that the political system needed to change, which would require raising future political leaders and the funding to support them.

Ahmad saw himself as a leader who helped young Lebanese become future leaders who would be equipped to work on themselves and the country's problems: "We want to inspire positive change for both individuals and organizations and to create empowered leaders for tomorrow." His company focused on four key areas: consultation, training, awareness programs, and character-building programs. Consultation consisted of introducing systems and techniques for personal and group development. Training involved special sessions on various issues, including leadership and effective communication. Awareness programs targeted parents, teachers, and NGO trainers and were designed to instill skills for raising youth with good character. Character-building programs focused on cultivating core ethical values in youth that would help their growth as moral people and responsible citizens. The programs in these four areas offered services to NGOs, grassroots organizations, universities, schools, and private companies.

I was struck by how Ahmad tied each of these areas to the country's politics and future. For example, he viewed the character-building programs as directly shaping the future of Lebanon: "You never know, one of those children might run the country, and we may have made the difference. Impacting them now may do well for this country." Ahmad was certain that some of the youth he engaged with would eventually become politically active, and he believed that the education he provided would equip them with relevant ethical values and skillsets for their future political engagement. Similar to Salem and others, he proudly emphasized that he continued to work in Lebanon out of an idealistic desire to support the Lebanese people, and that he had happily rejected well-paying job offers from consultancy companies in the United States and Canada. He drew considerable pride from his decision to stay, which, to Ahmad, symbolized his moral capacity to make sacrifices for Lebanon's sake.

Diasporan Entrepreneurial Activists' Sacrifice

Fadia and Salem emigrated in 2015. Salem accepted a job offer from an international consultancy in the United Arab Emirates, and Fadia was awarded a scholarship to study social entrepreneurship in London. They each explained this change of plans as a step that would help them become influential leaders in Lebanon after gaining experience and saving money abroad. For them, leaving Lebanon did not contradict working for nation-building but in fact constituted an important step toward it. Indeed, Lebanese diaspora communities have historically been central to Lebanon's economy and development. Some prominent Lebanese, such as Rafiq Hariri, became successful contractors in the Gulf and accumulated immense wealth, which they began to invest in construction, banking, and other major sectors in Lebanon during the early 1980s. Many other publicly well-known entrepreneurial émigrés returned after the long Lebanese War and invested in reconstruction efforts.

Most Lebanese viewed living abroad as prestigious and believed in the "state-supported mythology celebrating migration as a major Lebanese achievement."[18] During my first week in Lebanon in the summer of 2011, I unwittingly upset my neighbor, a jovial Sunni woman in her early sixties, when I heard the news that her daughter was moving to Canada and expressed compassion and wished for a quick reunion. Her face suddenly became serious, and she told me, "There's a principle you need to know. Whoever leaves doesn't come back. My two cousins who moved to France twenty years ago said they would return, but they're still there. They come in the summer to see the family, that's it. It's better for them abroad." I later observed many Lebanese proudly sharing their relatives' and friends' news of obtaining a visa, moving, and starting a comfortable life abroad, and I learned to properly congratulate them when I heard such news. Many Lebanese, including several activists, told me that anyone who had the opportunity to leave the country would do so. I also listened to many entrepreneurial activists proudly talk about how they adamantly resisted considerable family and peer pressure to leave, preferring to build their businesses in Lebanon and contribute to Lebanon's economy.

Yet, moving abroad was an unattainable dream for many young Lebanese, including some activists. Several middle-class female activists from what they called "conservative families" told me that their parents would not allow them to move abroad on their own. "I have to marry first and then move. But how will I focus on my studies if I am a newlywed woman?" a Sunni middle-class entrepreneurial activist who dreamed of studying public policy at a British institution told me in May 2014. In addition to the gendered barriers to mobility encountered by some female activists, many low-income young Lebanese did not have the required educational assets, such as degrees from top universities and fluency in English, to qualify for well-paying jobs abroad. Even some low-income activists who had strong résumés could not migrate because they did not have sufficient know-how or connections to help them prepare a competitive application package for Western institutions. While middle-class activists in Lebanon typically complained that "everyone is leaving," various social dynamics curtailed the mobility of many young Lebanese.

Entrepreneurial diaspora returnees to Lebanon received remarkable respect from local activists, who viewed the former as perfectly embodying ethical citizenship. When someone returned to Lebanon after studying or working abroad, especially from a North American or European country, it would initially raise suspicions that they had been unsuccessful. But when a diasporan was seen as returning to serve Lebanon through entrepreneurial projects, suspicion would turn into admiration for what was perceived as the returnee's sacrifice.

Contrasted with the image of "self-interested Lebanese" who were portrayed as focused only on their families and friends, entrepreneur diasporans were often praised by many for caring for the entire nation. Many activists in Lebanon also believed that by living abroad, outside the perceived nepotism of Lebanon's sectarian culture, diasporans acquired authentic professionalism and expertise. This respect from local activists enabled returning diasporans to forge productive social exchanges across sectarian boundaries.

Many Lebanese who had been living in North America and other parts of the global North began to return to Lebanon after 2011, when the Syrian War began to affect the country. I met around twenty returning diasporans who were middle-class professionals in their thirties and forties and led entrepreneurial initiatives in Lebanon in sectors such as educational consultancy, urban development, and environmental policy. Some of them had been born and raised in Western countries, and others had emigrated to the West and the Gulf while in their twenties. They told me they had come back to help deal with Lebanon's growing sectarian polarization and economic crisis. Self-identifying as activists and entrepreneurs, they joined Beirut's newly flourishing start-up culture and social entrepreneurship projects, which they viewed as political spaces offering creative solutions for Lebanon's problems.

AltCity, one of the most popular cafés in Hamra, was an example of such projects. David Munir Nabti, a Lebanese diaspora returnee and a co-founder of AltCity, told me during an interview in 2014 that after studying at Berkeley and Stanford, he had left a budding career in California to return to Beirut. Defining himself as a start-up trainer, activist, and futurist, David Munir sought to join political initiatives, foster collaboration, and create a community of entrepreneurs "in a place that needed it most." He embraced the entrepreneurial ethos of California's Silicon Valley, which approached social change through the idioms of managerial culture and business ethics, and thought its culture of positivity could benefit an unstable place like Lebanon, where mistrust and competition predominated. He viewed that ethos as a means to advance his political goals as an activist rather than to promote self-reliant individuals.

Entrepreneurial activism, as practiced and disseminated in spaces like AltCity, attracted many activists like Zeina and Fadia, who viewed networking in cafés as central to their entrepreneurial ethics of self-improvement. Zeina and Fadia praised AltCity for hosting a leading boot camp program and a variety of trainings designed to facilitate and mentor local start-ups like theirs. AltCity was also included and promoted in Daleel Madani. Most of the regular customers I met in AltCity were recent university graduates who were simultaneously working on launching two or three new start-ups or social entrepreneurship projects. These initiatives were seen as a means to foster individual flourishing and national economic growth and to cultivate autonomy and leadership, all of which ultimately aimed to solve Lebanon's social and political problems. Many activists believed that such projects could attract people from diverse political and social backgrounds, as well as help build national unity and political consciousness.

Since its inception, AltCity had brought together hundreds of activists in networking events and had hosted a wide variety of art exhibitions and public debates related to the Palestinian cause, Syrian refugees, and other politically sensitive topics. The entrepreneurialism promulgated at these events was a good example of entrepreneurial activism in its emphasis on new ideas for political causes and social good. For example, during an event organized to celebrate "Entrepreneurs Week" in November 2013, prizes were awarded to NGO activists who designed community-serving empowerment projects in a series of competitions on "Best Entrepreneurial Dreams." In such events and in broader civil society, the terms "social entrepreneurship" and "entrepreneurship" were used interchangeably, and entrepreneurs justified the value of their new ideas and projects as offering effective solutions for pressing problems in Lebanon. However, despite openly engaging with political issues and searching for political solutions to them, entrepreneurial activists in such spaces rarely formed ties of collective solidarity, instead pursuing political solutions through individual projects. Their crisiswork of ethical Politics was predominantly an individualistic project of enacting change.

Entrepreneurial Activists Competing in Elections

Disillusioned with the limited ability of civil society to achieve systemic change, and observing the dramatic impacts of the Arab uprisings and the Syrian War, civil society leaders like Gilbert began exploring strategies to directly target existing laws and policies. In 2013 and 2014, I participated in several workshops and talks in the office of Gilbert's consultancy, BRD, where he continued to work as an adviser and consultant. In addition to offering consultancy services to government institutions, civil society organizations, and local and international NGOs in Arab-majority countries, BRD also brought together various leftist activists and scholars from those countries and other parts of the world to discuss effective political interventions to challenge existing regimes.

When I met with Gilbert in his office in August 2013 for an interview, he clearly distinguished between "civil society activism" and "political activism," and highlighted how he and his team were transitioning into a more political movement:

> Civil society should remain. It's an important place for political socialization. But it's time to create a new political society that competes with the existing corrupt political society. Otherwise, there won't be change if there's no direct competition with the existing political structure.

Between 2013 and 2015, I heard many entrepreneurial activists in Lebanon criticize, as Gilbert did, the limited power of civil society to achieve systemic political change. Prominent civil society figures cooperated in devising new alliances, political movements, and public protests that would directly impact the political system. In July 2015, civil society mobilized in response to the suspension of garbage collection in Beirut, which created a public health crisis as piles of garbage accumulated on the streets. The Popular Movement (al-Hirak) that emerged drew more than 100,000 demonstrators to the city center to protest corruption. These influential "garbage protests," which accelerated in August of that year, were the turning point in civil society's transformation into a more durable and politicized coalition. In September 2015, independent civil society activists, including entrepreneurs, consultants, intellectuals, and artists, who had previously been unaffiliated with any political party, formed the political movement Beirut Madinati (Beirut, My City). The movement was supported by not only professional urban elites but also many of my activist and other unemployed interlocutors from low-income marginalized neighborhoods. They believed it offered tangible remedies for the deterioration of basic services such as garbage collection, electricity, and water.

Beirut Madinati competed in Beirut's May 2016 municipal elections with a platform that combined grassroots mobilization and technocratic governance. Threatened by Beirut Madinati's growing popularity, the existing political establishment joined forces under the Beirutis' List, which brought together major rival political parties under the leadership of Saad al-Hariri's Future Movement party. Beirut Madinati, in contrast, grounded itself in civil society and grassroots movements and presented itself as an alternative to the political establishment. The movement appropriated the grassroots tactics employed by civil society and relied on independent civil society activists to foster vibrant discussions in public spaces, including public assemblies, square encampments, and town halls. These events brought together different groups, in some instances including the urban poor and refugees, and it encouraged them to participate in formulating alternative strategies and policies. The movement also stressed the activist and entrepreneurial efforts of candidates whose professional expertise could effectively solve the everyday problems of Beirut residents, such as the lack of housing and public transportation. Given that many Lebanese viewed their politicians and civil servants as incompetent and corrupt, the language of entrepreneurial solutions and effective governance allowed the movement to successfully reach out across sectarian lines. Participating alongside thousands of other Lebanese, entrepreneurial activists viewed the pre-election campaign as a remarkable moment in the history of Lebanon.

Activists commonly saw Beirut Madinati candidates as ethical, praising their apparent autonomy from their sects of origin as well as from existing political parties and their clientelist networks of elite companies and families, all of which formed the backbone of the sectarian system. Fadia, for instance, found it particularly appealing that the candidates were young and educated professionals who were not from notable Lebanese families. These characteristics had two ethical implications for Fadia. First, the candidates would make trustworthy and patriotic politicians because they did not represent a particularistic sectarian interest. Second, they owed their success not to the support of their families but to merit; they were self-made and therefore autonomous. The formation of the Beirut Madinati movement, for Fadia, was the culmination of her dreams, a time when activists and entrepreneurs who loved their country finally sparked change:

> Everyone keeps saying nothing changes here. Things can change; we just need more positive people [*ashkhāṣ ījābiyya*] like the people in Beirut Madinati. People who have hope [*amal*] and *irāda*. If you look at them, you

see intellectuals, artists, architects, and professionals. All are entrepreneurs and activists, people who love their country and have a different mentality.

As a new political movement, Beirut Madinati surprised everyone in Lebanon and the Middle East by capturing about 40 percent of the vote. After this relatively close loss, Fadia wrote to me, "Change doesn't happen in the blink of an eye. But Beirut Madinati is what gives us hope that tomorrow will be better." Extensive local and global media coverage of the elections framed the results as an unexpected success for Lebanese people, represented by Beirut Madinati, against the sectarian system. A *Foreign Policy* article titled "Beirut's Lovable Losers," published on May 26, 2016, highlighted the role of an emergent leadership that could still challenge the political establishment by offering alternatives to existing political and social movements:

> In a region that seems overwhelmed by chaos and upheaval, even a minor election where *independent actors* [emphasis added] make their mark is a hopeful sign that a new generation of leaders may be rising—a generation that is trying to move beyond ideas of revolution, or even civil society activism, to change the status quo.[19]

Despite losing the elections, Beirut Madinati symbolized, for many journalists, intellectuals, and activists alike, the birth of a new politics that represented Lebanese people against the country's political class. The movement has remained active as a civil society organization, proposing pragmatic solutions to ongoing political conundrums. In May 2018, when Lebanon held its first parliamentary elections in nearly a decade, sixty-six civil society activists, including Gilbert, competed as part of Kulluna Watani (We Are All Our Nation), a broad civil society coalition. Even though only one activist candidate won a seat, many in Lebanon still considered it an important success, as Lebanon's election laws hampered the efforts of small political parties or independent groups to run for office. Also notable was the growing politicization of previously apolitical or cynical civil society activists.

Politicization But. . .

Translocal encounters between the middle class, the aspirational middle class, and the returning diaspora created new spaces in which leading civil society activists invoked entrepreneurialism in an effort to turn Lebanese into political subjects who could effectively work for change. Entrepreneurial activists sought to build autonomous and patriotic leaders who would enact an ethical Politics and participate in the formal political sphere. They appropriated an already well-institutionalized civil society as a space for cultivating moral leaders with tangible, effective projects. The local association of entrepreneurship with patriotism, leadership, and change amplified the political and moral underpinnings of using entrepreneurship for activism. Despite its successful mobilization of diverse groups for direct interventions in Politics, however, entrepreneurial activism produced a very restricted notion of the political that presented multiple problems.

Entrepreneurial activists' excessive focus on moral character and leadership in their crisiswork reflected their individualistic understanding of change, which contradicted shared activist goals such as fostering care, solidarity, and community. Entrepreneurial activists, claiming superior character and love for the nation, promised to effectively address the nation's problems and become the leaders for change. Nevertheless, despite articulating strong political ambitions, entrepreneurial activism could paradoxically foreclose political possibilities in its class-based formulations of moral individuals and political change. For instance, Gilbert's TED Talk imagined that an alternative Politics would be delivered by "outstanding individuals," rather than relying on collectivity and solidarity. The strong emphasis on the prominence of individual leadership in solving present crises echoed increasing global celebration of strong men in key positions such as technocrats, CEOs, celebrities, and even politicians as driving forces for positive change.

The focus on individual character also led entrepreneurial activists, in particular those from the middle class, to consistently downplay the inherent inequalities that market logics created. Unsurprisingly, I heard some leftist, anti-racist, and feminist activists in Lebanon criticizing entrepreneurial activists for ignoring the intertwined ills of colonialism, capitalism, patriarchy, and racism. Even though most entrepreneurial activists ostensibly welcomed and even encouraged the free discussion of political issues on civil society platforms, they were uncomfortable with—and refused to address—issues related to social inequality. In entrepreneurial workshops such as "Start Your Own Movement" and "Effective Communication," the participants conversed on a wide range of political issues, highlighting corruption, infrastructural collapse, and sectarian leaders as major problems. But workshop trainers tactfully changed the subject when participants raised questions such as "How might people who do not know English benefit from this workshop?" and

"Will we get certificates after we complete this training, and will we be able to find jobs?" In small enterprises or companies like Fadia's, exploitation of labor and hierarchies among employees were rarely addressed, even by those who self-identified as leftists. Entrepreneurial activists' refusal to engage with such social critiques and with broader questions about infrastructures of social inequality constricted the frontiers of the political and bounded the future possibilities of change.

The patriotism and related willingness to serve the nation invoked by entrepreneurial activists were similarly tied to exclusionary visions of national unity, citizenship, and the political. Despite their belief and investment in character development and ethical growth, entrepreneurial activists had little sympathy for the urban poor. They endorsed class-based discourses of incivility, as seen in the Live Love Lebanon video, which depicted tire-burning protesters, most of whom were poor Shiʿa, as violent, disorderly, and bad for activist morale and Beirut's public image. Like local mainstream media and other middle-class activists, many entrepreneurial activists portrayed marginalized communities who had little access to educational institutions or other urban resources—as embodiments of sectarianism, negatively characterizing them as family-oriented and therefore loyal to sectarian communities. The patriotic enterprise Live Love Lebanon's activists could connect with the American activist Maya Angelou but could not connect with the activism of street protesters from marginalized communities in Beirut. The "Lebanon" they loved was a nation they envisioned without the working class and poor. In proudly claiming to be autonomous, non-sectarian citizens with moral character, middle-class entrepreneurial activists obscured the various privileges undergirding this subject position. The concept of autonomy, as they employed it, was predominantly an exclusionary discourse, despite having also been invoked by some low-income activists in their advocacy for social mobility and other goals. The political and moral futures imagined by entrepreneurial notions of patriotism and service were bounded by class-based visions and practices.

The gendered language of leadership used by entrepreneurial activists was also criticized by some feminist and LGBTQ activists.[20] I met Joe, a self-identified queer activist working for a gender-focused human rights organization in Beirut, at the AltCity Café during an entrepreneurial event in February 2014. Joe later told me in an interview that they had problems with workshops on social entrepreneurship in their organization because these workshops promoted what they called, in English, "toxic masculinity." When I asked Joe to elaborate on what they meant, they gave examples of trainers explicitly praising being assertive, being a fighter, being tough, not being weak, and not giving up. They added that Lebanese culture overemphasized strength and resilience, and that leadership workshops naturalized this culture without showing sensitivity to the diverse experiences of Lebanese activists. Traits such as self-control, risk-taking, sacrifice, assertiveness, and courage were associated with culturally idealized values of masculinity in many parts of the Middle East.[21] The seemingly neutral ideals of entrepreneurial activism perpetuated, at times unwittingly, locally dominant gender norms. In endorsing and promoting ideas of leadership and change, many entrepreneurial activist men invoked images and assumptions of "strong" and "charismatic" Lebanese men as well as problematic, essentializing notions of "Lebanese resilience."

Hence, entrepreneurial activism was simultaneously a creative political response to Lebanon's long-standing problems and a site of classed elitism. It both politicized and depoliticized diverse groups in its contradictory practices that encouraged active political participation while discouraging radical questioning of historically accumulated privileges and inequalities. Such contradictions were also reflected in its cultivation of hope as part of ethical Politics. The message of hope that the entrepreneurial activists sought to convey as part of their crisiswork had contradictory implications, as did other projects of hope enacted by civil society activism in Lebanon. Focusing on "producing hope," an essential practice within crisiswork, reveals the affective and temporal trajectories of how abstract, elusive concepts of "change" and "future" were dreamed and actualized within diverse activist lifeworlds.

FIVE

Producing Hope

When we met in September 2013 for an interview, Layal, a prominent middle-class activist in her early thirties, spoke extensively about Lebanon's current problems. She emphasized that hope (*amal*) was essential and expressed concern about its absence among the Lebanese:

> Most Lebanese don't have hope. They think that they have no future. This is why everyone tries to emigrate. Despite all the problems, I have hope for this country. I want to stay and do something to change things. Some lose hope in their future and become puppets of sectarian leaders. Some others just accept the way things are and stop caring; they also become part of the system. They say, "This is Lebanon, no one can fix it." But it doesn't have to be like that. We must produce hope (*lāzim niṣnaʿ al-amal*); otherwise, we will lose this country.

Layal belonged to a well-known and influential Shiʿi family in the Bekaa Valley, but she had been raised in Beirut. She received her education at top schools in Lebanon and France and spoke three languages fluently. She was a stylish and self-confident young woman who radiated energy, as our mutual friends also pointed out. Because of her vivaciousness and strong public speaking skills, Layal was invited frequently to speak at well-attended public events, even though prominent speakers at such events tended to be middle-class Beiruti men from Christian and Sunni backgrounds. As an entrepreneurial activist who believed in the importance of self-empowerment for precarious communities, Layal collaborated with various NGOs in different cities and towns in Lebanon and the MENA region to offer motivational speeches and soft-skills workshops. In 2014, she founded an educational consultancy company that provided services to international and local NGOs. During our collaboration on several projects at a youth-focused NGO in central Beirut throughout 2014, I frequently heard her complain about various political and social problems in Lebanon and how they were not being adequately addressed—by both civil society projects and her own consultancy firm. However, she typically concluded such complaints by asserting the significance of maintaining hope.

Activists like Layal perceived hopelessness as a threat to their crisiswork because they believed that public sentiments of despair perpetuated crises. In February 2014, Layal led a half-day workshop titled "Leadership in Times of Crisis" at the NGO office where we collaborated. It included a series of fifteen-minute breakout discussion exercises, and one prompt in particular led to an animated conversation: "What is the #Lebanon2020 you want to live in?" In groups of four or five, around thirty participants from diverse backgrounds reflected on the question, imagining their country at the start of the new decade. Afterward, when representatives reported back on their group's conversation, we heard that most participants were extremely concerned about the worsening of political, economic, and other problems in the country. One representative commented, "My group believes that it's very difficult to think about 2020 or have hope about 2020 given the current situation," and then recounted the group members' experiences with public violence, infrastructural failure, unemployment, and heightened political polarization in the country. A twenty-four-year-old activist woman from my group, who volunteered at an active local NGO that focused on environmental problems, interjected that one can have fears and at times lose hope but still must continue fighting to save the country no matter what. Another activist, who worked as a public relations officer at the same NGO, supported her friend's interjection and added, "As activists, we try to bring good people together and provide them with hope. This is our role." Layal nodded animatedly as she listened to the two activists and commented, "Surely hope is very important. I also want to cultivate hope *(Anā baddī kamān izraʿ al-amal)* in this workshop. Despair just brings more crises and more despair."

Producing hope is foundational to crisiswork in Lebanon. In our individual meetings and during the many events and workshops they led, activists—most of whom were of the middle class and entrepreneurial—typically cited the lack of hope as a major problem that all Lebanese needed to fight against. They frequently used the phrases "producing hope" (*ṣināʿat al-amal*) and "cultivating hope" (*zirāʿat al-amal*) to describe their goals of motivating the younger generation to focus on the future and believe that things would get better. Middle-class activists like Layal designed programs and activities in partnership with various institutions, such as international organizations and donors, universities, banks, and private companies, that deliberately sought to instill hope among the youth—for both the future of the country and the future of Lebanese youth themselves. Various civil society groups in the country, including entrepreneurial activists, actively promoted hopefulness as an alternative ethico-political disposition against pervasive negative public feelings that apprehensively anticipated war or that despaired over Lebanon's many crises. They viewed being hopeful, and encouraging others to be hopeful, as both essential moral traits of activism and a panacea to Lebanon's perceived "sectarian" morality of disbelief in change and disengagement with other communities. For many activists, doing something about crises and working for change—core features of crisiswork—required that both activists and other Lebanese become hopeful about the future of the country.

Rather than studying hope as a normative concept in either celebratory or dismissive ways, as most scholars have done, I ethnographically trace how the crisiswork of Lebanese activists generates multiple interventions by problematizing the lack of hope in the country.[1] How is hope cultivated and to what effects? How do diverse Lebanese invoke, practice, and embody hope in ways that respond to lived and perceived experiences of crisis? In attending to the larger social and everyday processes in which diverse actors generate, maintain, and revitalize hope, one sees that being hopeful in Lebanon is not a quality of one's character or attitude but is a process of "becoming." I do not examine whether my interlocutors were hopeful or hopeless and do not assess their circumstances as hopeful or hopeless.[2] Hope for Lebanese activists is an "active work" of fostering ethical citizenship, which includes embodied pedagogies, moral trainings, and visual and sensory experiences.[3] Activist spaces reinforce becoming hopeful as both an individualistic and collective practice. As it does with cultivating the ethico-political dispositions of positivity, professionalism, and autonomy, Lebanese activists view producing hope as key for their crisiswork, which targets a multiscalar change in the sectarian system and culture.

Producing hope in Lebanon is a locally negotiated social process that is fraught with ambivalences and contradictions. Activists invoked visions of a hopeful future to provide alternative affects in the face of the present crises. They organized motivational public events that called participants to imagine "post-crisis" futures and new ways of being and acting. These events offered remarkable moments of togetherness and collective dreaming in which producing hope had contradictory effects. Activists' producing hope simultaneously expanded and bounded people's future horizons. Practicing hope provided young Lebanese with practical tools to tackle uncertainty in the present and to imagine better futures. It enabled some of them to transform their lifeworlds as they formed new connections, claimed agency, and felt more empowered in the present. Nonetheless, producing hope was also a project of affect management that aimed to control and discipline the affective orientations of Lebanese toward the past, present, and future as well as toward the nation, other communities, and themselves. Pedagogical practices such as having "realistic dreams" (e.g., hiking in Lebanon rather than emigrating to the United States) or "accepting deferral" (e.g., continuing to pursue job opportunities despite prolonged unemployment) bounded dreaming, and ultimately the future. Hence, not all dreaming and hoping practices and experiences were equally welcome. More crucially, many Lebanese found themselves more and more frustrated by experiencing unfulfilled dreams in the face of the country's worsening crises. Their hope transformed into resentment, despair, and cynicism. In this sense, many hope projects within Lebanese crisiswork operated through what Lauren Berlant calls "cruel optimism": excessive attachment to fantasies for a better life that ends up undermining one's flourishing because that life is unsustainable in the present.[4] Ironically, fostering hope and expectations for post-crisis futures could exacerbate negative experiences of new crises.

Imagining Post-Crisis Futures

The future-oriented politics of crisiswork dreamed of a stable Lebanon with national unity and of individuals with a strong sense of citizenship and national belonging. It imagined a peaceful non-sectarian society as not yet born and demanded that Lebanese youth hold onto hope until that society's birth. In the wake of the Syrian War, which affected political, economic, and social life drastically and increased fears of a new war in Lebanon, I frequently heard two questions from my interlocutors, both activists and others:

"When will these crises end?" and "Do you see any hope in Lebanon?" As anthropologists have demonstrated, the future is not an empty frame; it is a central political category that operates as a "cultural fact" in the present.[5] While almost everyone else in Lebanon talked about the future with complex sentiments of fear, anxiety, and anticipation of war, activists engaged in crisiswork to incite Lebanese to look toward the future with hope.

In approaching hope as an ethnographic object, one sees that in Lebanon, having hope or becoming hopeful required continual, active work. Producing hope was a collective practice of meaning-making—a model for action that sought to make sense of the present moment.[6] Civil society activists invoked hope to build a different knowledge about the present moment and to imagine a future collectivity that would be distinct from the existing ones. Many activists framed hope as a "principle": a major impetus for social change that encouraged people to focus on what is not yet.[7] Discourses and practices that invoked hope and dreaming were intrinsically linked to concerns about Lebanon and its future. The public events that were organized to produce hope rendered crisis a shared experience that could be endured through connecting and dreaming with other communities. In this sense, what seemed to be merely spaces of fun and leisure were generative of ambivalent sites of knowledge-making and world-making, rendering the production of hope an essential practice of crisiswork.

The motivational public events and workshops that middle-class Lebanese activists, particularly entrepreneurial activists, organized between 2012 and 2015 framed being hopeful and future-oriented as central to ethical citizenship and activism for change. Private companies and NGOs collaborated to plan large public events that brought together diverse Lebanese and involved leisurely activities and interacting with a select group of motivational speakers (Figures 7 and 8). Such events were popular because they framed Lebanon as a livable place in which public spaces, such as streets, were not sites of conflict, violence, and fear. For instance, many of my activist interlocutors articulated their appreciation of "Beirut by Bike," a popular bike rental shop located in downtown Beirut, by saying that biking across streets, some of which were controlled by confessional groups, made them feel free and mobile and gave them a sense of belonging to the city. Many local NGOs organized public biking events inside and outside of Beirut to promote their social causes. In these efforts of bringing together diverse Lebanese groups for fun activities, and thus fostering cross-sectarian interaction, activists sought to foster citizens that were non-sectarian and patriotic as well as hopeful and working for change.

FIGURE 7. Leaflet for the motivational public event "Innovating for Life."

FIGURE 8. Leaflet for the motivational public concert "One Lebanon: United for Tomorrow."

I was struck by the promotion of what one could call "public dreaming" practices, given that dreaming has typically been studied as an individual practice.[8] For many middle-class activists like Layal, hoping and dreaming were so important that they could not be left to people's individual experiences—they had to be produced in public spaces. Middle-class activists pointed out that the lack of hope and pervasiveness of despair were not only consequences of but also reasons for Lebanon's being stuck in crises. Targeting the widespread depiction of life in Lebanon as "without a future" (*mā fī mustaqbal*), they fostered both collective and individual dreaming practices to cultivate hope among Lebanese youth, as they believed only hopeful Lebanese could build the nation's future. In particular, during motivational public events, middle-class activists taught dreaming practices through various technologies of imagination that aimed to build a hopeful self and to reconfigure people's relationships with the country's past, present, and future. In doing so, they sought to mobilize the Lebanese youth for social and political change. Yet, the very efforts to produce hope also obscured existing social inequalities and frustrations with the deferral of dreams. The TEDx LAU conference in September 2013, which was entitled "Realistic Dreamer," is a good example of how such motivational events had contradictory impacts on people's affective and temporal experiences.

A GROWING SOCIAL MOVEMENT

I felt lucky when one of my interlocutors, who was on the event's organizing committee, found me a ticket for the "Realistic Dreamer" TEDx LAU event in September 2013.[9] TEDx talks were highly popular among middle-class Lebanese activists, who participated in them as organizers, speakers, volunteers, and audience members. In addition to the well-attended TEDx Beirut talks, major universities also organized their own independent TEDx talks. Between 2011 and 2015, ten day-long TEDx events, each hosting an audience of 1,000 to 2,000 people, were organized in the chic auditoriums of Beirut. The majority of TEDx talks in Lebanon were in English, and only a few of them were in Arabic. Many Lebanese activists praised the events to me as unique spaces that provided people with hope and an experience of change. In addition to attending the live events, many Lebanese gathered at small NGOs and in people's homes to watch popular TEDx talks, which prompted lively conversations about political problems, social life, and the future of Lebanon. In the three local youth-empowerment NGOs where I volunteered, we frequently watched and discussed motivational TEDx talks on YouTube from Lebanese and non-Lebanese speakers on the significance of activism and working for change.

As with many other motivational public events in Lebanon, the "Realistic Dreamer" event highlighted the power of hope in engaging with crises as well as the strength and potential of Lebanese culture. On the first page of the small event booklet that was handed out to attendees, the event coordinator Reine Azzi, a middle-class civil society activist who worked in an international NGO, welcomed the participants: "Our message is one of hope. We consider ourselves to be romantic dreamers. . . [the ellipses are in the text] those who want to concretize beautiful inspirational ideas while realizing their full potential and limitations. . ."[10]

The message of hope had a massive material presence on the LAU campus that day. Miscellaneous small activities, such as games, puzzles, and photography, were held at festively decorated platforms, booths, and boards spread throughout the campus. Motivational posters and fun exercises, which asked "What is your biggest dream? What do you dream for Lebanon? Where do you see yourself in five years?" invited event participants to interact closely with the theme of the event. The members of the large organizing team, most of whom self-identified as entrepreneurs and activists, were intentionally welcoming and cheerful, and looked positive and hopeful throughout the day. They regarded this one-day event as part of a broader movement in Lebanon and in service of a higher national cause that would bear fruit in the future. Some of the participants also described the event in English as the epitome of a quiet but growing social movement in Lebanon:

> A number of political analysts have reported that the Arab Spring all but missed Lebanon; yet such thinking dismisses the significance of the quiet social movement that is occurring in the country's enlightened corners. TEDx LAU is one of the firm anchors of this movement as it brings people of different stripes together to share and exchange ideas.[11]

The phrase "enlightened corners" frames prestigious Lebanese universities as distinguished sites of progress and casts event participants as members of a quiet social movement. The hierarchical distinction between the "enlightened" parts of the country and the rest portrays universities as primary actors for change. The use of the word "movement" and the reference to the Arab Spring implies that activism in TEDx events and similar spaces was as important for Lebanon as the national protests and collective struggles for change were for other Arab countries. Many participants framed the event as proof of LAU's "rich vein of activism," that "LAU is not an ivory tower," and that educated members of the LAU community were willing to "fight for Lebanon."[12]

Like many public events in Beirut organized by activists, TEDx LAU generated conversations about Lebanon and the Lebanese people that juxtaposed two common exceptionalist narratives about the country: that it is an unchanging and incomparable land of sectarian divisions, *and* that it is a land of peacefully coexisting diversity. The event had deep political meanings for many participants because it offered a shared space where Lebanese from different confessional backgrounds could interact civilly. For many during the event, TEDx LAU demarcated a modern and cosmopolitan enclave that was distinct from the majority of urban Beirut, where sectarian symbols were historically displayed, including on the LAU campus in other days.[13] "At least there are such events that unite us," Wissam, a Druze middle-class activist participant, who was about to complete his bachelor's degree in economics at LAU, told me during the event. He described how sectarian tensions and confrontations had recently increased among students on many campuses in Beirut and how Lebanese society was more polarized than ever. He brought up incidents that showed how even AUB and LAU campuses were highly politicized spaces where student groups that belonged to conflicting political alliances confronted each other during university elections and protests. Some of the other participants I spoke with that day similarly praised such events as unique symbols of national coexistence and jokingly referred to the event as "very non-Lebanese" (i.e., for having an atmosphere of unity in a peaceful and non-confrontational way). Yet, not everyone viewed the event as contradicting Lebanese culture. Arguing that the recent context of polarization had led to the isolation of Lebanon's communities, some other activists described the amicable mingling of diverse groups on the LAU campus as "reflecting the essence of Lebanon."

Inside LAU's large auditorium, together with an enthusiastic crowd, I watched twelve high-profile, professional guest speakers with cheerful personas deliver moving speeches. Tom Fletcher, the British ambassador to Lebanon and one of the most popular speakers, offered an enthusiastic message of hope.[14] Addressing the audience as "believers," "optimists," "inspirers," and "creators," Fletcher maintained that "anyone who has doubts about

Lebanon's future should come here today." He also characterized Lebanon as "the frontline for coexistence," which he said the LAU campus exemplified that day, and added, "If we can show that we can coexist here in this room, in Beirut, in Lebanon, across the region, we can show we can coexist anywhere in the world." When he praised the participants for demonstrating coexistence, positivity, resilience, and willingness to "fight for this Lebanon," the audience applauded vigorously. Even though Fletcher's focus was Lebanon and its problems, the solutions he promoted, such as positivity, resilience, and creativity, resonated with the neoliberal logics of social interventions in Britain and other countries.

The other speakers were highly successful, professional Lebanese, most of whom had lived and worked in North America and Europe. They presented their talks as part of a broader collective political effort in Lebanon rather than as an educational or leisure activity. Instead of apologetically praising Lebanon, they used the podium as a space for crisiswork and expressed their desire to undo the negative effects of crises. Mohamad J. Hodeib's "On the Root of Change" was one of the popular talks.[15] Hodeib, a research assistant at the Issam Fares Institute for Public Policy, was a self-identified Lebanese art activist who helped form several collectives. Speaking in Arabic, Hodeib talked at length about the negative impacts of sectarianism, such as poverty, street barricades, and political corruption, on everyday life in Lebanon. He asserted that, as a young Lebanese man, his dreams were beyond the boundaries of sectarian formations. He also called on the Lebanese youth, whom he described as desiring to live in dignity, to strengthen their sense of belonging to Lebanon and to work for a revolution against sectarianism. Sabine Jizi, another speaker who was enthusiastically received by the audience, was a prominent laughter yoga instructor in Lebanon. She also owned and managed a small company called "I laugh you." Framing her company as a movement, Jizi emphasized how laughing helps people stay healthy and live in harmony with society.[16] After she led a mini session of laughter yoga, the audience was visibly elated. While this experiential activity mainly focused on embodying feelings of relaxation, happiness, and positivity at the individual level, it shared the ultimate goal of the other speakers and event activities—to inspire hope and change within the larger Lebanese society.

Most speakers encouraged the audience to participate in civil society and fight against crises by becoming activists, entrepreneurs, or volunteers. They reminded the audience of the possibility of a brighter future, a future that would be attainable if they believed in it and worked with others to attain it. My activist interlocutors, and their friends whom I met at the event, praised the professionalism of the event organization, the speakers, and the quality of the activities. They asserted that the event space uniquely showcased the civilizational capacities of Lebanon, particularly by hosting high-skilled Lebanese professionals who designed projects that addressed the country's problems. Being able to interact with accomplished Lebanese who cared about Lebanon and its problems led many of them to believe that they could become like these speakers and that there was hope for the country.

For many Lebanese activists, prestigious public events like TEDx LAU represented a model of what was otherwise an abstract dream of a better country. Aesthetically designed as leisure activities, TEDx events in Lebanon combined the globalized practices of Silicon Valley entrepreneurialism with post-war longings for a united Lebanon. Civic interactions among young, educated Lebanese from different sects in well-maintained upscale spaces were celebrated as a model of a united and developed future nation, which had achieved peaceful coexistence. Creating the fantasy of a modern, civilized community served to provide a sense of hope and joy at a time of great uncertainty. In addition to articulating a different experience of "now," the TEDx LAU event also asked the audience to imagine a different future.

#LEB2020: BELONGING TO THE FUTURE

One of the hallmarks of the TEDx LAU event in September 2013 was the huge blackboard (Figure 9) located in a central place outside the auditorium building. The rich aesthetics of the blackboard, which student volunteers worked on, invited the participants to share their present complaints and future dreams. Popular complaints such as "I hate current politicians" were featured together with messages of hope. By asking the audience, "What would you like to change?" the board invited them not only to imagine and believe in a bright future but also to participate in its making. Collectively dreaming by writing on the board made an otherwise abstract, unknown future an experiential reality in the present.

The message on the blackboard clearly demanded that the audience ignore the past and the present in favor of tomorrow: "Regret is for the slaves of the Past, Uncertainty is for the sons of the Present, hope is ours, the children of Tomorrow, of 2020!" It encouraged the young Lebanese attending the event to imagine themselves as belonging to the future. In other

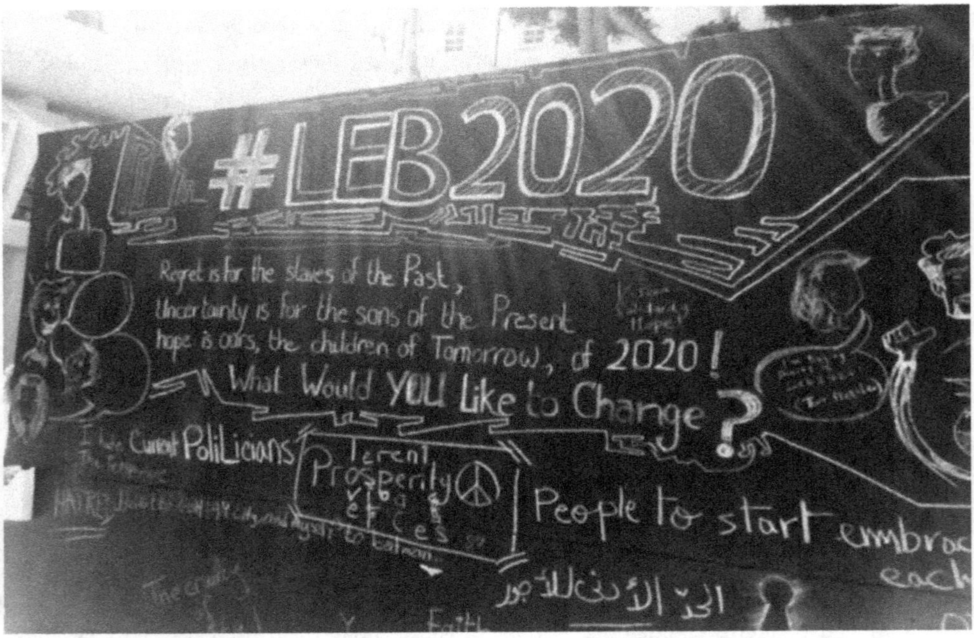

FIGURE 9. Blackboard at the TEDx LAU event. Photo by Author.

motivational public events that civil society activists organized, I frequently encountered a similar discourse of denigrating the present and the past and valorizing the future. This forthright denigration reflected a public consensus to avoid speaking about the past and the contested histories of war and violence, which had emerged after the long Lebanese War.[17] Civil society activists viewed the present as a "protracted now"[18] of sectarianism and war, and they condemned people's focus on the past and the present as being negative. Even though many activists sought to utilize the present to cultivate new ways of being and acting, they also viewed the present as sharing the same problems of the past, such as violence, polarization, infrastructural failure, and corruption. Given this widespread negative perception of the present in a society where many were carrying burdens of the past, numerous activists celebrated the future as a site of new potentialities and looked forward to a new Lebanon that would be devoid of its past and present problems.

The hashtag #LEB2020, which featured prominently on the blackboard, promised a better Lebanon in seven years' time. It visualized 2020 as a stable near future that could bracket past and present problems: one neither so close that it could be dismissed as "unrealistic," nor so distant that it would create despair. For many participants with whom I spoke that day, 2020 was near enough to raise the hope of finally having a good life. They hoped that by the time they entered their late twenties or early thirties, Lebanon would have solved its problems and become a place where they could have a stable job and start a family.

Hashtagging the beginnings of future decades, such as "#2020" and "#2030," was a common feature of many public events that local and international NGOs in Lebanon organized. For instance, a major UNDP Lebanon meeting in October 2015 used #Lebanon2030 and #Agenda2030 on event brochures and social media to convey the organization's commitment to solving environmental problems. In both Lebanon and other parts of the global South that are tainted by public perceptions of crisis, the punctuation of a future time period is used as a key technique to inspire dreaming and working toward those dreams.[19] The technique encourages hope by demarcating a tangible point in the near future after which things would be different and better.

Anthropologist Jane I. Guyer argues that "the evaporation of the near future in theory and public representations" has become a far more demanding problem since the 1970s.[20] According to Guyer, many people worldwide struggle with worsening short-term prospects and the increasing uncertainty of the near future, prompting an excessive focus on the long-term future. Through events such as TEDx talks, activists in Lebanon sought to address the sentiment of enforced presentism, which they saw as resulting from the widespread idea that things cannot change in Lebanon, and fears of uncertainty, as resulting from the apparent decline of the near future. Targeting the pervasive public fear that harder times would come in the near future, activists' punctuation of a new decade encouraged young Lebanese to actively work toward alternative near futures and remain hopeful until their efforts came to fruition. A focus on 2020 promised to expand future horizons and evoked new possibilities in 2013.

The TEDx LAU in September 2013 also invited participants to see themselves as part of an abstract universal humanity that accomplished change through hope, rather than as residents of a chaotic and divided country who were overwhelmed by crises. In other activities at the same event that day, I saw similar efforts to reorient affect and connect the participants to other global actors who overcame difficult circumstances through hope. Quotes on various posters, such as "I have a dream" (Martin Luther King) and

"Be the change you wish to see in the world" (Gandhi), called on the audience to identify with political figures in different parts of the world who had struggled against the arduous circumstances of their time. Such cross-cultural references convey that, since hope and dreaming brought success to other nation-building and state-making efforts, they might help Lebanon turn the page on sectarianism. The invocation of such actors who overcame the political obstacles confronting them renders being hopeful as essential to overcoming crises and creating change. In imagining themselves as part of a universal humanity with moral, exemplary stories, event participants were encouraged to concretize change and believe in its possibility. Through dreaming practices that called them to be ethical citizens who could struggle with hope as other peoples did in their own countries, participants were asked to believe that they had the agency to change themselves, their society, and their country.

DREAMS FOR THE UNEMPLOYED

A Lebanese friend, who was a leftist activist, called my attention to the demand for a minimum wage, which was the only Arabic sentence on the blackboard. This demand inserts class-specific anxieties among the more vaguely formulated political demands of peace, faith, and coexistence. Although most of the participants were middle-class students and graduates from elite universities, I saw some of my activist interlocutors from non-elite universities who belonged to disadvantaged communities. They told me that they were at the event out of curiosity and were happy to meet with people from different backgrounds. They were also interested in activities that were designed to address the growing discontent of a precarious community of job seekers who had low-paying jobs or were unemployed.

Joefish, one of the most popular activities of the day, asked participants to forget who they were and to dream of performing a different occupation. The Joefish ID tags (Figure 10), designed to attach to one's collar, offered a creative exercise for dreaming other ways of being. The ID tags asked participants to imagine a change in their present statuses: "I am a. . . But I wish I were a. . ." Joefish fliers framed dreaming of a new occupation as a way of dreaming of a new life: "Ever wondered what your life would be like if you had chosen a different career?"

The dreaming practice in Joefish targeted two pitfalls of hopelessness at once: First, it reoriented one's temporal focus from the present to the future.

“HELLO!
MY NAME IS .... FISH.
I AM A ....
BUT I WISH I WERE A ....”
#TEDXLAU
/JOEFISHPAGE
@JOEFISHTWEET
@JOEFISHINSTA #THECROSSROAD #JOEFISHWORLD
joefish
TEDxLAU

FIGURE 10. Joefish ID Tag.

Second, it reoriented one's desire for a highly sought-after occupation toward a more attainable yet enjoyable one. An open-ended question, which seemed to invite boundless dreaming, in fact prepared participants for the possibility that they might not have the upward mobility that the wider society expected from them. Despite the “I wish. . .” sentence, which invited one to desire anything, the instructions on the distributed activity flier carefully managed this process by offering relatively achievable job alternatives such as dancer, designer, DJ, chef, and humanitarian worker. Even though the well-paying occupations of interior architect and engineer were included on the flier, the two most well-respected occupations that most Lebanese parents fiercely pressured their children to pursue—doctor and lawyer—were not listed. Other occupations such as financial manager, banker, and consultant, which were popular among many young Lebanese, were also not mentioned. Instead, careers that were flexible and low-paying but sounded like cool alternatives in a cosmopolitan city were highlighted. In Lebanon, one could become a DJ, dancer, chef, or designer by attending a series of trainings and workshops that readily gave certificates to participants. These recommended positions were also easier to obtain than the more competitive and popular occupations.

Activities like Joefish sought to address the “temporal insecurities” that characterize globalized experiences of poverty and inequality.[21] By creating imaginative alternatives for the job market and having people embody these alternatives in the present, the temporal and affective technologies employed in those activities respond to the lived economic insecurities of the present. Imagining themselves in alternative jobs encourages young people to think of the job market, unemployment, and social respectability in different ways. For example, by including dream jobs that do not require formal university education, the activity expanded what counts as respectable work. However, these attempts to broaden future horizons do not necessarily articulate a critique of the economic system or the inequalities generated by that system. By redefining the boundaries of dreaming, such activities seek to prepare participants for an increasingly insecure job market in which only a small minority would be employed in "dream" jobs. The technologies of dreaming employed in activities like Joefish simultaneously expand future horizons and curtail more radical articulations of dissent.

With all these ambivalences and contradictions, the dreaming practices in the Joefish activity rendered what was usually experienced as an abstract "uncertain" future as instead individually and collectively desirable in the present. Instructions on the fliers guided participants through several interactive activities, such as taking group pictures or posting their dream jobs on social media. The participants were asked to visualize a positive future experience, embody that experience in the present, and share it with others. Sharing talks, pictures, comments, and other memories from the event on social media further expanded the present by turning a temporary individual experience of joy into a noteworthy collective experience. Such practices created a longer social life for the event, rendering seemingly fleeting activities more durable. Practices like taking a photo or wearing a Joefish tag turned an abstract dream of a future job into an experience that was affectively tangible and concrete in the present as well as memorable in the future. In these experiential moments, hope became a lived reality—albeit an ephemeral one—and rendered otherwise uncertain future dreams more attainable.

I saw about twenty activist interlocutors from diverse confessional and class backgrounds participate in the TEDx LAU event, and most of them viewed their experiences at the event as essential to dealing with the manifold crises facing Lebanon. They participated in all of the activities and took many individual and group photos in front of the activity panels. My conversations with them after the event reflected their cheerful optimism and feelings of agency. "Once you choose hope, anything is possible," commented Rola, a low-income Christian activist who at the time was unemployed and volunteering for an NGO. She told me that she had been depressed for several months because of the recent crises, and that the event significantly lifted her spirits and helped her continue her daily tasks and activism. When I asked her how one could choose hope or what one should do when one chooses hope, she responded by discussing specific practices, such as talking about positive things, being grateful for what one had, thinking about one's future dreams rather than one's past failures, not watching too much political news, exercising, and doing yoga. She described hope as concretely experienced through bodily practices such as smiling, dressing well, and going outside and socializing with others without fear. Just as Rola did, other low-income Lebanese said motivational events enabled them to learn important skills like stress management, and thus to maintain their mental health and well-being while pursuing their dreams. Civil society activities such as TEDx LAU events, empowerment workshops, and soft-skills trainings were widely seen by diverse activists as fostering well-being and a sense of normalcy, hence making their crisiswork possible.

By introducing a prospective momentum to the present, which was widely perceived as in crisis, TEDx LAU and similar events created new forms of "self-knowledge" and "collective agency."[22] Throughout all the 2013 TEDx LAU activities, speakers and participants invoked dreaming and hope to feel better in the present moment and produce a different knowledge about everyday life, which had been experienced predominantly as overwhelming, uncertain, and frightening. After the event, I joined a group of middle-class activists who decided to hang out at a nearby café. One participant told us, "It is these kinds of events that give me hope for the future of Lebanon." When I asked "How so?" she listed several ways she benefited: seeing many people together who were positive, passionate, successful, hardworking, and inspiring; "breathing a different air"; and renewing her motivation. Moreover, she pointed out, the LAU campus had been a secure and comfortable space. Several others shared her optimism and emphasized that, by being involved in public events and connecting with different communities, they had become more optimistic, self-driven, and open-minded. One of them who was on the event organizing committee said: "I see people changing, finding hope. You have to plant seeds everywhere, and today we planted lots of seeds."

Producing hope as a deliberate activist project of affect management thus became central to crisiswork's cultivation of subjects that believed in and worked for change. Middle-class activists believed that being future-oriented and hopeful marked a good, responsible citizen who would have the potential to transform the country. The connection between ethical citizenship and hopefulness is not unique to Lebanon. A futuristic politics characterized different projects of modernity and nation-making in other locales. Yet, in contrast to many communities around the world in which public actors invoked past experiences to shape people's horizons of expectations, most motivational public events in Lebanon focused heavily on the future, novelty, invention, and innovation.[23] Still, there were a few exceptions in which producing hope harnessed accounts of a memorable and inspiring past.

Future Rising on a Glorious Past

The popular documentary *The Lebanese Rocket Society* (2012), co-directed by Joana Hadjithomas and Khalil Joreige, is a good example of producing hope by unearthing the unrecognized past accomplishment and the unrealized potential of well-educated, talented, and resourceful patriotic Lebanese. The filmmakers, inspired by discovering a 1964 commemorative Independence Day postage stamp that displayed a rocket with a Lebanese flag, sought to document the long-forgotten but successful rocket research program of the early 1960s. The rocket program, initially called the Haigazian College Rocket Society, comprised the ambitious US-educated Lebanese Armenian professor Manoug Manougian and his seven undergraduate students.[24] The Society performed numerous rocket launches between 1960 and 1966 at the modest Haigazian University, which had been established in 1955 to cater to Lebanese Armenian students and had recently become a more diverse institution that attracted students from different ethnicities and sects. As the experiments of the program began to be successful, the Lebanese government and the army provided financial and logistic support. The group changed its name to the "Lebanese Rocket Society" and began naming its rockets after an iconic symbol of the nation, the cedar tree. Three of the launches were successful, including Cedar 4, which crossed the Kármán Line—an imagined boundary between Earth's atmosphere and outer space sixty-two miles above sea level—and which the 1964 Independence Day stamp commemorates. The team's work was closely monitored by representatives from the

CIA, Mossad, and the KGB, some of whom directly contacted Manougian several times. In the wake of the 1967 Six-Day War, also known as the third Arab–Israeli war, the program was forced to terminate by unnamed foreign governments. Its extraordinary success in rocket science was eventually erased from the collective memory, as demonstrated by the interviews the filmmakers conducted with diverse Lebanese.

The documentary presents the success of the program as a unique inspiration for the Lebanese, particularly the youth who lost hope in the country. It underscores the capacity of educated, hardworking youth to produce scientific progress and develop their nation. Yet the documentary's political message is ambivalent. It nostalgically portrays pan-Arabism, which was an influential anti-Western ideology in Lebanon and the broader region in the 1960s. At the same time, it implicitly criticizes anti-Western Hizbullah[25] and other factions in the region for weaponizing rockets and encourages "students from across the Middle East to fire rockets skywards, rather than at each other."[26] The documentary ends with a ten-minute animated sequence that depicts what Lebanon might have accomplished by 2026 if the rocket program had not been stopped. In that imagined future, Lebanon continues its productive scientific research, protects its border and sovereignty by deploying satellites, and achieves economic independence by surveying offshore oil. Beirut has an underground metro system and the "Lebanese" people, all of whom adopt Western-looking and secular dress, enjoy world-class infrastructure as well as a peaceful public life. Lebanon is finally able to claim its place among the developed and advanced nations of the world.

The counterfactual history that the documentary proposes suggests that past and present crises might have been prevented. The wars and conflicts might not have occurred, and the country's well-known businesses might have flourished without interruption, if only the commitment to scientific research—which Manougian's team exemplified—had endured. A successful rocket launch, the rocket flying and crossing borders, is a powerful metaphor for the ultimate modernist idea of individual and collective progress. The most optimistic message of the documentary is that it remains possible to create this future because Lebanon still has the same potential that led to the Lebanese Rocket Society in the 1960s. The story of interrupted progress, which the documentary convincingly articulates, invokes a temporal gap that the nation experienced after the long Lebanese War and offers solutions to overcome this gap. Lebanon's problems, the documentary conveys, result from outside interventions that prevent the nation from thriving. By encouraging the audience to connect to positive memories—to a past when youth passionately and successfully pursued their dreams—the documentary fosters patriotism and encourages dreaming for and believing in a better future during present crises.

I first watched the documentary on March 28, 2013, at Metropolis Empire Sofil theater in Ashrafieh—a major Christian-majority neighborhood in Beirut—during an *avant-première* (preview) co-organized by the feminist collective Nasawiya and a related NGO, the Anti-Racism Movement.[27] The two organizations had sold tickets for $13 each, with the revenue said to support their activities. The auditorium was at full capacity, and the audience—predominantly young, urban, middle-class-looking, and secularly dressed Lebanese—included many activists from civil society groups. I accompanied two middle-class activist friends, who had told me a week before that I should not miss the *avant-première* because many activists would come. At the salon, I greeted several friends and activist interlocutors who were curiously looking around to see who was there. The documentary began a little late and lasted for ninety-five minutes. The deep quietness in the room, together with the engaging story, made me think that the filmmakers had produced an iconic documentary.

The documentary was followed by a long and rapturous applause, and the audience seemed unanimously moved by its primary message—the potential of the Lebanese to carry their country to the level of civilized nations. I was struck by this rare moment of collective euphoria, which contrasted sharply with the sentiments of hopelessness and cynicism that dominated public life at the time. My two activist friends, who had frequently complained about Lebanon's problems previously, were moved to tears. Following the ovation, the three major subjects of the documentary—the Lebanese Armenian scientist and professor Manoug Manougian, who had initiated and led the rocket program; Hampar Karageozian, one of Manougian's students on the team; and Harry Koundakjian, the photographer who documented the experiments—had a discussion on stage. Their conversation was also frequently interrupted by applause, and the energetic crowd asked many questions.

The speakers, who called attention to the directors' concept of a "collective dream," emphasized the inspirational power of the documentary and explained how the Lebanese can learn from those who lived in the 1960s, who had pursued their dreams to accomplish extraordinary things with very limited resources. They offered the Lebanese public, in particular activists who worked for change, what they had long been searching for: a past to be proud of and a future to hope for. As we left the theater, I overheard people around us commenting "I'm impressed" and "I can't believe this is real." One of my activist friends told our group: "What is unimaginable now was imaginable before."

The documentary had a vibrant afterlife in shaping civil society in Lebanon. I heard many activists discuss the film during their meetings and reflect on the importance of science and education for building an independent and strong Lebanon. In 2014, a local youth-empowerment NGO in Beirut started a program on rocket science. It taught low-income Shiʿi youth scientific skills and provided motivational training to cultivate self-confidence and hopefulness. Lebanese TV channels covered the documentary and the history of the Lebanese Rocket Society,[28] and Lebanese bloggers wrote favorable reviews of the documentary and suggested that it would continue to inspire activists.[29] "This documentary will become an instant classic and will move a whole generation of Lebanon's increasingly vocal activists," wrote Joey Ayoub, a well-known activist, researcher, and writer, in his blog in April 2013. Over the next few years, I heard many Lebanese interlocutors, as well as friends from the Lebanese diaspora in the United States, enthusiastically praise the documentary for "reflecting the true essence of Lebanon" and for "giving hope to many Lebanese." As they did with other public events like TEDx LAU, many middle-class activists appreciated the documentary's depiction of well-educated youth as agents of change, and of educational institutions as main sites for this change.

The documentary received remarkable global recognition and won numerous accolades. It was screened at large festivals and local documentary theaters across the United States, Canada, Europe, Latin America, and the Middle East. It won the "Best Feature Documentary Award" at the Doha Film Festival and the Top Award at the Hong Kong Film Festival. Major media outlets, such as the BBC and *Smithsonian Magazine*, reviewed the documentary, interviewed Manougian, and highlighted the exceptional potential of the Lebanese and Lebanon.[30]

The Lebanese Rocket Society and the rich conversations it generated represent a different way of producing hope that renders the past inspiring and motivating, rather than dark and dreadful. In contrast to public events such as TEDx LAU, which ask participants to focus only on the future, the documentary frames the past as a potential source of collective and individual inspiration. The documentary seeks to cultivate agency by encouraging the audience to imagine a thriving Lebanon as not only a future possibility but an experience that already took place and could be modeled again in the present. In doing so, it powerfully weaves together "space of experience" (present past) and "horizon of expectation" (future made present)[31] and offers a collective narrative about modernity and progress that dislodges the centrality of sectarianism. According to historian Reinhart Koselleck, the gap between space of experience and horizon of expectation, produced by modernity's temporal logics of rupture between the past and the future, was the source of modern sentiments of crisis. In the modernist conception of history, the linear notion of progress, which emerged in the middle of the eighteenth century, favored newness and futurity over remembrance of the past. This notion of progress also rendered past experience as irrelevant and framed the future as an open-ended horizon of expectations. The documentary challenges the public tendency to disavow Lebanon's past, instead choosing to foreground positive spaces of experience. In doing so, it effectively contests a widespread, pessimistic view that something is inherently wrong with Lebanon and offers a more coherent, collective narrative that connects the past, present, and future.

Pedagogies of Dreaming

In late 2012, several of my interlocutors insisted that I attend an event called "The Dream Matcher" to see a "different picture" (*ṣūra mukhtalifa*). When I asked them what they meant by "different picture," they told me that the event brought together people from diverse backgrounds, and that its structure of fun activities offered a unique experience.

The Dream Matcher event was launched in January 2012 at AltCity, a popular café in Hamra which was frequented by activists and entrepreneurs. In few months, the event gained popularity and began to attract diverse groups of young Beirut residents. The event was advertised in English:

> Join us at the BEST networking event in Lebanon, a one-of-a-kind event where dreams come true! Our previous events in Beirut, Lebanon were a great success. In Silicon Valley a few participants commented that it is "the best networking event they ever attended." Join us and you might be

> lucky enough to find a match who would make a dream of yours come true, be it learning a language, meeting a celebrity, getting hypnotized, playing a musical instrument, visiting a place, or even trying an extreme sport. Your imagination is your limit. You might even be luckier to be the one to make someone else's dream come true![32]

Throughout 2013, this advertisement was posted on Facebook and sent through a variety of email lists, including the largest event-coordinating internet platform in the country, Lebtivity, which advertised the event on its calendar. Lebanon's major media outlets also promoted the event series. As the success of the event series grew, the organizers licensed many trainers and public speakers to execute the event format in other Lebanese cities and overseas, including in Dubai, Istanbul, and Madrid. A Syrian activist interlocutor, who had been living in Beirut since 2013, told me on WhatsApp that a Dream Matcher event was hosted in Homs, Syria, in October 2017. The event organizers publicized the events between 2017 and 2023 as "Lebanon's longest running networking event" and "Lebanon's most successful networking event."[33]

Ali Chehade, who founded the Dream Matcher and was its main organizer in Beirut, received numerous accolades from the media, which portrayed him as a successful entrepreneur who offered Lebanese a new and alternative culture of networking.[34] Having graduated from the Department of Communication Arts at LAU in 2007, Ali received a Fusion Arts Exchange Program Scholarship for a six-week workshop at the University of Southern California. Following formal training at the AMIDEAST office in Beirut, he was awarded a Fulbright Scholarship to enroll in a master of arts program in professional media and media management at Draper University. During our interview in 2014, the youth program coordinator at the AMIDEAST Beirut Office cited Ali as an example of a successful young beneficiary who "turned their dreams into concrete projects." Ali continued participating in the professional events in the United States after completing his master's degree. For instance, he experimented with the Dream Matcher event format during his visit to Stanford University in 2013 to attend the international AMENDS (American Middle Eastern Network for Dialogue at Stanford) conference, a student initiative that annually brings together youth from across the globe.

The Dream Matcher events in Beirut occurred on the first Wednesday of each month. I participated in the event five times during 2013 and 2014 and observed the types of people who attended, the issues they discussed, and how they responded to each other's dreams. Participants were mainly young university graduates in their twenties and early thirties, most of whom were unemployed or underemployed. They came from various parts of Lebanon and were remarkably diverse in terms of their political and sectarian affiliations. For instance, at each event, I saw a couple of young women who wore headscarves as well as glowing makeup and fashionable outfits, which contrasted with the more secular dress of the urban middle-class female participants.

The events were scheduled at 8:00 p.m. Tickets were sold for $10 and included one soft drink, redeemable at the entrance of the café. Participants were welcomed at the door by a young, smiling, energetic team, who asked them to fill out a short form. Once we were registered and our nametags and table numbers were pinned to our shirts, we were sent to our randomly assigned tables. There were around nine to twelve tables in the café space, each with the capacity to seat five to seven people. Because the organizers wanted participants to mingle with strangers, we were not allowed to choose who we sat with.

The event usually began with a speech by Ali about the significance of having dreams and, more importantly, having "dreams that are worth pursuing." Both Ali's introductory speech and the fliers that sat on the big rectangular tables of the café carefully guided how participants thought about and wrote down their dreams. The fliers gave concrete instructions and provided specific descriptions and examples of realistic dreams. In Step 1, we were asked to write down three of our dreams on three different stickers and post them on the Dream Wall. The flier defined a dream as "any goal you wish to achieve" and stated that "the people who will turn dreams to reality are around you tonight." The instructions on the flier further categorized dreams under three headings: High Match Rate, Low Match Rate, and Very Low Match Rate. Goals like learning Spanish, learning photography, taking a road trip around Lebanon, and visiting a chocolate factory were under the High Match Rate category; getting a job at Google and traveling to Australia were listed under Low Match Rate; and world peace, marrying Angelina Jolie, and flying to Mars were categorized under Very Low Match Rate. As with activities at the TEDx LAU event, the Dream Matcher activities provided clear instructions for how to dream in ways that would yield positive results.

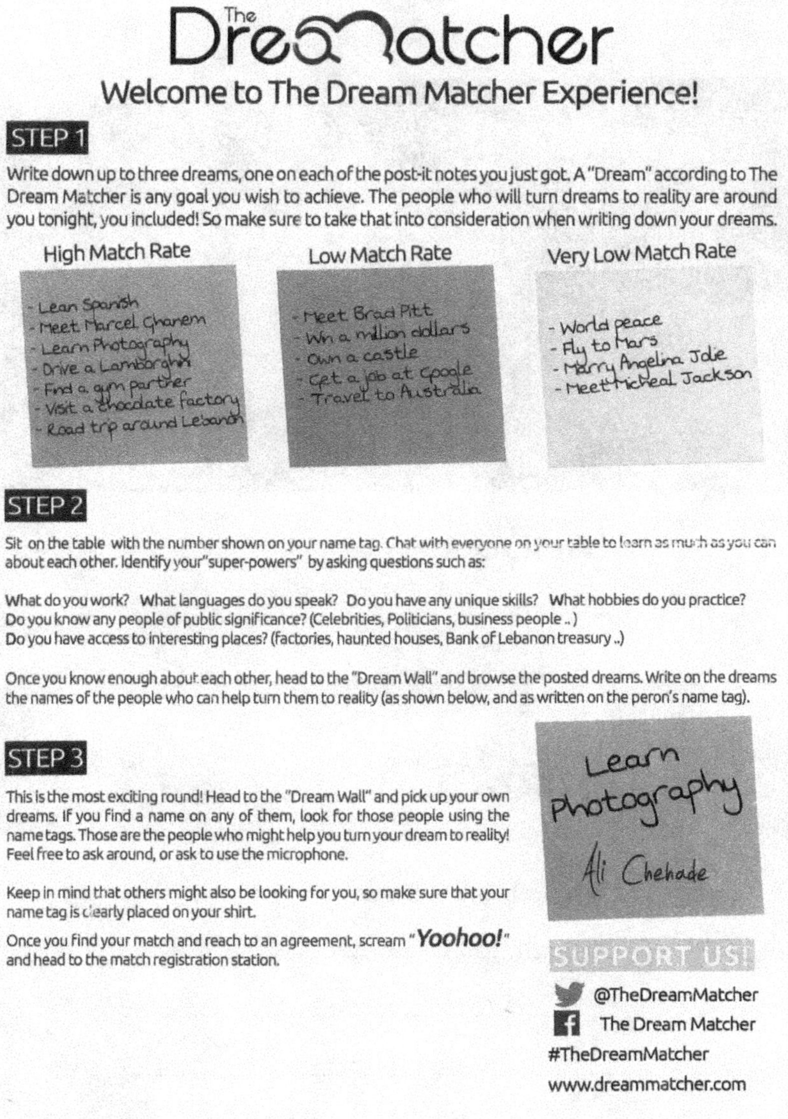

The DreamMatcher

Welcome to The Dream Matcher Experience!

STEP 1

Write down up to three dreams, one on each of the post-it notes you just got. A "Dream" according to The Dream Matcher is any goal you wish to achieve. The people who will turn dreams to reality are around you tonight, you included! So make sure to take that into consideration when writing down your dreams.

High Match Rate

- Lean Spanish
- Meet Marcel Ghanem
- Learn Photography
- Drive a Lamborghini
- Find a gym partner
- Visit a chocolate factory
- Road trip around Lebanon

Low Match Rate

- Meet Brad Pitt
- Win a million dollars
- Own a castle
- Get a job at Google
- Travel to Australia

Very Low Match Rate

- World peace
- Fly to Mars
- Marry Angelina Jolie
- Meet Micheal Jackson

STEP 2

Sit on the table with the number shown on your name tag. Chat with everyone on your table to learn as much as you can about each other. Identify your "super-powers" by asking questions such as:

What do you work? What languages do you speak? Do you have any unique skills? What hobbies do you practice?
Do you know any people of public significance? (Celebrities, Politicians, business people ..)
Do you have access to interesting places? (Factories, haunted houses, Bank of Lebanon treasury ..)

Once you know enough about each other, head to the "Dream Wall" and browse the posted dreams. Write on the dreams the names of the people who can help turn them to reality (as shown below, and as written on the peron's name tag).

STEP 3

This is the most exciting round! Head to the "Dream Wall" and pick up your own dreams. If you find a name on any of them, look for those people using the name tags. Those are the people who might help you turn your dream to reality! Feel free to ask around, or ask to use the microphone.

Keep in mind that others might also be looking for you, so make sure that your name tag is clearly placed on your shirt.

Once you find your match and reach to an agreement, scream "***Yoohoo!***" and head to the match registration station.

Learn Photography
Ali Chehade

SUPPORT US!

@TheDreamMatcher
The Dream Matcher
#TheDreamMatcher
www.dreammatcher.com

FIGURES 11. A pamphlet and two sides of a ticket. The Dream Matcher event. December 4, 2013.

Your TICKET to fulfill
Your DREAMS!

Location: Beirut
Date: 4/12/13
Price: $10

The DreaMatcher™

Matches I found:

Name Contact

Name Contact

Name Contact

FIGURES 11. (Continued)

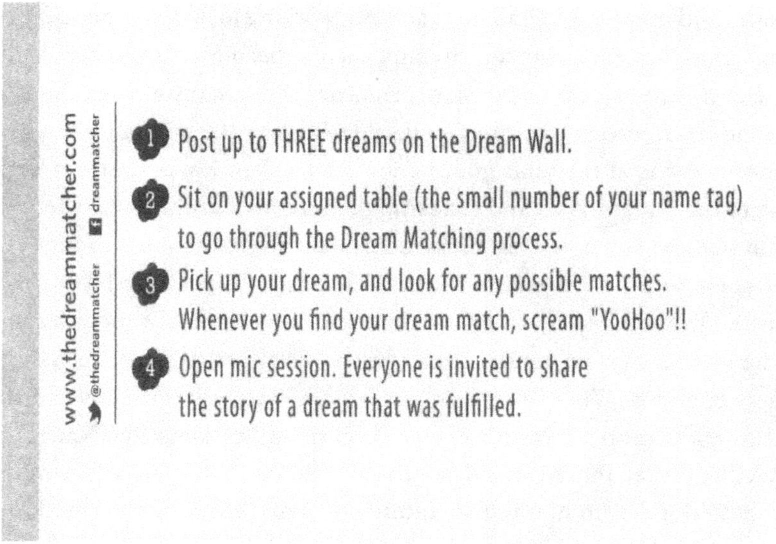

www.thedreammatcher.com
@thedreammatcher
dreammatcher
1 Post up to THREE dreams on the Dream Wall.
2 Sit on your assigned table (the small number of your name tag) to go through the Dream Matching process.
3 Pick up your dream, and look for any possible matches. Whenever you find your dream match, scream "YooHoo"!!
4 Open mic session. Everyone is invited to share the story of a dream that was fulfilled.

FIGURES 11. (Continued)

When we moved to Step 2, which asked participants to chat with everyone at their table and learn as much as they could about each other's lives, there was usually an awkward silence at the beginning. Writing down and posting dreams anonymously felt exciting, but sharing one's dreams at a table among strangers was not easy. My dreams such as "adopting an orphaned child" or "starting a book club in Arabic" were often unappealing to the others at the table. They were not impossible but did not match the other participants' entrepreneurial dreams, such as founding a consulting company for the environment or starting a cosmetics business that would showcase the true natural beauty of Lebanese women. Nevertheless, I had a variety of interesting conversations. Some of the participants at my table turned out to be passionate entrepreneurs who were trying to launch two or three new start-ups or social entrepreneurship projects simultaneously. I was impressed by the extensive details some of them provided about their efforts to advance their projects. For instance, a bright Armenian Lebanese man in his late twenties from a low-income background dreamt of opening Armenian restaurants in different parts of Lebanon. In addition to thoroughly researching successful restaurants in Lebanon, he had already contacted several local political figures for help in finding suitable locations. In contrast to what most activists organizing such events assumed, many young Lebanese were already filled with hopes and dreams and had been actively working to achieve them. Nevertheless, most of their "concrete" dreams, such as becoming a successful entrepreneur or traveling the world, were primarily individualistic, even though some could be framed as contributing to the society or the nation.

Once everyone at the table got to know each other, it was time for Step 3: going to the Dream Wall and checking the posted dreams to see whether we could help realize any. The sticky notes were posted in one of four categories classifying the dreams: "Visit," "Learn," "Meet," and "Other" (Figure 12). In the "Learn" category, the dreams were mostly about learning a new language or musical instrument or practicing performance arts such as acting. The "Visit" category included predominantly North American and European countries and, occasionally, places like Nepal or an eco-village that the educated youth considered "alternative." Almost no one posted a dream about love, family, or marriage at the events I attended, possibly because the Dream Matcher was commonly seen as a professional networking event. The "Meet" category included both "realistic" and "unrealistic" dreams: meeting a tango partner or a famous football player. Some of the dreams in the "Other" category were "driving a Ferrari," "building my own house," "becoming a TV presenter," "skydiving,"

FIGURE 12. The Dream Matcher Event, Reading Stickers. December 4, 2013. Photo by Author.

"singing in an Arabic band," and "publishing a children's book." At each stage, Ali and his assistants actively guided the participants by visiting the tables, making sure everyone had gotten to know each other, and encouraging quieter participants to speak up.

With the expectation of finding something relevant to their own interests, each participant read the notes that others had posted on the huge windows of the café. There were also instructions for matching dreams with each other: if you thought the dream on a sticky note matched your own dreams or abilities and you could help make that dream come true, you were supposed to write your name at the bottom. Around a hundred anonymous dreams hung on the café windows, waiting for someone to help realize them. More than 90 percent of the posts were in English; the rest were in Arabic. In the events I attended, I noticed that very few participants wrote their names on someone else's sticker. But the three organizers on AltCity's event team wrote their own names on many, particularly on dreams related to basic computer skills, photography, or language skills. The organizers encouraged the participants to be involved in this collaborative activity and support each other to make their dreams come true.

The Dream Matcher aligned well with the broader middle-class activist framework of crisiswork, which focused on cultivating ethical citizenship and non-sectarian culture and selfhood. Ali later told me during a long interview in March 2014 that one of the major goals of the Dream Matcher was to bring together Lebanese from different confessional communities. Even though the Dream Matcher was mainly promoted as a motivational networking event that offered a cosmopolitan experience, this comment about fostering peaceful coexistence among the Lebanese revealed Ali's additional political goals. He emphasized the uniqueness of the Dream Matcher event: "There are other entrepreneurship-related networking events in Beirut. But here, you have to talk to strangers, it is required, the structure of the event forces people to speak to others." He went on to explain that the Lebanese found it hard to interact with strangers because Lebanon's history of war and sectarianism had created divisions and polarized the country. Then he offered a moral critique of "selfish Lebanese people," which I had heard from many Lebanese, activists and others, since my first visit to Beirut. Ali, like many of my interlocutors, referred to the selfishness of the Lebanese as a fact that everyone, including me, apparently agreed with: "As you also probably know, Lebanese culture is opportunistic; people are very selfish. We don't think of others." He hoped that through events like the Dream Matcher the culture would change and Lebanese people would become more open to and supportive of others.

Ali's vision reflected the middle-class fantasy of self-enclosed and conflicting Lebanese communities.[35] In his live interviews with major Arab media outlets during 2013 and 2014, Ali similarly explained that the rationale behind the Dream Matcher was to overcome conflict and divisions in Lebanon. For instance, in his live interview with LBC—a prominent Lebanese TV channel—Ali proudly connected the event to larger political goals, such as reconciliation and coexistence (*al-ʿaysh al-mushtarak*): "We, the Lebanese society, are not used to sitting and chatting with people we do not know. We do not share our desires and dreams with others. For this reason, the Dream Matcher is a very different and beautiful idea."[36] Ali also viewed the event as a crucial site of affect management that helped Lebanese become happier and more positive. In an interview in August 2015 with Future TV—a pro-Sunni channel founded by Rafiq Hariri in 1993—Ali responded to the program presenter's question about the origin of the Dream Matcher. He said, in Arabic, "I am the kind of person who gets very happy when helping people with anything. This feeling, I believe, exists in everyone; it's human psychology. When we open a door for someone, we feel like a superman, happy, and relaxed for many hours."[37]

Promoting dreaming entailed more than fostering cross-sectarian interaction, altruism, and individual happiness. The complex pedagogies of dreaming (e.g., cultivating realistic dreams, fostering well-being, and promoting peaceful coexistence) that were employed at the TEDx LAU, the Dream Matcher, and similar events, conveyed middle-class concerns about growing aspirations for social mobility in Beirut. Some of the representatives from youth programs in consultancy companies and prominent banks I talked to similarly distinguished between "practical/attainable dreams" (*aḥlām ʿamaliyya*) and "fictitious/improbable dreams" (*aḥlām khayāliyya*). Those representatives criticized Lebanese youth for chasing dreams of wealth without adequately considering their individual capabilities and social circumstances. "Everybody wants to open a new business," a youth program representative in one of the largest Lebanese banks told me in March 2014. He continued, "It's a nice dream. But it's impossible for everyone to open a business. It requires preparation, connections, experience, and much more. We help our youth better assess their circumstances and make better decisions about their future." A few months prior, in October 2013, a youth program coordinator at a prominent consultancy company in Beirut had told me, "You ask high schoolers now, 'What is your dream?' and they tell you earning a million dollars. This is not a dream. A dream is your purpose in life that would fulfill you and also help others around you." These middle-class criticisms of popular aspirations for becoming rich reveal an inherent contradiction in the way that "dreaming" was held up as an ideal: The message was that Lebanese youth should freely dream, but they also needed guidance on how to dream in ways that conformed to the class status quo. Ambivalences and contradictions continued to characterize middle-class projects of hope and dreaming as desired better futures were continually deferred.

Unfulfilled Hopes and Critiques of Deferral

What happens to a dream deferred?
Does it dry up like a raisin in the sun?
Or fester like a sore—
And then run?
Does it stink like rotten meat?
Or crust and sugar over—
like a syrupy sweet?
Maybe it just sags
like a heavy load.
Or does it explode?[38]

Producing hope as a political and social practice poses several moral questions about political change, solidarity, and responsibility. For example, who would be accountable if the "seeds planted" during the TEDx LAU event in 2013 did not bear fruit by 2020? The broadened horizon of expectation within the modernist teleology of such events promises of a better tomorrow that is based on an assumption of continuous progress. Over time, however, the deferral of modernity's promises of progress and change, and the unfulfilled hopes that result, might culminate in a sense of crisis, worthlessness, and fatigue.[39] Many older activist cohorts in Lebanon expressed intense frustration with the unmet promises of activism. For example, Sama, a then forty-two-year-old leftist Lebanese-Palestinian activist who had long worked for the Palestinian cause, was highly critical of motivational public events that targeted change through producing hope. Her complaints during our Skype conversation in September 2016 exemplified such frustrations:

> I remember the discourses of Rafiq Hariri. They were exactly the same as the public events you mention: Hope, willpower, we can do it, forgo the past, you should continue working, blah, blah, blah. I also remember the promises of spring (*wuʿūd al-rabīʿ*) that Hariri made when he became PM the first time. "By spring, Lebanon will have electricity and infrastructure," and so on. The spring passed, and nothing happened. We had accumulated debt, social inequalities deepened. It became a joke in the late 1990s—if anyone does not do as promised, they say (*wuʿūd al-rabīʿ*). The situation is even worse now, and you have many people ageing in this country and becoming more and more frustrated with unfulfilled hopes.

Sama's comments about the optimistic discourses of future and change, which the motivational public events I attended promoted, conveyed frustrations about the empty rhetoric of hope that had brought nothing but disappointment. Optimistic depictions of the future did not mean much to Sama, given her personal experience of decades of deferred hopes, unfulfilled promises, and political deception. Sama viewed civil society activism as resembling mainstream Lebanese politics, in contrast to many Lebanese activists that typically construed themselves as alternatives to corrupt Lebanese politicians. We discussed whether a progressive activist project should refrain from making future promises or raising hope for better futures, but our conversation on this was inconclusive. Both Sama and I still continue to ponder the question.

During my fieldwork and in subsequent years, I heard many of my experienced activist interlocutors express disillusionment with civil society projects and movements for change. Casual conversations were replete with frustrated expressions of endless waiting. A rich tapestry of everyday phrases symbolized local frustration with the still-not-coming aspect of "yet to come."[40] The most popular and bitterly humorous phrase that described the frustration with waiting was *nayyamūnā*. Literally translated as "they [the political class] made us sleep," the phrase was used to describe the idea that "we were waiting too much, so we became bored, then tired, and then fell asleep." Several proverbs described frustration over deferred dreams, such as, "Here we are waiting, until Allah helps us" (*Hayyna nāṭrīn la-Allah yfarrijhā*) and "Here we are waiting, we don't have anything else to do but wait" (*Hayyna nāṭrīn, mā fī shī warānā*).

Thus, producing hope could also lead to the dynamic that Berlant termed "cruel optimism"—the promises of a good life prompt dreams, such as job security and political equality, that are increasingly unattainable for many because of the inherent problems and structural inequalities of the social system.[41] The very pursuit of dreams could undermine one's well-being through frustration, disappointment, and stuckness. Optimism becomes cruel insofar as people who ardently pursue unattainable dreams become depressed and traumatized when structural conditions shatter those dreams.

Therein lies the main paradox of middle-class crisiswork's production of futuristic hopes. Being hopeful—particularly in contexts like Lebanon where crises are felt as both chronic and worsening—centers on cultivating a subjectivity that focuses on the future while ignoring the past and present. When the long-awaited "post-crisis" future (e.g., of 2020 or 2030) eventually becomes the present, and ultimately the past, profound disappointment arises. Yet, because the future-oriented middle-class crisiswork dictates uninterrupted production of hope, Lebanese activists often refuse to collectively talk about disappointment, which they view as a "negative" emotion that undermines their agency. Consequently, the possibility of productive engagements with problems in existing activist projects and with negative affects such as disappointment, disillusionment, and suspicion are curtailed. "I am only disappointed with the Lebanese political class. Civil society is doing its best," Layal told me in the summer of 2016, when I asked her what she felt about the "failure" of the activist-led Beirut Madinati movement in that spring's municipal elections. She then changed the subject. Other interlocutors reacted similarly to my questions about failure or disappointment about activism. Only a few Lebanese activists I met rigorously reflected upon their "failed" projects or activities and where they might have gone wrong.

It is not that activists did not feel disappointment; I witnessed them expressing disappointment as an individual feeling, but they explicitly refused to acknowledge and discuss it collectively. When activists viewed a project as a "failure," they typically described it as "an experience" (*tajruba*) to learn from and called for positivity and hope, asking everyone to avoid discussions of "negative" incidents. Evading the past by recasting it as an abstract field of experiences that does not need deeper reflection, however, could prevent meaningful change in existing strategies and practices. In its cruel optimism of relentlessly hanging onto hope for a post-crisis future, crisiswork rejects a constructive collective engagement with both experiences of failure and feelings of disappointment. The futurism of crisiswork ironically bounds activist futures.

Many Lebanese found themselves more and more frustrated as their dreams went unfulfilled and the country's crises worsened. Though many motivational public events held between 2012 and 2015 had envisioned a better Lebanon by 2020, that year was instead one of the most difficult in the country's recent history. On August 4, 2020, the detonation of 2,750 tons of ammonium nitrate in Beirut's port killed 218 people and injured about 7,000.[42] Amid plummeting public trust in state institutions and ongoing mass protests against corruption, the World Bank characterized Lebanon's situation in 2020 as one of the worst economic crises globally since the mid-nineteenth century. When Layal and I had a video chat on WhatsApp in March 2021, she was still shocked by and sad about the accelerating crises in the country. She had lived since 2020 in Dubai, where she had moved her consultancy company from Beirut. After we talked at length about the developments in 2020, she remarked,

> Do you remember that we had mentioned #Lebanon2020 in our workshops? I had really believed that things would be different in 2020. Look at us now. I didn't completely lose my hope for Lebanon, but it's different now. It's more than a crisis. I don't know what to call it.

This was not the first time a Lebanese activist lamented the worsening crises and grieved the loss of hope for a better future. My fieldnotes are filled with numerous instances of such grief. Not everyone or every suffering in Lebanon, however, was seen as worthy of grieving. Most Lebanese activists viewed refugees and migrant workers in Lebanon as obstacles to producing present hopes and post-crisis futures. Identifying the Lebanese as primary victims of Lebanon's crises and of agents of change, and refusing to acknowledge Others' contributions to crisiswork, they bounded futures of collective and just liberation.

SIX

Exceptional Victimhoods

On the evening of September 24, 2013, leading Lebanese activists from diverse backgrounds filled AltCity Café in Beirut to attend the "Social Good Summit," an annual conference that is organized by the UNDP and takes place simultaneously in major cities across the globe. The year's theme was the use of social media for sustainable advocacy and social change. Nearly fifty activists and journalists, who represented different organizations and movements with diverse political positions, sat around small marble tables. They looked around and greeted participants they knew. A little before 6 p.m., I headed to a table with Hala, a Sunni middle-class activist friend who worked at a local environmental advocacy NGO (whose story was shared in Chapter 2). We each greeted several activists from prominent advocacy organizations in Beirut, whom we knew, and then enjoyed free canapés and drinks.

Marie, one of the activists at our table, was a low-income Armenian Lebanese woman who had been volunteering for several years with feminist organizations. She asked me the names of the few participants I had greeted and said she was hoping to meet new people at the event, including the "high-profile" activists that UN events tended to attract. Having interviewed her before, I knew that by "high-profile" she meant successful, leading middle-class figures in Beirut civil society. Marie was right—even though the event was open to the public, most speakers and participants were well-known, middle-class professionals who had a long trajectory of participation and leadership in civil society organizations and campaigns.

The event included three sessions focused on strategies for the effective use of social media in promoting activist causes. The first two sessions went smoothly. Like other events organized by international organizations, the presentations and follow-up discussions took place in Arabic and English. Many participants seemed enthusiastic about the topic and the event. They expressed appreciation for the informative presentations by Ayman Itani, a social media professor at LAU, and Khodor Salamah, an experienced activist and blogger. The final session, however, which focused on the need to represent Syrian refugee voices in Lebanon on social media, led to fierce debate among the audience.

Many representatives of leading Lebanese advocacy groups confronted the session's presenter Patricia Khoder, a senior reporter at *L'Orient-Le Jour*, for bringing up this issue, which they deemed "disrespectful to the sensitivities of Lebanon." They were upset at being called to attend to and engage with Syrian refugees and their problems. A female activist in her late twenties, who represented a well-known local organization that focused on women's rights, did not hide her anger: "I am angry. We, the Lebanese, suffer more, but nobody talks about us; it is all about Syrians. Okay, let's talk about them. But please with practical solutions (*ḥulūl ʿamaliyya*) that benefit all of us." Several others joined and articulated a scale of suffering that prioritized the problems of Lebanese: "We have so many problems now, why are we helping them?" "We are the victims (*al-ḍaḥāyā*), no one sees that." "Lebanon cannot carry all these." "Our system already does not work; it was already suspended, and now they [Syrians] stop it fully." "We already have many unemployed people; how can we have jobs for all of them?"

Patricia Khoder respectfully listened to the participants' complaints and tried to explain how fostering communication between host and refugee communities could potentially help address these issues. Yet, most participants seemed unconvinced. After the event ended, several Lebanese activists I knew continued to share their frustrations about the session. They were upset about their perception that Syrian refugees were placed at the center of many international meetings and felt that the problems of Lebanese were overlooked in favor of Syrian refugees' problems. They believed that Lebanon had been going through "exceptional" times and that "too much" was demanded of Lebanese people.

Crisiswork—in its hyper-focus on Lebanese problems understood as emanating from the nation's exceptional crises—systematically invokes victimhood. In a context in which international humanitarian aid was increasingly shifting its attention to Syrian refugees—even as Lebanon's political and economic circumstances were deteriorating—civil society meetings, such as the Social Good Summit, could potentially turn into spaces where hierarchies of victimhood are articulated. Lebanese activists often used the English term "victim" and the Arabic term *ḍaḥiyya* (victim) to refer to an imagined category of Lebanese civilians who were not sectarian but were negatively affected by issues related to sectarianism.

In this context, "victimhood" not only constitutes a descriptor of a social fact or a collective narrative; it is a crucial invocation of both political and moral capital—a claim for care for groups designated as victims.[1] In comparing the scope of the manifold crises Lebanese and Syrians faced, many Lebanese activists in civil society demanded that more attention be given to Lebanon's problems and the everyday struggles of the Lebanese. They did not deny that Syrians in Lebanon needed urgent support, but they believed that the Syrian War had disproportionately affected the Lebanese population and that these repercussions were invisible. In making the ethical and political choice to prioritize Lebanon and the Lebanese, many activists explicitly refused to engage with the predicament and suffering of Syrian refugees.

In contrast, some activists critiqued the idea of prioritizing Lebanese people's problems, although they were well aware that they represented a minority voice within Beirut's prominent civil society circles. Hala, for instance, expressed her frustration, not with Khodor's session, but with the audience's intense negative response. She had several Syrian relatives, and as an adherent to Arab nationalism, she strongly believed in solidarity between Lebanese and Syrian people. She actively supported various displaced Syrian activists in Lebanon with their grassroots projects that offered financial aid, food, and legal assistance to displaced Syrian families. While the audience fiercely debated the role of Lebanese civil society, Hala told me about a new project she was working on with Syrian activists. Overhearing our conversation, Marie smiled at us and commented, "Lebanese are racist, right?" (*al-libnāniyyīn ʿunṣuriyyīn, mish hayk?*). I remained silent, but Hala smiled and responded, "Yes, I'm with you (*anā maʿik*), but don't say that to others here." Because Christian communities tended to be more outspoken against Syrian refugees, Marie probably felt the need to showcase her own pro-refugee views.

Syrian refugees and Lebanon's other refugee and migrant communities were popular topics of discussion among activists, who exhibited a multiplicity of shifting positions on these issues. Many activists, echoing discourses circulating in the wider society, blamed Syrians for further disrupting Lebanon's already fragile order. They viewed both the Syrian War and the related refugee crisis as dragging the country into further polarization and violence. Other activists did not directly blame Syrians for Lebanon's disorder, and instead accused Western countries of burdening already "weak" countries like Lebanon with their refusal to accept more refugees into Europe or to provide more aid. They shared the more general concern, however, that the Syrian refugee presence threatened Lebanese stability and nation-building—just as the presence of Palestinian refugees was often believed to have historically produced the same effect—and likewise refused to focus their activism on Syrian refugees. Other activists, such as Hala and Marie, endorsed what became an increasingly popular explanation for public incidents of discrimination against Syrians and other refugee and migrant communities: Lebanese racism. While this explanation tended to characterize Lebanese responses to Syrians and others as unacceptable or inhumane, it unwittingly perpetuated Lebanese exceptionalism by depicting racism as an inherent quality of the Lebanese. In framing racism as an inherent character quality of an individual or a community, such explanations also glossed over complex histories of nation-state formation, colonial racialization practices, and global structures of racial capitalism that affected Lebanon.[2]

Crisiswork in Lebanon is essentially built upon the material, physical, and affective labor of various refugee and migrant communities whose presence in and contributions to Lebanese activist lifeworlds are systematically invisibilized. Syrian refugees, similar to Palestinian and Iraqi refugees, participate in activist spaces, taking up numerous roles such as protesters, volunteers, campaign organizers, project coordinators, workshop trainers and participants. Nevertheless, and in order to be accepted, many of them choose to conceal their ethnic backgrounds, seeking to pass as Lebanese. Migrant workers from countries such as Ethiopia and Bangladesh regularly perform cleaning services in spaces activists frequented such as NGO offices, hotel conference rooms, college auditoriums, cafés, and restaurants. They offer, among other forms of labor, cleaning, cooking, nursing, and childcare for activists and their family members, helping many Lebanese endure the complex daily impacts of crisiswork. This tremendous amount of labor frees time and offers myriad resources for activists, including some low-income activists, and their crisiswork, yet it is remarkably unacknowledged. Despite their involvement in almost all aspects of daily life, migrant and refugee communities are continually made to feel by many Lebanese, including activists, excluded and unbelonging to Lebanon.

Many Lebanese activist interlocutors were highly cognizant of the exploitative conditions that refugee and migrant communities endured in Lebanon and other countries. Some of these activists were even involved in well-funded humanitarian and developmental projects assisting refugees and migrants and actively contributed to raising awareness about their marginalization. Yet there was a tacit refusal to recognize, engage with, and collaborate with marginalized communities in the day-to-day life of crisiswork. What made these communities' predicaments so invisible or peripheral to activists' crisiswork? How might one productively understand this apparent indifference, or event contempt, for displaced Syrians and other refugee and migrant communities in Lebanon?

Examining the post-September 11 context, cultural theorist Judith Butler addresses the question of how some people's suffering may become ungrievable.[3] Focusing specifically on discourses and practices related to wars and military operations, Butler suggests that grievability is a central premise for a valuable and sustainable life.[4] Mainstream discourses frame some lives as more valuable, and hence more worthy of grieving when harmed, than others. In particular, refugee and migrant bodies are often framed as a threat to security and national stability, particularly in globally circulating discourses concerning receiving countries. As a result, their suffering and death are denied grievability.[5] Dispossessed mobile communities have been historically dehumanized and rendered disposable in multiple contexts.[6] Thus, the loss of socially privileged individual and collective lives is more readily mourned than those of socially marginalized groups.

Nevertheless, in the Lebanese context, a refusal to grieve for certain communities is an expression of not only exclusionary power but also precariousness and vulnerability. In this sense, displaced Syrians and other refugee and migrant communities are denied grievability because they are deemed *both* less valuable *and* less worthy of victim status than the Lebanese. In this context, understanding this rendering of certain communities' suffering as unworthy of grief requires attending to the complex historicity of collective memory and of narratives of exceptionalism and victimhood in Lebanon.

In examining the ungrievability of Syrian refugees and other marginalized communities, I focus on the internal contradictions of activists' crisiswork, which I contextualize within uneven histories of colonialism, nation-making, and dynamics of belonging and exclusion in Lebanon. As previously discussed, crisiswork—the multiplicity of activist responses to the nation's crises—is not immune to practices of exclusionary identification of particular individuals and communities as obstacles to desired political and social change. The uneducated urban and rural poor, who were widely depicted as an obstacle to building a collective national identity and a progressive sense of citizenship, were the primary "others" of activists' crisiswork. In particular, some activists denigrated low-income Shiʿi communities, who were portrayed as lacking proper codes of urbanity and cultural taste, for being deeply loyal to political and religious leaders in ways that perpetuated violence and incivility. Yet, since the beginning of the Syrian War, racializing representations and attitudes toward displaced Syrians tended to replace, or at least diminish, the previously more pervasive prejudice among activists against the urban poor, suggesting a reordering of exclusionary hierarchies.

I use the term "exceptional victimhood" to refer to how victimhood and exceptionalism narratives interlace to render displaced Syrians, migrant workers, and other marginalized people in Lebanon ungrievable. Lebanese activists' crisiswork was premised on unexamined and taken-for-granted narratives of exceptional victimhood. Many activists believed that Lebanon—which they saw as nearing collapse—was an exceptionally victimized nation. At the same time, they and many other Lebanese saw themselves as an exceedingly "qualified" people who faced exceptionally strenuous trials, such as the repercussion of the Syrian War on Lebanon's already precarious state of affairs. An underlying thread in activists' otherization of different communities was their fear that what they perceived as an exceptionally fragile order was further weakened, potentially in unrepairable ways, and with the Lebanese as the primary victims. Representations of Lebanon as a nation subjected to exceptional trials and crises throughout its history—yet also gifted with exceptional human potential—were widely used to justify the refusal to care for Syrian and other refugee and migrant communities. Moreover, the historical memory of a nation almost always in crisis because of outside forces is fundamental to understanding the post-Syrian War moral frameworks of victimhood and related grievances that render Lebanese lives more grievable than others.

Activists articulated multiple, competing victimhoods by invoking Lebanese exceptionalism. Similarly to crisis narratives, narratives of victimhood and exceptionalism are not monolithic—they are, rather, heterogeneous, open-ended, contradictory, and disjunctive. Activists' ambivalent interpretations of multiple variants of such narratives mobilized contradictory political and cultural practices within diverse lifeworlds. Examining how and why Lebanese activists experienced the mounting effects of the Syrian War, as well as with the growing presence of displaced Syrians in Lebanon, shows how crisiswork could function simultaneously as a colonizing and a decolonizing endeavor. Correspondingly, contextualizing and historicizing the ungrievability of specific Others in Lebanon reveal how activist practices may perpetuate and also contest ongoing legacies of colonialism.

Syrian Refugees and Lebanese Activists

Between 2011 and 2014, more than a million registered Syrian refugees arrived in Lebanon, making the tiny country host to the largest refugee population per capita in the world. In 2015, the total number of Syrians in Lebanon, including unregistered refugees and migrants, surpassed a quarter of Lebanon's previous population of 4.4 million.[7] During this period, there were also other refugees and asylum seekers, including those from Sudan and Iraq, but they did not receive much attention from local media nor were they prioritized by humanitarian organizations such as the United Nations High Commissioner for Refugees (UNHCR).[8] Framing the massive Syrian displacement through discourses of emergency and crisis, UNHCR and other prominent international organizations—including European embassies and cultural centers as well as development and human rights groups—turned their attention on Syrian refugees. For Western stakeholders, civil society efforts in Lebanon needed to be channeled to humanitarian interventions for Syrian refugees.

Throughout 2013, Michel Aoun and Samir Geagea, the leaders of the two major Christian parties in Lebanon, publicly claimed that Syrian refugees in Lebanon constituted a significant danger to the country.[9] In 2014, the Lebanon's Council of Ministers adopted a policy focused on encouraging Syrians to return to Syria, and the Lebanese General Security Directorate introduced new and more stringent requirements for Syrians' applications for new residency permits or for renewing the old ones. Increasingly, after 2015, Lebanese political authorities resorted to detentions, deportations, evictions, residency restrictions, and other coercive tactics to pressure refugees to return to Syria. Anti-refugee rhetoric continued to be deployed by political actors to strengthen the support of their constituencies. For instance, Gebran Bassil, who was the son-in-law of Lebanon's president Michel Aoun and served as Minister of Foreign Affairs between 2014 and 2020, actively promoted xenophobic anti-refugee rhetoric. In October 2017, as a response to public debates about the increasing number of assaults and incidents of discrimination against Syrian refugees, he tweeted, "We are racist in our Lebanese identity."[10] In February 2019, he stated that Syrian refugees had to return to their country because they posed an existential threat to Lebanon and their stay in Lebanon would spread terrorism into Europe.[11] Whether Bassil meant that "terrorists" among displaced Syrians would infiltrate European countries or that they would foment terrorism in Lebanon and elsewhere was unclear. What was clear is that he sought to associate Syrians with terrorism to justify Lebanon's unwelcoming policies against refugees. In another tweet on June 2019, he claimed that Lebanese were genetically superior to Syrians.[12]

Bassil's provocative comments received strong backlash from diverse circles of intellectuals and activists. Their condemnations of his racism, however, often reduced the problem to individual incivility, missing a robust critique of how such political rhetoric and accompanying policies frequently translated into institutional and daily practices of discrimination. Displaced Syrians and migrants in Lebanon, particularly those from working-class and poor groups, experienced discrimination, bullying, and physical harassment on an everyday basis.[13] Framing racism as an individual problem also obscured how numerous institutions, including civil society organizations, were complicit in the otherization of refugee and migrant communities.

The ungrievability of Syrian refugees must be situated within complex colonial legacies as well as within competing projects of nationalism in Lebanon. For centuries, Lebanon's political, social, and economic history has been strongly tied to Syria. The current territories constituting modern Lebanon were part of Bilad al-Sham or Greater Syria, a historical political entity that comprised areas within the contemporary borders of Syria, Jordan, Lebanon, Israel, and Palestine. Leading intellectual figures in Lebanon during the nineteenth century, such as Butrus al-Bustani, endorsed Syrianism and cherished the idea of a Greater Syria and its Arab culture.[14] After Le Grand Liban (Greater Lebanon) was founded in 1920 as a separate entity from other Syrian territories—and went under French colonial rule until its independence in

1943—many Lebanese Christians abandoned Arabism or Syrianism in favor of Lebanese nationalism. With limited initial success, the Maronite Christian intellectual and political elites of post-independence Lebanon fostered "Lebanism," seeking to cultivate a Lebanese identity distinct from other Arab identities, especially from Syrian identity. As in other colonial contexts, the French colonial mandate as a legal/institutional complex in Lebanon crafted particular political and ethno-religious identities that were later deployed to animate conflict and violence.[15]

After 1943, strong social and economic relations, including kinship relations, between various Lebanese and Syrian communities continued in the border zone between the two countries and in other areas of Lebanon. Until the onset of the Syrian War in 2011, crossing the borders between the two countries was like traveling between different cities in the same country. Lebanon had no visa requirements for Syrian citizens and vice versa. Before the Syrian War, many small traders and low-income Lebanese citizens frequently crossed the border to benefit from inexpensive medical, commercial, and other services in Syrian cities. Offering low-cost manual labor, Syrian workers were essential to Lebanon's economy before, during, and after the long Lebanese War.[16] Syrian middle classes also frequently visited Lebanon to participate in educational, cultural, and artistic activities.

Many Lebanese activists, as did many others in Lebanese society, held negative views about Syria and Syrian refugees for myriad historically situated reasons. In 1976, early in the long Lebanese War, Syrian forces entered Lebanon and established a military presence following an invitation from Suleiman Frangieh, the Lebanese president at the time. Many Lebanese from diverse confessional and political backgrounds referred to the Syrian military presence as a politically dark period when Lebanon experienced numerous human rights violations. Lebanese activist interlocuters in their thirties and forties described their mistreatment at checkpoints by the Syrian army as "still-traumatizing" memories. After the Lebanese War ended in the early 1990s, Syria's continued military presence and the so-called the Syrian tutelage (*al-wiṣāya al-sūriyya*) of Lebanon were widely criticized. In the early 2000s, the Syrian government's involvement in the day-to-day politics of Lebanon was increasingly condemned. Some groups blamed the Syrian state for the assassination of Lebanese Prime Minister Rafiq Hariri in February 2005. The assassination sparked massive public demonstrations against Syria, which led to the withdrawal of Syrian military forces from Lebanon in

April 2005. Following this withdrawal, Syria's influence on Lebanon's domestic politics continued to be a source of political tension.

With the outbreak of the Syrian War and resulting refugee displacement, however, sentiments of fear and anxiety were pronounced more publicly. Syrian refugees, who were predominantly Sunni Muslim, were seen by some Lebanese as threats to a fragile power balance, either between Christians and Muslims, or between the Sunni and the Shiʿa, in Lebanon. Many drew parallels to Lebanon's long war, which they believed had been precipitated by Palestinian refugees who were also predominantly Muslim. Increasingly after 2012, the fragility of Lebanon in the face of the Syrian conflict became a widely shared narrative, a vulnerability further amplified by the fear that Lebanon was about to become a battlefield between pro-Assad and anti-Assad groups in the country.

Arising from diverse factors—such as the influence of sectarian leaders' political rhetoric and of culturally shaped perceptions of Syria—anti-Syrian refugee views were more strongly voiced among Lebanon's Christian communities, whereas the country's Sunni groups were more sympathetic toward Syrian refugees, at least publicly. Among Lebanese activists, approaches toward Syrian refugees depended less on one's confession and more on one's historical ties and political commitments. Activists who expressed solidarity with Syrian refugees came from diverse confessional and class backgrounds. Some religious, Sunni activists characterized their support for Syrian refugees—especially those fleeing Assad's oppressive regime—as an expression of Muslim brotherhood. Yet most activists, secular or religious, did not share this sentiment. Instead, those who supported Syrian refugees tended to view Syria and Lebanon as ideological allies in Arab nationalism or Arab leftism, or they came from families with strong historical ties to Syria, through kinship or trade connections, for instance. They organized gatherings and panels and submitted petitions to counteract growing discrimination against Syrians.

Other activist groups expressed support for Syrian refugees using a liberal, humanitarian discourse that framed refugees as innocent victims of war. These groups expressed compassion toward Syrian refugees and wanted to offer humanitarian assistance, including educational programs and poverty-reduction strategies. Yet they received strong backlash from others. For example, in early 2014, at a youth-focused NGO where I volunteered, the project coordinator's decision to give donated clothes to Syrian refugees created a tense controversy, and several activists left the NGO because they believed that the Lebanese poor should have remained the priority of humanitarian assistance. I also frequently witnessed many activists taking different positions on Syrian refugees in different contexts. For example, some activists who expressed commitment to working with refugees in their activist circles might have voiced negative opinions about refugees in their family circles, and vice versa. Independently of these contradictions and ambivalences, prevalent discourses of "deservedness" and "worthiness" typically construed Lebanese as main subjects and objects of crisiswork, and refugees and migrant workers as deepening crises and disturbing the locals, hence obstructing Lebanese crisiswork.

All activists, regardless of their background or their perspectives on other issues, shared one common concern—the rise of sectarian identity politics in Lebanon. They observed that heightened political and sectarian tensions were causing many Lebanese to take refuge in their confessional relationalities, thereby interrupting civil society efforts to build Lebanese identity and belonging. I frequently heard activists lament that their nation-building efforts had been wasted now that, as a consequence of polarization, many Lebanese had "relapsed to their former sectarian selves." Many activists also accused the political class of taking advantage of the situation. In particular, the Lebanese parliament's postponement of the June 2013 parliamentary elections, which it justified as a response to the destabilizing effects of the Syrian War, led to various protests throughout 2013 and 2014. For protesters, the indefinite suspension of elections meant not only the suppression of citizens' political rights and agency but also the growing dysfunctionality of state institutions, given that critical political decisions were being deferred indefinitely. Thus, without necessarily holding any prejudice against the Syrian state or Syrian refugees, some activists were simply upset that their years of advocacy, peacebuilding, and empowerment work were lost to the changing political and social landscape. The observed persistence of sectarian belongings and the deterioration of the political process meant for many that their crisiswork of building non-sectarian futures was obstructed by outside forces. Particularly, those activists who centered their crisiswork around promoting belief in change through fostering social entrepreneurship and hope mourned the growing despair and disbelief in change they observed among the youth.

Many activists saw the Syrian War and the related refugee influx as an existential threat to crisiswork: sectarianism and war were making a massive reappearance and the hope in the possibility of "fixing" Lebanon was dissipating. They were particularly worried about the growing sentiment of "nothing changes in this country" and found it debilitating to discuss problems they believed were insoluble. The request for "practical solutions," voiced by some during the UN Social Good Summit, was an example of a common frustration about how the Syrian War's multifaceted effects caused some activists to feel powerless and despondent. In particular, activists in leadership roles whose crisiswork focused on bringing about multiscalar change considered the Syrian War's effects on Lebanese political institutions as insurmountable challenges that threatened their crisiswork. While they acknowledged that many of the problems exacerbated by the Syrian War were structural and endemic to Lebanon's longer history of sectarianism, rather than caused by displaced Syrians, this recognition did little to assuage their feelings of helplessness and gridlock. Because crisiswork—as practiced by the middle class, in particular—was so often articulated through idioms of "active citizenship," "creating change," and "producing hope," any social or political problem for which activists could not offer a solution was experienced as undermining their efforts. Hence, the very experience of not being able to "do something," that is, of reduced agency, was inherently frustrating for many middle-class activists.

There was also a shared concern that civil society projects that involved nation-building and state-making in Lebanon would pause indefinitely because of the shift in humanitarian aid toward Syrian refugees. Beginning in late 2012, donors began to focus their funding on projects for Syrian refugees, and new international NGOs opened up offices in Lebanon to assist Syrians. Additionally, many journalists, researchers, activists, volunteers, and professionals of various kinds arrived to Lebanon from different parts of the world to participate in the growing infrastructure of humanitarian aid for Syrian refugees. Throughout my fieldwork, I heard many civil society activists complaining that foreign donors only cared about Palestinians and Syrians, and that "nobody cares about the Lebanese." The loss of major funding sources led many activists working in Western-sponsored projects and NGOs to become dismayed and resentful. As with many NGOs in other Arab-majority societies, many Lebanese NGOs operated through "an economy of victimhood that is ultimately dependent on funding provided by states in the Global North."[17] In that sense, victimhood was a performance of deservedness of financial and other forms of support. The perceived tension between the growing victimhood of the Lebanese and the global invisibilization of their precariousness led many activists to further question the promise of crisiswork in civil society.

While there was a general discomfort with the Syrian presence in Beirut, activists also articulated specific civilizational, classed, gendered, and generational complaints. Syria was perceived by some urban, middle-class Lebanese, including activists, as an "uncivilized" Arab state and Syrians as devoid of "civility." The stereotypical images of the cruel Syrian soldier and of the poor, ignorant Syrian worker—pervasive for at least three decades before the Syrian War—depicted Syrians as incompatible with the "modernness" of Lebanon and the Lebanese. Some middle-class activists, in particular those who focused on empowerment rather than advocacy and human rights, did not shy away from expressing derogatory comments about the "vulgarity" of Syrians. They depicted the Syrian dialect of Arabic as barbaric (*lahja hamajiyya*) and rude (*lahja dafesh*), Syrians' manners in public spaces as uncivil and ignorant, and Syrians as broadly failing to adapt to norms of Western modernity and urbanity.[18] Many of my activist and non-activist Lebanese interlocutors said they had been "shocked" to observe that many poor Syrians did not know how to behave in public, raise a child, or clean their bodies.

Ironically, humanitarian NGO activities that served Syrian refugees played a significant role in producing and reproducing anti-Syrian rhetoric. Activists who worked on projects targeting Syrian refugees could participate in the development of a public discourse that regarded Syrians in Lebanon, whether refugees or not, as contaminants. In a well-known, local humanitarian NGO—where, in 2013, I had volunteered for two months teaching English to Syrian children—salaried and volunteer NGO participants, who all called themselves activists, adamantly tried to "civilize" Syrian children by activities such as teaching them personal hygiene practices of using soap and brushing teeth, assuming they did not already know these practices. They considered Syrian children and their families as health threats that needed to be contained. Throughout my stay in Lebanon, I heard numerous, vivid stories from my neighbors, friends, and their extended families that fearfully described how Syrian refugees spread diseases such as polio, measles, and tuberculosis. When I asked where and how they heard this information, most of them pointed to a relative who worked at an NGO that served displaced Syrians. Humanitarian and relief NGOs that focused on Syrian refugees published a number of reports in Arabic and English that documented how the spread of disease within this population threatened public health in Lebanon, the MENA region, and the entire globe.

Various Lebanese low-income activists also talked about the increased Syrian presence in Beirut with sentiments of fear and victimhood; however, they articulated these sentiments in concrete, experiential language, rather than in abstract terms. For instance, during strolls through Hamra and on Beirut's seaside with a group of low-income activists with whom I was volunteering at a youth-focused environmental NGO, our conversations often included anxious remarks about the dangers posed by Syrians to public health, public safety, and the urban environment. As we passed numerous Syrian children begging, laboring, and playing on the streets of central Beirut and other neighborhoods, I was struck by how many of the activists shared anecdotes that blamed Syrians for problems such as disease, unemployment, and crime that plagued their neighborhoods and families. In their accounts, Syrian refugees constituted a social problem, the impact of which tangibly influenced their loved ones.

In contrast to middle-class Lebanese activists whose narratives focused on how Syrians degenerated the distinctively cosmopolitan culture of Beirut, making it "look like any other Arab city," low-income activists tended to center their narratives on complaints about economic and social disempowerment. Some low-income Lebanese activists, for instance, were concerned with the growing upper-class Syrian presence in central neighborhoods in Beirut. As we walked through Hamra, they pointed to the luxurious cars parked along the streets carrying Syrian plates, newly opened Syrian-owned coffee shops and restaurants, and posters of young Syrian singers on billboards. They drew my attention to the fact that, in the same spaces where little Syrian children tried to sell roses to passing pedestrians and poor veiled Syrian women sat on the pavement holding babies and begging, the elite Syrian public presence was also growing. These contrasts facilitated the process of withdrawing one's sympathy for poor Syrian refugees, as the presence of "rich Syrians" in Beirut served as a justification for refusing to engage with the suffering of displaced Syrians. Though their experiences and rationales differed from those of middle-class activists, most low-income activists likewise refused to care about Syrian refugees or show solidarity with Syrian activists. Widely articulated narratives of fear and fragility were entangled with taken-for-granted ideas about the superiority of Lebanon and the Lebanese.

The Social Life of Lebanese Exceptionalism

During a conversation in September 2019, Joanne—a Lebanese graduate student who was pursuing a master's degree in public policy at a prestigious US university—suddenly looked uncomfortable and changed the subject when I mentioned Nadia, another Lebanese woman who had just entered the same program of education. I asked Joanne whether I had said or done something to upset her. She seemed nervous yet open to talk, and she asked me not to share with Nadia what she was about to say. When I replied "sure," she took a long sigh and continued: "She also told me that she's Lebanese. But I don't believe that. Her English is so bad; she cannot be Lebanese."

Having grown up in a middle-class Maronite Christian family in Beirut, Joanne spoke English and French fluently. Almost all her relatives and friends of her same age were fluent in English and French. For her, the command of these two languages was an essential characteristic of being a well-educated, professional, urban Lebanese. As an activist who offered trainings on citizenship rights to low-income communities in different parts of Lebanon, Joanne knew that some poor Lebanese did not speak any foreign languages. But she believed that any Lebanese who could make it to the United States for work or study must have a strong command of English. Joanne thus inferred from the new student's poor command of English that she was a Palestinian or Syrian who purported to be Lebanese as a means of social acceptance in the United States. What struck me was how certain she was about her inference. Nadia had told me that she had Lebanese citizenship, had grown up in a low-income Lebanese Shiʿi family, and had come to the United States through marriage.

The truth about Nadia's identity is less important here. What is more interesting is how Joanne's comments revealed that fluency in English or French was central to the imagination of an authentic Lebanese identity in contemporary Lebanon and among diasporan Lebanese living in the West. For many middle-class Lebanese, including activists, a good education demonstrated by strong language skills distinguished the Lebanese from other Arab nationalities. Middle-class Lebanese not only claimed superiority through exceptional language skills but also believed that other Arabs acknowledged and exploited Lebanese superiority, as seen in Joanne's assumption that Nadia was trying to pass as Lebanese.

Proficiency in English and French, as well as the ability to naturally code-switch between English, French, and Arabic, marked modernness, urbaneness, and culturedness in contemporary Lebanon.[19] Even though it was difficult for many low-income classes to attain fluency in these three languages, I met some low-income Lebanese activists who achieved proficiency by studying at prestigious educational institutions with the financial support of well-off family members or scholarships from charity organizations. Proficiency in several languages was more than a signature feature of middle-class belonging in Lebanon. As my conversation with Joanne exemplifies, in certain contexts and for specific audiences, language skills were also key to being recognized as Lebanese.

The prevalent discontent toward the growing presence of displaced Syrians in Lebanon exacerbated public anxieties about language. While businesses in many parts of Lebanon were criticized for hiring Syrian workers in order to lower employment costs, many upscale establishments in middle-class neighborhoods of Beirut sought to showcase "authenticity" and sophistication by not hiring Syrians. Many low-income Lebanese activists mentioned that their bosses in small stores, cafés, bars, and restaurants in chic, tourist areas of Beirut explicitly asked them to speak English or French to the clientele to avoid being mistaken for Syrians. For some in Beirut, speaking Arabic in a Lebanese dialect was not sufficient proof of one's "Lebaneseness." Because Syrians could pick up the Lebanese dialect relatively quicky and also because the Lebanese dialect was considered "too Arab" by some Lebanese, speaking English and French became, paradoxically, a crucial distinguishing feature of Lebanese identity.[20] Recognizing these subtle linguistic politics of belonging, middle-class Syrians deliberately deployed English and French as a subversive strategy to pass as Lebanese. I heard from many middle-class Syrian activists in Beirut that they and their Syrian friends and relatives were frequently harassed for their dialects and at times were explicitly asked to speak in the Lebanese dialect. Speaking in English and French, or code-switching as they spoke in the Lebanese dialect, enabled some of the displaced Syrians to avoid discrimination.

These particular interlacements of Lebanese politics of language, authenticity, and belonging are inflected with the historical legacies of Lebanese exceptionalism, which emphasize Lebanon's differences from and superiority to other Arab countries, on the one hand, and its closeness to the Western world, on the other.[21] During the nineteenth and twentieth centuries, prominent Maronite Christian thinkers imagined Lebanon not as part of an Arab civilization but as a heir to the Phoenicians—an ancient eastern

Mediterranean civilization prosperous during the first millennium BCE that had Byblos as its capital and contained key territories corresponding to the modern Lebanese cities of Beirut, Sidon, and Tyre.[22] In accordance with this view, the Phoenician establishment of colonies throughout the Mediterranean was framed as a story of origin that would have bestowed modern day Lebanon with a cultural kinship with Euro-Mediterranean states like Spain and Italy. Similarly, modern Lebanese polyglotism was regarded as a proud inheritance of these Phoenician ancestors.[23] Lebanon's "Westernness" also echoed in the European imaginary, which had referred to Lebanon as the "Switzerland of the Middle East" and to Beirut as the "Paris of the Middle East" until the long Lebanese War. Mostly owed to its open markets, flexible banking system, and urban elites' self-identification as liberal and cosmopolitan, diverse local elites and Westerners had promoted the country as a bastion of freedom and progress in a region filled with "authoritarian" and "traditional" Arab countries.

Identification with the Phoenicians was not very strong among contemporary Lebanese; however, allusions to Phoenician heritage continued to shape many public projects. Many Lebanese, including Maronite Christians, explicitly joked about the idea that Lebanese were Phoenicians and not Arabs. Moreover, many activists considered the claim of Phoenician inheritance and its association with Maronite Christian ideology as dangerously divisive. I met only a few middle-class activists—all of whom were Maronite Christians—who proudly endorsed the Phoenician origin claim and rejected their Arab heritage. Nevertheless, diverse national plans could invoke pride in the Phoenician heritage and express a desire to revive Beirut as the "Paris of the Middle East" when undertaking post-war public projects. Sunni Prime Minister Rafiq Hariri and his local and regional allies, for example, reclaimed such history when orchestrating the reconstruction of downtown Beirut. Moreover, the connection between Phoenician history and the modern nation of Lebanon was still part of school curricula and treated as scientific fact by various public actors. One of my middle-class activist interlocutors, a secular Druze woman in her late thirties, sent me the research article "Genetic Study Suggests Present Day Lebanese Descend from Biblical Canaanites," published on July 27, 2017, on the University of Cambridge website.[24] This research project—conducted by a team including researchers from Cambridge University's Department of Archaeology and Anthropology and led by the Wellcome Trust Sanger Institute—was widely distributed and debated in local Lebanese media and blogs in 2017. Hence, despite the loss of credibility of Phoenicianism as a political ideology, the debate over the ancestry of the Lebanese continued to be a popular discussion topic in formal media and social media.[25]

A "good" education, including proficiency in Western languages, was central to contemporary middle-class Lebanese exceptionalist discourses. Most of my middle-class activist interlocutors, from diverse confessional backgrounds, viewed present-day Lebanon as exemplifying many of the positive qualities of Western civilization and believed that Lebanon was the most modern and cultured Arab country.[26] They often justified this belief by arguing that Lebanon was home to the best educational institutions in the region. Many middle-class families I visited also argued that the exceptional value attributed to education distinguished Lebanon from other Arab countries. Some middle-class activists, for instance, cited a high investment in the education of their children as a distinguishing feature of the Lebanese. Even families who were politically aligned with Arab nationalist or pro-Syrian parties considered Lebanon superior to other Arab countries in educational infrastructure and cultural life. Lebanese commonly characterized several colleges and high schools in Beirut as top-tier institutions, unmatched by their counterparts in Syria, Jordan, and elsewhere in the region.

Many middle-class activists perpetuated Lebanese exceptionalism in their class-based narratives about "Lebanese prestige." Some middle-class activists invoked encounters with other Arabs in educational, NGO-related, or work-related meetings in different cities in the region, such as Amman, Dubai, and Istanbul, to praise the exceptional quality of Lebanese education and the unparalleled social capital it provided. They presented these encounters as evidence of the distinct and outstanding "etiquette" of the Lebanese. For my interlocutors, "etiquette" functioned as a multivocal signifier, encompassing cultural and embodied knowledge on how to dress, speak, and use body language but also the effective display of managerial skills such as networking, public speaking, and marketing. Having etiquette endowed someone with "prestige"—another widely used term in describing Lebanese's distinctive attention to social standing and presentability. While some activists mocked the idea of "Lebanese prestige" and poignantly criticized a culturally shared obsession with appearances, this self-conception broadly circulated as a source of national pride. I even heard some activists who had lived or worked in sub-Saharan African countries describe Lebanese as "bringing culture" to those lands.

Not surprisingly, naturalized ideas of Lebanese exceptionalism often led to negative assumptions about the education and culture of Syrians, including Syrian activists. In many spaces shared by Lebanese and Syrian middle-class activists, I observed how Lebanese activists systematically questioned or dismissed the knowledge and competence of their well-educated Syrian counterparts. Many Syrian activists expressed frustration with the condescending and exclusionary practices they faced when collaborating with Lebanese activists on various NGO or grassroots projects. Some Syrian activists, who had been in Lebanon for several years, mentioned feeling pressured to hide their identities and to try to pass as Lebanese in various professional settings, including civil society spaces, in order to be taken seriously. Palestinian activists described similar pressures. Performing Lebanese identity markers enabled some Syrian and Palestinian activists to avoid potential suspicion, discrimination, and exclusion, yet it also rendered them invisible within Lebanese civil society.

Middle-class activists' crisiswork—which painted Lebanon as a Western nation and, therefore, superior to other Arab countries and the global South, more generally—generated a sense of innate giftedness that perpetuated the historical legacies of Lebanese exceptionalism. Taken-for-granted ideas about Lebanese cultural superiority often translated into exclusionary discourses and practices toward displaced Syrians, including well-educated Syrian activists, within both activist spaces and other spaces of everyday life. Nevertheless, narratives of exceptionalism also conveyed sentiments of vulnerability and victimhood. In the eyes of many, an exceptionally resourceful and talented nation was also a nation with an exceptionally unlucky fate.

"Too Much"

On a sunny afternoon in early May 2013, I was sitting in the office of a prominent local advocacy organization that promoted active citizen participation in enacting social and political reforms. The office was located on the third floor of an old, renovated four-story building in one of the main streets of Ashrafieh. The space had been deftly transformed from a high-ceilinged and large-windowed three-bedroom family apartment into a vibrant and friendly office. Maha, one of the leading project managers in the organization, had invited me, after our initial interview several days before, to observe the daily routine at the office.

A secular woman in her mid-thirties from a prominent Maronite Christian family, Maha displayed a lean, toned physique and a self-confident demeanor. She wore a casual ponytail and no makeup, yet her attire spoke plainly of her class. Her well-fitting and skillfully combined outfit—a button-up striped knit top from an internationally renowned Lebanese designer, white stretch cotton, skinny pants from Ralph Lauren, and shiny cherry-colored vintage loafers—displayed her ability to purchase expensive brands and wear them comfortably. Like many other middle-class activists I met from diverse confessional backgrounds, she did not consider dressing in expensive brands as contradicting her activist profile. As an active supporter of several Lebanese feminist groups, she believed that looking elegant and taking care of herself did not undermine her feminist practice. She went to the gym every morning before work and frequented luxurious beauty salons and spa centers near her apartment in downtown Beirut.

Maha was eager to discuss the organization's activities and to hear about my experiences in Lebanon. I spent the early part of my six-hour visit in a spacious balcony chatting with her about various issues, such as the Syrian War, Hizbullah's politics, Lebanese activists' struggles with their "sectarian" families, the best cafés in Ashrafieh for working solo, and Turkish soap operas. It was a somewhat typical day for an active and popular NGO in Beirut. Peter, a Swedish man in his early thirties and one of the paid project managers, quietly worked on a grant application for an international NGO that was due the following day. He had initially traveled to Lebanon in late 2008 to study Arabic and decided to stay longer when, in 2009, he found a salaried position in Maha's NGO.[27] After he finished his work on the grant application, Peter ran a mentoring session with a small group of undergraduate interns from AUB and LAU who were writing a policy paper on agricultural development in Lebanon. The students seemed to enjoy their collaborative work and conversations. When we gathered for lunch at a chic French café on the same street, all of them were friendly and curious about my life in California and touristic places in Türkiye. Throughout the day, several activists stopped by to briefly discuss upcoming meeting plans or just to say hi to everyone. Probably because Peter was not fluent in Arabic, everyone spoke English, with occasional sprinkles of Arabic phrases.

When we returned from lunch around 3 p.m., I saw an Ethiopian maid in a pink-colored uniform finishing her daily, hour-long cleaning of the office.[28] She, like most domestic migrant workers at other NGOs, was practically invisible. Nobody in the office greeted her or spoke to her, except to scold her for imperfectly completed tasks. I did not feel comfortable talking to Maha about the maid, as our relationship was new, and I knew from experience that this was not the right occasion.[29] Indeed, when I had opened up a conversation about maids or directly engaged with maids at several other NGO offices, I was often treated by activists as a naïve visitor who was not aware of the consequences of "spoiling" migrant workers.[30] Similar to other middle-class Lebanese, these activists held taken-for-granted racializing representations of domestic workers such as ungrateful and immoral. Some activists told me stories about the "uncivilized," "embarrassing," and "strange" practices of domestic workers as they cleaned or cooked in these offices.

Within the logics of racial capitalism undergirding the operation of many NGOs in Beirut, the labor of Westerners like Peter and that of migrant workers, like the maids, was assessed in completely different terms—the former were precious assets and the latter flawed disposables. Some Lebanese activists were genuinely concerned about discrimination against migrant workers, and several NGOs and social movements in Lebanon promoted the rights of migrant workers and fought against their political, legal, and social racialization.[31] Nevertheless, most of my activist interlocutors either engaged in Lebanon's widespread anti-migrant rhetoric or were indifferent to discrimination against migrant workers, a position that was consistent with their attitude toward Syrian refugees.

The relaxed office atmosphere was not disrupted when a brisk, white British woman in her late forties arrived for an appointment. Maha hosted her in the common meeting room, which allowed the rest of us to participate in the conversation. The British woman was a representative of a well-known, prestigious international think tank based in London. She was touring successful advocacy organizations in major cities of the Middle East to introduce her institution and offer collaboration. At the beginning of the meeting, she spent about ten minutes describing her think tank's activities in the areas of "democratization in the Middle East" and "sustainable development." Then, she took out brochures and booklets from her elegant, brown leather tote bag and explained her think tank's interest in offering trainings to Maha's organization on developing policies for legal reforms and active citizenship. Maha and Peter asked the representative several questions about the nature of the proposed collaboration. The think tank did not provide direct funding but assisted local NGOs in application processes for international and local funding. It also covered expenses for several project participants to be trained in London and different cities in the global South. In addition, it offered free consultancy services and guidance on research and development. Its funding was provided by the British government and private donors.

Such proposals for partnership from Western organizations were not uncommon for successful Lebanese NGOs. When the think tank representative left, Maha told us that thanks to their achievements in engaging with the Lebanese parliament over the past decade, her NGO had been contacted by many international policy-makers, think tanks, donor agencies, and consultancy companies based in the United States, Canada, and European countries. After the founding of the NGO in the mid-2000s, its co-founder—who was Maha's friend as well as her boss—made agreements with numerous such actors to recruit and train talented Lebanese youth on policy-making, advocacy, lobbying, and leadership skills. In addition to participating in free trainings and workshops organized by international consultancy companies and think tanks, their NGO received substantial Western funding to educate and mobilize people in various urban and rural parts of Lebanon to actively work with their local political representatives on issues such as women's empowerment, waste management, and strengthening public schools.

Maha's proud review of her NGO's achievements took a sharp turn after about ten minutes: "And, of course, as you know, the Syrian situation changed everything. We are not sure what to do now. There is not much funding, and we also don't want Western funding anymore." Maha explained how the organization had recently decided to reduce their dependency on international—especially Western—funding. Receiving money from Western institutions, most of which were hostile to Hizbullah's military and political activities, tarnished the NGO's reputation for political neutrality and independence among some local communities and politicians. Western funding made the organization and its members susceptible to common accusations of working for Western, rather than Lebanese, interests. "We are now searching for ways to become more independent so that we can connect better with all Lebanese communities," Maha said.

I was not surprised by these comments, as several other activists at prominent advocacy NGOs I spoke to throughout 2013 had shared similar concerns. Peter asked Maha whether the board had considered his recommendation to repurpose the NGO's previous empowerment projects targeted to rural Lebanese women to instead serve displaced Syrian women. He added that there were more "neutral" funding opportunities available through the UNHCR, and also through several European and Middle Eastern organizations. Maha replied, "I don't know. There isn't any set decision yet, but we prefer self-financing. All donors have some expectations." She then followed with the idea to use their strong volunteer base to collaborate with reliable Lebanese companies and entrepreneurs for upcoming projects. She also smiled and told Peter, "Don't worry, we will find money for you too. We cannot lose you." In other prominent advocacy NGOs, as well as in Maha's, the presence of Western employees was believed to make the organization look more professional and prestigious in the eyes of Western donors and the general public.

Dima, one of the female volunteers from AUB, who had been chatty and jovial throughout the day, sulked as she listened to Maha and Peter's conversation. Speaking hesitantly, she added, "I don't want to sound racist, but our lives are drastically changing because of the Syrian War and refugee crisis." She recounted how her brother's visa application to Britain to attend a conference had been rejected the week before. She was surprised because her brother had traveled to other parts of Europe for NGO trainings in 2010 and 2011, and he had easily obtained visas. She told us how she came from a well-known Shiʿi family, and given her father's education in Paris and the family's reputation for being liberal and secular, none of its members had had any problems obtaining visas before. Her brother, who was preparing to complete a master's degree in environmental sciences at AUB and had applied to several British universities for doctoral studies, was shocked by the visa rejection. He and his family interpreted the visa denial as indicative of the increased security measures of European states against all Arabs because of the growing Syrian refugee crisis. Another volunteer from a middle-class Druze family added that she knew two other students from AUB who had recently been denied visas by the US Embassy. I had also heard similar news from several middle-class Lebanese recently, but I kept quiet to avoid inflaming an already sensitive conversation about the negative impacts of the Syrian War on Lebanon. Others supported Dima by commenting that her brother's years of work had been wasted because of corrupt, blood-thirsty Arab politicians and their blind followers that made all Lebanese look "bad." Maha added, "They consider all Lebanese potential terrorists now. I understand the fear about Syrians because their culture is different. But Lebanese adapt well to the West, they [Western embassies] know that." After thanking everyone for their support, Dima shrugged and added, "This is Lebanon (*haydā Libnān*), you can lose everything in one day because of a stupid war that you have no connection with. This is our history; we are victims of never-ending corruption and hatred. Now, it's just too much."

Growing restrictions on Lebanese mobility became a central node in the middle-class victimhood narrative regarding the Syrian War's impact on Lebanon. Middle-class Lebanese activists typically blamed visa rejections on the intensifying Syrian refugee crisis. Rather than criticize European states, most of them accused various political actors in Syria, Lebanon, and the broader Middle East of causing a catastrophic war with far-reaching negative consequences for everyone. Deploying common orientalist tropes such as "despotic leaders and their blind followers" and "violent, fanatic Muslim men" to explain the complex impacts of the Syrian War, most middle-class activists interpreted the increased racialized border security policies of various European states as a neutral technocratic policy response. In this narrative, most young Lebanese felt further victimized by being treated like Syrians and other Arab nationals and, therefore, by being denied the exceptional status they assumed they deserved.

The shared collective belief in Lebanon's Western proximity, exceptional liberal education, and cultural sophistication as justification for their worthiness, as articulated by Dima and Maha, was often invoked by many middle-class activists to render Lebanese suffering more grievable. Moreover, as Dima's "this is Lebanon" and "never-ending" comments illustrate, activists often attributed an exceptional quality to their perceived experiences of victimhood, even though they acknowledged that people in other countries in the region also shared such experiences. Sudden loss or trauma could happen anywhere, but in the activists' narratives, they were more likely to happen in Lebanon. Because Lebanon was broadly construed as continually suffering from crises, corruption, and violence, the Lebanese people's suffering was framed as exceptional. Prevalent sentiments that reflected a shared sense of historical trauma—Lebanon has always suffered, suffered more, or has suffered enough—paradoxically normalized victimhood and rendered it exceptional, generating conflicting narratives of exceptional victimhoods.

Western states implemented strict visa regulations after September 11, 2001, constricting the mobility of populations in Arab-majority countries.[32] In subsequent years, elaborate infrastructures of security and surveillance were arranged globally. Despite this, prior to the Syrian War, well-educated urban middle-class Lebanese still enjoyed a certain degree of international mobility.

Several middle-class activist interlocutors mentioned that even during tense periods—such as in the early 2000s, when several European cities were targeted in bombings linked to Islamic organizations, or during the July 2006 War between Israel and Lebanon—highly educated middle-class Lebanese were still eligible for visas from various Western countries. After the Syrian War began, travel restrictions expanded to cover larger segments of Lebanese society, a dynamic that extended to many other countries in the region. Many young middle-class Lebanese found it more difficult to secure work visas for attractive labor markets in the Gulf, in cities such as Dubai, Abu Dhabi, and Jeddah. Several of my interlocutors also emphasized that Gulf countries discriminated against Shiʿi visa applicants from Lebanon, which reflected those countries' general geopolitical strategy of supporting Sunni political groups in Lebanon. Increasingly after 2014, I heard various Lebanese activists complain about the difficulty of obtaining visas for work and education in different parts of the world.

Widespread public conversations regarding the more stringent visa policies newly adopted across the world were indicative of growing middle-class grievances against the effects of current political developments on their individual mobilities and livelihoods. Several of my activist interlocutors harshly condemned such grievances as "selfish," "spoiled," and "individualistic." Yet middle-class protestations against limited mobility—which could indeed be framed as selfish or disproportionate, particularly in the context of the catastrophic death toll and associated calamities undergone by Syrian refugees—do not result from individual moral shortcomings. Given the context of Lebanon's protracted and scaffolded crises, these grievances rather reflect historically built moral frameworks that are mobilized as attempts to work through accumulated and unresolved legacies of collective suffering. My middle-class interlocutors often recounted stories in which they endured a double victimization—first, by being forced to emigrate to have a decent life due to Lebanon's endless crises and, second, by being denied the chance to do so, again due to these crises. Given the taken-for-granted perceptions of timeless, *longue durée* collective suffering, seemingly small travel restrictions felt extremely daunting for many Lebanese. "It's too much" was a typical comment I heard from many activists to express their feelings about the daily and sometimes mundane effects of the Syrian War on their lives. The "it" in the statement "it's too much" refers to more than the current experience of crisis—it encompasses the "all" that Lebanon has endured since its foundation. It also expresses the excess of a transgenerational experience of crisis that overwhelms the individual's capacity and resources and ultimately communicates a collective grievance.

Middle-class grievances and resulting victimhood narratives about mobility and migration were inherently tied to gender, sexuality, and marriage.[33] During a movie night at her feminist collective in Ashrafieh in October 2013, Maha looked unusually sad and distracted. When her friends pressed her about what had happened, she was unwilling to talk. A week later, during a group outing at a bar in Mar Mikhail—a popular neighborhood with renovated restaurants, cafés, art galleries, and small stores—she decided to bring up the difficult topic. She had just broken up with her fiancé, a secular, middle-class Lebanese Sunni man who had lived and worked in Dubai since 2011. He had told Maha several weeks before that he could not handle their long-distance relationship and had started dating a French coworker some months ago. As Maha recounted the details of her break-up, lamenting that her ex-fiancé had humiliated her by portraying her to common friends as an obsessive lover, her voice became shaky and she began sobbing. Her close friend Jana, a middle-class queer LGBTQ activist in her early thirties, listened to Maha empathetically. She gave Maha a strong hug and consoled her: "Please don't cry, my dear. He's not worth it. You'll find a better one." Maha quickly gathered herself together, wiped her tears, and explained that she felt worried about her future prospects. Pointing out how hard it had been for her to meet a compatible man like her fiancé, she lamented that "all good men are outside [Lebanon]." The group then began a lively conversation about the "crisis of marriage" (*azmat al-zawāj*), which was framed as an exceptional problem, similar to many other problems in Lebanon.

As I listened to Maha, Jana, and another feminist activist discussing the chronic shortage of marriageable men in Lebanon, I recalled many similar conversations with Lebanese female interlocutors from diverse backgrounds. Many young Lebanese women referred to a low ratio of young Lebanese men to young Lebanese women as a depressing social fact caused by the mass, work-related emigration of Lebanese men since the long Lebanese War.[34] During an interview in the summer of 2012 with the female president of a successful advocacy NGO in Beirut, I was struck by her response to my question about the reasons for her success: "I think it's about being passionate, genuine, and things like that. But then you still can't find a husband with those qualities. All the guys I'm attracted to are not here. We have a social problem; we don't have enough men in this country." Some interlocutors even provided precise statistics for what they viewed as an exceptionally uneven gender ratio responsible for what they saw as a chronic marriage crisis in Lebanon. For example, that night, Jana said she had recently read in a Lebanese newspaper that, for every four single Lebanese women, there was one unmarried Lebanese man.

Given the absence of reliable census data in contemporary Lebanon, it was hard to assess the accuracy of such statistics or the actual reasons for any demographic imbalance. Yet, one thing was clear: female activists from diverse economic and political backgrounds felt disproportionately affected by the country's crises, which they believed caused marriageable men to leave the country, making it extremely difficult for Lebanese women to find a suitable partner. "Many Lebanese men go abroad and marry foreigners," Jana said, and continued, "My father went to Sierra Leone while my mother was pregnant with me. Then, we learned that he married someone else there." Beyond the emigration issue, female activists had more general critiques of the gender dynamics of marriage in Lebanon. They complained that men enjoyed the socially sanctioned privilege of waiting until their forties to marry, and when they were finally ready, they preferred younger women to enhance their chances of having children. Maha's group similarly lamented Lebanon's unequal social expectations, which pressured women to engage in serious relationships and get married in their twenties while permitting men to date casually.

Maha, who had been listening silently for a while, sarcastically thanked Jana for her helpful reminder that many Lebanese women shared a similar fate. Then, she expanded on her break-up, this time situating it in the context of the Syrian War: "Our plan was that he would return to Beirut last month and we would buy a house here. But the situation. . .he got very scared with explosions and everything. He did not want to return. I did not want to leave Lebanon. We were fighting a lot." Jana smiled and said, "We don't choose anything in this country, my dear. We don't choose whom to love, either." Maha's friends perceived her fiancé's betrayal as an ordinary yet still grievable incident; they shared her sense of victimhood in the context of the Syrian War.

(De)Colonizing Civil Society

The crisiswork of middle-class Lebanese activists, such as Maha and Jana, was filled with ambivalences and contradictions. They variously affirmed and rejected dominant discourses and practices that were rooted in colonial designations of identity and difference. I use the term "(de)colonizing" to capture the fluid relationality between colonizing and decolonizing practices of crisiswork in Lebanon. Many activists simultaneously engaged in practices of colonization and decolonization, meaning that they perpetuated and reproduced, and challenged and contested, colonial legacies. Despite operating within a position of privilege in a political space traversed by colonial traces of Western hegemony and related local inequalities, middle-class activists also participated in decolonizing discourses and practices.

Maha and Jana, for instance, were very critical of the "racist" rhetoric of politicians such as Gebran Bassil and carefully distinguished themselves from the "sectarianism" they observed in their social circles. As did several other secular Maronite activists, Maha criticized her "sectarian Christian friends" who discriminated against Muslims and who continued to circulate wartime divisions such as "East and West Beirut." Maha frequently referred to a childhood friend, who never left the perceived safety of Ashrafieh to visit Hamra or downtown, as an extreme example of how Maronite Christians could manifest their sectarianism. Maha had hoped that, if she had married a Sunni Lebanese man, she would contribute to the creation of a non-sectarian Lebanon. Likewise, by participating in cross-sectarian movements and alliances, she was proud to contribute to anti-sectarian politics. In contrast to other Maronite Christians I met, who lamented the growing marginalization and disempowerment of Christians in Lebanon, she explicitly acknowledged the privileges that the Maronite community had historically accrued from French colonialism and dreamed of a non-sectarian society that could cultivate a sense of belonging for Lebanese from all confessions. In so doing, Maha questioned and invited others to question the privilege and differential power she enjoyed as a consequence of a colonially created and maintained system of distinctions.

Maha's feminist collective included middle-class participants from diverse confessional and political backgrounds, and many participants expressed pride in this diversity. They collaborated with other collectives and grassroots initiatives that organized awareness campaigns, protested gender-based violence, and advocated for gender equality and LGBTQ rights in Lebanon. I also heard some of them discuss strategies for resisting "colonial" (*istiʿmārī*) and "Western" (*gharbī*) feminist norms and for generating alternatives to the hegemonic models of both Lebanese and Western femininity. They argued that Western-style feminism was complicit in both consumerist culture and Western interventions in the Middle East. They also shared a desire to create alternative feminist practices in Lebanon. Many activists viewed practices such as postponing marriage, traveling alone, and refusing to wear makeup as acts of resistance against imposed models of Lebanese womanhood. Most of them aspired to be successful and independent women who showed solidarity with other women and LGBTQ communities in Lebanon. I personally learned valuable insights from feminist activists like Maha and Jana, who critically analyzed everyday manifestations of patriarchal structures in Lebanon. Yet, I also found their refusal to closely engage with classed and racialized hierarchies and inequalities troubling.

As I continued to visit Maha's NGO in the following months—and joined some of the board meetings and more informal reunions among the core body of volunteers—I was struck by similar conversations about "creating alternatives" to historically entrenched sectarian and patriarchal structures. During an informal meeting in February 2014, Farid, the organization's president and a secular Sunni man in his late thirties, proudly recounted to me how five activist friends from diverse confessional backgrounds had initially founded the entity in early 2000s as a grassroots organization. In 2007, they converted the organization into an NGO in order to better execute advocacy projects and engage with diverse local actors. Farid explained why the organization was undergoing a new transition in 2014: "But now, we want to become more political because politics in the parliament stopped. We [civil society] need to step in. That's why we work on forming political coalitions." He was very critical of Western donors and organizations, which he characterized as operating with "colonial thinking" (*tafkīr istiʿmārī*), and as creating competition and fomenting disunity among activists. Farid explicitly criticized US organizations for instigating animosity between various groups in Lebanon, and he believed that the United States and European countries shared responsibility for the Syrian War with Iran and Türkiye. In their questioning of the viability of the Western-funded model of NGO activism, which inherently enforced competition among activists, experienced activists like Farid searched for alternative political solidarities that could potentially transcend the colonial infrastructures of Lebanese civil society activism.

Nevertheless, middle class-led crisiswork largely functioned within colonizing frames. Most Lebanese activists refused to "work toward liberations that are always plural"[35] and thus missed the opportunity to struggle alongside Lebanon's Others. Both Maha's NGO and collective turned a blind eye to displaced Syrians and avoided collaboration with Syrian activists. During a dinner I had with several Syrian activists in March 2014, a middle-class Syrian activist who was pursuing a master's degree in economics at AUB critiqued Farid for ignoring their requests for a meeting to discuss potential collaboration on citizenship rights and for discouraging other Lebanese activist groups from collaborating with them. I did not hear Farid talk negatively about Syrian refugees, but I did notice that none of the NGO's projects focused on refugees and none of the conversations among its participants engaged with refugee issues.

Lebanese activists' solidarity was vital for Syrian activists, as the Lebanese legal system made it extremely difficult for displaced Syrians to establish any civil society organization in Lebanon or be legally employed in NGOs. Middle-class Syrian activists had many privileges compared with poor Syrian refugees, but they still needed the support of Lebanese collaborators to materialize their projects. Some Syrian activists were arrested because of their political activities, which further led Syrian activists to be cautious of their public presence in Lebanon.[36] Given their active and deliberate invisibilization, as instigated by the political and legal system in the country, Syrian activists found Lebanese activists' refusal of solidarity profoundly discouraging.

In contrast to privileged subjects in the global North who implicitly or explicitly benefit from colonizing frameworks and agendas, Lebanese activists' racialization of Syrian refugees and other Others expressed both relative power and privilege as well as powerlessness and disempowerment. The ambivalent oscillation between exceptional victimhood and exceptional giftedness foregrounds the refusal to engage with Syrian refugees and collaborate with Syrian activists. Imagining their lives in Lebanon as vulnerable and fragile, many activists saw it as their right to ignore the everyday realities of violence and discursive erasure that Syrian refugees faced. Focusing on problems such as constriction of international travel and finding a marriageable partner, Lebanese activists construed themselves as exceptionally victimized by someone else's war. As a result, many activists became complicit in the continuing criminalization of refugees and their public ungrievability, and their crisiswork continued to refuse to build solidarity with Others.

Problematizing the victimhood narratives of Lebanese activists does not deny their difficult experiences or the value of their crisiswork, but it does call attention to the complex implications of claiming victimhood as a collective identity. Victimhood narratives often fail to recognize the suffering of marginalized Others. In addition to outright racializing and discriminating practices, indifference was vital to rendering Syrian refugees ungrievable. Victimhood narratives also obscured how Lebanese enjoyed numerous privileges in employment, access to formal institutions, and various other social and cultural rights that Palestinians and Syrians, who were subject to multiple forms of formal and informal exclusion in the country, did not. As citizens of Lebanon, many activists, particularly the middle-class ones, derived national, class, and racial privileges from unequal hierarchies of power. These privileges were often obscured through naturalized narratives of Lebanese exceptionalism. Cultural superiority and giftedness were invoked to claim sympathy for Lebanese suffering and justify indifference to others' suffering.

Naturalization of the historically constructed identity categories within dominant frames of crisiswork further undermined the possibility of extending solidarity, care, and grief to Lebanon's otherized communities. By reaffirming colonial distinctions that mapped diverse ethnic and religious groups in the Middle East onto civilizational hierarchies, and by claiming distinct qualities for Lebanese in these imagined hierarchies, many activists unwittingly aligned with sectarian, class-based, and racialized cultural logics of power in Lebanon. They perpetuated colonial legacies by taking for granted the dynamic and shifting nature of identities among Arab communities, as well as confessional and ethnic divisions among Lebanon's residents, and by treating those identities and divisions as static categories. Reification of historically created cultural distinctions also obscured how global and regional conditions impacted diverse communities in Lebanon in uneven ways. Refugees and migrant workers were not only the most marginalized and exploited groups in the country, they were also the ones impacted most by the legacies of Western colonialism and its racializing border policies. Despite growing limitations, Lebanese citizens were still more capable of international travel and other forms of mobility.

In addition to the ongoing legacies of Western colonialism and its racializing border policies, Lebanon was also shaped by—and in turn shaped—racial capitalism that rested on the exploitation of displaced Syrians and other migrant workers. Refugees and migrant workers, who were construed as ungrievable, threatening, burdensome, and ungrateful subjects, were nevertheless the ones who made possible livable lives for many Lebanese. They were pillars of the daily running of Lebanese capitalism as well as activist crisiswork in multiple contexts, including NGO offices and apartments where activists and their families lived. By laboring in low-paid jobs within civil society—jobs that most Lebanese did not want—or by passing as Lebanese to participate in diverse activities organized by civil society, they were invisibilized yet significant contributors to activists' crisiswork. Exceptional victimhood, a foundational narrative of crisiswork, obstructed the possibility of cross-national solidarities and bounded Lebanon's futures.

CONCLUSION

"People Will Unite at the Right Time"

In late July 2014, a week before I was to return home from my long fieldwork, I hosted a dinner at my place. In attendance was Manal, the optimistic and energetic low-income activist from the Introduction, as well as several other activists. The political atmosphere was particularly tense at the time; Israel had launched a war on Gaza on July 8 that would last for 50 days and kill more than 2,250 Palestinians. Our conversation took on a pessimistic and cynical tone as Manal's friends expressed their worries about ongoing clashes between various armed groups in Lebanon and at the Lebanese–Syrian border, as well as their concerns that many Lebanese activists did not care much about the Gazans. We also talked about stalled NGO projects as well as hiring pauses and unpaid salaries in the private sector. Seeking to add a note of hope, Manal commented, "People will unite at the right time, I'm sure." After 2014, Lebanon went through new episodes of turbulence, which aggravated the sentiments of crisis among its diverse inhabitants. I was physically distant most of the time, with the exception of summer visits, but I continued to regularly communicate with my key interlocutors, and I met and interviewed about a dozen others, including virtually. These conversations helped me recognize the "unfinished" nature of "the storytelling" of individual and collective struggles against crises within activist lifeworlds.[1]

Crisiswork continued to enable many in Lebanon to imagine and experiment with the afterlives of crises, even as new crises emerged. The collectively shared perceptions of crisis generated not only immense anxiety and frustration but also new ethico-political visions and struggles for change. As

Carol Hakim, a historian of Lebanon, wrote, "Periods of crisis are often associated with turmoil and disarray; at the same time, they represent fertile ground for reformation and innovation."[2] Political unrest in twenty-first-century Lebanon was intertwined with multiple social struggles, just as it had in nineteenth- and twentieth-century Lebanon. The growing interest in activism as a response to the Syrian War continued after 2015 as more and more activists demanded that civil society directly participate in electoral politics. The massive Garbage Protests in the summer of 2015—which responded to the vast piles of uncollected waste across the country—and the subsequent formation of Beirut Madinati prior to the municipal elections in May 2016 marked the transformation of Lebanese civil society into a more active and politicized platform. Both events brought together diverse groups that sought to create an alternative to the existing political system. In the following years, most of my activist interlocutors enthusiastically collaborated with other activists to create viable political projects and programs.

On October 17, 2019, Manal's hopeful prediction of unification was realized as the largest mass protests in Lebanon since 2005 drew more than a million people from diverse backgrounds into the streets. The spontaneous and rapidly growing public demonstrations came to be called the October Revolution or the October Uprising. The protests were sparked by proposed tax increases on a number of everyday items, but drew on broader popular frustration and anger that had built up over 2019 as Lebanon's economic crisis led to chronic shortages of basic necessities such as bread and fuel. Many of my interlocutors referred to that moment as the first time that diverse groups acted in solidarity against the political establishment. "All of them means all of them" (*killun yaʿnī killun*)—the most popular chant during the October protests—articulated a unified voice against all sectarian leaders and their parties. The Lebanese government resigned on October 29, 2019, after only two weeks; nevertheless, the mass protests continued.

All of my activist interlocutors from diverse class backgrounds and competing political positions participated in the October protests, which they viewed as a landmark event in their years of crisiswork. Many of them, upset by Western media's depictions of the October Uprising as a sudden outburst of anger and frustration, underlined that these protests would not have happened without years of work by Lebanese activist groups.[3] They believed that activist practices such as rallies, campaigns, advocacy work, workshops, trainings, grassroots organizing, aid distribution, and caring for each other had been a necessary foundation for the prolonged, impactful, and unified uprisings—a foundation obscured by much of the Western media.[4] Not surprisingly, middle-class civil society activists in the protests were strikingly more visible than others in prominent global media outlets because of those activists' fluency in English, French, and globalized human rights discourses, even as various other civil society groups, such as workers' unions and teachers' unions, were also present.

Throughout October and November, activists from NGOs, collectives, social movements, and coalitions gathered along with other residents of Lebanon to protest the state. Even though downtown Beirut was the epicenter of the uprisings, numerous groups who felt precarity more palpably—including poor Lebanese citizens, refugees, and migrant workers—also participated in protests across Lebanon and fiercely decried their impoverishment. These weeks of ongoing protests brought together different groups across class, sect, gender, regional, and generational lines, and for many of my interlocutors, this was their first mass protest. Whereas some had been reluctant to take part in the Garbage Protests of 2015, either out of distrust in the possibility of change or out of fear that "some political groups are controlling the protests," they were all moved by the spirit of unity they witnessed in 2019. Moreover, the national protests led more people to self-identify as activists. Some of my interlocutors, who previously had been skeptical of activism in general, told me in 2019 and 2020 that they found purpose and hope in street protests, regardless of whether such protests brought substantial change, and decided to become more active in civil society as a result.

Over the course of 2019, what began as angry demonstrations turned into a peaceful, festive, carnival-like celebration in downtown Beirut, which many families participated in (Figures 13 and 14). Activists organized public assemblies, square encampments, and town halls in Beirut and other cities. Improvised food stalls and a variety of events made it possible for many Beirut residents to spend long hours in the aspirational spaces of revolution. Some of my interlocutors organized twice-daily teach-ins that attracted hundreds of curious Beirutis to discuss Lebanon's problems and possible solutions to them. Many Lebanese found purpose and joy in becoming part of this unfolding political and social mobilization, uniting against a corrupt political establishment and collectively working on solutions. Nevertheless, not everyone equally felt this euphoria. I was told by some leftist activist interlocutors that some of the working-class protesters felt alienated by "festive" activities

FIGURE 13. Protests on Independence Day, November 22, 2019. Downtown Beirut. Photo by Jude Chehab.

FIGURE 14. Diverse Lebanese protest and chant in downtown Beirut. The symbol of a raised fist reads "thawra" (revolution). November 13, 2019. Photo by Jude Chehab.

at the protests, such as yoga classes and weddings, and accused the middle classes of depoliticizing the protests. Some of my practicing Muslim activist interlocutors also felt excluded by the "too-secular" character of the festivities and were upset by some teach-ins that conflated religiosity with sectarianism, representing both as outdated systems that needed to change.

It was not only working-class or pious activists who struggled with differences in perspective. Many activists had to confront profound disagreements over what "change" actually meant. In November and December 2019, I heard the following statement from many of my activist interlocutors: "We mostly agree on what we don't want, but we don't agree on what we do want." Many activists in Lebanon had abstract dreams of a stable non-sectarian system but did not have concrete ideas about how to realize it. They perceived the revolution less as a utopian process of creating an entirely new system and more as a normalization of everyday life in Lebanon. Activists adhering to certain utopian ideals or concrete political visions, on the other hand, had profound disagreements with each other. For example, those with specific socialist or secularist agendas that they envisioned replacing the confessional power structure found it hard to convince many Lebanese to completely overthrow the existing system. Not everyone agreed with ideas such as that Hizbullah should completely disarm or that Lebanon could have a Muslim rather than a Christian president. Such dilemmas revealed the tensions within crisiswork, which sought to construct a shared identity that could potentially transcend myriad differences.

Middle-class crisiswork invited Lebanese from diverse backgrounds to imagine themselves as part of a nation in crisis with shared hardships and the strength to overcome those sufferings. In doing so, it transformed individual and collective perceptions of crisis in Lebanon into shared aspirations of national identity and belonging. However, by flattening history into a single narrative of people's unified struggle against a corrupt system, middle-class crisiswork made it almost impossible to productively engage with differences and disagreements. Its narrative of unity against crisis glossed over social hierarchies and inequalities that unevenly affected different groups in Lebanon. Because middle-class activists idealized the potential of civil society to bring all Lebanese together, they often perceived social differences as uncomfortable or even potentially dangerous. They feared that focusing on such issues would undermine consensus and contribute to despair and cynicism. Even some low-income activists, who were well aware of their disadvantaged positions vis-à-vis middle-class activists, explicitly argued that it was not helpful to discuss social differences and structural inequalities.

Given this historical commitment to cultivating a shared identity and sidestepping questions of difference, many activists felt a sense of debility and confusion as they observed after the October Uprising that deep ideological and other differences persisted; forsaking sectarian loyalties and sharing a sense of belonging to Lebanon were not sufficient to cultivate political agreements. Despite people's shared grievances against the sectarian system, the nation was still not united. Activists' reluctance to productively recognize and engage with the nation's classed, gendered, legal status–based, and ideology-based fractures bounded the futures of their crisiswork.

Nevertheless, perhaps more than it illuminated crisiswork's limitations, the October Uprising expanded its repertoire of political practices. For instance, some of my middle-class activist interlocutors, whose main goal had been changing the sectarian culture, began to explicitly articulate concerns over social justice and economic inequality. Demands for universal health care and the improvement of public education, which had not commonly been raised in previous mass protests, became more pervasive. Many protesters carried banners calling for the abolition of the *kafala* system—a sponsorship system that led to the widespread abuse of hundreds of thousands of migrant workers, the majority of whom were from Ethiopia, Sri Lanka, Bangladesh, the Philippines, Nepal, and Sudan. The protests enabled growing public awareness of racial and gender inequalities, and of the activities of antiracist, feminist, and queer groups in Lebanon that focused on these issues. There was also some advocacy for, and solidarity with, refugees and people in prison, though those demands were not as widely expressed as others.

Protests, which were the epicenter of crisiswork in Lebanon during the October Uprising, gave rise to unexpected collaborations and solidarities. For example, during the Garbage Protests of 2015, most of my activist interlocutors were not interested in building alliances with activists around the world, and only a few imagined themselves as part of a larger, international community of discontent. During the nationwide protests of 2019, however, many activists expressed solidarity with and appropriated tactics from other activists in Iraq, Chile, and elsewhere. For instance, in May 2020, Salem and several other middle-class entrepreneurial activists, whose stories were in Chapter 4, told me that they had joined international virtual reading groups on racism and capitalism, and that "Lebanese must learn from activists in

Latin America." They found those groups particularly helpful for understanding how global processes affected Lebanon's problems such as unemployment and youth emigration, and how "we" (the Lebanese) needed global solutions for seemingly local problems.

Protests also became sites of innovation and experimentation with alternative political and cultural frameworks, as they did in other global contexts.[5] Some middle-class activist interlocutors, for instance, enjoyed meeting and collaborating with other activists, and in the process they became more open to engaging with strategies they had previously considered "too radical," such as drawing graffiti on walls or burning tires. In January 2020, the brutal suppression of Lebanon's ongoing protests by state security forces further politicized some middle-class activists. This was particularly true of the protests that targeted the country's corrupt banks, where tear gas, live ammunition, and metal pellets were deployed against protesters. Several of them who worked in humanitarian NGOs began to participate in street demonstrations for the first time in 2019 and 2020. They told me that experiences such as being injured by tear gas or rubber bullets had reinforced their activist identities and "radicalized" them. Throughout 2020 and 2021—in defiance of Covid-19 restrictions and national lockdowns—hundreds of poor Lebanese gathered to express their anger at widespread poverty and hunger, clashing with security forces in violent demonstrations. In solidarity with their struggle, my middle-class interlocutors would use their platforms to elevate these marginalized voices, and on occasion would join the demonstrations themselves. Similar to developments in different parts of Latin America, what began as "civic activism" within Western-funded civil society organizations could transform into "uncivic activism," which transgressed the prescriptions of neoliberal institutions and created unexpected political openings.[6]

The new government that was appointed in January 2020 failed to deliver on its promises, and Lebanon faced one of the largest economic and financial crises in its history. The economy and the banking system collapsed further as Lebanon's currency, which had been pegged to the US dollar since 1990, lost more than 70 percent of its value in June 2020. The twelve-month inflation rate rose to 120 percent in August 2020, and average food inflation grew by 254% over the year.[7] Food insecurity and severe fuel shortages began impacting more than half of the population, 80 percent of which were estimated to live below the poverty line. Some of my middle-class and low-income Lebanese interlocutors, who had previously volunteered for local NGOs to distribute food to Syrian refugees, told me that they never thought that they would be on the receiving end of food donations one day. Precarity increasingly characterized middle-class lives, radically shaping aspirations and trajectories for many. Middle-class activist interlocutors such as Sara and Ziad from Chapter 3, who had previously been against emigration, now viewed it as inevitable. Many of them also began to save money and significantly restrict leisure activities, such as going to cafés or traveling for vacations. At the same time, already precarious groups such as refugee and migrant communities experienced even more severe poverty and hardship, and hundreds of unpaid migrant domestic workers were abandoned by their employers, who could no longer afford to pay their salaries. They gathered in crowds outside of their respective consulates and embassies, desperately seeking repatriation.

"Cherry on Top"

On August 4, 2020, the detonation of 2,750 tons of ammonium nitrate, which had been unsafely stored at the Port of Beirut since 2014, killed 218 people and injured about 7,000.[8] The victims included nationals from Lebanon, Palestine, Syria, Ethiopia, Pakistan, Bangladesh, France, and the United States. The explosion destroyed thousands of buildings, displaced more than 300,000 residents, and caused extensive damage to urban infrastructure, health facilities, and private businesses. The Lebanese government resigned on August 10, 2020, in response to angry protesters who filled downtown Beirut. However, this did little to quell the increasing political unrest. The country's economic and political problems, as well as the people's frustrations with the Lebanese political class, continued to worsen.

After the explosion, numerous international organizations, media outlets, and policy-makers began to describe Lebanon more frequently as a country in severe crisis. Crisis as such gained an omnipresent reality, imagined as encompassing all aspects of everyday life. In addition to "the Lebanese crisis," many in Lebanon continually talked about the currency crisis, unemployment crisis, fuel crisis, bread crisis, food crisis, electricity crisis, water crisis, waste crisis, and Covid-19 crisis. The word "crisis" helped many articulate their daily struggles in ways that called attention to the severity of specific circumstances. It also enabled them to interpret their experience within a specific sense of historicity. Many Lebanese compared the economic crisis, which had worsened in early 2020, to the weak economies of the First World

War and the long Lebanese War, which were collectively remembered as the most difficult periods in the nation's history.

The explosion revived public narratives about life and death as many portrayed the Lebanese government as "killing its citizens." "We are dying a thousand deaths in this country," Dana, the low-income NGO volunteer from Chapter 3, wrote to me a few days after the explosion. Many other activists shared experiences of severe hardship, anxiety, and trauma during online meetings with other activists and on their social media accounts. All of my activist interlocutors described the blast as a life-changing event. For many of them, the initial days of shock and frustration were followed by years of trauma and grief. Hala, a middle-class environmental activist whose story of founding a healing collective appeared in Chapter 2, told me in August 2021, around the one-year anniversary of the blast, "It wasn't only the port, it was our hearts, dreams, and future that exploded. I'm still grieving. I've lost my faith in humanity." She called the port explosion, in English, the "'cherry on top' of all the Lebanese crises." From 2020 onwards, as living conditions collapsed and political instability deepened, the dominant public affects were rage, despair, and fatigue. The worsening of the country's conditions left many activists feeling disillusioned and resigned, and some of my activist interlocutors emigrated to different countries.

Nevertheless, many of my activist interlocutors continued their ethico-political project of crisiswork: They participated in public protests, joined collectives that discussed resistance strategies, repurposed previous projects on entrepreneurialism and self-development, assisted in grassroots efforts to aid impoverished communities, and tried to take care of themselves and others. They resisted a sense of resignation by building and participating in networks of solidarity in multiple spaces, including protests, NGO offices, and online platforms. For instance, several days after the blast, Nour—the low-income Shiʿi activist from Chapter 1—began to get actively involved in relief efforts. Despite her grief, she volunteered to help manage the social media platforms of two Lebanese NGOs, one focused on food distribution and the other on psychosocial services. The figure of a young Lebanese holding a broom and a shovel, clearing away the explosion debris, became a symbol of the initial relief efforts. Numerous small volunteer groups set up tents and distributed hot meals, food boxes, hygiene kits, clothes, and in some cases cash assistance to affected families. Diasporan Lebanese from across the world also contributed to these efforts in multiple ways, further inspiring the activists based in Lebanon. I was particularly struck by the prevalence of idioms of care (*ihtimām*) and solidarity (*taḍāmun*) even among activists who had grown cynical after the waning of the 2019 protests. Seemingly banal NGO activities such as distributing food or managing a social media page became political practices that brought together previously isolated activists, enabling them to make sense of a traumatic period through mutual support. What emerged was a particular "ethics of immediacy," an urgency to help the blast-affected areas that wove together care, solidarity, togetherness, sociality, and community.[9] This ethics interlaced the October 2019 uprising with the post-explosion humanitarian efforts and maintained the struggles for justice taking place in mass protests within everyday spaces, ultimately expanding the scope of crisiswork.

Individual and collective healing was another important component of activists' meaning-making out of unbearable events. Through their relief efforts, many Lebanese participants sought, as several of my interlocutors put it, "to heal and help other people heal" (*ta-itʿāfā wa sāʿid al-nās yitʿāfū*). Similar to activists in other contexts, Lebanese activists experienced healing through connecting with others and imbued their healing process with political meanings.[10] Many of them interpreted post-explosion solidarity as helping to heal their trauma from the multiple crises the country had experienced in the previous years. They created venues in which activists interacted with others with similar traumas and experienced group belonging—processes that enabled collective healing. For activists caring for the affected communities, each other, and themselves, crisiswork was a multiscalar fight against the physical, social, and psychological destruction caused by a corrupt state. In the context of generalized trauma, grief, and debilitation, caring for oneself and one's loved ones gained new significance. If the well-known feminist mantra "everything is political" highlights the impacts of politics on the minutiae of everyday life, then activist politics in Lebanon suggest that every miniscule effort, including cultivating personal well-being, might affect politics.

De-Exceptionalizing Crises

The port explosion reinforced portrayals of Lebanon as being exceptionally plagued by crises. Yet, many other countries experienced their own sense of crisis in the early 2020s, including the Covid-19 crisis, financial crisis, energy crisis, and ecological crisis. Public discourses in many precarious contexts around the globe commonly invoked the language of crisis to interpret complex economic, political, and social challenges. Lebanese activists were aware of problems elsewhere but largely believed that the level of state dysfunctionality in Lebanon was particularly severe. Nevertheless, some activists, particularly those that interacted with international communities, questioned the exceptionality of crises in Lebanon. A Syrian activist interlocutor, who moved from Beirut to Istanbul in 2021 to work at an NGO, told me in late 2022 that he found himself "running from one crisis into another," referring to his continuing racialization as a Syrian in Türkiye's deteriorating economy. Many activists in Lebanon, particularly the older cohort, increasingly reflected on how problems such as corruption, violence, and poverty had global roots and hence required global solidarities. There were also growing reflections on how Lebanon could adopt egalitarian and just economic models.

The potential for lived experiences of crises to be generative of political possibilities was also not limited to Lebanon; it resonated in many parts of the world. For example, in the first months of the Russia–Ukraine War in 2022, some Polish citizens perceived themselves as implicated in a severe crisis, which motivated them to support displaced Ukrainians.[11] The very uncertainty created by the Russian invasion of Ukraine, and the fear that Russia would target Poland and other nearby countries in the future, mobilized some Polish citizens to act as "agents of history" to fight for the future and "remake the world."[12]

Lebanon was also one example among many global contexts in which increasing levels of precarity generated new forms of mobilization and politicization rather than depleting political agency. For instance, in Greece during the 2010s, rising poverty and inequality demoralized many but also created a sense of urgency that proliferated "unconventional resistance actions such as alternative economies, solidarity collectives, and barter networks."[13] Grassroots solidarity initiatives in Athens offered caring systems of the commons and created values such as "relationality, conductivity, care and repair, which may nurture a transformative politics for a world in crisis, yet against crisis regimes."[14] These examples reveal the open-ended and ever-shifting ethico-political frameworks of activist lifeworlds and their dynamic entanglements with both translocal encounters. New visions for change continually emerge from shared sentiments of crisis.

In many other places, experiences of crisis mobilized diverse groups who took to the streets to decry their dire living conditions. Throughout 2019 and 2020, various protests took place globally alongside those in Lebanon. In countries such as Iraq, Algeria, Ecuador, Colombia, Chile, India, and Hong Kong, hundreds of thousands of protesters reacted against multiple forms of power and inequality affecting their daily lives. More and more people began to see themselves as political subjects who were passionate for change. In most of these contexts, the profound heterogeneity of participants led to unexpected alliances.[15] As protesters encountered people from other communities, they shared their experiences of precarity and marginalization, leading to the emergence of new practices of solidarity, care, and knowledge-making. For example, during the Chilean protests of 2019, growing experiences of crisis created an awareness that "Chile's neoliberal system was experiencing an unexpected and sudden collapse," which led to "a strong new participation by middle-class people demanding in-depth change."[16] As they did in Lebanon, collectively shared sentiments of crisis in Chile generated new solidarities among diverse local groups.

These global protests reveal the dynamic, ambivalent, and indeterminate nature of activism, as well as the unintended consequences of what were often dismissed as "failed revolutions." In different parts of the world, crisiswork, with all its contradictions and ambivalences, generates a "meeting place,"[17] whereby encounters among differently situated groups create possibilities for distilling competing crisis narratives into projects of change and for reimagining past, present, and future lifeworlds.

"Let Them Know About Our Situation"

As I work on completing this book in December 2024, many in Lebanon, including my interlocutors, have found themselves in what they consider to be the most devastating crisis of their lifetimes. Since October 2023, they had been vigilantly observing Israel's genocidal campaign against the Palestinians. During the same period, cross-border fires between Hizbullah and the Israeli army had intensified, and thousands of Lebanese had been internally displaced. In September 2024, Israel escalated its attacks on Lebanon and began a full-fledged war on the country. On September 17 and 18, thousands of pagers and walkie-talkies exploded across Lebanon, killing forty-two and injuring more than 3,500 civilians. In the following weeks, Israel initiated a ground invasion of southern Lebanon, and Israeli strikes across different parts of Lebanon killed around 4,000 people and injured many more by late November. In addition to assassinating key leaders and senior commanders of Hizbullah, including Hassan Nasrallah, Israeli attacks caused substantial damage to agriculture, housing, and other vital infrastructure throughout Lebanon.

Throughout October and November 2024, together with my interlocutors in the diaspora, I was devastated to watch the destruction of many parts of Lebanon inhabited by diverse religions and ethnicities, including mixed neighborhoods of central Beirut and various towns mainly occupied by Maronite Christians. Medical, educational, peacekeeping, humanitarian, financial, and media infrastructures in different parts of the country, including several UN facilities, were repeatedly targeted by Israeli forces. Some places, such as al-Bustan in the south and Bashoura in central Beirut, reported the use of phosphorus bombing by the Israeli army. According to UN reports, over 25 percent of Lebanon received evacuation orders from Israel, and more than 1.2 million people, including refugees and migrants, were displaced. Observing thousands of displaced people fill Beirut's already overwhelmed shelters and streets, and numerous countries quickly evacuate their citizens from Lebanon, led many Lebanese to once again feel stuck in dire crises, and some to fear sectarian strife and complete chaos. Given the shockingly rapid and broad destruction of many parts of the country, together with my interlocutors, I felt anger at the mainstream Western media for representing the Israeli war on Lebanon as a series of strategic, targeted operations against "terrorist groups."

I feel obliged to pass on what several close activist interlocutors in Beirut and in the diaspora, who knew I was about to finalize my book, wrote to me in late 2024: "Let them know about our situation." My activist interlocutors in Lebanon regularly uploaded vivid photos of the bombing and destruction that they witnessed on social media as they voiced their shock, fear, and anger. Some sent me photos of their destroyed family houses and farms in South Lebanon and elsewhere and added that I "should let everyone know" about these. The relentless, buzzing sound of Israeli military drones became part of the lived experience of war and continually traumatized them. Many of my interlocutors, the majority of whom belonged to Shiʿi communities, were displaced from south Beirut to central Beirut, and some others who had the resources to do so temporarily escaped to different parts of the world.

Hospitals were overwhelmed, and most universities and schools moved to online education so they could allocate their physical spaces to displaced communities. Despite war and ruination, some activists were able to maintain their crisiswork in schools, workplaces, restaurants, cafés, and even nightclubs, all of which opened their doors and reoriented their services to support the displaced communities.

Israel's unforeseen bombings of mixed and populated central Beirut neighborhoods, such as Ras al-Naba and Zuqaq al-Blat, which they conducted with the excuse of targeting Hizbullah, caused immense shock and fear among all Beirut residents. Such sentiments heavily characterized everyday affects in Beirut, including within middle-class activist lifeworlds. On November 23, Lara, the middle-class activist in Chapter 1, lost a close relative in the Basta neighborhood of central Beirut during an Israeli missile attack that killed thirty civilians. I had already felt utterly devastated since November 18, the day an Israeli airstrike hit the Mar Ilyas neighborhood, where I had lived during my long fieldwork. I also felt helpless for not being able to do anything other than contributing to the fundraising and awareness-raising efforts of my activist interlocutors. The unpredictability and viciousness of Israel's war in Lebanon globally connected all Lebanese and their allies through shared trauma. They processed new experiences of war within the prism of lived past ones and anticipated future ones.

Given the immediacy of this destructive war, it is too early to analyze its implications on activist and other lifeworlds in Lebanon in depth. All Lebanese activists condemned Israeli brutality, yet only some centered their crisiswork on this issue. Activists such as Hala, Manal, and Nour actively organized meetings to support Palestinian rights and devoted all their resources to documenting the Israeli state's crimes and Palestinians' suffering. Amid continuing Israeli bombing of their country, they were angry with the international community for "abandoning" Lebanon and Palestine. Many also criticized the Lebanese state for not doing anything about Israeli attacks or supporting the affected communities. Given Lebanon's already grim economic situation and dysfunctional state, this ruthless war aggravated their fears about the country's future.

Following the fragile sixty-day ceasefire agreement between Hizbullah and Israel, which began on November 27, many displaced Lebanese started returning to homes filled with rubble and dust, while many continued to be displaced, as their houses had been destroyed entirely. My interlocutors and their families were disheartened, tired, and confused. In early December, the sudden fall of the Assad regime—one of Hizbullah's closest allies—in Syria increased the concerns of activists sympathetic toward Hizbullah about Israel's growing influence in the region. Some other activists celebrated the regime change in Syria and the weakening of Iran's regional influence, but had doubts and worries of their own. Similar to 2012 and 2013, everyone in Lebanon anticipated that the seismic changes within Syria's political landscape would profoundly shape the future of Lebanon. As happened after the long Lebanese War and 2006 July War, activist lifeworlds began reflecting on post-war reconstruction, national unity, and political change. Despite the dominant sentiments of fear, uncertainty, and grief, many of my activist interlocutors emphasized the importance of activism given the continuing dysfunctionality of state institutions—Lebanon had been without a president for two years, and the state had recently been accused of mismanaging international aid. When Joseph Aoun was inaugurated as the new president in January 2025 with bold promises of reform and reconstruction, most of my activist interlocutors found it hard to become hopeful. Their "radicalization"—transformation from liberal, civic activism into more critical, leftist visions of dissent and change—was accelerated by the brutality of war and ongoing economic and other crises.

I began this book with Manal and want to complete it with her. When we discussed the political situation on a video call in mid-December 2024, Manal looked tired and sad. I thanked her for her time and asked about her family and friends. In mid-November, she had told me that she had lost two people from her extended family to Israeli bombing and the houses of several family members were also destroyed. Manal's own apartment and belongings were intact, and she had not been displaced, but she narrated the stories of her family's and friends' losses as though they were her own. As I clumsily tried to express empathy and support, she smiled and said, "Don't worry, it's okay. We will get back to our struggles and cause. But this time, I'm not gonna hide; it is different."

In December 2024 Manal was thirty-eight years old. She had worked as a project manager at a local women's empowerment NGO since 2022, following intermittent employment in various NGOs between 2015 and 2022. She was still the cheerful and optimistic woman I had met in 2012, but she had less hope for Lebanon now. She told me during our video chat that she needed time to process "everything" that recently happened. The same could be said for most of my interlocutors, who ambivalently continued their activism while caring for their families, friends, and themselves amid lived experiences of wars, related traumas, and other predicaments. Yet, as you have seen in this book, pauses, reflections, rest, leisure, and even inaction are all part of crisiswork. I dearly hope that, in addition to letting readers know the multifaceted struggles for better futures within Lebanon's diverse activist lifeworlds, this book will ultimately contribute to the crisiswork of diverse communities in Lebanon and beyond.

Notes

Introduction: "We Must Do Something."

1. Except for several well-known public figures, I have changed the names of my interlocutors and any details that could expose their identity. Similarly, I have used pseudonyms for most NGOs and movements because some details might potentially undermine these entities' relationships with others, such as Western donors. Unless stated otherwise, all conversations with my interlocutors were originally conducted in Arabic. The Lebanese dialect of Arabic, with occasional use of English and French words, was the primary language used by all of my interlocutors in daily conversations. Most of the printed material, however, was in English. In some cases, Arabic versions of those materials were also provided.

2. Building upon the work of anthropologist Michael Jackson, I use the term "lifeworld" to describe the everyday, experiential world of dynamic and contingent intersubjective, embodied, and affective relationships, which encompass a complex web of political and ethical connections, engagements, and struggles. In this sense, the term "activist lifeworlds" includes all ideologies, discourses, practices, narratives, and social structures that activists encounter and experience. Michael Jackson, *Lifeworlds: Essays in Existential Anthropology* (Chicago: University of Chicago Press, 2013).

3. Zeinab Cherri, Pedro Arcos González, and Rafael Castro Delgado, "The Lebanese–Syrian Crisis: Impact of Influx of Syrian Refugees to an Already Weak State," *Risk Management and Healthcare Policy* 9 (2016): 170.

4. Kamal Salibi, *A House of Many Mansions: The History of Lebanon Reconsidered* (Berkeley: University of California Press, 1988), 130–40.

5. Philip S. Khoury, *Syria and the French Mandate: The Politics of Arab Nationalism, 1920–1945* (London: I. B. Tauris, 1987), 57.

6. On the history of competing nationalist projects in Lebanon, see Carol Hakim, *The Origins of the Lebanese National Idea: 1840–1920* (Berkeley: University of California Press, 2013). Hakim discusses how the idea of an independent Lebanon ruled by

Maronite Christians was seeded in the mid-nineteenth century by France, and Lebanese nationalism has since developed as an incoherent ideology. On how numerous Muslims, secularists, and others did not want a sectarian republic and fought against it, see Elizabeth Thompson, *Colonial Citizens: Republican Rights, Paternal Privilege, and Gender in French Syria and Lebanon* (New York: Columbia University Press, 2000).

7. John Gulick's earlier ethnographic work on al-Munsif, a predominantly Greek Orthodox Lebanese village, shows how rural Christian communities in Lebanon during the 1950s held strong loyalties to "Lebanon" despite their investment in kinship and sect-based ties and their deep connection to European and American economic and cultural networks. John Gulick, "Conservatism and Change in a Lebanese Village," *The Middle East Journal* 8, no. 3 (1954): 295–307.

8. Following other scholars of Lebanon, I use "long Lebanese War" or "Lebanese War" instead of "Lebanese Civil War" to recognize the global complexities of that period. See, for instance, Saree Makdisi, "Beirut, a City Without History?" in *Memory and Violence in the Middle East and North Africa*, ed. Ussama Makdisi and Paul A. Silverstein (Bloomington, IN: Indiana University Press, 2006), 201–14.

9. One of the camps was led by Maronite Christians who favored the existing political system and brought together Maronite-dominated Christian militia groups such as the Lebanese Forces, Marada Brigade, and Guardians of the Cedars. The other group was more heterogeneous and included the Palestinian Liberation Organization (PLO), Amal Party (representing the Shiʿa), Murabitun (representing the Sunnis of Beirut), Progressive Socialist Party (representing the Druze), Syrian Nationalist Party, Communist Party, and some other militia groups.

10. Ussama Makdisi, *The Culture of Sectarianism: Community, History, and Violence in Nineteenth-Century Ottoman Lebanon* (Berkeley: University of California Press, 2000).

11. Suad Joseph, "Pensée 2: Sectarianism as Imagined Sociological Concept and as Imagined Social Formation," *International Journal of Middle East Studies* 40, no. 4 (2008): 553–54.

12. For similar comparisons, see Ussama Makdisi, *Age of Coexistence: The Ecumenical Frame and the Making of the Modern Arab World* (Berkeley: University of California Press, 2021), 5; and Lara Deeb, "Beyond Sectarianism: Intermarriage and Social Difference in Lebanon," *International Journal of Middle East Studies* 52, no. 2 (2020): 217. This is just one instance where I challenge pervasive narratives of exceptionalism in Lebanon throughout this book. In continually comparing Lebanon with other global contexts, I reject the hegemonic idea of Lebanon as having exceptional crises.

13. For more details on the post-Ta'if state, see Michael C. Hudson, "Lebanon after Ta'if: Another Reform Opportunity Lost?" *Arab Studies Quarterly* 21, no. 1 (1999): 27–40; and Nisreen Salti and Jad Chaaban, "The Role of Sectarianism in the Allocation of Public Expenditure in Postwar Lebanon," *International Journal of Middle East Studies* 42, no. 4 (2010): 637–55. On anthropological analyses of state discourses and practices in contemporary Lebanon, see Suad Joseph, "The Public/Private—The Imagined Boundary in the Imagined Nation/State/Community: The Lebanese Case," *Feminist Review* 57, no. 1 (1997): 73–92; and Michelle Obeid, "Searching for

the 'Ideal Face of the State' in a Lebanese Border Town," *Journal of the Royal Anthropological Institute* 16, no. 2 (2010): 330–46.

14. Melani Cammett, *Compassionate Communalism: Welfare and Sectarianism in Lebanon* (Ithaca, NY: Cornell University Press, 2014).

15. Hannes Baumann, "Bringing the State and Political Economy Back In: Consociationalism and Crisis in Lebanon," *Nationalism and Ethnic Politics* 30, no. 1 (2024): 92.

16. For more discussion on "neoliberal sectarianism," which emphasizes how neoliberal policies solidified sectarian polarization by reinforcing peoples' dependence on sectarian elites and by preventing cross-sectarian solidarities, see Rima Majed, "Lebanon and Iraq in 2019: Revolutionary Uprisings against 'Sectarian Neoliberalism,'" TNI, October 27, 2021, www.tni.org/en/article/lebanon-and-iraq-in-2019; and Lara W. Khattab, "The Genealogy of Social and Political Mobilization in Lebanon under a Neoliberal Sectarian Regime (2009–2019)," *Globalizations* (2022): 1–18.

17. For detailed analyses and critique of the state-sponsored amnesia in Lebanon, see Sune Haugbolle, *War and Memory in Lebanon* (Cambridge: Cambridge University Press, 2010); and Sami Hermez, *War Is Coming: Between Past and Future Violence in Lebanon* (Philadelphia: University of Pennsylvania Press, 2017).

18. Erik Van Ommering, "Schooling in Conflict: An Ethnographic Study from Lebanon," *International Journal of Sociology and Social Policy* 31, no. 9/10 (2011): 547.

19. Bassel Akar and Mara Albrecht, "Influences of Nationalisms on Citizenship Education: Revealing a 'Dark Side' in Lebanon," *Nations and Nationalism* 23, no. 3 (2017): 547–70.

20. Bassel Akar and Mara Albrecht, "Influences of Nationalisms," 548.

21. Simon Haddad, "Cultural Diversity and Sectarian Attitudes in Postwar Lebanon," *Journal of Ethnic and Migration Studies* 28, no. 2 (2002): 291–306; Craig Larkin, "Remaking Beirut: Contesting Memory, Space, and the Urban Imaginary of Lebanese Youth," *City & Community* 9, no. 4 (2010): 414–42; and Nasser Yassin, "Sects and the City: Socio-Spatial Perceptions and Practices of Youth in Beirut," in *Lebanon After the Cedar Revolution*, ed. Are J. Knudsen and Michael Kerr (Oxford: Oxford University Press, 2013), 203–18.

22. Stuart Hall and Doreen Massey, "Interpreting the Crisis," *Soundings* 44 (2010): 57–71; Colin Hay, "Narrating Crisis: the Discursive Construction of the 'Winter of Discontent,'" *Sociology* 30, no. 2 (1996): 253–77; Stuart Hall, Chas Critcher, Tony Jefferson, John Clarke, and Brian Roberts, *Policing the Crisis: Mugging, The State and Law & Order* (London: Macmillan, 1978); Janet Roitman, *Anti-Crisis* (Durham, NC: Duke University Press, 2014); Sarah Muir, *Routine Crisis: An Ethnography of Disillusion* (Chicago: University of Chicago Press, 2021); Brian Goldstone and Juan Obarrio, eds., *African Futures: Essays on Crisis, Emergence, and Possibility* (Chicago: University of Chicago Press, 2017); and Joseph Masco, "The Crisis in Crisis," *Current Anthropology* 58, no. 15 (2017): 65–76.

23. Focusing on crisis sensibilities and governance of the "climate crisis" and "nuclear crisis" in the United States since the 1980s, for instance, Joseph Masco, in "The

Crisis in Crisis," 67, suggests that crisis talks are "counterrevolutionary" because their invocation of urgency does not allow for questioning why the crisis emerged in the first place or imagining alternative positive futures.

24. Anna Lowenhaupt Tsing, *The Mushroom at the End of the World: On the Possibility of Life in Capitalist Ruins* (Princeton, NJ: Princeton University Press, 2015); and Jarrett Zigon, *A War on People: Drug User Politics and a New Ethics of Community* (Berkeley: University of California Press, 2018).

25. Tsing, *The Mushroom at the End of the World,* 20.

26. Lori Allen makes a similar argument about Palestinian human rights activists. Despite the pervasiveness of cynicism, the desire and work for a nationalist idea of the Palestinian people and for an effective state undergirded political activism. See Lori Allen, *The Rise and Fall of Human Rights: Cynicism and Politics in Occupied Palestine* (Stanford, CA: Stanford University Press, 2013), 16–17.

27. Reinhart Koselleck, *The Practice of Conceptual History: Timing History, Spacing Concepts* (Stanford, CA: Stanford University Press, 2002).

28. Anthropologists have studied emotions and sentiments as social constructions that are bounded by cultural practices and tied to complex relations of power and subjectivity. See, for instance, Michelle Z. Rosaldo, "Toward an Anthropology of Self and Feeling," in *Culture Theory: Essays on Mind, Self, and Emotion*, ed. Richard A. Shweder and Robert A. LeVine (Cambridge: Cambridge University Press, 1984), 137–57; and Catherine A. Lutz and Lila Abu-Lughod, eds., *Language and the Politics of Emotion* (Cambridge: Cambridge University Press, 1990). Many of them have refrained from making sharp distinctions between the terms feeling, sentiment, emotion, and affect. While drawing insights from these works, my understanding of affect is also indebted to recent works by critical theorists that focus on the formative role of "affect" (defined as "public feelings" in broad circulation) in unearthing the mutual construction of public and intimacy. See, for example, Lauren Berlant, *The Female Complaint: The Unfinished Business of Sentimentality in American Culture* (Durham, NC: Duke University Press, 2008); Sara Ahmed, *The Promise of Happiness* (Durham, NC: Duke University Press, 2010); and Kathleen Stewart, *Ordinary Affects* (Durham, NC: Duke University Press, 2007).

29. Angela Garcia, *The Pastoral Clinic: Addiction and Dispossession along the Rio Grande* (Berkeley: University of California Press, 2010); Cheryl Mattingly, *The Paradox of Hope: Journeys through a Clinical Borderland* (Berkeley: University of California Press, 2010); and Veena Das and Clara Han, *Living and Dying in the Contemporary World: A Compendium* (Berkeley: University of California Press, 2015).

30. My analysis also builds on the work of linguistic anthropologists who compellingly linked affect, temporality, and everyday discourse. They point to a novel space of socio-linguistic analysis of "small world stories," where allegories and cosmologies become personal narratives and everyday talks. See, for example, Amy Shuman, *Other People's Stories: Entitlement Claims and The Critique of Empathy* (Chicago: University of Illinois Press, 2005).

31. Hermez, *War Is Coming,* 4.

32. See, for instance, Munira Khayyat, *A Landscape of War: Ecologies of Resistance and Survival in South Lebanon* (Berkeley: University of California Press, 2022); and Yasmine Khayyat, *War Remains: Ruination and Resistance in Lebanon* (Syracuse, NY: Syracuse University Press, 2023). Munira Khayyat and Yasmine Khayyat's works also show how struggles with lived experiences of war in Lebanon were unevenly distributed among the country's groups.

33. Cultural theorist Lauren Berlant studies crisis as a normalized affect and emphasizes adaptation through their concept of "crisis-ordinariness." Lauren Berlant, *Cruel Optimism* (Durham, NC: Duke University Press, 2011), 81. Anthropologist Ghassan Hage describes how in current times crisis is globally experienced as normalcy rather than an unusual state. See Ghassan Hage, *Alter-Politics: Critical Anthropology and the Radical Imagination* (Melbourne: Melbourne University Press, 2015), 10. Anthropologist Henrik Vigh similarly suggests that instead of a state of exception, crisis becomes a norm, a continuing experience, or a permanent condition. See Henrik Vigh, "Crisis and Chronicity: Anthropological Perspectives on Continuous Conflict and Decline," *Ethnos* 73, no. 1 (2008): 5–24.

34. Anthony Shadid and Nada Bakri, "For Lebanese, Crisis Has Become a Way of Life," *New York Times*, January 14, 2011.

35. Matt Bradley, "Lebanon Marks a Year without a President with a Shrug," *Wall Street Journal*, May 23, 2015.

36. For a compelling discussion on orientalism and its representation of non-West as passive and non-changing, see Edward Said, *Orientalism: Western Conceptions of the Orient* (London: Penguin, 1995).

37. *Cambridge Dictionary Online*, s.v. "activist (n.)," accessed March 20, 2024, https://dictionary.cambridge.org/dictionary/english/activist.

38. Alexei Yurchak, *Everything Was Forever, Until It Was No More: The Last Soviet Generation* (Princeton, NJ: Princeton University Press, 2005), 104–108.

39. Nitzan Shoshan, *The Management of Hate: Nation, Affect, and the Governance of Right-Wing Extremism in Germany* (Princeton, NJ: Princeton University Press, 2016).

40. As examples of ethnographies that document ambiguities in enactments of resistance and agency, see Soo Ah Kwon, *Uncivil Youth: Race, Activism, and Affirmative Governmentality* (Durham, NC: Duke University Press, 2013); Jessica Greenberg, *After the Revolution: Youth, Democracy, and the Politics of Disappointment in Serbia* (Stanford, CA: Stanford University Press, 2014); Sa'ed Atshan, *Queer Palestine and the Empire of Critique* (Stanford, CA: Stanford University Press, 2020); Pascal Ménoret, *Graveyard of Clerics: Everyday Activism in Saudi Arabia* (Stanford, CA: Stanford University Press, 2020); Jillian Schwedler, *Protesting Jordan: Geographies of Power and Dissent* (Stanford, CA: Stanford University Press, 2022); and Elliott Prasse-Freeman. *Rights Refused: Grassroots Activism and State Violence in Myanmar* (Stanford, CA: Stanford University Press, 2023).

41. For a critical reflection on the historical evolution and ambiguity of the term "activism" in the United States, see Astra Taylor, "Against Activism," *The Baffler* 30 (2016): 123–31. Critiquing growing individualism among activist groups in the

United States, Taylor interprets the ambiguities about what activism entails or who is an activist as reinforcing the cooptation of activist formations.

42. Hannah Arendt, *The Human Condition* (Chicago: University of Chicago Press, 1958), 24.

43. Arendt, *The Human Condition*, 9.

44. Feminist theorists have thoroughly criticized the theoretical distinction between the public and the private, and subsequent scholarship has shared and built on these critiques. For earlier examples of these critiques, see Floya Anthias and Nira Yuval-Davis, *Woman-Nation-State* (London: Macmillan, 1989); and Lila Abu-Lughod, ed., *Remaking Women: Feminism and Modernity in the Middle East* (Princeton, NJ: Princeton University Press, 1998). As a key example of theoretical critiques of Arendt's distinctions between public and private as well as between the political and the social, see Michael Warner, *Publics and Counterpublics* (New York: Zone Books, 2002).

45. Prathama Banerjee, *Elementary Aspects of the Political: Histories from the Global South* (Durham, NC: Duke University Press, 2020), 10.

46. Similar to some other anthropological works, I use the terms "moral" and "ethical" interchangeably. See, for example, Yurchak, *Everything Was Forever.* Avoiding any normative definition, I focus on "what counts as moral experience" within a given local context. See Jarrett Zigon, "On Love: Remaking Moral Subjectivity in Postrehabilitation Russia," *American Ethnologist* 40, no. 1 (2013): 202.

47. Even though all of my interlocutors self-identified as *nāshiṭ* in Arabic, some of them distinguished between "social activist" and "political activist" when describing their identities in English. Those who preferred the term social activist typically believed that the word "political" was too polluted to use for their activities. Also, most of them used the terms "activist" and "civil society activist" interchangeably.

48. Audre Lorde, *A Burst of Light: And Other Essays* (Mineola, NY: Ixia Press, 1988). For a compelling feminist analysis of how self-care becomes a political tool for contemporary American Black women, see Bianca C. Williams, *The Pursuit of Happiness: Black Women, Diasporic Dreams, and the Politics of Emotional Transnationalism* (Durham, NC: Duke University Press, 2018).

49. On the relationship between political struggles and demands for a dignified life in Lebanon, see Sami Hermez, "On Dignity and Clientelism: Lebanon in the Context of the 2011 Arab Revolutions," *Studies in Ethnicity and Nationalism* 11, no. 3 (2011): 527–37.

50. Sociologist Asef Bayat examines how everyday life is an important site for diverse political struggles, including revolutions, in different parts of the Middle East. See, for instance, Asef Bayat, *Revolutionary Life: The Everyday of the Arab Spring* (Cambridge, MA: Harvard University Press, 2021). Despite demonstrating how everyday life matters for subjectivities, practices, and ideas, Bayat's analysis also reifies binaries such as "ordinary lives" versus "extraordinary revolutions" and "the social" versus "the political."

51. On how kinship and family interact with activist struggles and political mobilizations, see Sian Lazar, *The Social Life of Politics: Ethics, Kinship, and Union Activism in Argentina* (Stanford, CA: Stanford University Press, 2017).

52. Suad Joseph, ed., *Gender and Citizenship in the Middle East* (Syracuse, NY: Syracuse University Press, 2000).

53. Holly Wardlow, *Wayward Women: Sexuality and Agency in a New Guinea Society* (Berkeley: University of California Press, 2006), 66. Wardlow theorizes seemingly insignificant everyday acts of refusal among the Huli women in New Guinea as "negative agency." For instance, to refuse to undertake tasks required by men such as doing the laundry or to refuse to speak when addressed allows the Huli women to disrupt the everyday workings of power.

54. Joanne R. Nucho, *Everyday Sectarianism in Urban Lebanon: Infrastructures, Public Services, and Power* (Princeton, NJ: Princeton University Press, 2016).

55. *Crisiswork* builds upon and contributes to a growing body of scholarship that has highlighted the role of affects and ethics in understanding political subjectivity. See, for example, Naisargi N. Dave, *Queer Activism in India: A Story in the Anthropology of Ethics* (Durham, NC: Duke University Press, 2012); Lazar, *The Social Life of Politics*; Susanna Trnka and Catherine Trundle, eds., *Competing Responsibilities: The Ethics and Politics of Contemporary Life* (Durham, NC: Duke University Press, 2017); Zigon, *A War on People*; and Mubbashir A. Rizvi, *The Ethics of Staying: Social Movements and Land Rights Politics in Pakistan* (Stanford, CA: Stanford University Press, 2019).

56. Danilyn Rutherford, "Affect Theory and the Empirical," *Annual Review of Anthropology* 45, no. 1 (2016): 288.

57. Kirsten L. Scheid, *Fantasmic Objects: Art and Sociality from Lebanon, 1920–1950* (Bloomington, IN: Indiana University Press, 2022), 58.

58. Tania Ahmad, "Intolerants: Politics of the Ordinary in Karachi, Pakistan," in *Impulse to Act: A New Anthropology of Resistance and Social Justice*, ed. Othon Alexandrakis (Bloomington: Indiana University Press 2016), 135–60.

59. Maple Razsa coined the term "subjective turn" as an analytical approach to the study of activism. See Maple Razsa, "The Subjective Turn: The Radicalization of Personal Experience within Occupy Slovenia," Society for Cultural Anthropology, February 14, 2013, https://culanth.org/fieldsights/the-subjective-turn-the-radicalization-of-personal-experience-within-occupy-slovenia; and Maple Razsa, *Bastards of Utopia: Living Radical Politics After Socialism* (Bloomington, IN: Indiana University Press, 2015).

60. Othon Alexandrakis, ed., *Impulse to Act: A New Anthropology of Resistance and Social Justice* (Bloomington, IN: Indiana University Press, 2016), 4.

61. Alexandrakis, *Impulse to Act*, 259.

62. See, for instance, Dave, *Queer Activism in India*; Lazar, *The Social Life of Politics*; Larisa Kurtović and Nelli Sargsyan, "After Utopia: Leftist Imaginaries and Activist Politics in the Postsocialist World, *History and Anthropology* 30, no. 1 (2019): 1–19; and Rizvi, *The Ethics of Staying*.

63. Razsa, *Bastards of Utopia*; Lynette J. Chua, *The Politics of Love in Myanmar: LGBT Mobilization and Human Rights as a Way of Life* (Stanford, CA: Stanford University Press, 2018); and Mateusz Laszczkowski, "Rethinking Resistance through and as Affect," *Anthropological Theory* 19, no. 4 (2019): 489–509.

64. Hans Peter Hahn, "Diffusionism, Appropriation, and Globalization: Some Remarks on Current Debates in Anthropology," *Anthropos* 103, no. 1 (2008): 191–202.

65. Lieba Faier and Lisa Rofel, "Ethnographies of Encounter," *Annual Review of Anthropology* 43, no. 1 (2014): 363.

66. Ilana Feldman, *Life Lived in Relief: Humanitarian Predicaments and Palestinian Refugee Politics* (Berkeley: University of California Press, 2018), 230.

67. Faier and Rofel, "Ethnographies of Encounter," 365.

68. On how decolonization is not a theory but a practice, see Silvia Rivera Cusicanqui, "Ch'ixinakax utxiwa: A Reflection on the Practices and Discourses of Decolonization," *South Atlantic Quarterly* 111, no. 1 (2012): 95–109.

69. A. Lynn Bolles, "Decolonizing Anthropology: An Ongoing Process," *American Ethnologist* 50, no. 3 (2023): 519.

70. Sarah Nimführ, "Can Collaborative Knowledge Production Decolonize Epistemology?" *Migration Letters* 19, no. 6 (2022): 787.

71. As scholars of decolonization note, the knower/known relationship undermines the possibility of non-Western peoples' participation in the knowledge production process. See Boaventura de Sousa Santos, *Epistemologies of the South: Justice against Epistemicide* (New York: Routledge, 2015); and Aníbal Quijano, "Coloniality and Modernity/Rationality," *Cultural Studies* 21, no. 2–3 (2007): 168–78.

72. Marcelo Diversi and Claudio Moreira, *Betweener Talk: Decolonizing Knowledge Production, Pedagogy, and Praxis* (London: Routledge, 2016).

73. For further discussion on "learning from others," see Carolina Alonso Bejarano, Lucia López Juárez, Mirian A. Mijangos García, and Daniel M. Goldstein, *Decolonizing Ethnography: Undocumented Immigrants and New Directions in Social Science* (Durham, NC: Duke University Press, 2019).

74. For a detailed discussion on the history of Lebanese civil society, see Paul W. T. Kingston, *Reproducing Sectarianism: Advocacy Networks and the Politics of Civil Society in Postwar Lebanon* (New York: SUNY Press, 2013).

75. Ussama Makdisi, *Artillery of Heaven: American Missionaries and the Failed Conversion of the Middle East* (Ithaca, NY: Cornell University Press, 2011).

76. Ruben Andersson, *No Go World: How Fear is Redrawing Our Maps and Infecting Our Politics* (Berkeley: University of California Press, 2019).

77. Catherine Besteman, *Militarized Global Apartheid* (Durham, NC: Duke University Press, 2020).

78. Michel Foucault, "Of Other Spaces," trans. Jay Miskowiec, *Diacritics* 16, no. 1 (Spring 1986): 22–27.

79. Homi K. Bhabha, "Dissemination: Time, Narrative, and the Margins of the Modern Nation," in *Nation and Narration*, ed. Homi K. Bhabha (New York: Routledge, 1990), 299. Emphasis in original.

80. Thompson, *Colonial Citizens*; Fawwaz Traboulsi, *A History of Modern Lebanon* (London: Pluto Press, 2007). On intra-sectarian class hierarchies in Lebanon, see Mahdi Amel, *Fi al-Dawla al- Taʿifiyya* [On the Sectarian State] (Beirut: Dar Al-Farabi, 1986).

81. James Ferguson, *The Anti-Politics Machine: "Development," Depoliticization, and Bureaucratic Power in Lesotho* (Minneapolis: University of Minnesota Press, 1994).

82. For a seminal work on how civil society activism in Arab-majority societies can display remarkably vibrant and democratic forms of politicization, see Sheila Carapico, *Civil Society in Yemen: The Political Economy of Activism in Modern Arabia* (Cambridge: Cambridge University Press, 1998).

83. Jonathan Rosa and Yarimar Bonilla, "Deprovincializing Trump, Decolonizing Diversity, and Unsettling Anthropology," *American Ethnologist* 44, no. 2 (2017): 201–8.

84. This imagination of civil society was aspirational rather than objective. A quarter of all organizations in Lebanon had direct affiliations with confessional parties. See Tania Haddad, "Governance of the Nonprofit Sector in Lebanon between Theory and Practice," *Journal of Civil Society* 19, no. 3 (2023): 334–35. Additionally, many non-partisan and non-sectarian NGOs were coopted by sectarian elites. See Janine A. Clark and Bassel F. Salloukh, "Elite Strategies, Civil Society, and Sectarian Identities in Postwar Lebanon," *International Journal of Middle East Studies* 45, no. 4 (2013): 731–49.

85. Some activists also distinguished between NGOs and smaller unregistered groups. Some activists belonging to unregistered informal groups often criticized NGO employees as not being authentic activists.

86. As of 2014, over 8,300 civil society organizations were registered with the Ministry of Interior and Municipalities. See Civil Society Facility South, "Mapping Civil Society Organizations in Lebanon," Beyond Reform and Development, April 16, 2015, https://eeas.europa.eu/archives/delegations/lebanon/documents/news/20150416_2_en.pdf.

87. For other works on activist socialities in Lebanon, see Sami Hermez, "Activism as 'Part-Time' Activity: Searching for Commitment and Solidarity in Lebanon," *Cultural Dynamics* 23, no. 1 (2011): 41–55; and Fuad Musallam, "The Dissensual Everyday," *City & Society* 32, no. 3 (2020): 670–93.

88. Raymond Williams, *Marxism and Literature* (Oxford: Oxford Paperbacks, 1977).

89. Partha Chatterjee, *The Nation and Its Fragments: Colonial and Postcolonial Histories* (Princeton, NJ: Princeton University Press, 1993), 92.

90. For a compelling theorization of middle-classness as having a shared cultural milieu and modern aspirations, see Keith D. Watenpaugh, *Being Modern in the Middle East: Revolution, Nationalism, Colonialism, and the Arab Middle Class* (Princeton, NJ: Princeton University Press, 2006). For a detailed historical analysis of the formation of middle-classness in modern Lebanon and how it was profoundly shaped by histories of emigration, see Akram Fouad Khater, *Inventing Home: Emigration, Gender, and the Middle Class in Lebanon, 1870–1920* (Berkeley: University of California Press, 2001).

91. Though there are no official numbers, it is estimated that twelve to fifteen million Lebanese live in the diaspora. Diaspora communities have historically been

central to Lebanon's economy and politics. Some of those diasporans, including Rafiq Hariri, returned to Lebanon in the 1980s and 1990s, and invested in Lebanon's construction, banking, and real estate sectors.

92. Ghassan Hage, *The Diasporic Condition: Ethnographic Explorations of the Lebanese in the World* (Chicago: University of Chicago Press, 2021).

93. In different parts of the Middle East as well, civil society activism is dominated by middle-class elites, particularly men, and is centered largely on NGOs. Also, see Asef Bayat, *Revolutionary Life.*

94. Michel Foucault, "Of Other Spaces."

95. Sherry B. Ortner, "Dark Anthropology and Its Others: Theory since the Eighties," *HAU: Journal of Ethnographic Theory* 6, no. 1 (2016): 47–73.

96. The term non-sectarian was widely used by diverse Lebanese activists, and it included various positions from secularism to liberal piety. Some activists, for instance, explicitly rejected the term secular (*ʿalmānī*), seeing it as an anti-religious concept.

97. Sune Haugbolle, "Social Boundaries and Secularism in the Lebanese Left," *Mediterranean Politics* 18, no. 3 (2013): 432. I use the term "nationalism" in this work to refer to both a post-colonial political project of state-building and the appearances of nationalism in everyday life—"banal nationalism." The latter term focuses on everyday symbols and discourses referring to national identity and attends to a variety of patriotic, abstract, and daily invocations of nationhood—of Lebanon and the Lebanese, in this study. See Michael Billig, *Banal Nationalism* (London: Sage, 1995).

98. Scheid, *Fantasmic Objects*, 32. Similar to Scheid's brilliant ethnography on Lebanese art and sociality, *Crisiswork* calls attention to aspirations and dreams in understanding contemporary Lebanon and underscores its activists' contingency and open-endedness.

99. In contemporary Yemen, Lisa Wedeen similarly observes how citizens formed national attachments and solidarities despite a "weak state" and historically entrenched political divisions. Lisa Wedeen, *Peripheral Visions: Publics, Power, and Performance in Yemen* (Chicago: University of Chicago Press, 2009).

100. Numerous ethnographies productively theorize sectarianism, linking it to discussions of memory (e.g., Hermez, *War is Coming*); space (e.g., Kristin V. Monroe, *The Insecure City: Space, Power, and Mobility in Beirut* (New Brunswick, NJ: Rutgers University Press, 2016); religion (e.g., Nada Moumtaz, *God's Property: Islam, Charity, and the Modern State* (Berkeley: University of California Press, 2021); gender (e.g., Maya Mikdashi, *Sextarianism: Sovereignty, Secularism, and the State in Lebanon* (Stanford, CA: Stanford University Press, 2022); and urban infrastructure and services (e.g., Nucho, *Everyday Sectarianism*). While these works document at length the impacts of sectarianism as a political, economic, and cultural system, there is little consideration of everyday cross-sectarian encounters and political formations.

101. Arjun Appadurai, *The Future as Cultural Fact: Essays on the Global Condition* (London: Verso, 2013); Yurchak, *Everything Was Forever*; and Morten Nielsen, "A

Wedge of Time: Futures in the Present and Presents without Futures in Maputo, Mozambique," *Journal of the Royal Anthropological Institute* 20 (2014): 166–82.

102. Greenberg, *After the Revolution*, 2.

Chapter 1: Crisis Narratives

1. Referring to those grammatical mistakes, a Lebanese American friend of mine also commented that the survey had "definitely" been prepared by a group of young students rather than by a high-ranking professional.

2. Paul Ricoeur, *Time and Narrative*, vol. 1, trans. Kathleen McLaughlin and David Pellauer (Chicago: University of Chicago Press, 1984), 52.

3. Alasdair MacIntyre, *After Virtue: A Study in Moral Theory* (New York: University of Notre Dame Press, 1981), 200–204.

4. Dorinne Kondo, *Worldmaking: Race, Performance, and the Work of Creativity* (Durham, NC: Duke University Press, 2018), 29.

5. For an insightful analysis on the role of traffic in shaping public life and sociality in Beirut, see Kristin V. Monroe, *The Insecure City: Space, Power, and Mobility in Beirut* (New Brunswick, NJ: Rutgers University Press, 2016).

6. On how the word "crisis" has acquired a globally ubiquitous presence in recent decades and has been increasingly used by publicly influential actors, such as politicians and scientists, see Didier Fassin, "Crisis," in *Words and Worlds: A Lexicon for Dark Times,* ed. Veena Das and Didier Fassin (Durham, NC: Duke University Press, 2021), 261–76.

7. Janet Roitman, *Anti-Crisis* (Durham, NC: Duke University Press, 2014), 16.

8. I thank my research assistant Amina Skouti for her diligent research on the history, etymology, and contemporary usage of *azma*. I also thank Dr. Abdulrazzak S. Aldhobhani and Dr. Mohammad R. Salama for recommending several important sources for this research.

9. *The Doha Historical Dictionary of Arabic*, s.v. "azma (n.)," accessed October 5, 2022, www.dohadictionary.org/dictionary/%D8%A3%D8%B2%D9%85%D8%A9.

10. Muhammad ibn Abu Bakr al-Razi, *Mukhtar al-Sihah* (Digital Library of India, 2020), https://archive.org/details/dli.ernet.432454/page/n9/mode/2up.

11. Major Lebanese media institutions were controlled by sectarian and political groups. For example, LBC was controlled by the Christian Lebanese Forces. On the connections between the Lebanese media sector and the sectarian patronage system, see Hatim El-Hibri, *Visions of Beirut: The Urban Life of Media Infrastructure* (Durham, NC: Duke University Press, 2021), 14.

12. Karim Al-Dahdah, You Know You're Lebanese When . . ., trans. and ed. Sabine Taoukjian (Beirut: Turning Point Books, 2011).

13. Peter Grimsditch and Michael Karam, *Life's Like That!: Your Guide to the Lebanese* (Beirut: Turning Point Books, 2004).

14. Naharnet Newsdesk, "Suleiman, Berri, Miqati: Dahieh Blast Must Prompt Lebanese to End Their Differences," July 3, 2013, www.naharnet.com/stories/en/

89898-suleiman-berri-miqati-dahieh-blast-must-prompt-lebanese-to-end-their-differences.

15. The March 14 coalition mainly included Sunni-led Future Movement party, the Christian Lebanese Forces, and other liberal parties and was known for its pro-Western stance. The March 8 coalition was led by Hizbullah and the Amal party and also included the Christian Free Patriotic Movement and other pro-Syrian parties. It was known for its pro-Iranian and pro-Russian stance. These alliances were more about geopolitical divisions than sectarian divisions.

16. See, for instance, the "Proudly Non-Smoking" campaign by Nudge Lebanon, a middle class-led Lebanese advocacy NGO that called businesses that complied with the ban "good corporate citizens." "'Proudly Non-Smoking' Campaign," Nudge Lebanon, n.d., https://nudgelebanon.org/proudly-non-smoking-campaign/.

17. For a brief review of different public opinions on the ban, see Matt Nash, "Lebanon Smoking Ban Draws Dismay and Delight," BBC News, September 4, 2012, www.bbc.com/news/world-middle-east-19478690.

18. Not all Lebanese felt critical and cynical when observing such public scenes. As Ghassan Hage suggests, Lebanese complaints about chaos or unruliness in public spaces can reflect "mischievous enjoyment," and many Lebanese felt proud to navigate daily challenges. Ghassan Hage, *The Diasporic Condition: Ethnographic Explorations of the Lebanese in the World* (Chicago: University of Chicago Press, 2021), 169.

19. For similar dynamics of self-orientalizing discourses of the local elites in China, see Tim Oakes, "China's Provincial Identities: Reviving Regionalism and Reinventing 'Chineseness,'" *The Journal of Asian Studies* 59, no. 3 (2000): 667–92.

20. Setha Low, *Behind the Gates: Life, Security, and the Pursuit of Happiness in Fortress America* (London: Routledge, 2004); and Sarah Muir, *Routine Crisis: An Ethnography of Disillusion* (Chicago: University of Chicago Press, 2021).

21. Muir, *Routine Crisis*, 11.

22. Globally, the progress of a nation has been measured through comparisons of its history with the histories of Western modernity and civilization. See, for example, James Ferguson, *Expectations of Modernity: Myths and Meanings of Urban Life on the Zambian Copperbelt* (Berkeley: University of California Press, 1999).

23. Klaus Schwab and Xavier Sala-i-Martín, "The Global Competitiveness Report, 2013–2024," World Economic Forum, 2013, https://www3.weforum.org/docs/WEF_GlobalCompetitivenessReport_2013-14.pdf.

24. See Chapter 6 for an in-depth discussion on Lebanese exceptionalism.

25. Behrooz Ghamari-Tabrizi, "Revolution," in *Words and Worlds: A Lexicon for Dark Times*, ed. Veena Das and Didier Fassin (Durham, NC: Duke University Press, 2021), 171.

26. Solidere's project of post-war reconstruction, which redesigned the city center to benefit transnational companies, led to the forced displacement of an estimated 2,600 families, most of whom were Shiʿa. For compelling critiques of the project and its impacts, see Najib B. Hourani, "Post-Conflict Reconstruction and Citizenship Agendas: Lessons from Beirut," in *Citizenship Agendas in and beyond the Nation-State*,

ed. Martijn Koster, Rivke Jaffe, and Anouk De Koning (London: Routledge, 2018), 74–89.

27. For a more detailed discussion on the relationship between politics and electricity distribution, see Joanne Nucho, *Everyday Sectarianism in Urban Lebanon: Infrastructures, Public Services, and Power* (Princeton, NJ: Princeton University Press, 2016).

28. May El-Khalil, a former Lebanese athlete who stopped her career after a serious accident, founded the Beirut Marathon Association in 2003. The marathon was framed as a non-sectarian and non-partisan event, and all participants were asked to wear white shirts and avoid colorful shirts that represented any political group. Because El-Khalil's team successfully engaged with diverse political groups in the country, the marathon was widely supported and many mixed and politically tense locations in diverse parts of Beirut were successfully securitized during the days of the event.

29. Invocation of resilience in Lebanon included, but was not limited to, the neoliberal idea of self-responsibility. On the historically shifting meanings and practices of the term resilience, see Roberto E. Barrios, "Resilience: A Commentary from the Vantage Point of Anthropology," *Annals of Anthropological Practice* 40, no. 1 (2016): 28–38.

Chapter 2: Imagining a Multiscalar Change

1. For more details on the incident, see "Teen in Beirut Bombing 'Selfie' Dies," Al Arabiya News, December 28, 2013, https://english.alarabiya.net/News/middle-east/2013/12/28/Teen-in-Beirut-bombing-Selfie-dies-.

2. Accusations that Hizbullah was behind the attack led some of the Sunni attendees at al-Chaar's funeral at the Khashoggi Mosque to boo the Sunni Grand Mufti Qabbani, whom they viewed as a Hizbullah ally. The unrest during the funeral was widely covered as a display of Lebanese Sunnis' rising anger against Hizbullah. See, for instance, Anne Barnard, "Funeral Turnout Shows Lebanon's Ebbing Morale," *New York Times*, December 29, 2013.

3. As an example of international coverage that linked the bombing to Lebanon's ongoing crises, see Kim Ghattas, "Mohamad Chatah Killing Targets Potential Lebanon PM," BBC News, December 29, 2013, www.bbc.com/news/world-middle-east-25536149.

4. For more details on the campaign, see Cordelia Hebblethwaite, "#BBCtrending: Lebanon's #Notamartyr Selfie Protest," BBC News, January 6, 2014, www.bbc.com/news/blogs-trending-25623299.

5. Lebanese use the term "normalcy" *(al-ḥayāt al-ṭabīʿiyya)* in a positive way to refer to a relaxed mode of being that is not subject to continual fear and anxiety. Studying war as both a real and imagined local category in Lebanon, Sami Hermez suggests that people seek to "sustain a sense of everyday normalcy" in the context of war. Sami Hermez, *War Is Coming: Between Past and Future Violence in Lebanon* (Philadelphia: University of Pennsylvania Press, 2017), 2.

6. I approach "the youth" in Beirut as a "social shifter," and thus as both a discursive construct and a social force. See Deborah Durham, "Youth and the Social Imagination in Africa: Introduction to Parts 1 and 2," *Anthropological Quarterly* 73, no. 3 (2000): 113–20.

7. Neoliberal agendas have globally promoted active citizenship to justify the erosion of welfare services and state responsibilities. For a compelling critique of this process, see Andrea Muehlebach, *The Moral Neoliberal: Welfare and Citizenship in Italy* (Chicago: University of Chicago Press, 2012). However, active citizenship cannot be reduced to neoliberal processes. For an interesting discussion on how the Lebanese education system fosters active citizenship and to what ends, see Bassel Akar, "Learning Active Citizenship: Conflicts Between Students' Conceptualisations of Citizenship and Classroom Learning Experiences in Lebanon," *British Journal of Sociology of Education* 37, no. 2 (2016): 288–312.

8. Lebanese civil society's ongoing dependence on Western donors and the implications of this dependence have been widely studied. See, for example, Caroline Nagel and Lynn Staeheli, "International Donors, NGOs, and the Geopolitics of Youth Citizenship in Contemporary Lebanon," *Geopolitics* 20, no. 2 (2015): 223–47. For how donor dependency and related processes of institutionalization impact civil society activism in other contexts, see Analiese Richard, *The Unsettled Sector: NGOs and the Cultivation of Democratic Citizenship in Rural Mexico* (Stanford, CA: Stanford University Press, 2016); and Saida Hodžić, *The Twilight of Cutting: African Activism and Life After NGOs* (Berkeley: University of California Press, 2017).

9. Various critical works examine, within the context of the global war on terror, Western geopolitical interests in promoting civil society. See, for instance, Jude Howell, "The Global War on Terror, Development and Civil Society," *Journal of International Development* 18, no. 1 (2006): 121–35.

10. Nikolas Kosmatopoulos, "The Birth of the Workshop: Technomorals, Peace Expertise, and the Care of the Self in the Middle East," *Public Culture* 26, no. 3 (2014): 529–58.

11. "Youth in Governance: Shaping the Future," *Lebanon Development Marketplace 2006*, n.d., 3.

12. "Youth in Governance: Shaping the Future," 3.

13. "Youth in Governance: Shaping the Future," 11.

14. USAID, Office of Transition Initiatives—Lebanon, n.d., www.usaid.gov/stabilization-and-transitions/closed-programs/lebanon.

15. Western donors have promoted youth participation in civil society globally to precipitate geopolitically desirable outcomes of societal change. See, for example, Jessica Greenberg, *After the Revolution: Youth, Democracy, and the Politics of Disappointment in Serbia* (Stanford, CA: Stanford University Press, 2014); and Mayssoun Sukarieh, "The Hope Crusades: Culturalism and Reform in the Arab World," *PoLAR* 35, no. 1 (2012): 115–34.

16. USAID, "Civic Activism Toolkit: A Hands-On Manual to Help Youth Activists Make Change in Their Communities," USAID, Office of Transition Initiatives, Lebanon Civic Support Initiative, Beirut, 2013.

17. For more details on how Lebanon's voting system reproduces sectarian structures, see Melani Cammett, "Sectarianism and the Ambiguities of Welfare in Lebanon," *Current Anthropology* 56, no. 11 (2015): 76–87.

18. By 2015, there were at least 117 officially registered and active "youth-relevant NGOs" that were independent of political parties and religious organizations. See Mona Harb, "Youth Mobilization in Lebanon: Navigating Exclusion and Seeds for Collective Action," Power2Youth Working Paper 16, Istituto Affari Internazionali, September 30, 2016, www.iai.it/en/pubblicazioni/youth-mobilization-lebanon.

19. Omnia El Shakry, "Youth as Peril and Promise: The Emergence of Adolescent Psychology in Postwar Egypt," *International Journal of Middle East Studies* 43, no. 4 (2011): 591–610.

20. "The Youth Advocacy Process: YAP," MASAR Organization, n.d., 1.

21. For an overview of the national youth policy process, see "The Youth Policy in Lebanon," The Youth Advocacy Process and The Youth Forum for National Youth Policies, February 2012, www.youthpolicy.org/uploads/documents/2012_Case_Study_Youth_Policy_Lebanon_Eng.pdf.

22. "National Youth Policy Action Plan," UNICEF and UNFPA, September 2022, https://lebanon.un.org/sites/default/files/2022-09/National%20Youth%20Policy%20Action%20Plan-Full%20Report.pdf.

23. Several ethnographies on Lebanon share similar observations and challenge the fantasy of Lebanese living in self-enclosed sectarian spaces. See Aseel Sawalha, *Reconstructing Beirut: Memory and Space in a Postwar Arab City* (Austin: University of Texas Press, 2010); and Kristin V. Monroe, *The Insecure City: Space, Power, and Mobility in Beirut* (New Brunswick, NJ: Rutgers University Press, 2016).

24. On the ambivalent aspects of policy-making in different global contexts, see Winifred Tate, "Anthropology of Policy: Tensions, Temporalities, Possibilities," *Annual Review of Anthropology* 49, no. 1 (2020): 83–99.

25. Greenberg, *After the Revolution*, 149.

26. For instance, on Brazil, see Carlos A. Forment, "The Democratic Dribbler: Football Clubs, Neoliberal Globalization, and Buenos Aires' Municipal Election of 2003," *Public Culture* 19, no. 1 (2007): 85–116.

27. Corruption is not a self-evident concept with agreed-upon definitions and characteristics. Powerful global actors, such as the World Bank, have defined corruption in ways that shift the blame from colonial history to local institutions. For a critical anthropological engagement with the concept of corruption, see Sarah Muir and Akhil Gupta, "Rethinking The Anthropology of Corruption: An Introduction to Supplement 18," *Current Anthropology* 59, no. 18 (2018): 4–15.

28. Pascal Ménoret's study of Islamic activists in Saudi Arabia also suggests that neutrality and being apolitical, as well as related efforts to present oneself as

professional and an expert, could paradoxically enable politics. Pascal Ménoret, *Graveyard of Clerics: Everyday Activism in Saudi Arabia* (Stanford, CA: Stanford University Press 2020).

29. Greenberg, *After the Revolution*, 148.

30. Greenberg, *After the Revolution*, 116–17. Many activists in Serbia, where Greenberg conducted her research, expressed a simultaneous commitment to progressive politics and expertise. In other contexts, such as Chile and India, local activists were similarly compelled to frame their knowledge as expertise and proudly identified as professionals and experts. See Julia Paley, "The Paradox of Participation: Civil Society and Democracy in Chile," *PoLAR* 24, no. 1 (2001): 1–12; and Julia Kowalski, "Between Gender and Kinship: Mediating Rights and Relations in North Indian NGOs," *American Anthropologist* 123, no. 2 (2021): 330–42.

31. See, for instance, Julia Elyachar, *Markets of Dispossession: NGOs, Economic Development, and the State in Cairo* (Durham, NC: Duke University Press, 2005); and Tania Murray Li, *The Will to Improve: Governmentality, Development, and the Practice of Politics* (Durham, NC: Duke University Press, 2007).

32. Bianca Williams offers a compelling feminist anthropological analysis of self-care in her ethnography on African American women traveling to Jamaica in pursuit of wellness and happiness. Williams suggests that this pursuit was a form of political resistance because it helped alleviate the substantial emotional costs of enduring racialized and gendered forms of hardship and marginalization in the United States. See Bianca C. Williams, *The Pursuit of Happiness: Black Women, Diasporic Dreams, and the Politics of Emotional Transnationalism* (Durham, NC: Duke University Press, 2018). In Lebanon, activists' pursuit of positivity had similar political meanings but went beyond that. Achievement of wellness in the present was seen as a precondition for effective and feasible collective politics.

33. Lynette Chua describes how LGBT activists in Burma encouraged queer Burmese to overcome negative feelings such as resignation resulting from social stigmatization and tried to instill in them feelings of confidence. Similar to Lebanese activists' politics, Burmese activists' focus on emotions did not prevent them from identifying legal, political, and police institutions as the main causes of queer suffering. Lynette J. Chua, *The Politics of Love in Myanmar: LGBT Mobilization and Human Rights as a Way of Life* (Stanford, CA: Stanford University Press, 2018), 23–25.

34. For a historical and ethnographic analysis of yoga practices in Lebanon, see Annabel Claire Turner, *Yoga Practices in Beirut* (MA thesis, American University of Beirut, 2015).

35. Michael Jackson, *How Lifeworlds Work: Emotionality, Sociality, and the Ambiguity of Being* (Chicago: University of Chicago Press, 2017), 21.

36. Jackson, *How Lifeworlds Work*, 60.

37. Jackson, *How Lifeworlds Work*, 60, citing Bronislaw Malinowski, *Argonauts of the Western Pacific: An Account of Native Enterprise and Adventure in the Archipelagoes of Melanesian New Guinea* (London: Routledge and Kegan Paul, 1922).

38. On how NGOs can be repurposed for collective healing in different global contexts, see Sarah D. Phillips, "Civil Society and Healing: Theorizing Women's Social Activism in Post-Soviet Ukraine," *Ethnos* 70, no. 4 (2005): 489–514.

Chapter 3: Aspirant Professionals

1. For other ethnographies on how social stratification and class shaped Lebanon's cultural landscape, see Lara Deeb and Mona Harb, *Leisurely Islam: Negotiating Geography and Morality in Shi'ite South Beirut* (Princeton, NJ: Princeton University Press, 2013); Kristin V. Monroe, *The Insecure City: Space, Power, and Mobility in Beirut* (New Brunswick, NJ: Rutgers University Press, 2016); Aseel Sawalha, *Reconstructing Beirut: Memory and Space in a Postwar Arab City* (Austin: University of Texas Press, 2010); and Kirsten L. Scheid, *Fantasmic Objects: Art and Sociality from Lebanon, 1920–1950* (Bloomington: Indiana University Press, 2022).

2. My concept of class-making builds on the work of French anthropologist Pierre Bourdieu, who emphasizes the contingency and open-endedness of class formations and struggles. Pierre Bourdieu, "What Makes a Social Class? On the Theoretical and Practical Existence of Groups," *Berkeley Journal of Sociology* 32 (1987): 1–17.

3. As with "moral," terms such as "immoral," "corruption," "sectarian," "non-sectarian," "local," "universal," "civil," "uncivil," "threat," and "backwards" were widely used by my interlocutors in both Arabic and English.

4. Jihad Makhoul and Lindsey Harrison, "Intercessory Wasta and Village Development in Lebanon," *Arab Studies Quarterly* 26, no. 3 (2004): 25.

5. As other anthropological accounts on Lebanon also point out, familial and sectarian connections did not necessarily contradict "modern" ideals of democracy, individuality, and citizenship. See Suad Joseph, "The Public/Private—The Imagined Boundary in the Imagined Nation/State/Community: The Lebanese Case," *Feminist Review* 57, no. 1 (1997): 73–92; and Nada Moumtaz, *God's Property: Islam, Charity, and the Modern State* (Berkeley: University of California Press, 2021).

6. Dana Halawi, "Widespread Favoritism Takes Toll on Economy," *Daily Star*, November 4, 2013.

7. Lojine Kamel, "Bala Wasta: No Connections, All Work," Beirut, November 27, 2012, www.beirut.com/l/19987.

8. As an example of the discussion on *wāsṭa* in the region, see Jumana Alaref, "Wasta Once Again Hampering Arab Youth Chances for a Dignified Life," *World Bank Blogs*, March 13, 2014, https://blogs.worldbank.org/arabvoices/wasta-hampering-arab-youth-chances-dignified-life.

9. I am grateful to Suad Joseph for pointing out that being a *wāsṭa* (as opposed to having it) could signify adulthood for many Lebanese.

10. In this survey, my Lebanese research assistants majoring in sociology and I created five specific intervals (e.g., 500–800 USD) for measuring monthly family income in one of the questions. We also asked about the current jobs of parents in another question.

11. Elizabeth Thompson, ***Colonial Citizens: Republican Rights, Paternal Privilege, and Gender in French Syria and Lebanon*** (New York: Columbia University Press, 2000), 15–71.

12. Colonial discourses have systematically portrayed Arabs as violent, uncivilized, and non-liberal. For an extended discussion on these portrayals and their wider implications, see Joseph A. Massad, ***Desiring Arabs*** (Chicago: University of Chicago Press, 2019).

13. Anthropologists typically study "professionals" as powerful actors with specialized knowledge and primarily focus on expertise and its enactments of knowledge, power, and authority. See, for instance, Vincent Ialenti, "Spectres of Seppo: The Afterlives of Finland's Nuclear Waste Experts," ***Journal of the Royal Anthropological Institute*** 26, no. 2 (2020): 251–68; and David Kloos, "Experts beyond Discourse: Women, Islamic Authority, and the Performance of Professionalism in Malaysia," ***American Ethnologist*** 46, no. 2 (2019): 162–75. As a result, there is little ethnographic inquiry into invocations of professionalism by less privileged communities. Carla Freeman's research on female workers in the informatics industry in Barbados offers rich insights. Carla Freeman, ***High Tech and High Heels in the Global Economy: Women, Work, and Pink-Collar Identities in the Caribbean*** (Durham, NC: Duke University Press, 2000). However, professionalism in Freeman's context is still restricted to a shared work identity and work space.

14. Pierre Bourdieu, ***Distinction: A Social Critique of the Judgement of Taste***, trans. Richard Nice (Cambridge, MA: Harvard University Press, 1984).

15. Mirko Noordegraaf and Willem Schinkel, "Professionalism as Symbolic Capital: Materials for a Bourdieusian Theory of Professionalism," ***Comparative Sociology*** 10, no. 1 (2011): 89.

16. Noordegraaf and Schinkel, "Professionalism as Symbolic Capital," 88, original emphasis.

17. The exact Arabic translation of the word "professional" is ***muḥtarif.*** But the usage of this term is limited to scholarly and highly intellectual contexts; I heard only a few of my interlocutors use it.

18. Ilana Gershon, ***Down and Out in the New Economy: How People Find (or Don't Find) Work Today*** (Chicago: University of Chicago Press, 2017). The job market culture in the U.S. studied by Gershon shares many similarities with other neoliberal contexts, including Lebanon. In Lebanon, soft-skills workshops were promoted by mainstream social policy and development agendas to build resilience suitable for neoliberal markets. Yet in the Lebanese case, as exemplified by Dana and others, learning market-oriented skills was also repurposed for other goals.

19. Deeb and Harb, ***Leisurely Islam***, 25.

20. Other ethnographies of Lebanon similarly point out how Lebanese activists critique civil society. See, for example, Sophie Chamas, "Activism as a Way of Life: The Social World of Social Movements in Middle-Class Beirut," ***Partecipazione e Conflitto*** 14, no. 2 (2021): 530–46; and Sami Hermez, "Activism as 'Part-Time' Activity: Searching for Commitment and Solidarity in Lebanon," ***Cultural Dynamics*** 23, no. 1 (2011): 41–55.

Chapter 4: Entrepreneurial Activism

1. Gilbert Doumit, "TEDxBeirut—Gilbert Doumit—Political Entrepreneurship," TEDx Talks, posted November 9, 2011, 12:47, www.youtube.com/watch?v=5r-5vUKwztY.

2. The term "political entrepreneur" has been used by political theorists since 1978 to refer to people who mobilize or organize masses, especially the poor, for a collective goal and a common good in ways that also benefit themselves individually. See, for instance, Philip Jones, "The Appeal of the Political Entrepreneur," *British Journal of Political Science* 8, no. 4 (1978): 498–504. Gilbert's focus, however, was more on political change for the purposes of nation-building and state-making.

3. As many anthropological works note, entrepreneurial subjectivity is a sine qua non of neoliberalism. See, for example, James Ferguson, "The Uses of Neoliberalism," *Antipode* 41, S1 (2010): 166–84; and Aihwa Ong, *Neoliberalism as Exception: Mutations in Citizenship and Sovereignty* (Durham, NC: Duke University Press, 2006).

4. For a compelling discussion on different meanings of self-reliance in relation to neoliberalism, see Johanna Bockman, "The Political Projects of Neoliberalism," *Social Anthropology/Anthropologie Sociale* 20, no. 3 (2012): 310–17.

5. Ong, *Neoliberalism as Exception*, 14.

6. For contrasting examples of entrepreneurialism being ostensibly apolitical, see Carla Freeman, *Entrepreneurial Selves: Neoliberal Respectability and the Making of a Caribbean Middle Class* (Durham, NC: Duke University Press, 2014); and Ong, *Neoliberalism as Exception*.

7. The entrepreneurial logics of flexible, risk-taking, and responsibilized market actors permeate a wide range of fields, such as intimacy and marriage, the arts, and refugee management. See Freeman, *Entrepreneurial Selves*; Jesse Weaver Shipley, *Living the Hiplife: Celebrity and Entrepreneurship in Ghanaian Popular Music* (Durham, NC: Duke University Press, 2013); and Lewis Turner, "'#Refugees Can Be Entrepreneurs Too!' Humanitarianism, Race, and the Marketing of Syrian Refugees," *Review of International Studies* 46, no. 1 (2020): 137–55.

8. Many scholarly articles mention the entrepreneurial character of the Lebanese as a widely agreed social fact that does not require any evidence. On how Lebanon is renowned for its entrepreneurial acumen, see, for instance, Zafar U. Ahmed and Craig C. Julian, "International Entrepreneurship in Lebanon," *Global Business Review* 13, no. 1 (2012): 25–38.

9. See Sune Haugbolle, "Social Boundaries and Secularism in the Lebanese Left," *Mediterranean Politics* 18, no. 3 (2013): 427–43. Haugbolle discusses how contemporary Lebanese civil society, including its leftist members, combined ideas of nationalism and secularism.

10. For a thorough analysis of the history of leftist movements in Lebanon, see Fadi A. Bardawil, *Revolution and Disenchantment: Arab Marxism and the Binds of Emancipation* (Durham, NC: Duke University Press, 2020).

11. Haugbolle, "Social Boundaries," 428–29.

12. In addition to civil society, the private sector, and state institutions such as the Beirut Municipality, major religious groups also actively promoted social entrepreneurship in Lebanon. For example, Omar Bortolazzi discusses how Shiʿi religious and political groups fostered social entrepreneurship. Omar Bortolazzi, "Harakat Amal: Social Mobilization, Economic Resources, Welfare Provision," *Journal of South Asian and Middle Eastern Studies* 45, no. 1 (2021): 37–65.

13. Some activist groups in Lebanese civil society explicitly opposed neoliberal economic policies. These included independents such as anti-racist and feminist groups and the movement the People Want (al-Shaʿb Yurid), as well as activists who were close to parties such as the Syrian Social Nationalist Party, the People's Movement (Harakat al-Shaʿb), and the Lebanese Communist Party. There were also Lebanese leftists who collaborated with global movements such as the Occupy movement in the United States. See Sami Hermez, "Activism as 'Part-Time' Activity: Searching for Commitment and Solidarity in Lebanon," *Cultural Dynamics* 23, no. 1 (2011): 41–55.

14. Whereas in other contexts such as Malaysia and Oman the state promoted entrepreneurial ideas to create loyal citizens, in Lebanon, civil society disseminated these ideas to promote activism for social change. See Sarah Kelman, "The Bumipreneur Dilemma and Malaysia's Technology Start-Up Ecosystem," *Economic Anthropology* 5, no. 1 (2018): 59–70; and Robin Thomas Steiner, "Cultivating 'Omani Ambitions': Entrepreneurship, Distributive Labor, and the Temporalities of Diversification in the Arab Gulf," *Economic Anthropology* 7, no. 1 (2020): 80–92.

15. Youmna Chamcham, "Live Love Beirut: The Story of a Movement," Vimeo, June 25, 2015, https://vimeo.com/131797617.

16. Freeman, *Entrepreneurial Selves*, 5.

17. Siobhan Magee, "'To Be One's Own Boss': Exceptional Entrepreneurs and Products That Sell Themselves in Urban Poland," *Ethnos* 84, no. 3 (2019): 436–57.

18. Ghassan Hage, *The Diasporic Condition: Ethnographic Explorations of the Lebanese in the World* (Chicago: University of Chicago Press, 2021), ix.

19. Kim Ghattas, "Beirut's Lovable Losers," *Foreign Policy*, May 26, 2016, https://foreignpolicy.com/2016/05/26/beiruts-loveable-losers/.

20. I did not conduct research on any LGBTQ-focused organization in Lebanon, but I met twelve LGBTQ activists who volunteered for, worked in, or were affiliated with organizations and collectives in which I did participate. All of these activists were middle-class Lebanese, though their confessional backgrounds varied.

21. On competing values of masculinity in Egypt, for instance, see Farha Ghannam, *Live and Die Like a Man: Gender Dynamics in Urban Egypt* (Stanford, CA: Stanford University Press, 2013).

Chapter 5: Producing Hope

1. Critical theorists praise hope for being central to building collective struggles for justice and equality. See Ernst Bloch, *The Principle of Hope*, vol. 1, trans. Neville Plaice, Stephen Plaice, and Paul Knight (Cambridge, MA: MIT Press, 1986); David Harvey, *Spaces of Hope* (Berkeley: University of California Press, 2000); and Mary

Zournazi, *Hope: New Philosophies for Change* (New York: Routledge, 2002). Many anthropologists similarly celebrate hope as an emancipatory feeling, and as a precondition for a progressive politics. Arjun Appadurai, for example, views hope as a precondition for any meaningful change. Arjun Appadurai, *The Future as Cultural Fact: Essays on the Global Condition* (London: Verso, 2013). Other critical accounts, however, point out how hope as a discourse could reproduce structural inequalities and violence. Ghassan Hage examines how unequal distribution of hope can be central to neoliberal governance. Ghassan Hage, ed., *Waiting* (Carlton Vic., Australia: Melbourne University Publishing, 2009). Mayssoun Sukarieh documents how the rhetoric of hope was used as a strategic tool for key policy reforms and public relations campaigns in the Middle East in ways that served Western colonial interests. Mayssoun Sukarieh, "The Hope Crusades: Culturalism and Reform in the Arab World," *PoLAR* 35, no. 1 (2012): 115–34. Very few ethnographies focus on how diverse communities talk about and experience hope. This is why several anthropologists rightly call for in-depth ethnographies of hope. See, for instance, Hirokazu Miyazaki, "Economy of Dreams: Hope in Global Capitalism and Its Critiques," *Cultural Anthropology* 21, no. 2 (2006): 147–72.

2. Several ethnographic works point out a growing sentiment of hopelessness within the communities they studied. See, for instance, Samuli Schielke, *Egypt in the Future Tense: Hope, Frustration, and Ambivalence before and after 2011* (Bloomington: Indiana University Press, 2015); and Daniel Mains, "Neoliberal Times: Progress, Boredom, and Shame among Young Men in Urban Ethiopia," *American Ethnologist* 34, no. 4 (2007): 659–73.

3. For examples of well-known ethnographic analyses of hope as "active work," see Cheryl Mattingly, *The Paradox of Hope: Journeys Through a Clinical Borderland* (Berkeley: University of California Press, 2010); and Hirokazu Miyazaki, *The Method of Hope: Anthropology, Philosophy, and Fijian Knowledge* (Stanford, CA: Stanford University Press, 2004).

4. Berlant's concept of "cruel optimism" suggests that people's fantasies of a good life ironically undermine their happiness because these fantasies are often unattainable, especially for disadvantaged communities. See Lauren Berlant, *Cruel Optimism* (Durham, NC: Duke University Press, 2011).

5. Appadurai, *The Future as Cultural Fact.* Numerous anthropological studies similarly emphasize how the category of the future is critical in understanding the present. For some key examples, see Vincent Crapanzano, *Imaginative Horizons: An Essay in Literary-Philosophical Anthropology* (Chicago: University of Chicago Press, 2004); Jane I. Guyer, "Prophecy and the Near Future: Thoughts on Macroeconomic, Evangelical, and Punctuated Time," *American Ethnologist* 34, no. 3 (2007): 409–21; and Charles Piot, *Nostalgia for the Future: West Africa After the Cold War* (Chicago: University of Chicago Press, 2010).

6. I build on Miyazaki's *The Method of Hope*, which frames hope as an active collective practice of meaning-making. Miyazaki views hope not as an emotion targeted toward the future, but as a model for action that seeks to make sense of the present

moment. However, I also situate hope within power relations and show that hope can be used to govern people and to control public sentiments of uncertainty.

7. Bloch, *The Principle of Hope.*

8. See, for instance, G. William Domhoff, *The Mystique of Dreams: A Search for Utopia through Senoi Dream Theory* (Berkeley: University of California Press, 1990); and Amira Mittermaier, *Dreams that Matter: Egyptian Landscapes of the Imagination* (Berkeley: University of California Press, 2010).

9. The acronym "TED" stands for "Technology, Entertainment and Design," and "x" indicates an independently organized local event version.

10. Reine Azzi, *Realistic Dreamer #TheCrossRoad* (Beirut, Lebanon: Lebanese American University, 2013), 1.

11. "Realistic Dreamers: Hundreds Attend the TEDxLAU Event Dubbed #The-CrossRoad," LAU News, September 10, 2013, www.lau.edu.lb/news-events/news/archive/realistic_dreamers.

12. "Realistic Dreamers: Hundreds Attend the TEDxLAU Event," LAU.

13. For a discussion on sectarian urban symbols, see Mona Fawaz, Mona Harb, and Ahmad Gharbieh, "Living Beirut's Security Zones: An Investigation of the Modalities and Practice of Urban Security," *City & Society* 24, no. 2 (2012): 173–95.

14. Tom Fletcher, "Lebanon 2020: Tom Fletcher at TEDxLAU," TEDx Talks, posted October 14, 2013, 10:31, www.youtube.com/watch?v=aAmPYKOHC_k&t=237s.

15. Mohamad J. Hodeib, "On the Root of Change: Mohamad Hodeib at TEDx-LAU," TEDx Talks, posted October 9, 2013, 8:50, www.youtube.com/watch?v=vN12i1LLE_w&t=438s.

16. Sabine Jizi, "I-Laugh-You: Sabine Jizi at TEDxLAU," TEDx Talks, posted October 14, 2013, 16:30, www.youtube.com/watch?v=ooICrvMMIiA.

17. For more in-depth discussion on the post-war public life of memory and the past, see Sune Haugbolle, *War and Memory in Lebanon* (Cambridge: Cambridge University Press, 2010); Sami Hermez, *War Is Coming: Between Past and Future Violence in Lebanon* (Philadelphia: University of Pennsylvania Press, 2017), 142–50; and Craig Larkin, *Memory and Conflict in Lebanon: Remembering and Forgetting the Past* (London: Routledge, 2012). Hermez, for instance, examines how active forgetting (*tanāsī*) was a pervasive cultural practice in contemporary Lebanon: *War is Coming,* 140–50.

18. Walid Sadek, "When Next We Meet: On the Figure of the Nonposthumous Survivor," *ARTMargins* 4, no. 2 (2015): 49.

19. For instance, on the punctuation of a future time in Palestinian NGO projects, see Ilana Feldman, *Life Lived in Relief: Humanitarian Predicaments and Palestinian Refugee Politics* (Berkeley: University of California Press, 2018), 212–16.

20. Guyer, "Prophecy and the Near Future," 410.

21. For examples of ethnographic studies on governance and experiences of temporal insecurities, see, for instance, Craig Jeffrey, *Timepass: Youth, Class, and the Politics of Waiting in India* (Stanford, CA: Stanford University Press, 2010).

22. Miyazaki, *The Method of Hope,* 27.

23. Future imaginations in many communal or national undertakings often involve invocations of the past. As examples of those cases, see Alexei Yurchak, *Everything Was Forever, Until It Was No More: The Last Soviet Generation* (Princeton, NJ: Princeton University Press, 2005); and Miyazaki, *The Method of Hope.*

24. As an ambitious twenty-five-year-old professor with a BS degree in Mathematics from the University of Texas and ongoing graduate work at the same department, Manougian came to Lebanon to work at Haigazian University between 1960 and 1966. He moved to the University of South Florida, Tampa, after he left his assistant professor position at Haigazian University in 1966.

25. The filmmakers also shared that they were surprised to find out that their web search results in 2009 for "Lebanese rocket" did not show anything about the Lebanese Rocket Society, but were all about Hizbullah and Israel targeting each other with missiles. See Joana Hadjithomas and Khalil Joreige, "On the Lebanese Rocket Society," e-flux Journal, March 2013, www.e-flux.com/journal/43/60187/on-the-lebanese-rocket-society/.

26. Mike McCahill, "The Lebanese Rocket Society-Review," *Guardian* (US edition), October 17, 2013, www.theguardian.com/film/2013/oct/17/lebanese-rocket-society-review.

27. Nasawiya (Feminist) was a well-known vocal Lebanese feminist collective established in 2010. It did advocacy work and mobilized many protests on areas of gender equality, human rights, citizenship, and democracy. The Anti-Racism Movement was a grassroots collective founded in 2010 by a group of activists at Nasawiya. Its goal was to collaborate with and support migrant workers, in particular domestic workers, to fight against racism in the country. It became a registered NGO in 2012 to increase the effectiveness of its operations. The Anti-Racism Movement was still active as of 2022, but Nasawiya ceased its operations by the end of 2014 due to internal disagreements.

28. See, for instance, an episode of a popular TV show aired by the LBC channel: "Kalam Ennas—Lebanese Rocket Society," LBC International, posted April 12, 2013, 18:43, www.youtube.com/watch?v=5OUmi4EBeFI.

29. See, for instance, Elia J. Ayoub, "The Unbelievable True Story of the 'Lebanese Rocket Society,'" *Hummus for Thought* (blog), March 12, 2013, https://hummusforthought.com/2013/03/12/lebanese-rocket-society-a-review/; Najib, "The Lebanese Rocket Society—The Strange Tale of the Lebanese Space Race," *Blogbaladi*, March 9, 2013, https://blogbaladi.com/the-lebanese-rocket-society-the-strange-tale-of-the-lebanese-space-race/.

30. Richard Hooper, "Lebanon's Forgotten Space Programme," BBC News, November 14, 2013, www.bbc.com/news/magazine-24735423; Peter Schwartzstein, "The Bizarre Tale of the Middle East's First Space Program," *Smithsonian Magazine*, October 17, 2016; and Rashed Aqrabawi, "Lebanon's Forgotten Space Race: In 1961, Manoug Manougian Aimed the Middle East at the Stars," VICE, July 17, 2013, www.vice.com/en/article/pggn4y/lebanons-forgotten-space-race-in-1961-manoug-manougian-aimed-the-middle-east-at-the-stars.

31. Reinhart Koselleck. *Futures Past: On the Semantics of Historical Time* (New York: Columbia University Press, 2004).

32. "The Dream Matcher Experience—Beirut (New Year's Edition)," Lebtivity, n.d., www.lebtivity.com/event/the-dream-matcher-experience-entrepreneurs-edition.

33. "Lebanon's Most Successful Networking Event: The Dream Matcher Experience," Beirut, March 2, 2016, www.beirut.com/en/45970/lebanons-most-successful-networking-event-the-dream-matcher-experience.

34. "Sweet Dreams (Are Made of This)," *Executive*, January 22, 2016, www.executive-magazine.com/special-report/entrepreneurship-in-lebanon/sweet-dreams-are-made-of-this.

35. See Chapter 2 for an analysis of this middle-class fantasy.

36. thedreammatcher, "The Dream Matcher Experience on LBC B-Beirut," LBC B-Beirut, posted October 18, 2013, 14:03, translated from Arabic to English by the author, www.youtube.com/watch?v=EInQJzoA9X8.

37. "Special Segment: An Interview with Ali Chehade," Future TV Alam Al-Sabah, posted August 30, 2015, 13:40, www.youtube.com/watch?v=dRxWL8uKzlA.

38. Langston Hughes, "Harlem," in *The Collected Poems of Langston Hughes* (New York: Vintage, 2020).

39. Major examples of these accounts include James Ferguson, *Expectations of Modernity: Myths and Meanings of Urban Life on the Zambian Copperbelt* (Berkeley: University of California Press, 1999); and Susana Narotzky and Niko Besnier, "Crisis, Value, and Hope: Rethinking the Economy: An Introduction to Supplement 9," *Current Anthropology* 55, no. 9 (2014): 4–16. The deferral of hope can bring resentment. See Vincent Crapanzano, "Reflections on Hope as a Category of Social and Psychological Analysis," *Cultural Anthropology* 18, no. 1 (2003): 3–32. It can also engender cynicism. See Lori Allen, *The Rise and Fall of Human Rights: Cynicism and Politics in Occupied Palestine* (Stanford, CA: Stanford University Press, 2013).

40. See Abdou Maliq Simone, *For the City Yet to Come: Changing African Life in Four Cities* (Durham, NC: Duke University Press, 2004). Simone conceptualizes "yet to come" as a temporal site of hope for various urban communities who invest in daily activities with manifold expectations.

41. Berlant, *Cruel Optimism*.

42. For a comprehensive and reliable report on the blast and its multidimensional impacts, see Lama Fakih and Aya Majzoub, "They Killed Us from the Inside: An Investigation into the August 4 Beirut Blast," Human Rights Watch, August 3, 2021, www.hrw.org/report/2021/08/03/they-killed-us-inside/investigation-august-4-beirut-blast.

Chapter 6: Exceptional Victimhoods

1. On how victimhood as a political construction invokes moral capital, see Didier Fassin and Richard Rechtman, *The Empire of Trauma: An Inquiry into the Condition of Victimhood* (Princeton, NJ: Princeton University Press, 2009); and Steffen

Jensen and Henrik Ronsbo, eds., *Histories of Victimhood* (Philadelphia: University of Pennsylvania Press, 2014).

2. Cedric J. Robinson, *Black Marxism: The Making of the Black Radical Tradition* (Chapel Hill, NC: UNC Press Books, 2020). Robinson coined the term "racial capitalism" to argue that modern capitalism was inherently a racializing system that was dependent on the enslaving, dispossession, and genocide of non-white marginalized populations. The creation of racial hierarchies was an intrinsic part of modern European nation-states and their economic growth. Others have applied this concept to understand dispossession and marginalization in diverse contexts. See, for example, Yousuf Al-Bulushi, "Thinking Racial Capitalism and Black Radicalism from Africa: An Intellectual Geography of Cedric Robinson's World-System," *Geoforum* 132 (2022): 252–62; and Justin Leroy and Destin Jenkins, eds., *Histories of Racial Capitalism* (New York: Columbia University Press, 2021).

3. Judith Butler, *Frames of War: When Is Life Grievable?* (London: Verso Books, 2016).

4. Butler also shows that grievability is a quality of "bodies that matter," referring to "lives worth protecting, lives worth saving, lives worth grieving." See Judith Butler, *Bodies That Matter: On the Discursive Limits of "Sex"* (New York: Routledge, 1993), 16.

5. On how migrant and refugee communities were racialized through ungrievability, see Nicholas de Genova, ed., *The Borders of "Europe": Autonomy of Migration, Tactics of Bordering* (Durham, NC: Duke University Press, 2017).

6. See Laleh Khalili, "Humanitarianism and Racial Capitalism in the Age of Global Shipping," *European Journal of International Relations* 29, no. 2 (2023): 374–97. Khalili provides an in-depth historical and theoretical discussion of the racialization of mobile subjects in different contexts.

7. Cathrine Thorleifsson, "The Limits of Hospitality: Coping Strategies among Displaced Syrians in Lebanon," *Third World Quarterly* 37, no. 6 (2016): 1071.

8. On UNHCR's over-focus on Syrian refugees compared to other refugee communities in Lebanon, see Maja Janmyr, "Sudanese Refugees and the 'Syrian Refugee Response' in Lebanon: Racialised Hierarchies, Processes of Invisibilisation, and Resistance," *Refugee Survey Quarterly* 41, no. 1 (2022): 131–56.

9. On Lebanese political actors' reactions to and problematic Lebanese media representations of Syrian refugees, see Bassem Chit and Mohamad Ali Nayel, "Understanding Racism Against Syrian Refugees in Lebanon," Civil Society Knowledge Centre, Lebanon Support, October 1, 2013, https://civilsociety-centre.org/paper/understanding-racism-against-syrian-refugees-lebanon.

10. "'We Are Racist': Lebanon FM Says on Refugees," Albawaba News, October 8, 2017, www.albawaba.com/news/we-are-racist-lebanon-fm-says-refugees-1031102.

11. "Gebran Bassil: al-Nazihun al-Suriyyun Yuhaddidun Wujud Lubnan" [Gebran Bassil: Displaced Syrians Threaten the Existence of Lebanon], CNN

Arabic, February 5, 2019, https://arabic.cnn.com/middle-east/article/2019/02/05/lebanon-gebran-bassil-syrian-refugees.

12. Walid El Houri, "There Is a Rotten Stench Coming from Lebanon," Open Democracy, June 13, 2019, www.opendemocracy.net/en/north-africa-west-asia/there-rotten-stench-coming-lebanon/.

13. See "Syrian Refugees in Lebanon Endure Racism, Deprivation of Rights, and Risks of Being Banished and Extradited to the Syrian Regime: No Protection, No Rights," Syrian Network for Human Rights, February 27, 2017, https://snhr.org/wp-content/pdf/english/Syrian_Refugees_in_Lebanon_Endure_Racism_Deprivation_of_Right_en.pdf. Also, see Liliana Riga, Johannes Langer, and Arek Dakessian, "Theorizing Refugeedom: Becoming Young Political Subjects in Beirut," *Theory and Society* 49, no. 4 (2020): 709–44.

14. Kais M. Firro, "Lebanese Nationalism versus Arabism: From Bulus Nujaym to Michel Chiha," *Middle Eastern Studies* 40, no. 5 (2004): 2. Firro offers a thorough historical analysis of how Maronite Christian elites formulated Lebanese nationalism as an alternative to Arabism or Arab Syrianism.

15. Mahmood Mamdani, "Beyond Settler and Native as Political Identities: Overcoming the Political Legacy of Colonialism," *Comparative Studies in Society and History* 43, no. 4 (2001): 651–64. Mamdani offers a compelling discussion about how colonial legacies impact contemporary political, legal, and social formations in diverse contexts. Homi K. Bhabha also describes how colonial political rule works through the fixation of porous social and ethnic identities. Homi K. Bhabha, *The Location of Culture* (London: Routledge, 1994). On how colonial mappings generate civilizational hierarchies, see Michel-Rolph Trouillot, *Global Transformations: Anthropology and the Modern World* (New York: Palgrave MacMillan, 2003).

16. John Chalcraft, *The Invisible Cage: Syrian Migrant Workers in Lebanon* (Stanford, CA: Stanford University Press, 2009).

17. Nour Abu-Assab, Nof Nasser-Eddin, and Roula Seghaier, "Activism and the Economy of Victimhood: A Close Look into NGO-ization in Arabic-Speaking Countries," *Interventions* 22, no. 4 (2020): 482.

18. A Lebanese activist friend told me that such condescending descriptions of dialect could also be deployed to characterize the language of some rural communities in Lebanon. In this sense, judgments over language expressed both classed and racialized anxieties with modernness and civility.

19. Linguistic anthropologists focusing on diverse contexts have widely argued that code-switching was not a linguistic necessity, but rather a strategy for class-making. See, for example, Shana Poplack, "Sometimes I'll Start a Sentence in Spanish Y TERMINO EN ESPAÑOL: Toward a Typology of Code-Switching," *Linguistics* 18, no. 7–8 (1980): 581–618.

20. Several Christian intellectuals attempted to make colloquial Lebanese a national language of Lebanon, while other Christian intellectuals treated French as a national language of Lebanon. Asher Kaufman, "'Tell Us Our History': Charles

Corm, Mount Lebanon and Lebanese Nationalism," *Middle Eastern Studies* 40, no. 3 (2004): 1–28.

21. Any discourse that views Lebanon as significantly different from other Arab countries may be considered part of Lebanese exceptionalism. In this sense, negative portrayals, such as Lebanon having incomparably horrific wars, violence, and hatred, also perpetuate Lebanese exceptionalism. For historical analyses on the emergence of Lebanese exceptionalism, see Maria B. Abunnasr, "The Making of Ras Beirut: A Landscape of Memory for Narratives of Exceptionalism, 1870–1975" (PhD dissertation, University of Massachusetts Amherst, 2013). For contemporary invocations of Lebanese exceptionalism, see Ghassan Moussawi, "Queer Exceptionalism and Exclusion: Cosmopolitanism and Inequalities in 'Gay-Friendly' Beirut," *The Sociological Review* 66, no. 1 (2018): 174–90.

22. Asher Kaufman, *Reviving Phoenicia: The Search for Identity in Lebanon* (London: Bloomsbury Publishing, 2014). Kaufman provides a rich analysis on the influence of Phoenicianism on Lebanese history and on both Christian and non-Christian Lebanese intellectuals.

23. Firro, "Lebanese Nationalism Versus Arabism," 24.

24. "Genetic Study Suggests Present-Day Lebanese Descend from Biblical Canaanites," University of Cambridge, July 27, 2017, www.cam.ac.uk/research/news/genetic-study-suggests-present-day-lebanese-descend-from-biblical-canaanites.

25. See, for instance, "Phoenician or Arab? A Never-Ending Debate in Lebanon," *Independent*, June 12, 2010, www.independent.co.uk/property/house-and-home/phoenician-or-arab-a-neverending-debate-in-lebanon-5547901.html; and Anthony Kantara, "New Study Proves Lebanese Ancestry Is Mostly Phoenician," *961*, June 27, 2017, www.the961.com/study-proves-lebanese-are-phoenicians/.

26. Other researchers also found that Beirut's residents distinguished themselves from other Arabs in the region, whom they characterized as traditional and backward. See, for instance, Moussawi, "Queer Exceptionalism."

27. I met numerous Western volunteer and paid NGO participants in Lebanese NGOs. Young professionals from Sweden, Denmark, Finland, and Switzerland, countries that most Lebanese viewed as less colonial in contrast to Britain and France, were particularly active in Lebanese NGOs that focused on youth, citizenship, and political reform. There were also volunteers from other countries such as China, India, and Japan who visited Lebanon to learn Arabic and gain professional experience in Lebanon's rich NGO world.

28. The majority of migrant workers in Lebanon during my fieldwork were women from Bangladesh, Sri Lanka, Kenya, Ethiopia, and the Philippines, and it was very common for businesses and families with middle-class or even low-income backgrounds to employ a domestic worker. During the 2010s, international and local media covered the abuse and exploitation of domestic migrant workers in Lebanon as well as rising rates of deaths and suicides among them. The *Guardian* published multiple articles focusing on the issue in 2012 alone. See, for instance, Nesrine Malik, "Lebanon Cannot Be 'Civilized' While Domestic Workers Are Abused," *Guardian*

(US edition), March 16, 2012, www.theguardian.com/commentisfree/2012/mar/16/lebanon-domestic-workers-abuse.

29. Foreign domestic workers were essential to the post-war Lebanese economy. For an in-depth discussion on domestic workers in Beirut and discrimination against them, see Sumayya Kassamali, "Migrant Worker Lifeworlds of Beirut" (PhD dissertation, Columbia University, 2017).

30. Denial of or lack of interest in domestic migrant workers' suffering was not new in Lebanon. During the 1990s, activists in Lebanese human rights NGOs justified the mistreatment of domestic female workers who came to Lebanon by accusing them of exaggerating their problems and being ungrateful to the Lebanese people. See Lina Abu-Habib, "The Use and Abuse of Female Domestic Workers from Sri Lanka in Lebanon," *Gender & Development* 6, no. 1 (1998): 52–56.

31. Examples of prominent NGOs and movements advocating domestic migrant workers' rights include the Lebanese Center for Human Rights, Anti-Racism Movement, and KAFA.

32. On how the post-September 11 context affected the mobilities of many communities in the Middle East, see Louise Cainkar, "No Longer Invisible: Arab and Muslim Exclusion after September 11," *Middle East Report* 224 (2002): 22–29.

33. My Lebanese activist interlocutors voiced diverse victimhood narratives. Here, I focus on several common ones to illustrate the connection between victimhood, exceptionalism, and ungrievability.

34. Public anxieties about the shrinking number of eligible grooms did not start with the long Lebanese War. During the 1890s, the problem of single women who had been unable to find husbands was pronounced in Lebanese towns that experienced rapid mass migration. On the gendered debates about emigration during the nineteenth century, see Akram Fouad Khater, *Inventing Home: Emigration, Gender, and the Middle Class in Lebanon, 1870–1920* (Berkeley: University of California Press, 2001).

35. Amahl A. Bishara, "Decolonizing Middle East Anthropology: Toward Liberations in SWANA Societies," *American Ethnologist* 50, no. 3 (2023): 396.

36. On how Syrian refugees in Lebanon kept a low public profile to avoid political pressure, see Zeina El-Helou, "Political Participation of Refugees: The Case of Syrian Refugees in Lebanon," International Institute for Democracy and Electoral Assistance, 2018, www.idea.int/sites/default/files/publications/political-participation-of-refugees-the-case-of-syrian-refugees-in-lebanon.pdf.

Conclusion: "People Will Unite at the Right Time"

1. João Biehl and Peter Locke, eds., *Unfinished: The Anthropology of Becoming* (Durham, NC: Duke University Press, 2017), x.

2. Carol Hakim, *The Origins of the Lebanese National Idea: 1840–1920* (Berkeley: University of California Press, 2013), 13.

3. In other contexts as well, such as Palestine, activists believed that protests were only one part of a long political struggle. See, for instance, Amahl A. Bishara, *Crossing*

a Line: Laws, Violence, and Roadblocks to Palestinian Political Expression (Stanford, CA: Stanford University Press, 2022).

4. Other scholars similarly observe that, during times of "abeyance" (the absence of mass mobilization), social movements in Lebanon continued their political strategizing and actively prepared for future mobilization. See, for instance, Carmen Geha, "Politics of a Garbage Crisis: Social Networks, Narratives, and Frames of Lebanon's 2015 Protests and Their Aftermath," in *Network Mobilization Dynamics in Uncertain Times in the Middle East and North Africa*, eds. Frédéric Volpi and Janine A. Clark (New York: Routledge, 2020), 78–92.

5. Jessica Greenberg, *After the Revolution: Youth, Democracy, and the Politics of Disappointment in Serbia* (Stanford, CA: Stanford University Press, 2014); and Maple Razsa, *Bastards of Utopia: Living Radical Politics After Socialism* (Bloomington: Indiana University Press, 2015).

6. Sonia E. Alvarez, Jeffrey W. Rubin, Millie Thayer, Gianpaolo Baiocchi, and Agustín Laó-Montes, eds., *Beyond Civil Society: Activism, Participation, and Protest in Latin America* (Durham, NC: Duke University Press, 2017).

7. "Lebanon Economic Monitor: Lebanon Sinking (To the Top 3)," World Bank, May 31, 2021, https://documents1.worldbank.org/curated/en/394741622469174252/pdf/Lebanon-Economic-Monitor-Lebanon-Sinking-to-the-Top-3.pdf.

8. For a comprehensive and reliable report on the blast and its multidimensional impacts, see Lama Fakih and Aya Majzoub, "They Killed Us from the Inside: An Investigation into the August 4 Beirut Blast," Human Rights Watch, August 3, 2021, www.hrw.org/report/2021/08/03/they-killed-us-inside/investigation-august-4-beirut-blast.

9. Amira Mittermaier, "Bread, Freedom, Social Justice: The Egyptian Uprising and a Sufi Khidma," *Cultural Anthropology* 29, no. 1 (2014): 55.

10. For instance, Megan Raschig, in her ethnographic research in the mostly Mexican enclave of East Salinas, California, shows how local projects of collective healing could become sites for new forms of activism and political engagement. See Megan Raschig, "Triggering Change: Police Homicides, Community Healing, and the Emergent Eventfulness of the New Civil Rights," *Cultural Anthropology* 32, no. 3 (2017): 399–423.

11. Elizabeth Cullen Dunn and Iwona Kaliszewska, "Crisis as Potential for Collective Action: Violence and Humanitarianism on the Polish–Ukrainian Border," *Anthropology Today* 39, no. 2 (2023): 18–20.

12. Dunn and Kaliszewska, "Crisis as Potential for Collective Action," 18–20.

13. Othon Alexandrakis, "Incidental Activism: Graffiti and Political Possibility in Athens, Greece," *Cultural Anthropology* 31, no. 2 (2016): 276.

14. Isabel Gutierrez Sanchez, "Care Commons: Infrastructural (Re) Compositions for Life Sustenance Through Yet Against Regimes of Chronic Crisis," *Urban Studies* 60, no. 12 (2023): 2456.

15. For a thoughtful comparison of the commonalities and differences among different protests during that period, see Shan Huang and Pablo Seward Delaporte,

"Global Protest Movements in 2019: Conclusion," *Cultural Anthropology*, November 24, 2020.

16. Denisse Sepúlveda Sánchez, Anne Lavanchy, Céline Heini, and Aline Acevedo, "Chile, October and November 2019: 'Feel' and Field-work in Times of Crisis," *Anthropology Today* 37, no. 2 (2021): 23.

17. Doreen Massey, *Space, Place, and Gender* (Minneapolis: University of Minnesota Press, 1994).

Bibliography

Abu-Assab, Nour, Nof Nasser-Eddin, and Roula Seghaier. "Activism and the Economy of Victimhood: A Close Look into NGO-ization in Arabic-Speaking Countries." *Interventions* 22, no. 4 (2020): 481–97.

Abu-Habib, Lina. "The Use and Abuse of Female Domestic Workers from Sri Lanka in Lebanon." *Gender & Development* 6, no. 1 (1998): 52–56.

Abu-Lughod, Lila, ed. *Remaking Women: Feminism and Modernity in the Middle East.* Princeton, NJ: Princeton University Press, 1998.

Abunnasr, Maria B. "The Making of Ras Beirut: A Landscape of Memory for Narratives of Exceptionalism, 1870–1975." PhD dissertation, University of Massachusetts Amherst, 2013.

Ahmad, Tania. "Intolerants: Politics of the Ordinary in Karachi, Pakistan." In *Impulse to Act: A New Anthropology of Resistance and Social Justice*, edited by Othon Alexandrakis, 135–60. Bloomington: Indiana University Press, 2016.

Ahmed, Sara. *The Promise of Happiness.* Durham, NC: Duke University Press, 2010.

Ahmed, Zafar U., and Craig C. Julian. "International Entrepreneurship in Lebanon." *Global Business Review* 13, no. 1 (2012): 25–38.

Akar, Bassel. "Learning Active Citizenship: Conflicts between Students' Conceptualisations of Citizenship and Classroom Learning Experiences in Lebanon." *British Journal of Sociology of Education* 37, no. 2 (2016): 288–312.

Akar, Bassel, and Mara Albrecht. "Influences of Nationalisms on Citizenship Education: Revealing a 'Dark Side' in Lebanon." *Nations and Nationalism* 23, no. 3 (2017): 547–70.

Al-Bulushi, Yousuf. "Thinking Racial Capitalism and Black Radicalism from Africa: An Intellectual Geography of Cedric Robinson's World-System." *Geoforum* 132 (2022): 252–62.

Al-Dahdah, Karim. *You Know You're Lebanese When. . .* Translated and edited by Sabine Taoukjian. Beirut: Turning Point Books, 2011.

Al-Razi, Muhammad ibn Abu Bakr. *Mukhtar al-Sihah*. Digital Library of India, 2020. https://archive.org/details/dli.ernet.432454/page/n9/mode/2up.

Alaref, Jumana. "Wasta Once Again Hampering Arab Youth Chances for a Dignified Life." *World Bank Blogs*, March 13, 2014. https://blogs.worldbank.org/arabvoices/wasta-hampering-arab-youth-chances-dignified-life.

Alexandrakis, Othon, ed. *Impulse to Act: A New Anthropology of Resistance and Social Justice*. Bloomington: Indiana University Press, 2016.

Alexandrakis, Othon. "Incidental Activism: Graffiti and Political Possibility in Athens, Greece." *Cultural Anthropology* 31, no. 2 (2016): 272–96.

Allen, Lori. *The Rise and Fall of Human Rights: Cynicism and Politics in Occupied Palestine*. Stanford, CA: Stanford University Press, 2013.

Alvarez, Sonia E., Jeffrey W. Rubin, Millie Thayer, Gianpaolo Baiocchi, and Agustín Laó-Montes, eds. *Beyond Civil Society: Activism, Participation, and Protest in Latin America*. Durham, NC: Duke University Press, 2017.

Amel, Mahdi. *Fi al-Dawla al- Taʿifiyya* [On the Sectarian State]. Beirut: Dar Al-Farabi, 1986.

Andersson, Ruben. *No Go World: How Fear is Redrawing Our Maps and Infecting Our Politics*. Berkeley: University of California Press, 2019.

Anthias, Floya, and Nira Yuval-Davis. *Woman-Nation-State*. London: Macmillan, 1989.

Appadurai, Arjun. *The Future as Cultural Fact: Essays on the Global Condition*. London: Verso, 2013.

Aqrabawi, Rashed. "Lebanon's Forgotten Space Race: In 1961, Manoug Manougian Aimed the Middle East at the Stars." VICE, July 17, 2013. www.vice.com/en/article/pggn4y/lebanons-forgotten-space-race-in-1961-manoug-manougian-aimed-the-middle-east-at-the-stars.

Arendt, Hannah. *The Human Condition*. Chicago: University of Chicago Press, 1958.

Atshan, Sa'ed. *Queer Palestine and the Empire of Critique*. Stanford, CA: Stanford University Press, 2020.

Ayoub, Elia J. "The Unbelievable True Story of the 'Lebanese Rocket Society.'" *Hummus for Thought* (blog), March 12, 2013. https://hummusforthought.com/2013/03/12/lebanese-rocket-society-a-review/.

Azzi, Reine. "Realistic Dreamer #TheCrossRoad." Beirut: Lebanese American University, 2013.

Banerjee, Prathama. *Elementary Aspects of the Political: Histories from the Global South*. Durham, NC: Duke University Press, 2020.

Bardawil, Fadi A. *Revolution and Disenchantment: Arab Marxism and the Binds of Emancipation*. Durham, NC: Duke University Press, 2020.

Barnard, Anne. "Funeral Turnout Shows Lebanon's Ebbing Morale." *New York Times*, December 29, 2013.

Barrios, Roberto E. "Resilience: A Commentary from the Vantage Point of Anthropology." *Annals of Anthropological Practice* 40, no. 1 (2016): 28–38.

Baumann, Hannes. "Bringing the State and Political Economy Back In: Consociationalism and Crisis in Lebanon." *Nationalism and Ethnic Politics* 30, no. 1 (2024): 85–102.

Bayat, Asef. *Revolutionary Life: The Everyday of the Arab Spring.* Cambridge, MA: Harvard University Press, 2021.

Bejarano, Carolina Alonso, Lucia López Juárez, Mirian A. Mijangos García, and Daniel M. Goldstein. *Decolonizing Ethnography: Undocumented Immigrants and New Directions in Social Science.* Durham, NC: Duke University Press, 2019.

Berlant, Lauren. *The Female Complaint: The Unfinished Business of Sentimentality in American Culture.* Durham, NC: Duke University Press, 2008.

Berlant, Lauren. *Cruel Optimism.* Durham, NC: Duke University Press, 2011.

Besteman, Catherine. *Militarized Global Apartheid.* Durham, NC: Duke University Press, 2020.

Bhabha, Homi K. "Dissemination: Time, Narrative, and the Margins of the Modern Nation." In *Nation and Narration*, edited by Homi K. Bhabha, 291–322. New York: Routledge, 1990.

Bhabha, Homi K. *The Location of Culture.* London: Routledge, 1994.

Biehl, João, and Peter Locke, eds. *Unfinished: The Anthropology of Becoming.* Durham, NC: Duke University Press, 2017.

Billig, Michael. *Banal Nationalism.* London: Sage, 1995.

Bishara, Amahl A. *Crossing a Line: Laws, Violence, and Roadblocks to Palestinian Political Expression.* Stanford, CA: Stanford University Press, 2022.

Bishara, Amahl A. "Decolonizing Middle East Anthropology: Toward Liberations in SWANA Societies." *American Ethnologist* 50, no. 3 (2023): 396–408.

Bloch, Ernst. *The Principle of Hope*, vol. 1. Translated by Neville Plaice, Stephen Plaice, and Paul Knight. Cambridge, MA: MIT Press, 1986.

Bockman, Johanna. "The Political Projects of Neoliberalism." *Social Anthropology/Anthropologie Sociale* 20, no. 3 (2012): 310–17.

Bolles, A. Lynn. "Decolonizing Anthropology: An Ongoing Process." *American Ethnologist* 50, no. 3 (2023): 519–22.

Bortolazzi, Omar. "Harakat Amal: Social Mobilization, Economic Resources, Welfare Provision." *Journal of South Asian and Middle Eastern Studies* 45, no. 1 (2021): 37–65.

Bourdieu, Pierre. *Distinction: A Social Critique of the Judgement of Taste.* Translated by Richard Nice. Cambridge, MA: Harvard University Press, 1984.

Bourdieu, Pierre. "What Makes a Social Class? On the Theoretical and Practical Existence of Groups." *Berkeley Journal of Sociology* 32 (1987): 1–17.

Bradley, Matt. "Lebanon Marks a Year without a President with a Shrug." *Wall Street Journal*, May 23, 2015.

Butler, Judith. *Bodies That Matter: On the Discursive Limits of "Sex."* New York: Routledge, 1993.

Butler, Judith. *Frames of War: When Is Life Grievable?* London: Verso Books, 2016.

Cainkar, Louise. "No Longer Invisible: Arab and Muslim Exclusion After September 11." *Middle East Report* 224 (2002): 22–29.

Cammett, Melani. *Compassionate Communalism: Welfare and Sectarianism in Lebanon.* Ithaca, NY: Cornell University Press, 2014.

Cammett, Melanie. "Sectarianism and the Ambiguities of Welfare in Lebanon." *Current Anthropology* 56, no. 11 (2015): 76–87.

Carapico, Sheila. *Civil Society in Yemen: The Political Economy of Activism in Modern Arabia.* Cambridge: Cambridge University Press, 1998.

Chalcraft, John. *The Invisible Cage: Syrian Migrant Workers in Lebanon.* Stanford, CA: Stanford University Press, 2009.

Chamas, Sophie. "Activism as a Way of Life: The Social World of Social Movements in Middle-Class Beirut." *Partecipazione e Conflitto* 14, no. 2 (2021): 530–46.

Chamcham, Youmna. "Live Love Beirut: The Story of a Movement." Vimeo, June 25, 2015. https://vimeo.com/131797617.

Chatterjee, Partha. *The Nation and Its Fragments: Colonial and Postcolonial Histories.* Princeton, NJ: Princeton University Press, 1993.

Cherri, Zeinab, Pedro Arcos González, and Rafael Castro Delgado. "The Lebanese–Syrian Crisis: Impact of Influx of Syrian Refugees to an Already Weak State." *Risk Management and Healthcare Policy* 9 (2016): 165–72.

Chit, Bassem, and Mohamed Ali Nayel. "Understanding Racism against Syrian Refugees in Lebanon." Civil Society Knowledge Centre, Lebanon Support, October 1, 2013. https://civilsociety-centre.org/paper/understanding-racism-against-syrian-refugees-lebanon.

Chua, Lynette J. *The Politics of Love in Myanmar: LGBT Mobilization and Human Rights as a Way of Life.* Stanford, CA: Stanford University Press, 2018.

"Civic Activism Toolkit: A Hands-On Manual to Help Youth Activists Make Change in Their Communities." USAID, Office of Transition Initiatives, Lebanon Civic Support Initiative, Beirut, 2013.

Clark, Janine A., and Bassel F. Salloukh. "Elite Strategies, Civil Society, and Sectarian Identities in Postwar Lebanon." *International Journal of Middle East Studies* 45, no. 4 (2013): 731–49.

Crapanzano, Vincent. *Imaginative Horizons: An Essay in Literary-Philosophical Anthropology.* Chicago: University of Chicago Press, 2004.

Crapanzano, Vincent. "Reflections on Hope as a Category of Social and Psychological Analysis." *Cultural Anthropology* 18, no. 1 (2003): 3–32.

Cusicanqui, Silvia Rivera. "Ch'ixinakax utxiwa: A Reflection on the Practices and Discourses of Decolonization." *South Atlantic Quarterly* 111, no. 1 (2012): 95–109.

Das, Veena, and Clara Han. *Living and Dying in the Contemporary World: A Compendium.* Berkeley: University of California Press, 2015.

Dave, Naisargi N. *Queer Activism in India: A Story in the Anthropology of Ethics.* Durham, NC: Duke University Press, 2012.

De Genova, Nicholas, ed. *The Borders of "Europe": Autonomy of Migration, Tactics of Bordering.* Durham, NC: Duke University Press, 2017.

De Sousa Santos, Boaventura. *Epistemologies of the South: Justice against Epistemicide.* New York: Routledge, 2015.

Deeb, Lara. "Beyond Sectarianism: Intermarriage and Social Difference in Lebanon." *International Journal of Middle East Studies* 52, no. 2 (2020): 215–28.

Deeb, Lara, and Mona Harb. *Leisurely Islam: Negotiating Geography and Morality in Shiʿite South Beirut.* Princeton, NJ: Princeton University Press, 2013.

Diversi, Marcelo, and Claudio Moreira. *Betweener Talk: Decolonizing Knowledge Production, Pedagogy, and Praxis.* London: Routledge, 2016.

Domhoff, G. William. *The Mystique of Dreams: A Search for Utopia through Senoi Dream Theory.* Berkeley: University of California Press, 1990.

Doumit, Gilbert. "TEDxBeirut—Gilbert Doumit—Political Entrepreneurship." TEDx Talks, posted November 9, 2011, 12:47. www.youtube.com/watch?v=5r-5vUKwztY.

"The Dream Matcher Experience—Beirut (New Year's Edition)." Lebtivity, n.d. www.lebtivity.com/event/the-dream-matcher-experience-entrepreneurs-edition.

thedreammatcher, "The Dream Matcher Experience on LBC B-Beirut," LBC B-Beirut, posted October 18, 2013, 14:03, translated from Arabic to English by the author, www.youtube.com/watch?v=EInQJzoA9X8.

Dunn, Elizabeth Cullen, and Iwona Kaliszewska. "Crisis as Potential for Collective Action: Violence and Humanitarianism on the Polish-Ukrainian Border." *Anthropology Today* 39, no. 2 (2023): 18–20.

Durham, Deborah. "Youth and the Social Imagination in Africa: Introduction to Parts 1 and 2." *Anthropological Quarterly* 73, no. 3 (2000): 113–20.

El-Helou, Zeina. "Political Participation of Refugees: The Case of Syrian Refugees in Lebanon." International Institute for Democracy and Electoral Assistance, 2018. www.idea.int/sites/default/files/publications/political-participation-of-refugees-the-case-of-syrian-refugees-in-lebanon.pdf.

El-Hibri, Hatim. *Visions of Beirut: The Urban Life of Media Infrastructure.* Durham, NC: Duke University Press, 2021.

El Houri, Walid. "There Is a Rotten Stench Coming from Lebanon." Open Democracy, June 13, 2019. www.opendemocracy.net/en/north-africa-west-asia/there-rotten-stench-coming-lebanon/.

El Shakry, Omnia. "Youth as Peril and Promise: The Emergence of Adolescent Psychology in Postwar Egypt." *International Journal of Middle East Studies* 43, no. 4 (2011): 591–610.

Elyachar, Julia. *Markets of Dispossession: NGOs, Economic Development, and the State in Cairo.* Durham, NC: Duke University Press, 2005.

Faier, Lieba, and Lisa Rofel. "Ethnographies of Encounter." *Annual Review of Anthropology* 43, no. 1 (2014): 363–77.

Fakih, Lama, and Aya Majzoub. "They Killed Us from the Inside: An Investigation into the August 4 Beirut Blast." Human Rights Watch, August 3, 2021. www.hrw.org/report/2021/08/03/they-killed-us-inside/investigation-august-4-beirut-blast.

Fassin, Didier. "Crisis." In *Words and Worlds: A Lexicon for Dark Times*, edited by Veena Das and Didier Fassin, 261–76. Durham, NC: Duke University Press, 2021.

Fassin, Didier, and Richard Rechtman. *The Empire of Trauma: An Inquiry into the Condition of Victimhood*. Princeton, NJ: Princeton University Press, 2009.

Fawaz, Mona, Mona Harb, and Ahmad Gharbieh. "Living Beirut's Security Zones: An Investigation of the Modalities and Practice of Urban Security." *City & Society* 24, no. 2 (2012): 173–95.

Feldman, Ilana. *Life Lived in Relief: Humanitarian Predicaments and Palestinian Refugee Politics*. Berkeley: University of California Press, 2018.

Ferguson, James. *The Anti-Politics Machine: "Development," Depoliticization, and Bureaucratic Power in Lesotho*. Minneapolis: University of Minnesota Press, 1994.

Ferguson, James. *Expectations of Modernity: Myths and Meanings of Urban Life on the Zambian Copperbelt*. Berkeley: University of California Press, 1999.

Ferguson, James. "The Uses of Neoliberalism." *Antipode* 41, Issue S1 (2010): 166–84.

Firro, Kais M. "Lebanese Nationalism versus Arabism: From Bulus Nujaym to Michel Chiha." *Middle Eastern Studies* 40, no. 5 (2004): 1–27.

Fletcher, Tom. "Lebanon 2020: Tom Fletcher at TEDxLAU." TEDx Talks, posted October 14, 2013, 10:31. www.youtube.com/watch?v=aAmPYKOHC_k&t=237s.

Forment, Carlos A. "The Democratic Dribbler: Football Clubs, Neoliberal Globalization, and Buenos Aires' Municipal Election of 2003." *Public Culture* 19, no. 1 (2007): 85–116.

Foucault, Michel. "Of Other Spaces." Translated by Jay Miskowiec. *Diacritics* 16, no. 1 (Spring 1986): 22–27.

Freeman, Carla. *Entrepreneurial Selves: Neoliberal Respectability and the Making of a Caribbean Middle Class*. Durham, NC: Duke University Press, 2014.

Freeman, Carla. *High Tech and High Heels in the Global Economy: Women, Work, and Pink-Collar Identities in the Caribbean*. Durham, NC: Duke University Press, 2000.

Garcia, Angela. *The Pastoral Clinic: Addiction and Dispossession along the Rio Grande*. Berkeley: University of California Press, 2010.

"Gebran Bassil: al-Nazihun al-Suriyyun Yuhaddidun Wujud Lubnan," [Gebran Bassil: Displaced Syrians Threaten the Existence of Lebanon]. CNN Arabic, February 5, 2019. https://arabic.cnn.com/middle-east/article/2019/02/05/lebanon-gebran-bassil-syrian-refugees.

Geha, Carmen. "Politics of a Garbage Crisis: Social Networks, Narratives, and Frames of Lebanon's 2015 Protests and Their Aftermath." In *Network Mobilization Dynamics in Uncertain Times in the Middle East and North Africa*, edited by Frédéric Volpi and Janine A. Clark, 78–92. New York: Routledge, 2020.

"Genetic Study Suggests Present-Day Lebanese Descend from Biblical Canaanites." University of Cambridge, July 27, 2017. www.cam.ac.uk/research/news/genetic-study-suggests-present-day-lebanese-descend-from-biblical-canaanites.

Gershon, Ilana. *Down and Out in the New Economy: How People Find (or Don't Find) Work Today*. Chicago: University of Chicago Press, 2017.

Ghamari-Tabrizi, Behrooz. "Revolution." In *Words and Worlds: A Lexicon for Dark Times,* edited by Veena Das and Didier Fassin, 166–84. Durham, NC: Duke University Press, 2021.

Ghannam, Farha. *Live and Die Like a Man: Gender Dynamics in Urban Egypt.* Stanford, CA: Stanford University Press, 2013.

Ghattas, Kim. "Beirut's Lovable Losers." *Foreign Policy,* May 26, 2016. https://foreignpolicy.com/2016/05/26/beiruts-loveable-losers/

Ghattas, Kim. "Mohamad Chatah Killing Targets Potential Lebanon PM." BBC News, December 29, 2013. www.bbc.com/news/world-middle-east-25536149.

Goldstone, Brian, and Juan Obarrio, eds. *African Futures: Essays on Crisis, Emergence, and Possibility.* Chicago: University of Chicago Press, 2017.

Greenberg, Jessica. *After the Revolution: Youth, Democracy, and the Politics of Disappointment in Serbia.* Stanford, CA: Stanford University Press, 2014.

Grimsditch, Peter, and Michael Karam. *Life's Like That!: Your Guide to the Lebanese.* Beirut: Turning Point Books, 2004.

Gulick, John. "Conservatism and Change in a Lebanese Village." *The Middle East Journal* 8, no. 3 (1954): 295–307.

Guyer, Jane I. "Prophecy and the Near Future: Thoughts on Macroeconomic, Evangelical, and Punctuated Time." *American Ethnologist* 34, no. 3 (2007): 409–21.

Haddad, Simon. "Cultural Diversity and Sectarian Attitudes in Postwar Lebanon." *Journal of Ethnic and Migration Studies* 28, no. 2 (2002): 291–306.

Haddad, Tania. "Governance of the Nonprofit Sector in Lebanon between Theory and Practice." *Journal of Civil Society* 19, no. 3 (2023): 330–45.

Hadjithomas, Joana, and Khalil Joreige. "On the Lebanese Rocket Society." e-flux Journal, March 2013. www.e-flux.com/journal/43/60187/on-the-lebanese-rocket-society/.

Hage, Ghassan. *Alter-Politics: Critical Anthropology and the Radical Imagination.* Melbourne: Melbourne University Press, 2015.

Hage, Ghassan. *The Diasporic Condition: Ethnographic Explorations of the Lebanese in the World.* Chicago: University of Chicago Press, 2021.

Hage, Ghassan, ed. *Waiting.* Carlton Vic., Australia: Melbourne University Publishing, 2009.

Hahn, Hans Peter. "Diffusionism, Appropriation, and Globalization: Some Remarks on Current Debates in Anthropology." *Anthropos* 103, no. 1 (2008): 191–202.

Hakim, Carol. *The Origins of the Lebanese National Idea: 1840–1920.* Berkeley: University California Press, 2013.

Halawi, Dana. "Widespread Favoritism Takes Toll on Economy." *Daily Star,* November 4, 2013.

Hall, Stuart, and Doreen Massey, "Interpreting the Crisis." *Soundings* 44 (2010): 57–71.

Hall, Stuart, Chas Critcher, Tony Jefferson, John Clarke, and Brian Roberts. *Policing the Crisis: Mugging, The State and Law & Order.* London: Macmillan, 1978.

Harb, Mona. "Youth Mobilization in Lebanon: Navigating Exclusion and Seeds for Collective Action." Power2Youth Working Paper 16, Istituto Affari Internazionali, September 30, 2016. www.iai.it/en/pubblicazioni/youth-mobilization-lebanon.

Harvey, David. *Spaces of Hope*. Berkeley: University of California Press, 2000.

Haugbolle, Sune. "Social Boundaries and Secularism in the Lebanese Left." *Mediterranean Politics* 18, no. 3 (2013): 427–43.

Haugbolle, Sune. *War and Memory in Lebanon*. Cambridge: Cambridge University Press, 2010.

Hay, Colin. "Narrating Crisis: The Discursive Construction of the 'Winter of Discontent.'" *Sociology* 30, no. 2 (1996): 253–77.

Hebblethwaite, Cordelia. "#BBCtrending: Lebanon's #Notamartyr Selfie Protest." BBC News, January 6, 2014. www.bbc.com/news/blogs-trending-25623299.

Hermez, Sami. "Activism as 'Part-Time' Activity: Searching for Commitment and Solidarity in Lebanon." *Cultural Dynamics* 23, no. 1 (2011): 41–55.

Hermez, Sami. "On Dignity and Clientelism: Lebanon in the Context of the 2011 Arab Revolutions." *Studies in Ethnicity and Nationalism* 11, no. 3 (2011): 527–37.

Hermez, Sami. *War Is Coming: Between Past and Future Violence in Lebanon*. Philadelphia: University of Pennsylvania Press, 2017.

Hodeib, Mohamad. "On the Root of Change: Mohamad Hodeib at TEDxLAU." TEDx Talks, posted October 9, 2013, 8:50. www.youtube.com/watch?v=vN12i1LLE_w&t=438s.

Hodžić, Saida. *The Twilight of Cutting: African Activism and Life After NGOs*. Berkeley: University of California Press, 2017.

Hooper, Richard. "Lebanon's Forgotten Space Program." BBC News, November 14, 2013. www.bbc.com/news/magazine-24735423.

Hourani, Najib B. "Post-Conflict Reconstruction and Citizenship Agendas: Lessons from Beirut." In *Citizenship Agendas in and beyond the Nation-State,* edited by Martijn Koster, Rivke Jaffe, and Anouk De Koning, 74–89. London: Routledge, 2018.

Howell, Jude. "The Global War on Terror, Development and Civil Society." *Journal of International Development* 18, no. 1 (2006): 121–35.

Huang, Shan, and Pablo Seward Delaporte. "Global Protest Movements in 2019: Conclusion." *Cultural Anthropology*, November 24, 2020.

Hudson, Michael C. "Lebanon After Ta'if: Another Reform Opportunity Lost?" *Arab Studies Quarterly* 21, no. 1 (1999): 27–40.

Hughes, Langston. *The Collected Poems of Langston Hughes*. New York: Vintage, 2020.

Ialenti, Vincent. "Spectres of Seppo: The Afterlives of Finland's Nuclear Waste Experts." *Journal of the Royal Anthropological Institute* 26, no. 2 (2020): 251–68.

Jackson, Michael. *How Lifeworlds Work: Emotionality, Sociality, and the Ambiguity of Being*. Chicago: University of Chicago Press, 2017.

Jackson, Michael. *Lifeworlds: Essays in Existential Anthropology*. Chicago: University of Chicago Press, 2013.

Janmyr, Maja. "Sudanese Refugees and the 'Syrian Refugee Response' in Lebanon: Racialised Hierarchies, Processes of Invisibilisation, and Resistance." *Refugee Survey Quarterly* 41, no. 1 (2022): 131–56.

Jeffrey, Craig. *Timepass: Youth, Class, and the Politics of Waiting in India*. Stanford, CA: Stanford University Press, 2010.

Jensen, Steffen, and Henrik Ronsbo, eds. *Histories of Victimhood*. Philadelphia: University of Pennsylvania Press, 2014.

Jizi, Sabine. "I-Laugh-You: Sabine Jizi at TEDxLAU." TEDx Talks, posted October 14, 2013, 16:30. www.youtube.com/watch?v=ooICrvMMIiA.

Jones, Philip. "The Appeal of the Political Entrepreneur." *British Journal of Political Science* 8, no. 4 (1978): 498–504.

Joseph, Suad, ed. *Gender and Citizenship in the Middle East*. Syracuse, NY: Syracuse University Press, 2000.

Joseph, Suad. "Pensée 2: Sectarianism as Imagined Sociological Concept and as Imagined Social Formation." *International Journal of Middle East Studies* 40, no. 4 (2008): 553–54.

Joseph, Suad. "The Public/Private—The Imagined Boundary in the Imagined Nation/State/Community: The Lebanese Case." *Feminist Review* 57, no. 1 (1997): 73–92.

"Kalam Ennas—Lebanese Rocket Society." LBC International, posted April 12, 2013, 18:43. www.youtube.com/watch?v=5OUmi4EBeFI&t=1s.

Kamel, Lojine. "Bala Wasta: No Connections, All Work." Beirut, November 27, 2012. www.beirut.com/l/19987.

Kantara, Anthony. "New Study Proves Lebanese Ancestry Is Mostly Phoenician," *961*, June 27. 2017. www.the961.com/study-proves-lebanese-are-phoenicians/.

Kassamali, Sumayya. "Migrant Worker Lifeworlds of Beirut." PhD dissertation, Columbia University, 2017.

Kaufman, Asher. *Reviving Phoenicia: The Search for Identity in Lebanon*. London: Bloomsbury Publishing, 2014.

Kaufman, Asher. "'Tell Us Our History': Charles Corm, Mount Lebanon and Lebanese Nationalism." *Middle Eastern Studies* 40, no. 3 (2004): 1–28.

Kelman, Sarah. "The Bumipreneur Dilemma and Malaysia's Technology Start-up Ecosystem." *Economic Anthropology* 5, no. 1 (2018): 59–70.

Khalili, Laleh. "Humanitarianism and Racial Capitalism in the Age of Global Shipping." *European Journal of International Relations* 29, no. 2 (2023): 374–97.

Khater, Akram Fouad. *Inventing Home: Emigration, Gender, and the Middle Class in Lebanon, 1870–1920*. Berkeley: University of California Press, 2001.

Khattab, Lara W. "The Genealogy of Social and Political Mobilization in Lebanon under a Neoliberal Sectarian Regime (2009–2019)." *Globalizations* (2022): 1–18.

Khayyat, Munira. *A Landscape of War: Ecologies of Resistance and Survival in South Lebanon*. Berkeley: University of California Press, 2022.

Khayyat, Yasmine. *War Remains: Ruination and Resistance in Lebanon*. Syracuse, NY: Syracuse University Press, 2023.

Khoury, Philip S. *Syria and the French Mandate: The Politics of Arab Nationalism, 1920–1945*. London: I. B. Tauris, 1987.

Kingston, Paul W. T. *Reproducing Sectarianism: Advocacy Networks and the Politics of Civil Society in Postwar Lebanon*. New York: SUNY Press, 2013.

Kloos, David. "Experts beyond Discourse: Women, Islamic Authority, and the Performance of Professionalism in Malaysia." *American Ethnologist* 46, no. 2 (2019): 162–75.

Kondo, Dorinne. *Worldmaking: Race, Performance and the Work of Creativity*. Durham, NC: Duke University Press, 2018.

Koselleck, Reinhart. *Futures Past: On the Semantics of Historical Time*. New York: Columbia University Press, 2004.

Koselleck, Reinhart. *The Practice of Conceptual History: Timing History, Spacing Concepts*. Stanford, CA: Stanford University Press, 2002.

Kosmatopoulos, Nikolas. "The Birth of the Workshop: Technomorals, Peace Expertise, and the Care of the Self in the Middle East." *Public Culture* 26, no. 3 (2014): 529–58.

Kowalski, Julia. "Between Gender and Kinship: Mediating Rights and Relations in North Indian NGOs." *American Anthropologist* 123, no. 2 (2021): 330–42.

Kurtović, Larisa, and Nelli Sargsyan. "After Utopia: Leftist Imaginaries and Activist Politics in the Postsocialist World." *History and Anthropology* 30, no. 1 (2019): 1–19.

Kwon, Soo Ah. *Uncivil Youth: Race, Activism, and Affirmative Governmentality*. Durham, NC: Duke University Press, 2013.

Larkin, Craig. *Memory and Conflict in Lebanon: Remembering and Forgetting the Past*. London: Routledge, 2012.

Larkin, Craig. "Remaking Beirut: Contesting Memory, Space, and the Urban Imaginary of Lebanese Youth." *City & Community* 9, no. 4 (2010): 414–42.

Laszczkowski, Mateusz. "Rethinking Resistance through and as Affect." *Anthropological Theory* 19, no. 4 (2019): 489–509.

Lazar, Sian. *The Social Life of Politics: Ethics, Kinship, and Union Activism in Argentina*. Stanford, CA: Stanford University Press, 2017.

"Lebanon's Most Successful Networking Event: The Dream Matcher Experience." Beirut, March 2, 2016. www.beirut.com/en/45970/lebanons-most-successful-networking-event-the-dream-matcher-experience.

"Lebanon Sinking (To the Top 3)." Lebanon Economic Monitor, Spring 2021. https://documents1.worldbank.org/curated/en/394741622469174252/pdf/Lebanon-Economic-Monitor-Lebanon-Sinking-to-the-Top-3.pdf.

Leroy, Justin, and Destin Jenkins, eds. *Histories of Racial Capitalism*. New York: Columbia University Press, 2021.

Li, Tania Murray. *The Will to Improve: Governmentality, Development, and the Practice of Politics*. Durham, NC: Duke University Press, 2007.

Lorde, Audre. *A Burst of Light: And Other Essays*. Mineola, NY: Ixia Press, 1988.

Low, Setha. *Behind the Gates: Life, Security, and the Pursuit of Happiness in Fortress America*. London: Routledge 2004.

Lutz, Catherine A., and Lila Abu-Lughod, eds. *Language and the Politics of Emotion*. Cambridge: Cambridge University Press, 1990.

MacIntyre, Alasdair. *After Virtue: A Study in Moral Theory*. New York: University of Notre Dame Press, 1981.

Magee, Siobhan. "'To Be One's Own Boss': Exceptional Entrepreneurs and Products That Sell Themselves in Urban Poland." *Ethnos* 84, no. 3 (2019): 436–57.

Mains, Daniel. "Neoliberal Times: Progress, Boredom, and Shame among Young Men in Urban Ethiopia." *American Ethnologist* 34, no. 4 (2007): 659–73.

Majed, Rima. "Lebanon and Iraq in 2019: Revolutionary Uprisings against 'Sectarian Neoliberalism.'" TNI, October 27, 2021. www.tni.org/en/article/lebanon-and-iraq-in-2019.

Makdisi, Saree. "Beirut, a City without History?" In *Memory and Violence in the Middle East and North Africa*, edited by Ussama Makdisi and Paul A. Silverstein, 201–14. Bloomington: Indiana University Press, 2006.

Makdisi, Ussama. *Age of Coexistence: The Ecumenical Frame and the Making of the Modern Arab World*. Berkeley: University of California Press, 2021.

Makdisi, Ussama. *Artillery of Heaven: American Missionaries and the Failed Conversion of the Middle East*. Ithaca, NY: Cornell University Press, 2011.

Makdisi, Ussama. *The Culture of Sectarianism: Community, History, and Violence in Nineteenth-Century Ottoman Lebanon*. Berkeley: University of California Press, 2000.

Makhoul, Jihad, and Lindsey Harrison. "Intercessory Wasta and Village Development in Lebanon." *Arab Studies Quarterly* 26, no. 3 (2004): 25–41.

Malik, Nesrine. "Lebanon Cannot Be 'Civilized' While Domestic Workers Are Abused." *Guardian* (US edition), March 16, 2012. www.theguardian.com/commentisfree/2012/mar/16/lebanon-domestic-workers-abuse.

Malinowski, Bronislaw. *Argonauts of the Western Pacific: An Account of Native Enterprise and Adventure in the Archipelagoes of Melanesian New Guinea*. London: Routledge and Kegan Paul, 1922.

Mamdani, Mahmood. "Beyond Settler and Native as Political Identities: Overcoming the Political Legacy of Colonialism." *Comparative Studies in Society and History* 43, no. 4 (2001): 651–64.

"Mapping Civil Society Organizations in Lebanon." Civil Society Facility South, Beyond Reform and Development, 2015. https://eeas.europa.eu/archives/delegations/lebanon/documents/news/20150416_2_en.pdf.

Masco, Joseph. "The Crisis in Crisis." *Current Anthropology* 58, no. 15 (2017): 65–76.

Massad, Joseph A. *Desiring Arabs*. Chicago: University of Chicago Press, 2019.

Massey, Doreen. *Space, Place, and Gender*. Minneapolis: University of Minnesota Press, 1994.

Mattingly, Cheryl. *The Paradox of Hope: Journeys through a Clinical Borderland*. Berkeley: University of California Press, 2010.

McCahill, Mike. "The Lebanese Rocket Society—Review." *Guardian* (US edition), October 17, 2013. www.theguardian.com/film/2013/oct/17/lebanese-rocket-society-review.

Ménoret, Pascal. *Graveyard of Clerics: Everyday Activism in Saudi Arabia*. Stanford, CA: Stanford University Press, 2020.

Mikdashi, Maya. *Sextarianism: Sovereignty, Secularism, and the State in Lebanon*. Stanford, CA: Stanford University Press, 2022.

Mittermaier, Amira. "Bread, Freedom, Social Justice: The Egyptian Uprising and a Sufi Khidma." *Cultural Anthropology* 29, no. 1 (2014): 54–79.

Mittermaier, Amira. *Dreams That Matter: Egyptian Landscapes of the Imagination*. Berkeley: University of California Press, 2010.

Miyazaki, Hirokazu. "Economy of Dreams: Hope in Global Capitalism and Its Critiques." *Cultural Anthropology* 21, no. 2 (2006): 147–72.

Miyazaki, Hirokazu. *The Method of Hope: Anthropology, Philosophy, and Fijian Knowledge*. Stanford, CA: Stanford University Press, 2004.

Monroe, Kristin V. *The Insecure City: Space, Power, and Mobility in Beirut*. New Brunswick, NJ: Rutgers University Press, 2016.

Moumtaz, Nada. *God's Property: Islam, Charity, and the Modern State*. Berkeley: University of California Press, 2021.

Moussawi, Ghassan. "Queer Exceptionalism and Exclusion: Cosmopolitanism and Inequalities in 'Gay-Friendly' Beirut." *The Sociological Review* 66, no. 1 (2018): 174–90.

Muehlebach, Andrea. *The Moral Neoliberal: Welfare and Citizenship in Italy*. Chicago: University of Chicago Press, 2012.

Muir, Sarah. *Routine Crisis: An Ethnography of Disillusion*. Chicago: University of Chicago Press, 2021.

Muir, Sarah, and Akhil Gupta. "Rethinking The Anthropology of Corruption: An Introduction to Supplement 18." *Current Anthropology* 59, no. 18 (2018): 4–15.

Musallam, Fuad. "The Dissensual Everyday: Between Daily Life and Exceptional Acts in Beirut, Lebanon." *City & Society* 32, no. 3 (2020): 670–93.

Nagel, Caroline, and Lynn Staeheli. "International Donors, NGOs, and the Geopolitics of Youth Citizenship in Contemporary Lebanon." *Geopolitics* 20, no. 2 (2015): 223–47.

Naharnet Newsdesk. "Suleiman, Berri, Miqati: Dahieh Blast Must Prompt Lebanese to End Their Differences." Naharnet, July 3, 2013. www.naharnet.com/stories/en/89898-suleiman-berri-miqati-dahieh-blast-must-prompt-lebanese-to-end-their-differences.

Najib. "The Lebanese Rocket Society—The Strange Tale of the Lebanese Space Race." *BlogBaladi*, March 9, 2013. https://blogbaladi.com/the-lebanese-rocket-society-the-strange-tale-of-the-lebanese-space-race/.

Narotzky, Susana, and Niko Besnier. "Crisis, Value, and Hope: Rethinking the Economy: An Introduction to Supplement 9." *Current Anthropology* 55, no. 9 (2014): 4–16.

Nash, Matt. "Lebanon Smoking Ban Draws Dismay and Delight." BBC News, September 4, 2012. www.bbc.com/news/world-middle-east-19478690.

"National Youth Policy Action Plan." UNICEF and UNFPA, February 2022. https://lebanon.un.org/sites/default/files/2022-09/National%20Youth%20Policy%20Action%20Plan-Full%20Report.pdf.

Nielsen, Morten. "A Wedge of Time: Futures in the Present and Presents without Futures in Maputo, Mozambique." *Journal of the Royal Anthropological Institute* 20 (2014):166–82.

Nimführ, Sarah. "Can Collaborative Knowledge Production Decolonize Epistemology?" *Migration Letters* 19, no. 6 (2022): 781–89.

Noordegraaf, Mirko, and Willem Schinkel. "Professionalism as Symbolic Capital: Materials for a Bourdieusian Theory of Professionalism." *Comparative Sociology* 10, no. 1 (2011): 67–96.

Nucho, Joanne R. *Everyday Sectarianism in Urban Lebanon: Infrastructures, Public Services, and Power.* Princeton, NJ: Princeton University Press, 2016.

Nudge Lebanon. "'Proudly Non-Smoking' Campaign," n.d. https://nudgelebanon.org/proudly-non-smoking-campaign/.

Oakes, Tim. "China's Provincial Identities: Reviving Regionalism and Reinventing 'Chineseness.'" *The Journal of Asian Studies* 59, no. 3 (2000): 667–92.

Obeid, Michelle. "Searching for the 'Ideal Face of the State' in a Lebanese Border Town." *Journal of the Royal Anthropological Institute* 16, no. 2 (2010): 330–46.

Ong, Aihwa. *Neoliberalism as Exception: Mutations in Citizenship and Sovereignty.* Durham. NC: Duke University Press, 2006.

Ortner, Sherry B. "Dark Anthropology and Its Others: Theory since the Eighties." *HAU: Journal of Ethnographic Theory* 6, no. 1 (2016): 47–73.

Paley, Julia. "The Paradox of Participation: Civil Society and Democracy in Chile." *PoLAR* 24, no. 1 (2001): 1–12.

Phillips, Sarah D. "Civil Society and Healing: Theorizing Women's Social Activism in Post-Soviet Ukraine." *Ethnos* 70, no. 4 (2005): 489–514.

"Phoenician or Arab? A Never-Ending Debate in Lebanon." *Independent*, June 12, 2010. www.independent.co.uk/property/house-and-home/phoenician-or-arab-a-neverending-debate-in-lebanon-5547901.html.

Piot, Charles. *Nostalgia for the Future: West Africa After the Cold War.* Chicago: University of Chicago Press, 2010.

Poplack, Shana. "Sometimes I'll Start a Sentence in Spanish Y TERMINO EN ESPAÑOL: Toward a Typology of Code-Switching." *Linguistics: An Interdisciplinary Journal of the Language Sciences* 18, no. 7–8 (1980): 581–618.

Prasse-Freeman, Elliott. *Rights Refused: Grassroots Activism and State Violence in Myanmar.* Stanford, CA: Stanford University Press, 2023.

Quijano, Aníbal. "Coloniality and Modernity/Rationality." *Cultural Studies* 21, no. 2–3 (2007): 168–78.

Raschig, Megan. "Triggering Change: Police Homicides, Community Healing, and the Emergent Eventfulness of the New Civil Rights." *Cultural Anthropology* 32, no. 3 (2017): 399–423.

Razsa, Maple. *Bastards of Utopia: Living Radical Politics after Socialism*. Bloomington: Indiana University Press, 2015.

Razsa, Maple. "The Subjective Turn: The Radicalization of Personal Experience within Occupy Slovenia." Society for Cultural Anthropology, February 14, 2013. https://culanth.org/fieldsights/the-subjective-turn-the-radicalization-of-personal-experience-within-occupy-slovenia.

"Realistic Dreamers: Hundreds Attend the TEDx LAU Event Dubbed #TheCross-Road." LAU News, September 10, 2013. www.lau.edu.lb/news-events/news/archive/realistic_dreamers.

Richard, Analiese. *The Unsettled Sector: NGOs and the Cultivation of Democratic Citizenship in Rural Mexico*. Stanford, CA: Stanford University Press, 2016.

Ricoeur, Paul. *Time and Narrative*, vol. 1. Translated by Kathleen McLaughlin and David Pellauer. Chicago: University of Chicago Press, 1984.

Riga, Liliana, Johannes Langer, and Arek Dakessian. "Theorizing Refugeedom: Becoming Young Political Subjects in Beirut." *Theory and Society* 49, no. 4 (2020): 709–44.

Rizvi, Mubbashir A. *The Ethics of Staying: Social Movements and Land Rights Politics in Pakistan*. Stanford, CA: Stanford University Press, 2019.

Robinson, Cedric J. *Black Marxism: The Making of the Black Radical Tradition*. Chapel Hill, NC: UNC Press Books, 2020.

Roitman, Janet. *Anti-Crisis*. Durham, NC: Duke University Press, 2014.

Rosa, Jonathan, and Yarimar Bonilla, "Deprovincializing Trump, Decolonizing Diversity, and Unsettling Anthropology." *American Ethnologist* 44, no. 2 (2017): 201–8.

Rosaldo, Michelle Z. "Toward an Anthropology of Self and Feeling." In *Culture Theory: Essays on Mind, Self, and Emotion*, edited by Richard A. Shweder and Robert A. LeVine, 137–57. Cambridge: Cambridge University Press, 1984.

Rutherford, Danilyn. "Affect Theory and The Empirical." *Annual Review of Anthropology* 45, no. 1 (2016): 285–300.

Sadek, Walid. "When Next We Meet: On the Figure of the Nonposthumous Survivor." *ARTMargins* 4, no. 2 (2015): 48–63.

Said, Edward. *Orientalism: Western Conceptions of the Orient*. London: Penguin, 1995.

Salibi, Kamal. *A House of Many Mansions: The History of Lebanon Reconsidered*. Berkeley: University of California Press, 1989.

Salti, Nisreen, and Jad Chaaban. "The Role of Sectarianism in the Allocation of Public Expenditure in Postwar Lebanon." *International Journal of Middle East Studies* 42, no. 4 (2010): 637–55.

Sanchez, Isabel Gutierrez. "Care Commons: Infrastructural (Re)Compositions for Life Sustenance through yet against Regimes of Chronic Crisis." *Urban Studies* 60, no. 12 (2023): 2456–73.

Sawalha, Aseel. *Reconstructing Beirut: Memory and Space in a Postwar Arab City*. Austin: University of Texas Press, 2010.

Scheid, Kirsten L. *Fantasmic Objects: Art and Sociality from Lebanon, 1920–1950.* Bloomington: Indiana University Press, 2022.

Schielke, Samuli. *Egypt in the Future Tense: Hope, Frustration, and Ambivalence Before and After 2011.* Bloomington: Indiana University Press, 2015.

Schwab, Klaus, and Xavier Sala-i-Martín. "The Global Competitiveness Report, 2013–2014." World Economic Forum, 2013. https://www3.weforum.org/docs/WEF_GlobalCompetitivenessReport_2013-14.pdf.

Schwartzstein, Peter. "The Bizarre Tale of the Middle East's First Space Program." *Smithsonian Magazine*, October 17, 2016.

Schwedler, Jillian. *Protesting Jordan: Geographies of Power and Dissent.* Stanford, CA: Stanford University Press, 2022.

Sepúlveda Sánchez, Denisse, Anne Lavanchy, Céline Heini, and Aline Acevedo. "Chile, October and November 2019: 'Feel' and Field-work in Times of Crisis." *Anthropology Today* 37, no. 2 (2021): 23–25.

Shadid, Anthony, and Nada Bakri, "For Lebanese, Crisis Has Become a Way of Life." *New York Times,* January 14, 2011.

Shipley, Jesse Weaver. *Living the Hiplife: Celebrity and Entrepreneurship in Ghanaian Popular Music.* Durham, NC: Duke University Press, 2013.

Shoshan, Nitzan. *The Management of Hate: Nation, Affect, and the Governance of Right-Wing Extremism in Germany.* Princeton, NJ: Princeton University Press, 2016.

Shuman, Amy. *Other People's Stories: Entitlement Claims and The Critique of Empathy.* Chicago: University of Illinois Press, 2005.

Simone, Abdou Maliq. *For the City Yet to Come: Changing African Life in Four Cities.* Durham, NC: Duke University Press, 2004.

"Special Segment: An Interview with Ali Chehade." Future TV Alam Al-Sabah, August 30, 2015, 13:40. www.youtube.com/watch?v=dRxWL8uKzlA.

Steiner, Robin Thomas. "Cultivating 'Omani Ambitions:' Entrepreneurship, Distributive Labor, and the Temporalities of Diversification in the Arab Gulf." *Economic Anthropology* 7, no. 1 (2020): 80–92.

Stewart, Kathleen. *Ordinary Affects.* Durham, NC: Duke University Press, 2007.

Sukarieh, Mayssoun. "The Hope Crusades: Culturalism and Reform in the Arab World." *PoLAR* 35, no. 1 (2012): 115–34.

"Sweet Dreams (Are Made of This)." *Executive,* January 22, 2016. www.executive-magazine.com/special-report/entrepreneurship-in-lebanon/sweet-dreams-are-made-of-this.

"Syrian Refugees in Lebanon Endure Racism, Deprivation of Rights, and Risks of Being Banished and Extradited to the Syrian Regime: No Protection, No Rights." Syrian Network for Human Rights, February 27, 2017. https://snhr.org/wp-content/pdf/english/Syrian_Refugees_in_Lebanon_Endure_Racism_Deprivation_of_Right_en.pdf.

Tate, Winifred. "Anthropology of Policy: Tensions, Temporalities, Possibilities." *Annual Review of Anthropology* 49, no. 1 (2020): 83–99.

Taylor, Astra. "Against Activism." *The Baffler* 30 (2016): 123–31.

"Teen in Beirut Bombing 'Selfie' Dies." Al Arabiya, December 28, 2013, updated May 20, 2020. https://english.alarabiya.net/News/middle-east/2013/12/28/Teen-in-Beirut-bombing-Selfie-dies-.

Thompson, Elizabeth. *Colonial Citizens: Republican Rights, Paternal Privilege, and Gender in French Syria and Lebanon*. New York: Columbia University Press, 2000.

Thorleifsson, Cathrine. "The Limits of Hospitality: Coping Strategies among Displaced Syrians in Lebanon." *Third World Quarterly* 37, no. 6 (2016): 1071–82.

Traboulsi, Fawwaz. *A History of Modern Lebanon*. London: Pluto Press, 2007.

Trnka, Susanna, and Catherine Trundle, eds. *Competing Responsibilities: The Ethics and Politics of Contemporary Life*. Durham, NC: Duke University Press, 2017.

Trouillot, Michel-Rolph. *Global Transformations: Anthropology and the Modern World*. New York: Palgrave Macmillan, 2003.

Tsing, Anna Lowenhaupt. *The Mushroom at the End of the World: On the Possibility of Life in Capitalist Ruins*. Princeton, NJ: Princeton University Press, 2015.

Turner, Annabel Claire. "Yoga Practices in Beirut." MA thesis, American University of Beirut, 2015.

Turner, Lewis. "'#Refugees Can Be Entrepreneurs Too!' Humanitarianism, Race, and the Marketing of Syrian Refugees." *Review of International Studies* 46, no. 1 (2020): 137–55.

USAID, Office of Transition Initiatives—Lebanon. n.d. www.usaid.gov/stabilization-and-transitions/closed-programs/lebanon.

Van Ommering, Erik. "Schooling in Conflict: An Ethnographic Study from Lebanon." *International Journal of Sociology and Social Policy* 31, no. 9/10 (2011): 543–54.

Vigh, Henrik. "Crisis and Chronicity: Anthropological Perspectives on Continuous Conflict and Decline." *Ethnos* 73, no. 1 (2008): 5–24.

Wardlow, Holly. *Wayward Women: Sexuality and Agency in a New Guinea Society*. Berkeley: University of California Press, 2006.

Warner, Michael. *Publics and Counterpublics*. New York: Zone Books, 2002.

Watenpaugh, Keith D. *Being Modern in the Middle East: Revolution, Nationalism. Colonialism, and the Arab Middle Class*. Princeton, NJ: Princeton University Press, 2006.

"'We Are Racist': Lebanon FM Says on Refugees." Albawaba News, October 8, 2017. www.albawaba.com/news/we-are-racist-lebanon-fm-says-refugees-1031102.

Wedeen, Lisa. *Peripheral Visions: Publics, Power, and Performance in Yemen*. Chicago: University of Chicago Press, 2009.

Williams, Bianca C. *The Pursuit of Happiness: Black Women, Diasporic Dreams, and the Politics of Emotional Transnationalism*. Durham, NC: Duke University Press, 2018.

Williams, Raymond. *Marxism and Literature*. Oxford: Oxford Paperbacks, 1977.

Yassin, Nasser. "Sects and the City: Socio-Spatial Perceptions and Practices of Youth in Beirut." In *Lebanon: After the Cedar Revolution*, edited by Are J. Knudsen and Michael Kerr, 203–18. Oxford: Oxford University Press, 2013.

"The Youth Advocacy Process: YAP." MASAR Organization, n.d.

"Youth in Governance: Shaping the Future," *Lebanon Development Marketplace 2006*. n.d.

"The Youth Policy in Lebanon." The Youth Advocacy Process and The Youth Forum for National Youth Policies, February 2012. www.youthpolicy.org/uploads/documents/2012_Case_Study_Youth_Policy_Lebanon_Eng.pdf.

Yurchak, Alexei. *Everything Was Forever, Until It Was No More: The Last Soviet Generation*. Princeton, NJ: Princeton University Press, 2005.

Zigon, Jarrett. "On Love: Remaking Moral Subjectivity in Postrehabilitation Russia." *American Ethnologist* 40, no. 1 (2013): 201–15.

Zigon, Jarrett. *A War on People: Drug User Politics and a New Ethics of Community*. Berkeley: University of California Press, 2018.

Zournazi, Mary. *Hope: New Philosophies for Change*. New York: Routledge, 2002.

Index

Page numbers in *italics* refer to figures and tables.